Maximizing Web Dynpro for Java

 **PRESS**

SAP PRESS is issued by
Bernhard Hochlehnert, SAP AG

SAP PRESS is a joint initiative of SAP and Galileo Press. The know-how offered by SAP specialists combined with the expertise of the publishing house Galileo Press offers the reader expert books in the field. SAP PRESS features first-hand information and expert advice, and provides useful skills for professional decision-making.

SAP PRESS offers a variety of books on technical and business related topics for the SAP user. For further information, please visit our website: *www.sap-press.com*.

Chris Whealy
Inside Web Dynpro for Java
2005, 356 pp., ISBN 1-59229-038-8

Karl Kessler, Peter Tillert, Panayot Dobrikov
Java Programming with the SAP Web Application Server
2005, 568 pp., ISBN 1-59229-020-5

Jörg Beringer, Karen Holtzblatt
Designing Composite Applications
2006, 192 pp., ISBN 1-59229-065-5

Andreas Schneider-Neureither
The ABAP Developer's Guide to Java
2005, 500 pp., ISBN 1-59229-027-2

Bertram Ganz, Jochen Gürtler, Timo Lakner

Maximizing Web Dynpro for Java

ISBN   1-59229-077-9

ISBN 13   978-1-59229-077-2

1st edition 2006

Translation: Lemoine International, Inc., Salt Lake City, UT
Editor: Stefan Proksch
Copy Editors: Nancy Etscovitz and John Parker, UCG, Inc., Boston, MA
Cover Design: Silke Braun
Layout Design: Vera Brauner
Production: Iris Warkus
Typesetting: Jan Carthaus Publishing, Radolfzell (Germany), www.carthaus.com
Printed and bound in Germany

Contents at a Glance

Contents

5   Web Dynpro and SAP NetWeaver Portal 151

6   Web Dynpro NavigationTester 197

10 Tips for the Installation, Configuration, and Administration 363

Appendix 467

1 Introduction

From the start, we agreed that we weren't going to write another reference manual for *Web Dynpro for Java*. Instead, we would discuss several examples to illustrate the countless possibilities that are made available to you by Web Dynpro for Java. Because they aren't typical scenarios—developing games or CD management programs using Web Dynpro—the examples that we chose to illustrate Web Dynpro's capabilities may surprise you at first. Nevertheless, we believe that these examples best illustrate many *best practices* that will be useful to you in your daily work with Web Dynpro.

Relevance to real-life projects

Furthermore, although we ended up writing a tome (i.e., 500 pages instead of the initially planned 350 pages), we soon discovered that by no means could we describe all the options afforded by using Web Dynpro for Java. On the one hand, this indicates the enormous scope of functions inherent in Web Dynpro; on the other hand, it might be an incentive to write a second volume.

Before we cite examples to describe the various options available to you in Web Dynpro, we'll give you a basic introduction to the Web Dynpro programming model in **Chapter 2**. In particular, we'll focus on the internal structure of the Web Dynpro runtime environment and how it is embedded into SAP NetWeaver.

Introduction

One of our major concerns was the consistent componentization of the Web Dynpro sample applications. The *SAP NetWeaver Development Infrastructure* (NWDI) in particular provides you with a very powerful functionality—it enables you to build your own Web Dynpro application with reusable units. We'll describe the usage of Web Dynpro components specifically in terms of using the *Web Dynpro GameStation* (see **Chapter 3**) and the *Web Dynpro MusicBox* (see **Chapter 8**). In **Chapter 9**, we'll describe the generic Web Dynpro development components that are reused in several places in the examples given in this book.

Componentization

Because service-oriented applications have become increasingly popular since the introduction of the *Enterprise Services Architecture* (ESA) or Enterprise SOA, we will discuss how web services are used within your Web Dynpro application by using the *Web Dynpro Google search* (see **Chapter 4**). Additionally, we'll address the differences between the declarative and dynamic creation of Web Dynpro UIs based on the display of search results.

We'll also describe the interaction between your Web Dynpro applications and the SAP NetWeaver Portal. Although Web Dynpro applications generally run outside the SAP NetWeaver Portal as well, there is a multitude of new possibilities available to you as soon as you start your Web Dynpro applications within the SAP NetWeaver Portal. Extended navigation options (see **Chapter 6** and **Chapter 7**) or the personalization options (see **Chapter 8**) are only two examples that are implemented in a very straightforward manner, particularly with regard to the Web Dynpro MusicBox. In addition to describing those functions, **Chapter 5** contains a general description of the steps required to start your Web Dynpro application within the SAP NetWeaver Portal.

Examples
All examples were created based on SAP NetWeaver 2004 (SP14) and tested to the best of our knowledge. We did our very best to ensure consistency with regard to structuring and naming conventions. In **Appendix A**, we also provide some recommendations on how to achieve a consistent and comprehensible description of your Web Dynpro applications, in particular, when using Web Dynpro components and Web Dynpro development components (DCs).

All examples in this book can be extended and modified. The generic functionalities can also be reused in your Web Dynpro applications; however, we cannot provide support if problems occur. Therefore, we would like to refer you to the Web Dynpro forum in the SAP Developer Network (see **Appendix B**) in the event that you need assistance. In this part of the appendix, you will also find more detailed information about the Feature2Sample matrix that helps you to select sample and tutorial applications in the SAP Developer Network. Here, you'll find plenty of material for the Web Dynpro technology that ideally supplements the contents presented in this book.

Because we know full well from working with Web Dynpro that, apart from the actual application development, the administration and configuration of the Web Dynpro runtime environment frequently causes problems, resulting in unresolved questions and discussions, this topic is extensively discussed in **Chapter 10**.

We would especially like to thank Manohar Sreekanth who helped us set up the NWDI landscape. Additionally, Udo Offermann supported us with his detailed knowledge of the SAP NetWeaver Portal. Reiner Hammerich gave us an understanding of the future SAP UI strategy in which Web Dynpro (for Java) will, of course, play a key role. Last but not least, we want to thank Karin Schattka, Thomas Chadzelek, Jens Ittel, Markus Cherdron, and Alfred Barzewski. Special thanks also go to the publishing company Galileo Press that gave us the opportunity to write this book. In particular, we would like to thank Stefan Proksch from the SAP PRESS editorial office who always supported us with his invaluable experience.

Acknowledgements

We hope that you will enjoy reading and testing the examples and we look forward to receiving your feedback.

Walldorf, Germany, July 2006

Bertram Ganz (*bertram.ganz@sap.com*)
Jochen Gürtler (*jochen.guertler@sap.com*)
Timo Lakner (*timo.lakner@sap.com*)

Web Dynpro for Java officially came to life with release of SAP NetWeaver 2004. It represents the new framework for programming SAP user interfaces and will be used for developing the future generation of SAP business applications. In this chapter, we will introduce the philosophy and the basic concepts of Web Dynpro and give you a short overview of the SAP NetWeaver system landscape.

2 Web Dynpro Architecture Concepts

Web Dynpro uses a model-based approach to application development. This enables the developer to create large parts of an application declaratively from a development environment and thus to enable very efficient design of user interfaces. By strictly separating the presentation of data from the concrete storage of data according to the *Model-View-Controller Design Pattern*, Web Dynpro applications are clearly structured and can easily be extended. Via a clearly defined interface for integrating models, different kinds of back ends can be used for procuring data. Web Dynpro's component-based development approach also makes it suitable for complex software projects where different groups design different parts of an application in parallel.

Strict separation, clear structure

For the SAP NetWeaver 2004 release, Web Dynpro is optimized for Web-based applications that can be executed on the *SAP Web Application Server*[1] (Web AS) and easily started from the *SAP NetWeaver Portal*. With the flexible Web Dynpro architecture, it will also be possible in future releases to use local installations of *smart clients*, such as Web Dynpro clients for Java, Windows or Flex, as the rendering technology. The rendering technology itself, however, is not relevant to the application developer when creating the user interfaces: Web Dynpro applications are client-independent and thus

Flexible implementation options

---

1 As of Release SAP NetWeaver 2004s: SAP NetWeaver Application Server.

executable in the web browser, in locally installed clients (Web Dynpro clients), and on mobile devices.

The tight integration of Web Dynpro in the *SAP NetWeaver Development Infrastructure* (NWDI) enables you to control the management, adaptation, and delivery of software throughout its entire lifecycle. The tight connection thus achieved between development environment and runtime environment facilitates the modification and maintenance of delivered Java applications; something that long has been common practice in the R/3 environment.

2.1 Architecture Concepts

Declarative programming model

Web Dynpro was developed to support highly declarative, model-driven application development. With this approach, one can create large portions of an application declaratively at design time; that is, without programming, using development tools like *SAP NetWeaver Developer Studio* or *SAP NetWeaver Visual Composer*. It is possible to clearly improve development productivity and the reliability of the developed applications in ways beyond the capability of traditional application development.

A model-driven approach like Web Dynpro's creates metadata that describes an application irrespective of the technology. Special code generators are then able to produce source code from the application metadata in which a developer can insert his or her own code in *custom coding areas* or *hook methods*. Application-specific code can thus be added: e.g., for event handling or the initialization of an application.

These programming hooks of the generated classes that can be used by an application developer are called by the Web Dynpro framework at different times during request processing. These times and the order of their processing are defined by the *Web Dynpro phase model*, which is shown in Figure 2.1.

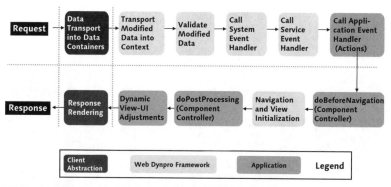

Figure 2.1 Web Dynpro Phase Model of Request Processing

Another goal in the development of Web Dynpro was to clearly structure the applications created using Web Dynpro by strictly following the Model-View-Controller (MVC) concept. This design pattern separates the presentation of data in a user interface from its representation in the back end, that is, there is a clear difference between the presentation layer (*view*) and the data layer (*model*). Both layers communicate via the *controller* that defines a clear contract and serves as a mediator between view and model. Due to the clearly defined interface of the controller, changes to the implementation of the model or view layer should not affect or only lightly affect the other layers. This principle of *designing by contract* simplifies the division of an application into different parts that then can be developed in parallel by different groups. For example, after specifying the controller interfaces, one developer group can take care of the backend integration while another one can deal with the creation of user interfaces.

Model-View-Controller

Figure 2.2 gives an overview of the most important logical parts of the Web Dynpro runtime. Essentially, it is divided into the *Web Dynpro Foundation Runtime* and the abstraction layers for integrating into different server platforms, to use different clients and different models.

Web Dynpro Foundation Runtime

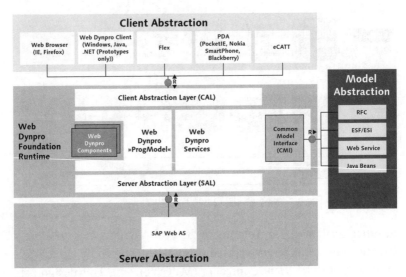

Figure 2.2 Main Modules of the Web Dynpro Runtime

Web Dynpro pro-
gramming model

The Web Dynpro Foundation Runtime is the core of the Web Dyn-pro runtime. Its central unit is the *Web Dynpro programming model* (ProgModel) which includes the phase model of request processing mentioned above. Other basic parts of the programming model are the extremely powerful and effective concept of reusable compo-nents and the data context for data exchange and flow between the used models, controllers, and views. These concepts will be described in detail using numerous examples throughout the follow-ing chapters of this book.

The Web Dynpro programming model also provides a large variety of user interface (UI) elements and layout procedures that you can use to easily create modern user interfaces. To name but a few exam-ples, these include the Table UI element and the Tree UI element. In the development environment, the supported UI elements can be placed in a work area per drag-and-drop, which enables a very quick prototyping of a user interface.

Generic services
and model
abstraction

Additionally, the Web Dynpro Foundation Runtime provides various *generic UI services* such as the simple or extended input help. Using the *Common Model Interface* (CMI), an interface is defined using which different models and back ends can be integrated in the Web Dynpro runtime. Examples for models already supported in SAP NetWeaver 2004 are the *Adaptive RFC Model* for integrating with

ABAP back ends or the *Web Service Model* for using Web services. More models will be added in the near future, such as the *Enterprise Services Framework* (ESF), which allows enterprise services to be used according to the service-oriented architecture supported by SAP.

We enable the use of Web Dynpro in different implementation scenarios by describing the connections of the Web Dynpro Foundation Runtime to the outside world via abstraction layers that represent clearly defined contracts for embedding the Web Dynpro runtime in different environments. As mentioned above, models are thus accessed via the CMI. The integration with the underlying server platform and the used client via the *Server Abstraction Layer* (SAL) and the *Client Abstraction Layer* (CAL) is defined as well.

Server and client abstraction

Theoretically, server abstraction enables you to run Web Dynpro in different runtime environments, although the SAP Web AS is currently the only supported platform. Client abstraction enables you to use different clients and rendering technologies for Web Dynpro and to thus achieve the client independence of Web Dynpro applications that was mentioned above. The standard clients in SAP NetWeaver 2004 are the HTML client—the web browser is used as a client—and the clients for mobile devices.

2.2 SAP NetWeaver System Landscape

The SAP Web AS is the central technology component of SAP NetWeaver. It is the application platform on which the enterprise software is run. In a homogeneous environment, the Web AS integrates many different infrastructure services with which business applications can be successfully built and executed. Examples of such infrastructure components are the SAP NetWeaver Portal, a J2EE-certified application server[2], or the Web Dynpro framework for creating user interfaces, to name but two.

The main components of a prototypical system landscape with SAP NetWeaver are illustrated in Figure 2.3.

A Web AS system provides a high degree of scalability and resilience, both crucial for the implementation of business-critical applications.

Web AS cluster environment

---

2 The J2EE engine implements the J2EE-1.3 standard in SAP NetWeaver 2004.

This results from the system's ability to group many application servers in a dialog instance and to group these in large composites in a cluster. Thus, the Web AS is suitable as an application platform for both small user groups and for enterprises that operate applications with large and very large user master records.

The *Web Dispatcher* is the central point of entry to the Web AS and uses a load distribution algorithm to distribute inbound requests to the available dialog instances. Every dialog instance in turn has its own load balancer, the *J2EE Dispatcher*. Its task is to evenly distribute inbound requests to the connected application servers.

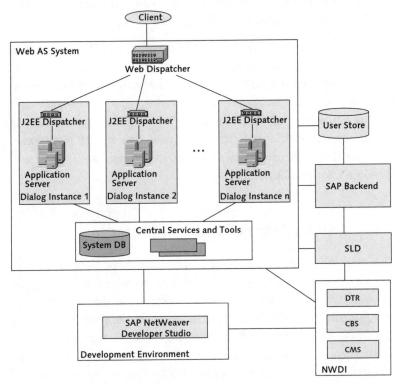

Figure 2.3 SAP NetWeaver System Landscape

To be able to centrally manage such a cluster, the Web AS provides various central services for sending messages or for locking resources within the cluster, as well as central tools for administration, configuration, and installation.

The Web AS does currently not support the option to assign a certain task to specific application servers in a cluster. For example, for isolating various applications it could make sense to plan a separate dialog instance for every group of the same kind of applications in order to achieve better robustness and performance. For example, if you want to operate the SAP NetWeaver Portal and Web Dynpro applications on different application servers for this reason, you currently need to install two separate Web AS systems.

The *SAP NetWeaver Developer Studio* is provided as a development tool. Based on the open-source product Eclipse, it was used to create the examples discussed in this book. In future releases of SAP NetWeaver, the *SAP NetWeaver Visual Composer* will additionally be available for declaratively creating user interfaces based on Web Dynpro.

SAP NetWeaver Developer Studio

The development environment is integrated with the SAP NetWeaver Development Infrastructure, which controls the life cycle of software. The source code of applications and other design-time objects is thus stored in the *Design Time Repository* (DTR) for versioning. Using the *Component Build Service* (CBS), the development components stored in the DTR can be built centrally. Finally, the integrated *Change Management System* (CMS) can be used to create, consolidate, and validate code lines and deploy them in the connected systems and to transport software changes to the different versions and code lines.

SAP NetWeaver Development Infrastructure

The descriptions of system and transport landscape are centrally stored in the *System Landscape Directory* (SLD). The SLD also integrates a naming service and thus serves as a central validation instance for the uniqueness of the names of used development components.

System Landscape Directory

Because of this comprehensive integration of development and runtime environment and because to the provided software infrastructure, Web AS is suitable for software projects of any size because it optimally supports working in teams, even—or especially—at a global level.

2.3   Summary and Perspective

To conclude this overview of basic concepts of Web Dynpro and the Web AS system landscape, we would like to summarize the most important benefits provided by Web Dynpro:

▶ The declarative, model-driven application development enables the creation of large parts of an application without having to write your own code. Code generators use the metadata to produce appropriate Java classes that are structured according to the MVC concept. For this reason and due to the component concept of Web Dynpro, an application can be split into separate parts and be developed by larger teams in parallel.

▶ Your own code can be inserted in the generated classes in custom coding areas that are then called by the Web Dynpro framework in specific phases during request processing.

▶ Web Dynpro supports numerous simple, complex, and graphical UI elements and thus enables you to easily create modern and user-friendly interfaces.

▶ Web Dynpro defines clear interfaces for integrating the most different models and clients and thus enables a very flexible implementation for different runtime environments and implementation scenarios.

Enterprise
Services
Architecture

What kind of function will Web Dynpro fulfill in future releases after SAP NetWeaver 2004? To answer this question, let us briefly outline the future SAP strategy. Over the next few years, SAP NetWeaver will focus on supporting the *Enterprise Services Architecture* (ESA), which is service-oriented application development. This means that applications are composed of enterprise services that encapsulate all semantic aspects of a service or business process and expose them via an appropriate interface. An example of such a service could be "Take an order." To prevent an application from having to recreate this process again and again to provide such functionality, the application relies on sophisticated enterprise services and is thus composed of higher-value blocks.

This standardization of the used enterprise services includes the possibility to standardize the user interfaces required for these services as well and to make them available to an application as *UI patterns*

(*UI building blocks*) that are simple to use. This simplification and uni-fication of the user interface means that business process experts without programming experience will be able to configure schematic user interfaces from standardized UI building blocks in the future.

In the years to come, SAP will therefore continuously promote the enhancement of an *enterprise services repository*. The SAP NetWeaver Visual Composer will serve as a modeling and configuration tool of business applications based on enterprise services and UI building blocks. From the user interfaces modeled using this tool, Web Dyn-pro applications will be generated that are run by the Web Dynpro runtime. Web Dynpro thus represents the strategically important technology component for creating user interfaces and for running applications. With the support of additional rendering technologies, smart clients will be available in addition to the web browser. These locally installed clients are based on different technologies and plat-forms such as Windows, Java, or Flex. This shows that the imple-mentation options of Web Dynpro will be continuously enhanced in the future.

Using the example of the GameStation application, you will be introduced step by step to the strategy of a component-oriented Web Dynpro developer. You will get to know the main benefits of Web Dynpro components for modularization of comprehensive applications in the NWDI component model. Further, you will learn how to use component interfaces to integrate new components in the GameStation application without changing the code.

3   Web Dynpro GameStation

3.1   Componentization Using the Example of the Web Dynpro GameStation

This chapter demonstrates the technical implementation of a component-based Web Dynpro application architecture using the example of an application named "Web Dynpro GameStation" (see Figure 3.1). The aim is to visualize the benefits of the component concept in a simple real-life example.

The architecture of the GameStation application is to be designed based on the Web Dynpro component model. For this purpose, a classification of special component types will be introduced that simplifies the development and organization of complex Web Dynpro applications.

Component-based application architecture

The GameStation application uses a concept of embedding additionally developed game applications at a later stage (*Deploy & Play*). This concept is based on using a *Web Dynpro component interface* for an abstract definition of a game component irrespective of its implementation. Due to this loose coupling between using component and implementation at the design stage, games can be deployed at a later stage and then be started from within the GameStation without having to change any code.

Deploy & Play using component interfaces

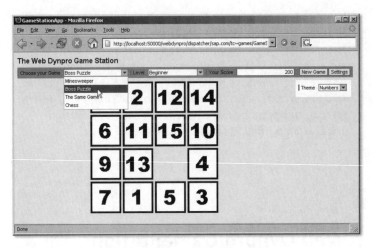

Figure 3.1 GameStation Application in the Web Browser

Note that the GameStation application presented here is not a typical business application with back-end integration. Therefore, many issues such as the use of Web Dynpro models or the internationalization of applications are not discussed. Despite this restriction, the GameStation application demonstrates numerous techniques, concepts, and ideas regarding the componentization of Web Dynpro applications that you can transfer to your own application architecture.

Web Dynpro DCs   In the next step, the development objects belonging to the GameStation are transferred to the component model of the SAP NetWeaver Development Infrastructure. Because the development objects belonging to the GameStation application are divided into separate *Web Dynpro Development Components* (Web Dynpro DCs), an efficient development process can be implemented that optimally meets such requirements as distributed development in teams, maintainability, reusability, and extensibility. Using the GameStation example, usage dependencies between Web Dynpro development components are explained based on *public part definitions*.

Implementation of component interfaces   Another section deals with the individual steps that are necessary to implement the previously defined game component interface using the Web Dynpro tools.

Creating a game component instance   The creation of game-component instances at runtime is particularly significant. While the GameStation component only uses a game-component interface at design time, it must create a concrete game-component instance for it at runtime. A *DeploymentManager* component determines the game components that are then deployed on the SAP Web AS. The implementation section will explain the use of the IWDComponentUsage API for programmatically creating game component instances.

For exchanging data across components, different kinds of context mapping are applied. While in *internal interface context mapping* the data source is within the embedded component, in *external interface context mapping* it is outside the embedded component. In the Game-Station application, both forms of interface context mapping are introduced, using real-life examples.

Server-side eventing is an important technique for communicating between Web Dynpro components. In the GameStation application, the handling of actions is delegated by the user to the root component via an eventing approach. You will thus get to know the definition of events and event handlers across components, and will deal with the possibility of *dynamic event subscription* using the IWDComponentUsage API.

The GameStation user interface and the navigation transitions are modeled in the navigation modeler of the Web Dynpro tools. This is done by embedding different component interface views within the central root component using the special ViewContainer UI element. The chapter concludes with a comprehensive discussion of component navigation and the calling of the initial view assembly when starting Web Dynpro applications.

Like all other applications presented in this book, you can download the Web Dynpro GameStation from the web page of this book under *http://www.sap-press.com*.

Margin notes:
Inter-component context mapping chains

Server-side eventing between components

Embedding of component interface views and navigation between components

3.2 Using Components to Create an Application Architecture

Let us begin with designing the application architecture of the GameStation. In the initial phase, we will remain on the level of various Web Dynpro entities like Web Dynpro applications, components, local dictionaries, or component interfaces. In a second phase, we will then transfer the developed architecture to the NWDI component model. The Web Dynpro entities belonging to the GameStation will then be stored in several separate Web Dynpro development components or Web Dynpro DCs.

3.2.1 First-Level Structure of the User Interface

In a first step we will design the first-level structure of the GameStation user interface. This means that we will divide the user interface into individual areas and will then consider how we can transfer these to component-based application architecture.

The presented GameStation application is characterized by a simple user interface where the actual playground is surrounded by four additional areas (see Figure 3.2):

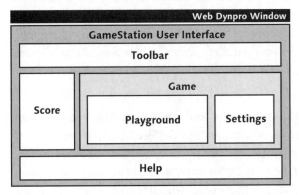

Figure 3.2 First-Level Structure of the GameStation User Interface

In the top position, a **Toolbar** for controlling the GameStation is displayed. Next to the **Playground** there are two areas for displaying the highest score (**Score**) and for editing the **Settings** of the game that is currently displayed. Underneath the playground, the user can optionally display a help text (**Help**) for the currently selected game.

For a game to be displayed in the GameStation application it must have two user interfaces. This means that a GameStation game must make two different user interfaces available to the using component: the actual user interface with the playground, and the UI for entering game settings.

This simple first-level structure of the GameStation user interface is the basis of all the following sections of this chapter. This structure is very appropriate for demonstrating the development of a component-based Web Dynpro application and to illustrate the corresponding technical background.

3.2.2 Disadvantages of Large Web Dynpro Components

When developing Web Dynpro applications, there is always the question of how to implement the componentization of the application. The most obvious, though in most cases wrong, approach is to develop the complete application within a single monolithic Web Dynpro component; this is referred to as *tight coupling*. Although the GameStation application could be developed according to this pattern by one or two developers with some effort, they would eventually realize that, for example, the extensibility of the GameStation application by new game implementations would not be feasible without completely redesigning and redeploying this one component.

Tight coupling

The development speed would also continuously decrease with the growth of the component because every new testing process of the application would involve a slower, non-incremental, build process. Even the presence of an additional developer could hardly alleviate this problem because the parallel development of a single Web Dynpro component in a team inevitably involves an intensive synchronization effort.

Slower development

Another disadvantage of monolithic Web Dynpro components is that they are difficult to maintain by other developers. Although all views and controllers are accessible in one place in such components, the analysis of application logic and view composition is difficult. Apart from the separation into component, custom, and view controllers, the components do not allow for any further organization (except for the implementation of certain naming rules for functional identification). In contrast to this approach, a modular component-based model has the benefit of developing hierarchically structured and functionally separated application architecture with clear usage dependencies and interfaces.

Difficult maintainability

3.2.3 Designing a Simple Component Architecture

In the next step, we will map the first-level structure of the Game-Station user interface to an architecture that consists of several Web Dynpro components. We already discarded the wrong approach of a single monolithic Web Dynpro component in the previous section, so that we will now determine what an appropriate component model for the GameStation could look like (see Figure 3.3).

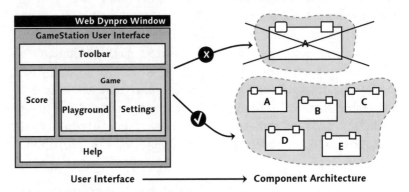

Figure 3.3 From the User Interface to the Component Architecture

Separation of Game and Game Console

Embedding of UI components using the ViewContainer UI element

The basic principle of the architecture of the GameStation application is to separate the game console from the games embedded therein by using separate Web Dynpro components. Figure 3.4 illustrates this simple component architecture. The GameStationComp component is the root component of the application (❶ to the left) and embeds a game component (for example, for the SameGame game) as a visual UI component (❷ to the left). The embedding is achieved by inserting the component interface view of the game component in the UI part of the GameStation (❶ to the right) into a ViewContainer UI element (❷ to the right). In the embedded GameStation-Comp component, the ViewContainer UI element represents a placeholder for the playground implemented by the game component.

To illustrate this usage dependency in the component diagram, the root component is connected to the UI port (component interface view) of the used game component by means of a connector. More details about the Web Dynpro component diagrams shown in the book can be found in Appendix A.

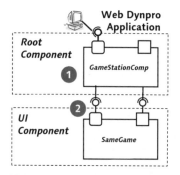 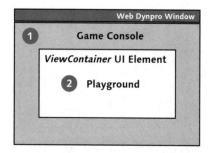

Figure 3.4 Separation of Game Console and Game in Separate Web Dynpro Components

Embedding a Second Component Interface View of the Game Component

UI components provide at least one visual interface or a component interface view to their using components. Additionally, a Web Dynpro component can expose additional interface views. In our case, in addition to the playground itself, the game component is to implement a user interface for editing the game settings and to make it available to the outside via a second component interface view.

Figure 3.5 shows how such a game component is structured. At their first level, the two views GameView (❶) and SettingsView (❷) contain two different view layouts, one for the actual playground and one for editing the settings. For an embedded component to be able to freely position both views within itself, these views must be separately available in two component interface views (❸ and ❹). For creating a second component interface view, you need to create an additional window within the game component in which the SettingsView view is inserted (❻) while the GamesView view is contained in the other window (❺). Please note that in the Web Dynpro component model, every window within a component is assigned exactly one component interface view as an outer visual interface (1:1 relation).

Web Dynpro component with two visual interfaces

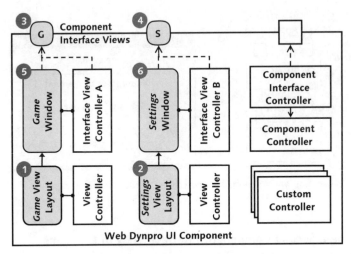

Figure 3.5 UI Component with Two Component Interface Views

At runtime, both interface views can only be displayed simultaneously if no view is contained more than once, which is the case here. The Web Dynpro runtime environment would report a duplicate view instance within the displayed view assembly via the following error message:

WDRuntimeException: Duplicate instance exception: There is already an instance of view <View-Name> in component <Component-Name>.

Figure 3.6 illustrates the embedding of a second component interface view of the same component using an additional UI port (❸ to the left).

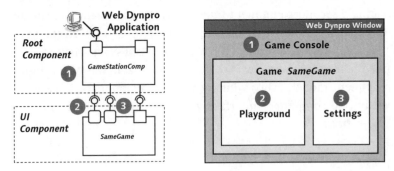

Figure 3.6 Displaying the Game Settings Using a Second Component Interface View

Separation of Root Component and UI Components

In the simplest case, the root component itself could implement the entire UI part of the GameStation and only transfer the actual playground and the game settings to a separate game component. However, to reduce the functionality of the root component as far as possible to that of a "component embedder" we will transfer the three UI areas of the GameStation component to separate UI components in the next step. The toolbar for selecting and starting a game and for setting the level of difficulty is contained in the separate `Toolbar` UI component (see Figure 3.7, ❸). The parts of the user interfaces for displaying the score (❹) and the help text (❺) are implemented by the two UI components `Highscore` and `Help`. These visual components, too, are inserted in the root component via `ViewContainer` UI elements.

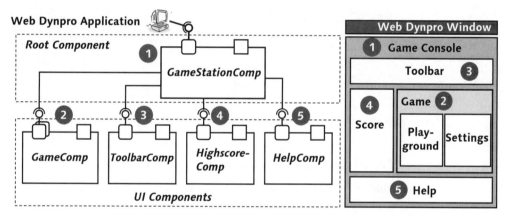

Figure 3.7 Outsourcing UI Components From the Root Component

3.3 Extensibility Using Component Interfaces

In the next step, we will extend the existing component architecture of the GameStation application by the critical characteristic of *exchangeability* of game components. Using this form of modularization, we can embed an abstract definition of the game component without any underlying implementation at design time. Only at runtime must the root component know an implementation of this defined game component in order to display it in the playground.

Web Dynpro com-
ponent interfaces This basic and to Java users familiar principle of separating design
and implementation can be implemented in Web Dynpro using *component interfaces* (or *component interface definitions*). A component
interface is the abstract description of the various interfaces and
model usages of a Web Dynpro component without associated
implementation. The interfaces of a Web Dynpro component
include the *component interface controller* at the controller level and
the optional *component interface views* at the UI level. While the component interface controller defines methods, events, and context
(see Figure 3.8, ❷), the component interface views (❶) are characterized by their *inbound* and *outbound plugs* for defining navigation
links.[1] For the component interface controller to be able to bind the
context to a specific *model* you also need to define its usage in the
component interface (❸).

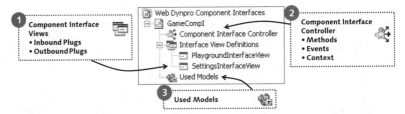

Figure 3.8 Component Interface Presented in the Web Dynpro Explorer

Comparison Between Component Interface and Component

Figure 3.9 shows a comparison between a component interface and
a component implementation. A component interface only comprises the definition of component interface views (**0..n**) as the visual
interfaces (Figure 3.9, ❶) of the component interface controller
(**1..1**) (❷) as the controller interface as well as the model usages (**0..n**)
(❸).

---

1 You cannot define startup and exit plugs in component interfaces because they are
only required in root components. The only Web Dynpro entity that can define
the usage of a root component is that of the Web Dynpro application. However,
since you cannot declare the usage of a component interface for a Web Dynpro
application (given that it is impossible to define or configure an associated implementation), the abstract description of root components using component interfaces is not feasible.

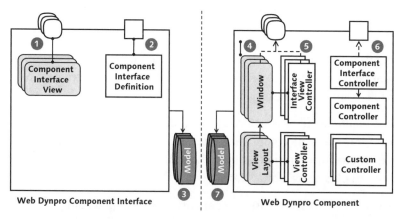

Figure 3.9 Comparing Component Interface to Component Implementation

In a component, the component interface views are implemented in two parts. First, the interfaces for the user interface of a component that are exposed to the outside are implemented within the component via their windows (Figure 3.9, ❹). A window contains the definition of a *view composition* that is defined by the connection of views or component interface views to navigation links. To the outside—that is, for visually embedding a Web Dynpro component in the view composition of another component—windows are represented by appropriate component interface views that themselves have inbound and outbound plugs. The second part of the implementation takes place in the component interface view controllers (❺) that carry out the event handling of inbound plugs and the triggering of outbound plugs.

Implementation of component inter-face views

The controller interface of a component interface is implemented by the component interface controller (Figure 3.9, ❻). Because this controller will be abstract[2] in the following SAP NetWeaver releases, it is advisable to delegate all implementation parts in the component interface controller to appropriate methods in the component controller. The model usages predefined by the component interface are accordingly defined in the implementing component (❼).

Implementation of the component interface controller

---

2 The component interface controller is then implemented by the component controller.

3.3.1 Component Interface of a Game Component

Component inter-
face = contract
between using
component and
implementation
The component interface of a game component specifies the contract between its using component and its implementation. In other words, it describes the demands of the GameStation component on a game component it uses and vice versa.

For example, the GameStation component requires two different user interfaces or component interface views, respectively, from a game: one for representing the playground and another one for editing certain settings for a game.

Data exchange via
interface context
mapping
The data exchange across components is determined using the context structure in the component interface controller. Keep in mind that the data exchange or the context mapping between GameStation (using component) and game (implementation) takes place in both directions. If the level of difficulty of a game is defined and stored outside the GameStation, it is only accessible in the game component itself via *external interface context mapping*. The isInputElement property of a context attribute for the level of difficulty is therefore to be assigned a value of **true**. The game component therefore makes one demand on its using component; that is, the provision of the level of difficulty that is stored externally. The settings that are specific to a game, however, should be stored in the game itself. If the associated context elements in the component interface controller of the game component are exposed to the outside, the embedded GameStation component can also access them via context mapping. In Section 3.7, we will deal with inter-component context mappings in more detail.

Component inter-
face method start-
Game()
In addition to the context structure, the component interface in the component interface controller of a game component requires the public method void startGame(). By calling this method, a game component can be started by its using component (GameStation component) from the outside. Table 3.1 shows the entire definition of a game component interface.

Web Dynpro component interface			
GameCompI			
General definition of a game component to be embedded in the GameStation component			
Component interface controller			
GameCompI			
Context definition and public methods in the interface controller of a game component			
Context	**Card.**	**Type**	**isInput**
Game	**1..1**		
˪Caption		**string**	
˪ContinueGame		**boolean**	
˪Description		**string**	
˪Name		**string**	
˪Score		**integer**	
GameSettings	**1..1**		x
˪Level		***com.sap.wdbp.game.Level*** (Dictionary Simple Type)	x
Methods			
void startGame()			
Component interface views			
PlaygroundInterfaceView		**SettingsInterfaceView**	
User interface for a playground		User interface for editing the settings belonging to a game	
Inbound Plugs		**Inbound Plugs**	
Default()		Default()	

Table 3.1 Definition of a Game Component Interface

3.3.2 Declaration of a Component Interface in the Web Dynpro Tools

The *Web Dynpro Explorer* displays the component interfaces included in a Web Dynpro DC in the **Web Dynpro Component Interfaces Definitions** node. The declaration of a new component interface is performed according to the following procedure:

1. In the Web Dynpro Explorer, open the node **Web Dynpro · Web Dynpro Component Interfaces**.

2. In the associated context menu, select the entry **Create Component Interface Definition**. A window for entering the component interface name and the package name are displayed (see Figure 3.10).

3. Enter the name of the new component interface. In parallel to Java interfaces, it should begin with the prefix I (here: IGame). It is recommended to create the component interfaces of a Web Dynpro DC in a separate package (for example, in the package *.cid).

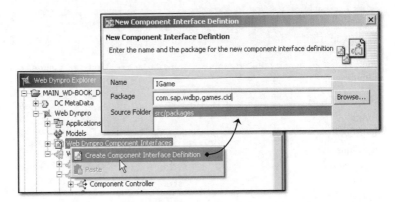

Figure 3.10 Declaration of a New Component Interface

4. For declaring the component interface controller, select the node of the same name **Web Dynpro · Web Dynpro Component Interfaces · IGame · Component Interface Controller** in the Web Dynpro Explorer. The perspective view belonging to the controller declaration is opened via a double click on the node or on the **Edit** context menu option (see Figure 3.11).

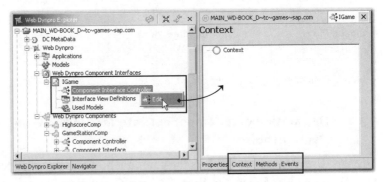

Figure 3.11 Declaration of the Component Interface Controller

5. In the **Context**, **Methods**, and **Events** tabs, declare the component-interface controller according to Table 3.1. Within a component interface definition, the **Implementation** tab is naturally not displayed. The **Properties** tab is shown but does not contain any

editable fields for defining controller usage dependencies because these depend on the implementation.

6. In the Web Dynpro Explorer, select the node **Web Dynpro · Web Dynpro Component Interfaces · IGame · Interface View Definitions** to add a component interface view. By selecting the context menu entry **Create Interface View**, a window is displayed where you can enter the interface view name (see Figure 3.12, ❶ and ❷). We recommend the suggested package name.

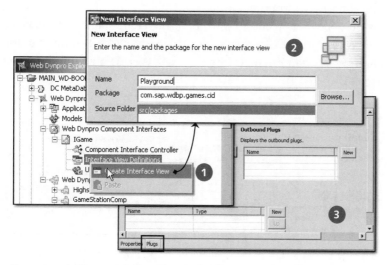

Figure 3.12 Adding an Interface View to the Component Interface

7. Because a game component is to have a second component interface view for displaying game settings, the previous step is to be repeated for the interface view named SettingsInterfaceView.

8. In the perspective view you can additionally define the inbound and outbound plugs (but no startup and exit plugs) belonging to an interface view, along with their parameters (see Figure 3.12, ❸).

3.3.3   Component Usages

To be able to integrate the component interface of a game component in the existing component architecture of the GameStation application, we will first deal with the central term of *component usage*. In the Web Dynpro programming model, the component usage is a variable using which the embedding component defines

Component usage as a variable for a component

the usage of another component. At design time, it is a placeholder for a used component, at runtime a component usage is associated to a corresponding component instance. If a component is to be used more than once you need to define two separate component usages. At runtime, the embedded component would then have two component instances of the same type.

Component usages must be explicitly declared in the using component at design time. It is not possible to create a component usage dynamically at runtime using controller code. Every component usage dependency declared in the using component is displayed in the Web Dynpro Explorer under the node **<Web Dynpro Components> · <Component Name> · Used Web Dynpro Components** (see Figure 3.13).

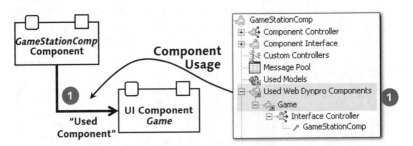

Figure 3.13 Presentation of the Component Usage Game in the Web Dynpro Explorer

After a component usage has been defined within the embedding component, up to three types of usage dependencies can be defined at controller or UI level, respectively, at design time (see also Figure 3.14):

1. **Component usage**

   A controller of the embedding component uses the component usage itself to control the lifecycle of the associated component instance. It is also possible to provide a component usage with the reference to another component usage of the same type. The used component usage can be accessed by a controller via the IWDComponentUsage API.

2. **Component interface controller**

   A controller of the embedding component uses the component interface controller of the component that is associated to the component usage. Thus, the context exposed in the component interface (for defining context mapping chains) and its methods and events are visible to the controller. The component interface controller provides its IExternal API as an interface to a using component.

3. **Component interface view (optional)**

A window or ViewContainer UI element can embed the component interface view of the component instance associated to the component usage. By using the inbound and outbound plugs defined by the component interface view, navigation links can be defined across components. Because faceless components do not have component interface views this usage dependency is only available to UI components.

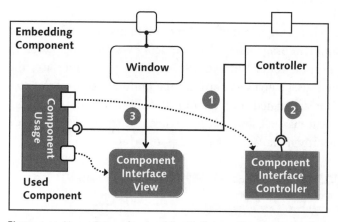

Figure 3.14 Usage Dependencies After Defining a Component Usage

Lifecycle Property of a Component Usage

To correctly understand component usages, you need to clearly distinguish between the entity of the component usage itself and the component instance to which it refers. At design time, the component usage is the usage dependency of the parent component with the embedded child component. In parallel, a variable in Java represents the usage of another object instance. The entity of the component usage is not identical to the actual component instance. As shown in Figure 3.14, this difference becomes obvious in that, apart from the component usage, the two interfaces of a Web Dynpro component—a component interface view and a component interface controller—can be used directly.

Difference between component usage and associated component instance

45

At runtime, an instance of the component usage of the type IWDComponentUsage points to the instance of the used component. At design time, the **Lifecycle** property can be defined for a component usage to specify the way of controlling the creation and destruction of the associated component instance at runtime (see Figure 3.15):

▶ **createOnDemand**
The Web Dynpro runtime environment itself performs the lifecycle management of the component instance belonging to the component usage. On demand, the component instance is created automatically and destroyed if necessary. For example, a UI component is created automatically as soon as its component interface view is contained in a *view assembly* for the first time or displayed in the user interface.

▶ **manual**
The lifecycle management of the component instance belonging to the component usage takes place explicitly via implementation in the application code. With its IWDComponentUsage interface, the component usage gives a controller the option to control the lifecycle of the associated component instance. That is, the controller can create it via IWDComponentUsage.createComponent(), if needed, or destroy it via IWDComponentUsage.deleteComponent().

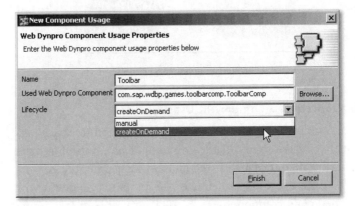

Figure 3.15 Definition of the Lifecycle Property of a Component Usage

Component Usages in the Referencing Mode

Additionally, a component usage A can use the IWDComponentUsage.enterReferencingMode(IWDComponentUsage componentUsage) method to refer to another component usage B of the same type (that is, a component usage that represents the usage of a component of the same type). Thus, component usage A refers to the same component instance as component usage B (if it exists). This *referencing mode* of component usages is implemented particularly when a central model component is used by several UI components. In SAP NetWeaver 2004, however, the referencing mode is only supported for faceless components without component interface view. More details about this technique can be found in Section 3.8.3.

3.3.4 Component Usages and Component Interfaces

A significant improvement for the design of component-based Web Dynpro applications is achieved by the combination of component usages and component interfaces.

In a simple case, a component usage points to the concrete implementation of a Web Dynpro component at design time. Due to this *tight coupling* at design time, the using component cannot use a different component implementation with the same functionality for such a component usage at runtime than the one that was specified at design time. To be able to use a different component implementation at runtime, a separate, second component usage dependency would have to be defined at design time for tight coupling. In more complex application scenarios, such an approach would not be feasible due to the required handling of numerous component usages.

Tight coupling of component usage and implementation

By using component interfaces for separating design and implementation, it is possible to decouple the tight relationship between using component and component implementation at the component usage level. In a *loose coupling*, a component usage points to an abstract component interface at design time without having to know the component implementation that will be associated at runtime. According to a plug-in concept, this implementation can be selected at runtime but does not need to be known at design time.

Loose coupling with component interfaces

Figure 3.16 shows a graphical comparison of tight and loose coupling between component usage and the corresponding component instance. To understand this more easily, consider the parallel between component usage and *variable*, component or component interface and *type* at design time, as well as component instance and *object* at runtime.

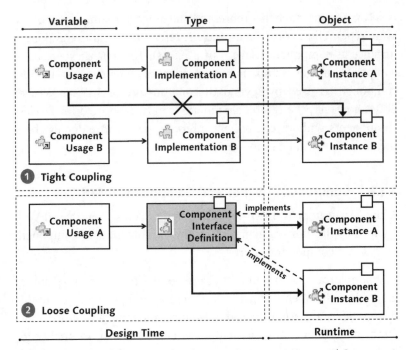

Figure 3.16 Tight and Loose Coupling Between Component Usage and Component Implementation

In a tight coupling (Figure 3.16, ❶) a component cannot point to the instance of another component at runtime other than the one that was already defined at design time. To meet this requirement in a tight coupling, a second component usage B that points to component B would have to be defined. This corresponds to the way a variable is typed with a class.

In a loose coupling using a component interface (Figure 3.16, ❷), a component usage can also point to different component instances at runtime as long as they implement the component interface that was used at design time. In parallel to Java, this corresponds to the typing of a variable using an interface.

Lifecycle and component interfaces

Knowing the considerations presented above it is now easy to understand why the lifecycle property of the component usage always has a value of **manual** when component interfaces are used (see Figure 3.17).

Figure 3.17 Lifecycle Property When Using a Component Interface

The Web Dynpro runtime environment cannot create a component interface itself without knowing an implementing component (**Lifecycle** with the value **createOnDemand**). In fact, it is the task of the application developer to programmatically create an appropriate component instance by calling one of the methods createComponent (String componentName) or createComponent(String component- Name, String deployableObjectName) in the IWDComponentUsage API. For this purpose, it either must know the fully qualified name of the implementing component or it might use, for example, the DeploymentManager component used in Section 3.6.2 that returns the component implementations deployed on the SAP Web Application Server for a specific component interface.

3.3.5 Embedding the Interface Definition of a Game Component in the Root Component

By using a Web Dynpro component interface, we can now implement the embedding or the *plug-in* of any game component in the GameStation component. Thus, the embedding of a game component can be defined at design time without knowing the implementation(s) available at runtime.

Figure 3.18 illustrates the GameStation architecture based on loose coupling. The GameStationComp root component (❶) no longer directly points to a component implementation via a component usage but only points to the independent component interface (❷). The two game components implementing this component interface, SameGameComp and MineSweeperComp, are not visible to the GameStation component at design time. Only at runtime, the embedding root component must create an instance of the corresponding game component (❸ and ❹).

> Loose coupling using component interface

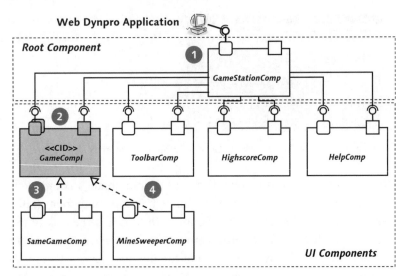

Figure 3.18 Embedding a Component Interface for the Game Component in the Root Component

Declaration and implementation when using component interfaces

By using a component interface at the component usage level, we can define all usage dependencies between components, controllers, windows, or views merely based on interfaces. It is also possible to define context-mapping chains or the subscription of events. Finally, in the controller implementation it is possible to program against the visible external interface of the component-interface controller associated to the component interface. At runtime, the corresponding component usage must then point to a runtime instance that implements the used component interface.

3.4 Embedding the GameStation in Web Dynpro DCs

Transfer to the NWDI component model

Now that we have designed the basic component architecture of the GameStation application in the previous steps, we will now transfer these in the next step to the *NWDI component model*. Only if the architecture of a Web Dynpro application was mapped to this component model can we begin with the real-life application development in SAP NetWeaver Developer Studio. Even though the Web Dynpro tools provide numerous re-factoring features for moving and renaming Web Dynpro entities at a later stage, the basic usage dependencies among them should have been defined beforehand.

See Appendix A for a basic introduction to the SAP NetWeaver Development Infrastructure and its component model.

3.4.1 Web Dynpro Development Components

The NWDI component model provides the special *Development Component type* (DC type) of *Web Dynpro Development Components* for storing Web Dynpro entities in an NWDI development system. In contrast to normal Web Dynpro projects, usage dependencies can be defined among Web Dynpro DCs, where the mutual visibility of DCs is restricted to the parts exposed in the *public parts*. A public part therefore can be regarded as the interface of a DC for its outer using component, where several public parts can be defined for one DC.

Figure 3.19 shows how one Web Dynpro component can be used by another across several DCs:

1. The Web Dynpro component to be used, component 2, is added to a public part of Web Dynpro DC 2. To create the associated *public part archive*, a DC build is then to be triggered (Figure 3.19, ❶).

2. Web Dynpro DC 1 defines the DC usage of Web Dynpro DC 2. The contents of all public parts of DC 2 are then available to be used in DC 1 (Figure 3.19, ❷).

3. Web Dynpro component 1 can now define the usage of component 2 as if it were contained in Web Dynpro DC 1 (Figure 3.19, ❸).

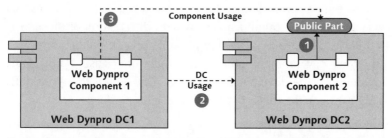

Figure 3.19 Usage Dependency Between Two Web Dynpro DCs and Public Part

Purpose of Public Parts

Because *Development Components* are containers of development objects, you can also define the purpose of public parts (*public part purpose*). In the NWDI component model, you need to generally distinguish between the two usage types **compilation** and **assembly**.

Compilation
The definition of a public part of the type **compilation** means that the development objects contained in the public part are required in the using DC for compiling, or in the Web Dynpro DC to be used for this public part for the build process. For this purpose, the using DC inserts the public part archive in its own Java build path. The public-part archive contains all Web Dynpro metadata files and class files that are required for generating the own DC archive. The DC archive of the used Web Dynpro DC must still be created and deployed separately, though, because the usage of a public part of the **compilation** type does not involve the extension of the own DC archive.

Assembly
Public parts of the **assembly** type must be defined when the development objects contained therein need to be grouped together, or *assembled*, to a larger unit at a higher level, i.e., by a using DC. A public part of this kind is not used to compile the parent DC, though. To achieve this, you need to define a second public part of the **compilation** type.

Public part
purpose =
compilation in
Web Dynpro DCs
To better understand the public part definition it is helpful to know that only the **compilation** usage type is relevant for Web Dynpro DCs. Public parts of the **assembly** type are required for embedding non-deployable DC types such as Java DCs or Library DCs in deployable DCs. Because Web Dynpro DCs are deployable themselves, public parts of the **assembly** type are not relevant.

Accelerated Development of Web Dynpro DCs

If a new public part is defined for a Web Dynpro DC, this means that every triggered DC build process involves the creation of the associated *public part archive*. The definition of several public parts with numerous development objects can therefore cause a noticeable slowdown of the development process. You should therefore definitely consider the following tip for accelerating the process.

Quick
DC build

> **Tip**
>
> Public part archives are newly created only if a *Development Component build process* (DC build) is triggered. If the development objects contained in the public part do not change, it is sufficient to run the normal and faster build process (see Figure 3.20). Particularly for larger Web Dynpro DCs, this procedure can considerably accelerate the development process for repeated testing.

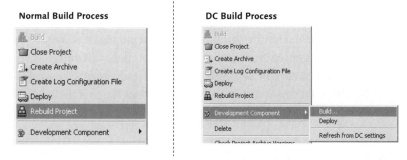

Figure 3.20 Normal Build As Opposed to a DC Build Process

3.4.2 DC Separation of the GameStation in the NWDI Component Model

After the conceptual preparation, we will now separate the architecture of the GameStation application shown in Figure 3.18 into three different Web Dynpro DCs. This naturally brings up the question of why it is necessary to divide a concise Web Dynpro application into several DCs, referred to later as *DC separation*: Would it not be sufficient to have a single Web Dynpro DC where all entities can be used directly without having to create additional DC usage dependencies and public-part definitions?

On closer examination, however, you will notice that the DC separation of Web Dynpro applications has considerable benefits that exceed the effort of creating additional definitions at the DC level by far.

Benefits of the DC separation of Web Dynpro applications

Accelerated Development Process

Because DCs are the build units of the Component Build Service (CBS), their number and size are particularly important for the optimization of the development process. Further, the SAP NetWeaver Developer Studio currently does not support an incremental build process for creating DC archives. Therefore, the overall size of a Web Dynpro DC immediately affects the total time required to newly deploy and test a DC archive (order of steps: **Rebuild Project**, **Create Archive**, **Deploy Archive**, and **Run Application**).

53

Regarding these prerequisites, the most effective method of optimizing the development process is to divide the development objects involved in a Web Dynpro application into separate DCs. By storing stable entities like component interfaces, models, dictionaries, or reusable components in separate DCs, the build process is accelerated for those DCs containing Web Dynpro components that change more frequently.

Extensibility of the GameStation Application

The architecture of the GameStation application is designed in a way that allows the integration of additional game components at a later stage without having to adapt the GameStation component to be embedded at design time or to redeploy it at runtime. In the DC component model, these requirements can be met simply by storing every game component in its own Web Dynpro DC.

Figure 3.21 illustrates how the DC of the GameStation application is actually separated. We apply the principle of separating GameStation and game components at a DC level as well and store every game implementation in its own Web Dynpro DC (❷ and ❸). The embedding GameStation component, the component interface defining a game component, and the Toolbar component are stored in another Web Dynpro DC (❶).

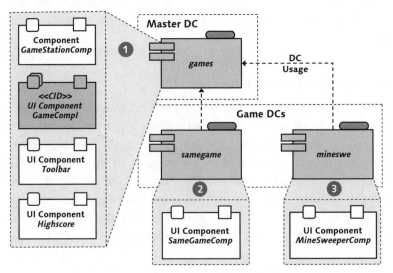

Figure 3.21 Simple DC Architecture of the GameStation Application

3.4.3 Defining Usage Dependency Between DCs

After the DC separation of GameStation and game components, you might wonder how the game-component interface defined in the first Web Dynpro DC can be implemented across several DCs. Figure 3.22 also illustrates the corresponding view of this architecture in the Web Dynpro Explorer of the Web Dynpro tools below the DC diagram. To implement the GameCompI component interface defined in the game DC in the sameGame DC, we will now make the definitions that were presented in a general form in Section 3.4.1 using a real-life example:

1. Adding the game component interfaces in the public part of the game DC

2. Defining a usage dependency between sameGame DC and the game component interface in the public part of the game DC

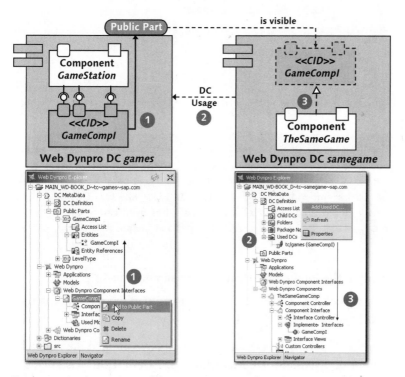

Figure 3.22 Implementation of the Component Interface of a Foreign Web Dynpro DC

Exposing the Component Interface in the Public Part of the game DC

At first, a new public part named GameCompI is added to the game DC (see Figure 3.22; ❶ top). In this public part, the component interface of the same name, GameCompI, is entered as a public part entity. The easiest way of adding a Web Dynpro entity to the public part of a DC is to use the context menu option **Add to Public Part** (see Figure 3.22; ❶ bottom).

Public part
purpose =
compilation

To be able to use or view the component interface in the game DC at design time at all the purpose of the public part must be assigned the value **compilation**. In the input dialog, select the **Provides an API for developing/compiling other DCs** checkbox (see Figure 3.23).

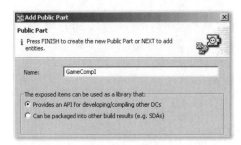

Figure 3.23 Adding a New Public Part to a Web Dynpro DC

Tip

For Web Dynpro DCs, you can always select the **compilation** usage type when defining the public part. The second usage type, **assembly**, is required for embedding *non*-deployable DC types like Java DCs or Library DCs in deployable DCs. Web Dynpro DCs, however, can be deployed directly so that they do not need public parts of the **assembly** type.

Defining the Public Part Usage in the sameGame-DC

The usage of the GameCompI public part entity of the game DC can then be defined in the sameGame DC:

▶ In the Web Dynpro Explorer, you first have to open the node element **<DC name>** · **DC MetaData** · **DC Definition** · **Used DCs** to select its context menu option **Add Used DC ....**

▶ In the **Add Dependency** display frame, you then directly select the public part entity of the GameCompI component interface. Open the nodes **<DC name>** · **DC MetaData** · **Public Parts** · **GameCompI** · **Entities** · **GameCompI** (see Figure 3.24).

▶ As a **Dependency Type**, enable the **Build Time (needed for compilation)** checkbox and then complete the definition of the public part purpose by clicking on **Finish**.

Because all DCs can use each other in the same way, they are dependant on each other. When defining a public-part purpose, you therefore need to specify which **dependency type** is to exist between the using DC and the DC providing the public part. As the public part entity GameCompI is required in the sameGame DC for both declaration and compilation, or for building the DC archive, respectively, we will select the **Build Time** dependency type.

Dependency type = build time

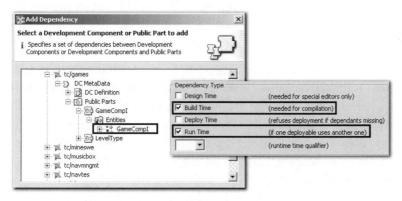

Figure 3.24 Definition of a Used DC Dependency in the Web Dynpro Tools

As a general rule, you need to specify the **Build Time** type as the public part dependency when using Web Dynpro DCs. Although the other two dependency types, **Deploy Time** and **Run Time**, are selectable for the public part purpose of Web Dynpro DCs, they are usually not required.

The selection of the **Deploy Time** dependency type causes the deployment of a Web Dynpro DC to be automatically canceled when a DC it uses is missing in the runtime system.

The **Run Time** dependency type is also to be selected when the public part contains a Java archive (JAR file) that must be visible in the using DC at runtime for class loading or instantiation. However, if the used public part contains Web Dynpro entities, the required runtime dependencies are automatically entered in the DC archive by the Web Dynpro tools, even without the **Run Time** dependency type being set. Still, it is advisable to always select the **Run Time** dependency type whenever you use public parts of other Web Dynpro DCs.

3.5 Implementation of a Component Interface

Section 3.4 described how a Web Dynpro component interface is to be inserted in the public part of the game DC to be used by other Web Dynpro DCs. Apart from the usage of a component interface at the component-usage level, its implementation is obviously of major importance. In this section, we will therefore demonstrate the implementation of the game-component interface in a separate Web Dynpro DC using the SameGame game as an example.

At first we assume that the usage dependency with the game component interface has already been defined in the sameGame DC. More specifically, the sameGame DC is already using the GameCompI public part entity of the game DC. This usage dependency is represented in the Web Dynpro Explorer by the node **Main_WD_BOOK_D~tc~ samegame~sap.com · DC MetaData · DC Definition · Used DCs · tc/games (GameCompI)**. The implementation of the game component interface is then effected in three consecutive steps.

1. **Create a new component**
   Creating a new Web Dynpro component.

2. **Define the implementation dependency**
   Automatic declaration of component interface views and component interface controller by selecting a component interface. The new component thus has an *implementation dependency* with the component interface.

3. **Implement the component**
   Implementation of the component interface in the component interface controller and in the component interface views by embedding views.

3.5.1 Creating a New Web Dynpro Component

In the first step, you need to create a new empty Web Dynpro component:

1. In the Web Dynpro Explorer, select the node **Web Dynpro · Web Dynpro Components**.

2. Open the context menu and select the option **Create Web Dynpro Component**.

3. A new window for entering component, window, view, and package names is displayed (see Figure 3.25). When entering these names, ensure that you end the component name with the suffix "Comp" and the view name with "View." The three package names should be the same, and every Web Dynpro component is to be stored in its own package name range. It is therefore a good idea to end the package name with "*.comp.<component name>."

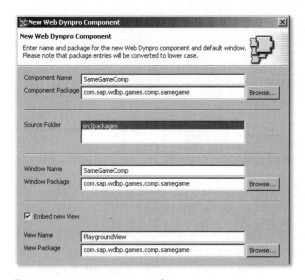

Figure 3.25 Creating a New Web Dynpro Component

3.5.2 Defining Implementation Dependencies

After its creation, a new Web Dynpro component is in an *initial* state. This means that at this time, it only contains its default controllers and a view that is embedded in the window defined during creation. A corresponding component interface view is attached to the window, and the component interface controller is in an empty state without methods, events, and context elements.

By defining an *implementation dependency* with the game-component interface, the newly created component becomes a game component. It then syntactically matches the specifications of the game component interface with regard to the declaration of its component-interface views and its component-interface controller.

Declaring the implementation of the game component interface

The implementation dependency between Web Dynpro component and component interface is declared according to the following procedure:

1. In the Web Dynpro Explorer, select the node **Web Dynpro · Web Dynpro Components · <component name> · Component Interface · Implemented Interfaces**.

2. In the context menu, select the **Add** option (see Figure 3.26).

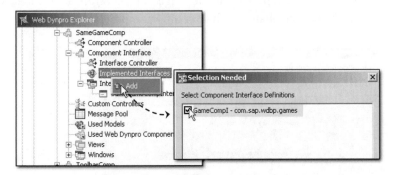

Figure 3.26 Adding an Implementation Dependency

3. In the displayed dialog box, select the component interfaces to be implemented and then press the **OK** button.

4. In the following two dialog boxes, confirm the definition of new windows (Playground and Settings) that are associated with the component interface views specified by the component interface.

The new component interface views PlaygroundInterfaceView and SettingsInterfaceView as well as the corresponding windows are then displayed in the Web Dynpro Explorer (see Figure 3.27). The interface controller of the SameGame component contains the start-Game() method, and its context contains the nodes Game and Game-Settings, including their context attributes.

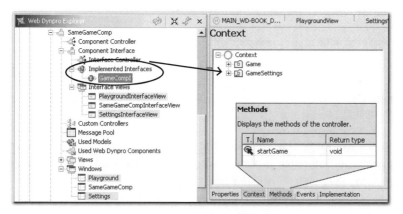

Figure 3.27 SameGame Component After Adding an Implementation Dependency

3.5.3 Completely Implementing the Component

After the declaration of an implementation dependency, the Same-Game component is syntactically but not semantically correct. Still missing is the full implementation of the controllers, windows, and views.

In this section, the most important aspects of the implementation part are outlined without comprehensively discussing all the details of a game implementation. Example components implementing the game component interface are available for download in the Website of this book.[3]

Controller Implementation

A game component is started by its using component by calling the startGame() method in the component-interface controller. This method is defined in the game-component interface and is implemented by delegation to the component controller. For this to work, the component controller must contain the same method in its IPublic API. After defining a controller usage dependency with the component controller, the startGame() method can be implemented in the component interface controller as shown in Listing 3.1.

Implementation of the sameGame() method

---

3 The games, SameGame and BossPuzzle, are implemented in the two Web Dynpro DCs MAIN_WD-BOOK_D~tc~bosspuzzle~sap.com and MAIN_WD-BOOK_D~tc~same-game~sap.com.

```
public void startGame() {
//@@begin startGame()
wdThis.wdGetSameGameCompController().startGame();
//@@end
}
```

Listing 3.1 SameGameCompInterface.java–Implementation of the startGame()
Method

In the component controller, the startGame() method triggers an
event[4] for starting a new game that is handled in the Play-
ground.java view controller (see Listing 3.2).

```
public void startGame() {
//@@begin startGame()
wdThis.wdFireEventStartGame();
//@@end
}
```

Listing 3.2 SameGameComp.java–Triggering the Events StartGame

Context mappings between component interface and component controller As a general rule, the component interface controller should fulfill
the function of a delegator to the component controller. Conse-
quently, no own data elements but only mapped context elements
need to be defined in the context of a component interface (see Section 3.7.1). Figure 3.28 shows the context mapping definitions
required to close the mapping chains.

In the component-interface controller, the Game node including its
attributes is to be mapped to the corresponding context elements in
the component controller (see Figure 3.28, ❶). The GameSet-
tings.Level context attribute in the interface controller does not
contain any data itself but obtains or references it from the embedding GameStationComp component by *external interface context mapping* (see Figure 3.28, ❷ and Section 3.7.2). In the component controller, the context elements GameSettings and Level are mapped to
these two Input elements in the interface controller context.

---

4 Section 3.8 contains more detailed information on server-side eventing.

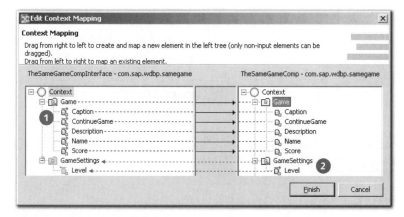

Figure 3.28 Context Mappings Between Component and Component Interface Controller in a Game Component

The game component interface defines the two component interface views `Playground` and `Settings`. On the inside of the game component, their implementation represents the two windows `Playground` and `Settings` (see Figure 3.29). The actual user interface is finally implemented at the lowest level in the layout of the two views `PlaygroundView` and `SettingsViews`. In the navigation modeler, a view can be newly created and at the same time embedded in the presented window (see Figure 3.30).

Embedding views in windows

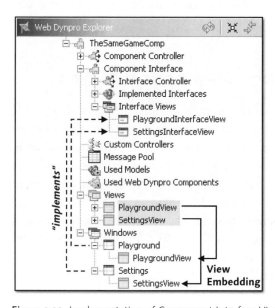

Figure 3.29 Implementation of Component Interface Views

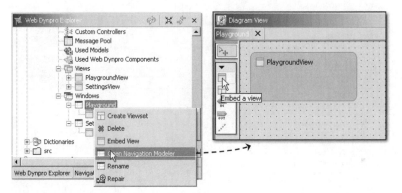

Figure 3.30 Navigation Modeler for Embedding Views in Windows

Further implemen-
tation steps To fully implement a game component, the following steps still need to be carried out:

▶ Definition and mapping of view contexts

▶ Event handling of the `StartGame` event in the `PlaygroundView`

▶ Dynamic view modification for presenting the playground

▶ Event handling of actions triggered on the playground by the user

▶ Implementation of the `SettingsView` for entering game settings

Because this chapter focuses on the componentization of Web Dynpro applications, these further implementation steps are not discussed here.

3.6 Creating Game Components at Runtime

A major benefit of the GameStation application architecture is the loose coupling between the root component and the game component embedded via the component interface. At the design time t_D (see Figure 3.31), the GameStation component only defines a usage or *component usage dependency* with the `GameCompI` game component interface. As we saw in Section 3.3, this component interface can already define all dependency types like (external) interface context mapping, event subscription, method calls at the interface controller level, the embedding of component-interface views, or the definition of navigation links.

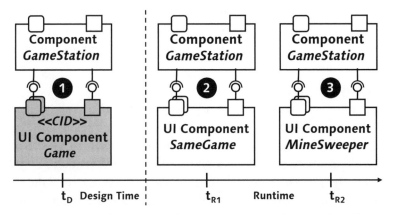

Figure 3.31 Using Component Interface at Design Time and Late Binding of Component Instances

At runtime, however, the GameStation component has the task of assigning component instances to the component usage that implements the game component interface. If several component implementations of this kind exist on the SAP Web AS at runtime, it is also possible to play several games in a row on the GameStation (Figure 3.31, ❷ and ❸). These points in time are referred to as t_{R1} and t_{R2} in Figure 3.31. A component usage is only a variable at runtime, pointing to a concrete component instance.

In the remaining parts of Section 3.6, we will deal with the questions of how the lifecycle of game components is controlled within the GameStation component at runtime, how the available game implementations are determined, and how these are selected by the user.

3.6.1 IWDComponentUsage API

The component instance associated with a component usage is programmatically created and destroyed via the IWDComponentUsage API. For creating such an instance, this interface provides the three-times overloaded createComponent() method, and for its destruction the deleteComponent() method. To understand the usage of these methods, we will first explain some terms that are relevant in this context:

▶ **Deployable object = Web Dynpro DC**
  In the Web Dynpro API, deployable object is an alternative term for Web Dynpro Development Component. In the NWDI component model, the Web Dynpro DC represents the unit for deploy-

ing Web Dynpro development objects (components, component interfaces, model, dictionaries) at design time. The deployable object is the name of this unit within the Web Dynpro runtime environment.

▶ **Deployable object name**
The fully qualified name of a deployable object in a Web Dynpro DC is composed of its vendor name and its name segments. The vendor name and the first name segment are separated by a slash (/); the name segments themselves are connected via tildes (~). A Web Dynpro DC named `company.com/ui/forms/address` therefore results in the deployable object with the name `company.com/ui~forms~address`.

▶ **Active component**
An active component is an existing component instance.

▶ **Referencing mode**
Under certain conditions, a component usage A can point to another component usage B to delegate the lifecycle control of the component instance to be used. With regard to component usage B, component usage A is then in *referencing mode*[5]. More details about this technique can be found in Section 3.8.3.

▶ **Fully qualified name**
The fully qualified name of a Web Dynpro component comprises its package name and its component name connected with a period. The `AddressComp` component in the package `com.company.app.booking.ui.address.comp` therefore has a fully qualified name of `com.company.app.booking.ui.address.comp.AddressComp`.

Using the create-Component() method
At first we want to point out that the `IWDComponentUsage.createComponent()` method can only be called without parameters if the associated component usage does not point to a component interface but to a component implementation. In which Web Dynpro DC it is contained and which name it has are determined by the Web Dynpro runtime environment, from the metadata of the component usage defined at design time. If the lifecycle property of such a component usage was additionally assigned, the value **createOnDemand** the `createComponent()` method does not need to be called at all.

---

5 In SAP NetWeaver 2004, you can use the referencing mode only for faceless components without component interface views.

However, if the component usage (see Figure 3.32, ❶) points to a component interface (❷) as in this example, the Web Dynpro runtime environment must be informed which component implementation (❸ or ❹) is to be used for creating a new component instance. In this case, the lifecycle property of the component usage has the value **manual**; that is, the component instance *must* be created via a method call.

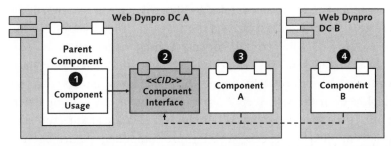

Figure 3.32 DC Affiliation of Component Interface and Implementing Component

Depending on the Web Dynpro DC containing the implementing component, the name of the deployable object—i.e., the associated Web Dynpro DC—must be passed to the IWDComponentUsage API along with the fully qualified component name when the createComponent() method is called.

In our application architecture, the root and the game components are in different Web Dynpro DCs (*deployable objects*). As a result, the method IWDComponentUsage.createComponent(String component-Name, String deployableObjectName) is to be called for creating game component instances within the GameStation component (see Figure 3.33).

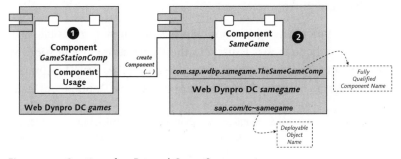

Figure 3.33 Creation of an External Game Component

3.6.2 DeploymentManager Component

Determining the deployed game components at runtime

At design time, GameStation and game components are loosely coupled via a game-component interface. This means that the declarations and the application coding take place in the GameStation component without knowing the components implementing a game. Does this statement also apply to *manual*[6] lifecycle management? That is, could we really operate without knowing the fully qualified component and DC names at design time when we programmatically create a component instance via the `IWDComponentUsage` API? In this case, no code line could contain **String** values such as `com.sap.wdbp.samegame.TheSameGameComp` or `sap.com/tc~samegame`. Instead, the information about the game components that are deployed on the SAP Web AS at runtime would have to be determined via a specific service API. In the GameStation architecture, this task is fulfilled by a special Web Dynpro component named `DeploymentManagerComp` (DeploymentManager), where the data exchange between the components `GameStationComp` and `DeploymentManagerComp` is exclusively established by the definition of context mapping dependencies.[7] The `GameStationComp` component first stores the fully qualified name of the game component interface in its own component controller context, then creates the DeploymentManager component, and finally can access information about the deployed game components found by the DeploymentManager.

3.6.3 Final Architecture of the GameStation Application

With the DeploymentManager component, we have completed the design of the GameStation application architecture (see Figure 3.34) and applied essential Web Dynpro concepts such as componentization and component interfaces.

The DeploymentManager component is the first non-visual Web Dynpro component that is used in the GameStation application by the root component `GameStationComp` (Figure 3.34, ❶). The component diagram in Figure 3.34 therefore shows the DeploymentMan-

---

6 A component usage that points to a component interface always has the lifecycle property **manual**. This means that the creation and deletion of component instances must be programmed in the application code.

7 Section 3.7 provides detailed information on the data exchange across component boundaries using normal or external interface context mappings.

ager component (**❷**) without the port icon used for representing component interface views.

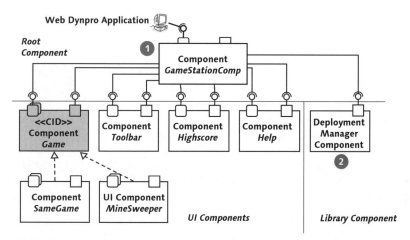

Figure 3.34 Final Component Architecture of the GameStation Application with the DeploymentManager Component

Figure 3.35 shows the presentation of the GameStationComp component in the Data Modeler of the Web Dynpro tools. On the left-hand side, all five components used by the GameStationComp component are represented by component usage icons. Context- mapping dependencies between different controller contexts are symbolized by arrows. Double arrows are displayed when context-mapping dependencies were defined in both directions.

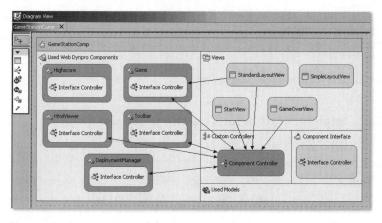

Figure 3.35 Representation of the GameStationComp Component in the Data Modeler

Table 3.2 presents the specification of the DeploymentManager component at the level of its component-interface controller. Apart from the elements contained in the interface context, the DeploymentManager component exposes neither methods nor events.

Web Dynpro component (faceless)				
DeploymentManagerComp				
Web Dynpro library component for determining all Web Dynpro components that are deployed on the SAP Web Application Server and implement a given component interface.				
Component interface controller				
DeploymentManagerComp				
Context definition and public methods in the interface controller				
Context	**Card.**	**Type**	**Mapping to component context**	**isInput**
Implementing-Components	0..n		x	
▶ DOName		**string**	x	
▶ DOPart		**WDDeployableObjectPart**	x	
▶ DOShortName		**string**	x	
▶ FullName		**string**	x	
▶ ShortName		**string**	x	
RequestedInterface	1..1			x
▶ FullName		**string**		x
Methods	**Events**			
none	none			

Table 3.2 Specification of the DeploymentManager Component

3.6.4 Implementation for Creating Game Component Instances

We first assume that all context-mapping dependencies between the components GameStationComp and DeploymentManagerComp have been defined (see Figure 3.36). The DeploymentManager thus can access the fully qualified name of the game component interface to be implemented. The GameStationComp component stores this name in its own component controller context and enables the DeploymentManager to access it by closing the context-mapping chain using *external interface context mapping* (see Figure 3.36, ❶).

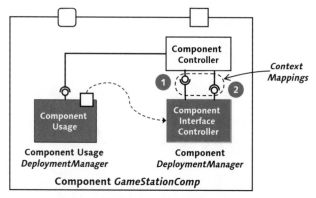

Figure 3.36 Using the DeploymentManager and Its Interface Controller in the GameStationComp Component

The DeploymentManager then determines all game components that are deployed on the SAP Web AS and that implement the specified game component interface. The associated information about the found component implementations such as the fully qualified component name or the name of the associated deployable object (Web Dynpro DC) is stored by the DeploymentManager component in the context of its own component-interface controller. Via context mapping (see Figure 3.36, ❷), the GameStationComp component then can access this information and use it for creating game component instances.

Function of the Deployment-Manager component

Let us now have a look at the implementation part that is required for creating a game component instance using the DeploymentManager component.

Implementation in the GameStationComp.java Controller Class

In the wdDoInit() hook method, when initializing the GameStation component controllers, we first store the fully qualified name of the com.sap.wdbp.games.GameCompI game component interface in the context. Then we create an instance of the used DeploymentManager component and populate the list of the game components deployed on the SAP Web AS (see Listing 3.3).

```
public void wdDoInit() {
  //@@begin wdDoInit()
  wdContext.currentGameInterfaceElement().setFullName(
    "com.sap.wdbp.games.GameCompI");
  wdThis
    .wdGetDeployment ManagerComponentUsage()
    .createComponent();
  updateGameList();
  //@@end
}
```

Listing 3.3 GameStationComp.java–Initialization of the GameStation Component Controller

Determining the game names to be displayed The private method `updateGameList()` in the GameStation component controller implements the determination of game names to be displayed in a dropdown list in the user interface. For this purpose, a `for` loop accesses all elements in the `DeployedGames` context node previously populated by the DeploymentManager. Because the DeploymentManager can only determine technical names for the deployed game components, we need access to the individual game components themselves each of which has the game name to be displayed in the UI. Therefore, every deployed game component is temporarily created in the `updateGameList()` method and destroyed immediately after copying the game name in the context. This name is then stored in the `Deployed Games.Caption` context attribute. Note that this context attribute named `Caption` is not contained in the mapped node `DeployedGames` but was added at a later stage as an unmapped attribute (see Figure 3.37).

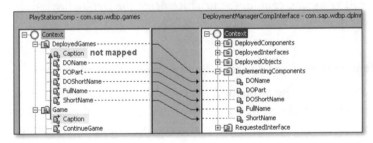

Figure 3.37 Adding the Unmapped Caption Attribute in the Mapped Context Node DeployedGames

Mapped and unmapped attributes can therefore be *mixed* in the same node in Web Dynpro.[8] In this way, we do not need to define an additional context node DeployedGamesCaptions and can also simplify the required application code.

The updateGameList() method is implemented in the closing application code area (*user coding area*) of the GameStation component controller that is contained between the lines //@@begin others and //@@end (see Listing 3.4).

```
//@@begin others
private void updateGameList() {
  IPublicGameStationComp
    .IDeployedGamesElement deployedGameElement;
  IWDComponentUsage iGameUsg=
    wdThis.wdGetGameComponentUsage();
  for (int i= 0;
    i < wdContext.nodeDeployedGames().size(); i++) {
    deployedGameElement= wdContext.nodeDeployedGames()
      .getDeployedGamesElementAt(i);
    iGameUsg.createComponent(
    deployedGameElement.getFullName(),
    deployedGameElement.getDOName());
    deployedGameElement.setCaption(
      wdContext.currentGameElement().getCaption());
    iGameUsg.deleteComponent();
  } // close for-loop
}
//@@end
```

Listing 3.4 GameStationComp.java–Method for Creating a List of Game Names

After copying the game names to the Deployed Games context node, they can be displayed in an IWDDropDownByIndex UI element of the Toolbar UI component and selected by the user. In the onStartNew-Game() event handler of the GameStation component controller, the selected game component instance is finally created. This event handler is linked to a server-side event in the Toolbar UI component that is triggered in the action event handler for the selection of a game in the user interface (see Figure 3.38 and Section 3.8.1).

---

8 This is only true under the following condition: The corresponding context node must not be bound to a structure. In that case, however, the additional attribute could be added in a **non-singleton** type child node with cardinality **1..1**.

Figure 3.38 Display of Game Names in a Selection List

Creation of Game Component Instances in the Application Code

Creating a game component instance

We will now deal with that part of the application code that implements the creation of a component instance belonging to the selected game (see Listing 3.5). After selecting a game in the user interface, the lead selection of the DeployedGames node is set to the corresponding node element on the server side. This element can be directly referenced via wdContext.currentDeployedGamesElement(). To be able to select a new game during the running game, you first must check that the component usage already points to an active game component instance. If this is the case, this instance must first be destroyed by calling the IWDComponentUsage.deleteComponent() method before a new instance can be created. The component is created by transferring the fully qualified name of the game component and the corresponding deployable object name using the IWDComponentUsage.createComponent() method. Both **String** values were previously stored in the selected node element of the DeployedGames node of the DeploymentManager.

```
public void onStartNewGame(
  com.sap.tc.webdynpro.progmodel.api.IWDCustomEvent
    wdEvent) {
//@@begin onStartNewGame(ServerEvent)
IPublicGameStationComp
  .IDeployedGamesElement selectedGameElement=
wdContext.currentDeployedGamesElement();

IWDComponentUsage iGameUsg=
wdThis.wdGetGameComponentUsage();

if (iGameUsg.hasActiveComponent()) {
  iGameUsg.deleteComponent();
}
iGameUsg.createComponent(
  selectedGameElement.getDOName(),
  selectedGameElement.getFullName());
wdThis.wdGetGameInterface().startGame();
```

```
//@@end
}
```

Listing 3.5 GameStationComp.java–Event Handler for Starting the Game Component Selected by the User

3.7   Inter-Component Context Mapping

In the Web Dynpro programming model, the concept of *context mappings* enables you to reference global context data across controllers. The original data stored in a *data context* thus can be referenced by several mapped contexts of other controllers so that extensive copying of this data can be avoided.

By defining context-mapping dependencies in Web Dynpro, data can be exchanged not only across controllers but also across components. The context of the component-interface controller is very important in this respect because it is included in every possible context mapping chain across components.[9] For a better understanding, we therefore refer to the inter-component context mapping as *interface context mapping* from now on (interface stands for component interface controller) to distinguish it from normal context mapping in component, custom or view controllers.

Interface context mapping

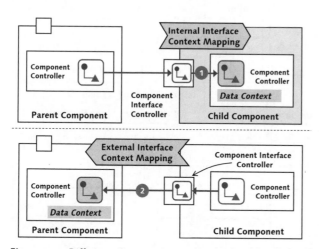

Figure 3.39 Difference Between Internal and External Interface Context Mapping

9 As component interface views do not contain a separate context, the component interface controller provides the only context interface of a Web Dynpro component.

There are two kinds of inter-component context mapping: *external* and *internal* interface context mapping. The diagrams shown in Figure 3.39 already illustrate the most important differences between these two types of interface context mapping: the location of the data context, and the location where the interface context mapping is defined.

3.7.1 Internal Interface Context Mapping

Data context lies within the component

Normally, the data context is included in the component itself. To make this data available to an external component, you only need to define a context mapping from the component-interface controller to the own component controller or custom controller (see Figure 3.40, ❶). Because this mapping dependency can be defined in the component-interface controller itself and within the component, it is referred to as *internal* interface context mapping. Whenever a Web Dynpro component wants to make its own data context visible to the outside (to other components), it must define an internal interface context mapping.

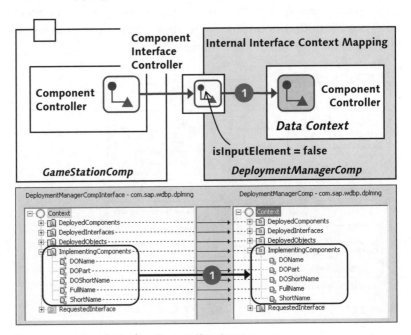

Figure 3.40 Internal Interface Context Mapping

Figure 3.40 illustrates internal interface context mapping using the example of the DeploymentManager-component. In the component controller, the context node `ImplementingComponents` stores the implementations found for a component interface. To expose this context data to the outside, an internal mapping towards this context node is defined in the interface controller context. For all context elements involved, the **isInputElement** property is set to a value of **false**.

> **Tip**
>
> In the component-interface controller, do not define any data context but only mapped or externally mappable context elements (with the **isInputElement = true** property). This way, you can avoid having to implement supply functions for context nodes in the interface controller. We recommend this approach because the implementation of the component interface controller will be moved to the component controller in subsequent releases of SAP NetWeaver. The migration of existing Web Dynpro applications to subsequent releases is easier the more strictly the component interface controller is defined and implemented as a mere delegator controller to the component controller already part of SAP NetWeaver 2004. This applies when no data context elements are defined and all methods in the interface controller delegate their implementation to the component controller.

3.7.2 External Interface Context Mapping

The second kind of interface context mapping is shown in the lower diagram in Figure 3.39 and in Figure 3.41. In some applications, it is necessary to access *external* data contexts from a Web Dynpro component. Such a component is intentionally developed so that it cannot be run independently but is dependent on its later using component (an embedded component) to fulfill its function.

Data context lies outside the component

In the GameStation application, the DeploymentManager component is such a component. For determining the game components deployed on the SAP Web AS, it requires the fully qualified name of the game component interface from its using component (the Game- StationComp component). Because the DeploymentManager component does not know its using component, it cannot map its interface context (context of the component interface controller) to the data context of its using component. Instead, it first flags the respective context elements as special input elements to obtain their input or their data from outside, that is, from the using component. This flag is achieved by assigning a value of **true** to the **isInputElement** property of a context element (context node or context attribute).

External definition
of interface context
mapping

The actual interface context mapping takes place in a second step outside the component on the part of the using component. The name *external* interface context mapping is attributed to the fact that the using component defines the context mapping from the component interface controller to its own component controller. The essential difference from the *internal* interface context mapping is that the data context is outside the component and the interface context mapping must therefore be defined externally in the outside component that is using the component (see Figure 3.41, ❷).

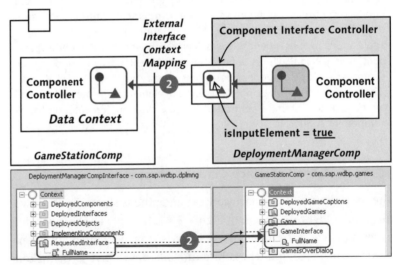

Figure 3.41 External Interface Context Mapping Between DeploymentManager and GameStation Context

Tip

To display context-mapping dependencies between two Web Dynpro controllers in Web Dynpro Explorer, you can use the node marked with an arrow beneath a controller. If you double-click on this node, a window is opened that displays the context mapping defined between the two controllers (see Figure 3.42).

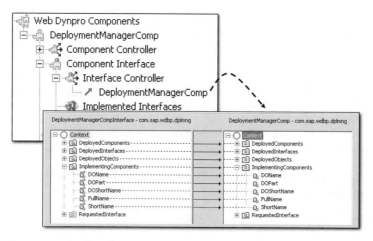

Figure 3.42 Display of Context Mapping Dependencies Via Controller Usages in Web Dynpro Explorer

3.7.3 Declaration of External Interface Context Mapping

Two separate declaration steps are required for a child component to be provided with data by its parent component via external interface context mapping, In the first step, the interface context of the child component is to be prepared so that in the second step it can be mapped to the data context of the embedding parent component at the component-usage level. In the following section, both steps are described in more detail using the example of the external interface context mapping between DeploymentManager and playground component.

Set the IsInputElement Properties in the Child Component to True

We assume that, in the interface controller context of the DeploymentManager component, the **1..1** node **RequestedInterface** and the string attribute FullName contained therein have been defined. At runtime, the element in the node **RequestedInterface** should point to the respective data element in the component controller context of the embedding GameStation component. In other words, it is supposed to obtain the context data from the external component. Those elements of an interface context that are to be provided with data from outside via external interface context mapping are therefore referred to as *input elements* and are assigned a value of **true** for their **isInputElement** property.

isInputElement = true

1. In Web Dynpro Explorer, open the node **Web Dynpro Components · DeploymentManagerComp · Component Interface · Interface Controller, and in the context menu select the Edit** option (see Figure 3.43, ❶).

2. In the perspective view **DeploymentManagerCompInterface**, open the **Context** tab.

3. Select the node **RequestedInterface** and then open the corresponding **Properties** tab.

4. Assign a value of **true** to the **isInputElement** property (see Figure 3.43, ❷).

5. Repeat the previous two steps for the FullName context attribute.

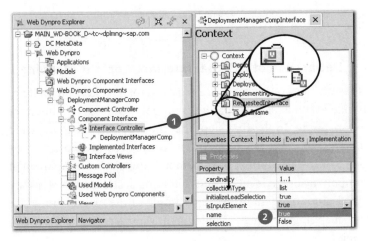

Figure 3.43 Setting the isInputElement Property

The first part of declaring the external interface context mapping is thus completed. The two context elements RequestedInterface and FullName were flagged as input elements **(isInputElement = true)** and are now marked with a slightly different icon in the context-perspective view. Because no actual context mapping has been defined, the tip of the arrow is missing. However, you can see a special mark for representing input elements (see Figure 3.43, on the top right).

To better understand this first part of external interface context mapping, we will shortly point out another interpretation: For an external component to be able to map the interface context of an embedded component to its own context, input elements must have been defined in the interface context. By setting the **isInputElement** property to **true**, a context element is identified as externally mappable at a later stage or mappable in the external using component at a later stage.

> **Note**
>
> Please note that context attributes immediately under the root node (*top-level context attributes*) cannot be declared as input elements and are thus not externally mappable. Instead, these attributes are to be defined using the **isInputElement = true** property in an independent context node of a cardinality of **1..1**.

Declaring External Interface Context Mapping in the Parent Component

In the second step, the external interface context mapping between DeploymentManager and GameStation component can now be defined. In this way, the FullName attribute (fully qualified name of a component interface) in the interface context of the DeploymentManager is to reference the same attribute in the data context of the GameStation component controller. Figure 3.44 shows the presentation of these external interface context mappings in the Web Dynpro tools.

The external interface context mapping is declared according to the following procedure:

1. In Web Dynpro Explorer, open the node **Web Dynpro Components · GameStationComp**, and in the context menu select the **Open Data Modeler** option.

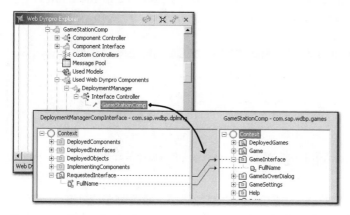

Figure 3.44 External Interface Context Mapping from the DeploymentManager to the GameStation Component

2. In the toolbar of the Data Modeler, select the **Create a data link** icon (see Figure 3.45, ❶).

3. Move the mouse pointer over the rectangle **DeploymentManager · Interface Controller** in the area **Used Web Dynpro Components** (❷).

4. Keep the mouse button pressed and move the mouse pointer from there over the rectangle **Component Controller** (Figure 3.45, ❸ and ❹).

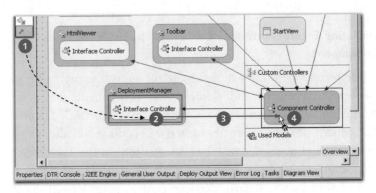

Figure 3.45 Defining the Data Link in the Data Modeler

5. This opens the input dialog for defining an (external) context mapping dependency. Move the mouse pointer on the left side in the **DeploymentManagerCompInterface** area over the **Requested-Interface** context node (Figure 3.46, ❶).

6. Keep the mouse button pressed and move the pointer from there to the right, over the node **GameInterface** in the context of the GameStation component controller (Figure 3.46, ❷).

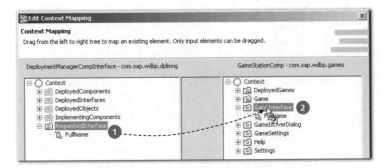

Figure 3.46 External Interface Context Mapping Via Drag-and-Drop in the Context Mapping Wizard

7. In the second dialog step, enable the **RequestedInterface** and **FullName** checkboxes (see Figure 3.47). Then click on **OK**.

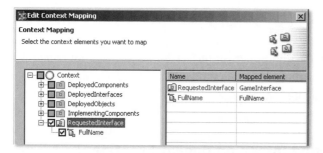

Figure 3.47 Selection of the Context Elements to be Mapped

8. In the last dialog step, the defined context mapping dependency is illustrated using arrows (see Figure 3.48).

9. Finish the definition of the external interface context mapping by clicking on the **Finish** button.

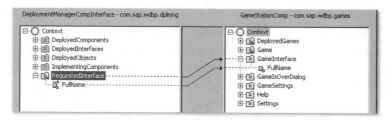

Figure 3.48 Presentation of the External Interface Context Mapping in the Last Dialog Step

Using External Interface Context Mapping

After the definition of the external interface context mapping, the mapping chain between the component controllers of the components GameStationComp and DeploymentManagerComp is completely defined (see also Figure 3.41). In both controllers, the typed context APIs IPublicDeploymentManagerComp.IRequestedInterface<Node, Element> and IPublicGameStationComp.IGameInterface<Node,Element> can be used to access the data context stored in the Game-Station component:

▶ wdContext.currentGameInterfaceElement().setFullName("com.
  sap.wdbp.games.GameCompI")

Stores the fully qualified name of the component interface in the context attribute `GameInterface.FullName` of the GameStation component controller

▶ `wdContext.currentRequestedInterfaceElement().getFull Name()`
Accesses the component interface name in the DeploymentManager component controller that is required for determining the deployed components

3.8   Using Inter-Component Eventing

Server-side eventing—triggering and handling events in controllers— plays an important part in component-based Web Dynpro applications when implementing the application logic. It is required in particular when a child component must delegate the implementation of the application logic to its own parent component. The child component can never define a usage dependency with its parent component because this implies a cyclic dependency. Thus, the child component cannot use the `IExternal` API of its parent component for a method call. To still delegate the application logic to the parent component, the child component can use the technique of server-side eventing. It enables the child component to delegate the handling of its own events to the parent component without actually using it. To achieve this, the parent component must subscribe to the event of its child component and implement the appropriate event handler.

3.8.1   Server-Side Eventing Between Child and Parent Component

The GameStation application implements inter-component eventing within the two components `ToolbarComp` and `GameStationComp`. This makes it possible to delegate the handling of actions (for example, starting the selected game, or displaying game settings) in the `ToolbarView` to the embedding `GameStation` component (see Figure 3.49). The following sections explain the procedure for applying server-side eventing across components.

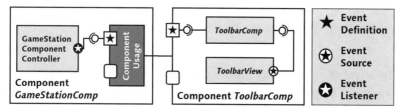

Figure 3.49 Server-Side Eventing Across Components

Declaring an Event in the Interface Controller of the Toolbar Component

To make an event known across several components it must be defined in the component-interface controller of the component that triggers the event.

1. In Web Dynpro Explorer, open the node **Web Dynpro Components · ToolbarComponent · Component Interface · Interface Controller**, and in the context menu select the **Edit** option.

2. In the **ToolbarCompInterface** perspective view that is then displayed, go to the **Events** tab (see Figure 3.50).

3. For declaring a new event, select the **New** button.

4. In the following dialog box, enter the name of the event (for example, "startNewGame"). If no parameters are to be passed with the event, click on **Finish**. Otherwise, you can use the next dialog to define event parameters.

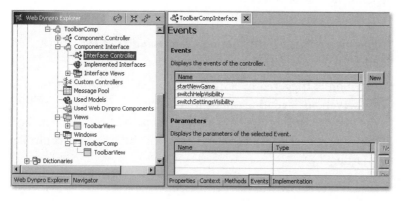

Figure 3.50 Event Declaration in the Component Interface

After declaring an event in the component interface controller, its IPublic API is automatically extended by the wdFireEvent<Event-

Name>() method, for example wdFireEventStartNewGame().[10] This method can then be called by the component controller.

Implementing a Method in the Component Controller of the Toolbar Component

Generally, it is advisable to have view controllers not directly communicate with the component interface controller but only with the component or custom controller. To still be able to trigger the component interface event StartNewGame in a view controller, the component controller must provide an appropriate startNewGame() method in its IPublic API that in turn delegates to the component interface controller (see Listing 3.6).

```
public void startNewGame( )
{
  //@@begin startNewGame()
  wdThis.wdGetToolbarCompInterfaceController()
    .wdFireEventStartNewGame();
  //@@end
}
```

Listing 3.6 ToolbarComp.java–Triggering the Event StartNewGame in the Component Controller

Naturally, the IPublic API of the component interface controller is only visible in the component controller after an appropriate usage dependency has been defined.

Triggering an Event in the Action Event Handler of the ToolbarView Controller

If an action is triggered by a user in the view layout of the Toolbar view, server-side eventing can be used to delegate its event handling in the view controller upwards to the component controller, which in turn triggers the StartNewGame event in the interface controller (see Listing 3.7).

---

10 Note that in contrast to this, the triggering methods wdFireEvent<Eventname>() are added in the IPrivate API instead of the IPublic API for events in component and custom controllers. If you want those events to be triggered from other controllers, you must use additional public methods.

```
public void onActionStartNewGame(
  com.sap.tc.webdynpro.progmodel.api.IWDCustomEvent
  wdEvent )
{
  //@@begin onActionStartNewGame(ServerEvent)
  wdThis.wdGetToolbarCompController().startNewGame();
  //@@end
}
```

Listing 3.7 ToolbarView.java–Calling the startNewGame() Method in the View Controller

Declaring an Event Handler in the GameStation Component Controller

In the GameStationComp component, a component usage dependency with the Toolbar component is defined so that the toolbar interface controller can be used in all controllers of the GameStation component. An event handler for the event StartNewGame exposed by the component ToolbarComp is to be declared in the component controller of the GameStation component as follows:

1. In the GameStation component controller, first define the usage of the interface controller belonging to the Toolbar component. In the **Properties** tab, click on the **New** button, and in the following dialog select the node **Toolbar · Toolbar (Web Dynpro Component Interface Controller)** (see Figure 3.51). The toolbar component usage itself only needs to be declared when the associated IWDComponentUsage API needs to be accessed, for example for the programmatic lifecycle management of the toolbar component instance.

Subscribing an event handler to an event

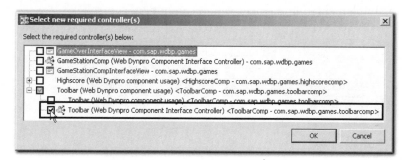

Figure 3.51 Usage of the Toolbar Interface Controller

2. For declaring an event handler, go to the **Methods** tab and select **New**.

3. In the first dialog **New Method**, mark the **Event handler** entry and then click on **Next**.

4. In the second dialog, enter the name of the event handler `onStart-NewGame()` (see Figure 3.52).

5. In the **Event source** field, select the entry **Toolbar (Web Dynpro Component Interface Controller)**; in the field **Subscribed event**, select the entry **startNewGame <ToolbarCompInterface ...>** as well as the checkbox **Create event handler parameters according to subscribed event**. Then click on **Finish**.

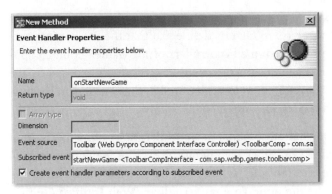

Figure 3.52 Declaring an Event Handler

The **Methods** tab displays the newly added event handler `onStart-NewGame()` (see Figure 3.53). The relations illustrated in Figure 3.49 between event trigger, event definition, and event listener are thus completely declared, so that only the actual event handling needs to be implemented in the playground component controller.

T.	Name	Return type	Event source	Subscribed event	
	onStartNewGame	void	Toolbar (Web Dynpro ...	startNewGame <Toolb...	
	onSwitchHelpVisibility	void	Toolbar (Web Dynpro ...	switchHelpVisibility <T...	
	switchSettingsVisibility	void	Toolbar (Web Dynpro ...	switchSettingsVisibility...	
	getHelpButtonText	void			
	getSettingsButtonText	void			
	showSimpleLayout	void			
	showStandardLayout	void			
	startGame	void			

Figure 3.53 Display of Declared Controller Methods in the GameStation Component Controller

Implementing an Event Handler in the GameStation Component Controller

The implementation of the `onStartNewGame()` event handler includes creation of the game component selected in the toolbar component. More details have already been presented in Section 3.6.4, regarding Listing 3.5.

3.8.2 Dynamic Event Subscription

Here we briefly want to mention the potential to dynamically logon the event handler `onStartNewGame()` to the event `StartNewGame` in the interface controller of the `Toolbar` component at runtime using application code. In addition to dynamic subscription, it is also possible to dynamically un-subscribe event handlers.

Subscribing an event handler at runtime using an API

The dynamic event subscription can be implemented easily via the `IWDComponentUsage` API. In a static case, the event controller (controller in which the event is defined) and the event name need to be defined for an event handler (see Figure 3.54).

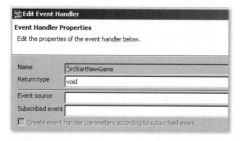

Figure 3.54 Definition of the onStartNewGame Event Handler Without Statically Defined Event Subscription

In a dynamic case, this mapping is achieved by passing identifier objects of the types `IWDEventId` and `IWDEventHandlerId` to the `IWDComponentUsage` API using the `addEventHandler(IWDEventId event, IWDEventHandlerId eventHandler)` method. The identifier objects are automatically created by the Web Dynpro runtime environment and can easily be addressed in the application code using constants.

Thus, the constant `WD_EVENT_START_NEW_GAME` is created for the `StartNewGame` event in the `IExternal` API of the toolbar component interface controller. In the same way, a constant is created in the

IPrivate API as soon as an event handler has been defined in the corresponding controller. For the onStartNewGame() event handler in the GameStation component controller, this is the constant WD_ EVENTHANDLER_ON_START_NEW_GAME.

Dynamically sub-scribing an event handler to an event

For the implementation of dynamic event subscription, these facts result in the application code shown in Listing 3.8.

```
//@@begin javadoc:wdDoInit()
/** Hook method called to initialize controller. */
//@@end
public void wdDoInit()
{
  //@@begin wdDoInit()
  ...
  wdThis.wdGetToolbarComponentUsage().addEventHandler(
  wdThis.wdGetToolbarInterface()
    .WD_EVENT_START_NEW_GAME,
  wdThis.WD_EVENTHANDLER_ON_START_NEW_GAME);
  //@@end
}
```

Listing 3.8 GameStationComp.java–Dynamic Event Subscription

3.8.3 Method Calls as a Substitute for Server-Side Eventing

In the server-side eventing discussed in Section 3.8.1, the event was defined in the embedded child component so that the parent component could subscribe to it (child component contains event source, parent component contains event listener).

External event subscription is not possible

In inter-component eventing, however, the reverse case can occur. The embedded child component is to react to an event in the parent component; the child component contains the event listener, while the parent component contains the event source. Is it possible to implement this eventing type as well in the Web Dynpro component model? Currently, the answer is no.

Similarity to external interface context mapping

This is due to the technique of external interface context mapping, whereby child component contains data listener or mapped context, and parent component contains data source or data context, respectively. In this mapping type, the interface context mapping must be defined outside of the child component itself within the parent component. In parallel, an event handler would have to be externally subscribed in the component interface of the child component to an event of the parent component. However, such an *external event subscription* is currently not supported in the Web Dynpro programming model. Therefore, the only alternative solution to this problem is to replace server-side eventing with method calls. Let us have a look at the following application case.

Referencing Mode and Passing Component Usages to Child Components

In Section 3.6.1 describing the IWDComponentUsage API, the referencing mode was introduced which enables the component usage of component A to point to the component usage of the same type of component B. In component-based Web Dynpro applications, it is thus possible to use a single-model component instance in several UI components. The lifecycle management of the model component instance would be controlled at the component usage level by the root component. However, the various UI components would use this central model component instance only in referencing mode without influencing its lifecycle management.

Referencing the component usage of another component

Figure 3.55 illustrates the described component architecture. Via external event subscription, it would very easily be possible to pass a reference to the own model component usage from the root component to all UI components. When firing the ModelCompCreation event, you would only have to pass a variable of the IWComponent-Usage type (see Listing 3.9).

```
//@@begin javadoc:wdDoInit()
/** Hook method called to initialize component
 * controller MasterComp.java. */
//@@end
public void wdDoInit()
{
  //@@begin wdDoInit()
  wdThis.wdGetModelComponentComponentUsage()
    .createComponent();
  // THIS IS NOT POSSIBLE IN SAP NetWeaver 2004 ...
  // (requires missing external event subscription)
  wdThis.wdFireEventModelCompCreation(
    wdThis.wdGetModelComponentComponentUsage());
```

```
//@@end
}
```

Listing 3.9 MasterComp.java–Firing an Event in the Parent Component

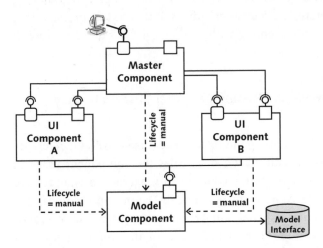

Figure 3.55 Using a Central Model Component in Referencing Mode

Method calls as a
substitute for
server-side
eventing

As external event subscription is not yet possible in SAP NetWeaver 2004, so you need to pass the reference to the model component usage of the master component to the two UI components via two method calls. The UI components must implement the reference-ModelComponent(IWDComponentUsage modelCompUsg) method in their interface controller (see Listing 3.10).

```
//@@begin javadoc:wdDoInit()
/** Hook method called to initialize component
 * controller MasterComp.java. */
//@@end
public void wdDoInit()
{
  //@@begin wdDoInit()
  wdThis.wdGetModelComponentComponentUsage()
    .createComponent();
  // THIS IS POSSIBLE ...
  // (call public methods instead of firing an event)
  wdThis.wdGetFirstUIComponentInterface()
    .referenceModelComponent(
  wdThis.wdGetModelComponentComponentUsage());
  wdThis.wdGetSecondUIComponentInterface()
    .referenceModelComponent(
      wdThis.wdGetModelComponentComponentUsage());
```

```
   //@@end
}
```

Listing 3.10 MasterComp.java–Method Calls for Passing the Model Component Usage to the Two UI Components

When there are several event recipients, this approach requires the repeated call of the same method in the IExternal API of the child components and is therefore not as elegant as firing an event without knowing the event recipients. However, because the master component knows its embedded UI components, the method call is a feasible solution.

The referenceModelComponent(IWDComponentUsage modelCompUsg) method in the component interface controller of the used UI component delegates to the same method in the component controller (see Listing 3.11).

Implementation of the interface controller of the UI component

```
public void referenceModelComponent(
   com.sap.tc.webdynpro.progmodel.api.IWDComponentUsage
   modelCompUsg )
{
   //@@begin referenceModelComponent()
   wdThis.wdGetFirstUICompController()
      .referenceModelComponent(modelCompUsg);
   //@@end
}
```

Listing 3.11 FirstUICompInterface.java–Delegation of the referenceModelComponent() Method to the Component Controller

In the component controller, the model component usage of the UI component finally changes to referencing mode, so that from then on it points to the model component usage of the master component (see Listing 3.12).

Referencing mode

```
public void referenceModelComponent(
   com.sap.tc.webdynpro.progmodel.api.IWDComponentUsage
   modelCompUsg )
{
   //@@begin referenceModelComponent()
   wdThis.wdGetModelComponentComponentUsage()
      .enterReferencingMode(modelCompUsg);
   //@@end
}
```

IWDComponent-Usage.enter-ReferencingMode()

Listing 3.12 FirstUIComp.java–Using the Passed Model Component Usage in Referencing Mode

3.9   Using Component Interface Views

The usage of *component interface views* plays an important part in the componentization of Web Dynpro applications. In Section 3.2, we used these visual interfaces of Web Dynpro components when designing component-based application architecture, in order to modularize the GameStation application at the user interface level.

In this section, we will switch from the design to the declaration and implementation level to deal with some real-life aspects of handling component interface views.

3.9.1   Component Interface Views

Definition of component interface views

A component interface view is the visual interface of a Web Dynpro component that can be used for building structured componentized Web Dynpro user interfaces. Every window within a Web Dynpro component is assigned exactly one component interface view.[11] If a UI component is used by another component, that component can use every exposed component interface view like one of its own views. The name *interface view* is used because the visual interface of a Web Dynpro component behaves like a normal view for its using component:

▶ **Declaration of navigation links**
Like views, component interface views can have *inbound* and *outbound plugs* that are used for declaring navigation transitions via navigation links.

▶ **Embedding in view sets and view areas**
Like views, component interface views can be embedded in *view sets* or *view areas*. Using view sets and view areas, several views can be positioned in a window via predefined layouts (T layout, grid layout).

▶ **Embedding in** ViewContainer **UI elements**
Like views, component interface views can be embedded in ViewContainer UI elements. As opposed to view sets, ViewContainer UI elements have the advantage that the embedded views and component interface views can be positioned in a more flexible

---

11 If a component contains several windows, it also contains several component interface views.

way and irrespective of the runtime via data binding. Using view sets and view areas, the settings defined at design time can no longer be changed programmatically (by controller coding).

3.9.2 Embedding Component Interface Views in ViewContainer UI Elements

Let us now start to further examine the embedding of the UI components belonging to the GameStation application and of the game component interface in the root components. The perspective views and modeling interfaces of the Web Dynpro tools to be used for this purpose play an important part in this respect (see Figure 3.56):

1. **Web Dynpro Explorer**
   Enables the hierarchical embedding of component interface views in windows, view areas, and `ViewContainer` UI elements.

2. **Navigation Modeler**
   As an alternative to the Web Dynpro Explorer, enables the graphical embedding of component interface views within a specific window.

3. **View Designer**
   Enables the exact positioning of `ViewContainer` UI elements within a layout view specifically used for this purpose.

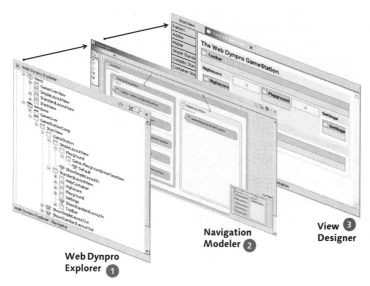

Figure 3.56 Presentation of Component Interface Views and ViewContainer UI Elements in the Web Dynpro Tools

Component interface views are embedded in `ViewContainer` UI elements using two separate steps:

1. Adding `ViewContainer` UI elements in the view designer of the layout view

2. Adding component interface views in the navigation modeler of the window that contains the layout view and then defining navigation transitions by adding navigation links between inbound and outbound plugs

Step 1 – Declaration of a Layout View in the Root Component

Layout views contain ViewContainer UI elements

Layout views are normal Web Dynpro views that are specifically used for embedding and positioning `ViewContainer` UI elements. By using a specific container layout like a `Matrix`, `Grid`, or `Flow` layout at the `RootContainerUIElement` or `TransparentContainer` level, the embedded `ViewContainer` UI elements can be positioned in a very flexible way. You also can add more UI elements like `Group`, `HorizontalGutter`, `InvisibleElement`, or `TransparentContainer` in the layout view.

> **Tip**
>
> Always embed component interface views in `ViewContainer` UI elements of layout views. In comparison to view sets and view areas, this method gives you many more possibilities for positioning interface views. In addition to using special UI elements like `TransparentContainer` or `InvisibleElement`, it is also possible to change the state of the UI element properties via data binding to appropriate context attributes at runtime (show and hide; change heights and widths).

StandardLayout-View in the GameStation-Comp root component

The first layout view of the GameStation application is contained in the `GameStationComp` root component and is named `StandardLayoutView`. The root component uses the four UI components `ToolbarComp`, `HighscoreComp`, `HTMLViewerComp`, and the UI component interface `IGame` which itself has two component interface views (`Playground` and `Settings`). Therefore, five different component interface views can be embedded altogether in the `StandardLayoutView` layout view.

In the first step, the embedding of the component interface views begins with adding five new `ViewContainer` UI elements to the view layout:

1. In the Web Dynpro Explorer open the node **Main_WD-BOOK-D~tc~games~sap.com · Web Dynpro · Web Dynpro Components · GameStationComp · Views · StandardLayoutView**.

2. In the context menu, select the **Edit** option. This opens the perspective view `Layout` for declaring the UI elements contained in the `StandardLayoutView`.

3. In the `Outline` perspective view, add an appropriate `ViewContainer` UI element for every component interface view to be displayed. In the selection list for the **Type** field, this UI element is named `ViewContainerUIElement`.

4. Exactly arrange and position the embedded `ViewContainer` UI elements using additional UI elements, if necessary. Avail yourself of the possibilities provided by different container layouts (`Grid`, `Matrix`, `Row`, `Flow`) as well as additional UI elements such as `TransparentContainer` or `InvisibleElement`.

Figure 3.57 shows the rectangular presentation of `ViewContainer` UI elements in the view designer. The views or component interface views embedded in the `ViewContainer` UI elements are not displayed in the view designer. In fact, the view designer only serves for exactly positioning the `ViewContainer` UI elements and for declaring their properties.

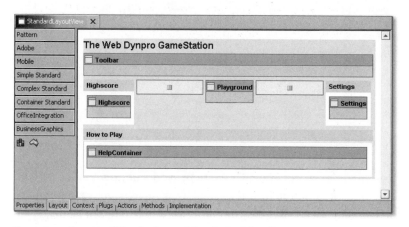

Figure 3.57 Layout of StandardLayoutView in the View Designer

Step 2 – Embedding Component Interface Views in the Navigation Modeler

Opening the navigation modeler

In the second step, the component interface views are embedded in the respective ViewContainer UI elements using the navigation modeler.

1. In Web Dynpro Explorer, open the node **Main_WD-BOOK-D~tc~games~sap.com · Web Dynpro · Web Dynpro Components · GameStationComp · Windows · GameStationComp**.

2. In the context menu, select the **Open Navigation Modeler** option.

3. This opens the navigation modeler with a graphical representation of the view composition defined in the GameStationComp window.

Declaration of the view composition

The view composition is declared in the navigation modeler and represents the set of all view assemblies that can be reached in a window via navigation links. The view assembly is an arrangement of views and component interface views presented in the application window at runtime t_R. Via navigation transitions, the user changes from one view assembly to the next.

Presentation of ViewContainer UI elements in the navigation modeler

The ViewContainer UI elements contained in a view are presented in the navigation modeler as light-colored empty rectangles that are additionally provided with the associated UI element ID (see Figure 3.58).

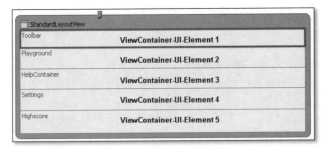

Figure 3.58 Presentation of ViewContainer UI Elements in the Navigation Modeler

In a single ViewContainer UI element, you can now embed at least one view or component interface view. If several views are embedded, exactly one active view or empty view at a time can be displayed at runtime. The transition from one view to another is achieved via normal navigation transitions.

1. In the toolbar of the navigation modeler, select the top icon, **Embed a view**.

Embedding component interface views

2. Move the mouse pointer to an empty rectangle representing a `ViewContainer` UI element (see Figure 3.59, ❶), and press the mouse button once.

3. In the following dialog box, select the radio button **Embed Interface View of a Component instance** (❷) and click on **Next**.

4. In the next dialog box, all component instances (or component usages) used by the GameStation component are displayed. First open the node of the UI component to be embedded, and then select the name of the wanted component interface view (❸). Finish the last dialog step with **Finish**.

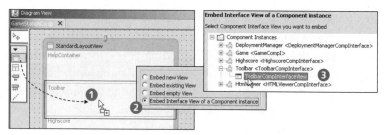

Figure 3.59 Adding a Component Interface View to a ViewContainer UI Element

After this second step, the component interface views embedded in the `ViewContainer` UI elements are displayed like normal views in the navigation modeler (see Figure 3.60).

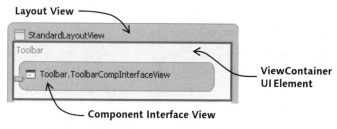

Figure 3.60 Presentation of Component Interface Views in the Navigation Modeler

Note that no children—i.e., no embedded views or component interface views—are displayed for `ViewContainer` UI elements in the outline perspective view used for editing view layouts. They are exclusively presented hierarchically in the Web Dynpro Explorer as well as graphically in the navigation modeler (see Figure 3.61).

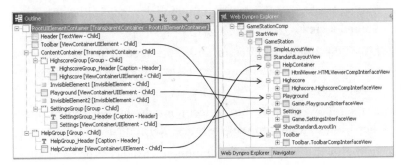

Figure 3.61 Different Presentation of ViewContainer UI Elements

3.9.3 Navigating to the Initial View Assembly Using Start View and URL Parameters

Starting the GameStation application with different display options

In addition to the actual user interface that was previously presented for our GameStation application, we should be able to display only the playground without the surrounding areas. In this simple case, the SameGame game is to be displayed by default without the user interface of the embedding GameStation game console (Standard-LayoutView). The display mode is to be addressed immediately after the application start via URL parameter.

To meet this requirement, the following problems must be solved:

▸ How can the default view initially displayed in the GameStation-Comp window be changed at runtime?

▸ How are URL parameters read when the application is started?

Declaring the Start View for Initial Navigation

If two views are directly integrated in a Web Dynpro window, we have to decide at design time already, when setting the **default** property, which of the two views is to be displayed at application startup.

Auxiliary view

Now we aim at using a URL parameter to set the default view that is displayed in the GameStationComp window when the GameStation application is started. To solve this *default view problem,* we use an additional auxiliary view named StartView whose outbound plugs are required to trigger the initial navigation toward the desired actual default view. At design time, we assign the **default = true** property to the `StartView`. This specifies that the `StartView` controller is created by the Web Dynpro runtime environment in any case when the application is started and can be used to fire outbound plugs.

To define two navigation links between the views `StartView`, `StandardLayoutView`, and the `IGame` component interface view, we will add two new outbound plugs named `ShowStandardLayoutOut` and `ShowSimpleLayoutOut` to the `StartView`.

Definition of two outbound plugs

In the navigation modeler, starting at the `StartView`, we can then define two new navigation links (see Figure 3.62), the outbound plugs of which are triggered depending on the value of the `mode` URL parameter when the application is started.

Definition of two navigation links

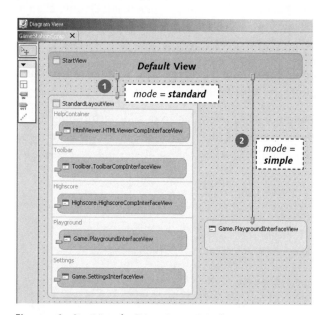

Figure 3.62 StartView for Triggering an Initial Navigation Transition

Reading URL Parameters at Application Startup

The second task refers to the reading of URL parameters when the application is started. It can be solved easily if you make use of the automatic transport of URL parameters to corresponding startup-plug parameters of the component interface views. This special service of the Web Dynpro runtime environment is based on the fact that the value of a URL parameter is passed to the parameter of the

URL parameters are automatically passed to parameters of the same name in the startup plug event handler

same name in the startup-plug event handler of the component interface view controller. For this to be possible, the parameter of the same name and of the **String** type must have already been defined in the startup plug at design time. If this has been done, the corresponding URL parameter value can be accessed directly in the startup-plug event handler without having to use additional code. The following steps are needed.

Declaring the parameter mode in the startup plug event handler

1. In Web Dynpro Explorer, open the node **Main_WD-BOOK-D~tc~games~sap.com · Web Dynpro · Web Dynpro Components · GameStationComp · Component Interface · Interface Views · GameStationCompInterfaceView**.

2. In the context menu, select the **Edit** option.

3. In the GameStationComp-InterfaceView perspective view, change to the **Plugs** tab and select the **Default** startup plug.

4. Using the **New** button, open the **New Parameter** dialog box.

5. Assign the name "mode" and the **string** type to the parameter and finish the dialog step with **Finish**.

After the mode parameter has been declared, the startup-plug event handler onPlugDefault() is accordingly extended by the Web Dynpro tools (see Listing 3.13).

```
//@@begin javadoc:onPlugDefault(ServerEvent)
/** Declared validating event handler. */
//@@end
public void onPlugDefault(
  com.sap.tc.webdynpro.progmodel.api.IWDCustomEvent
    wdEvent,
  java.lang.String mode) {
  //@@begin onPlugDefault(ServerEvent)
  ...
  //@@end
}
```

Listing 3.13 GameStationCompInterfaceView.java–Startup Plug Event Handler

Firing Outbound Plugs in the StartView Using Server-Side Eventing

In the first step, we defined the additionally needed auxiliary view StartView along with its outbound plugs and navigation links. We then read the URL parameter mode in the component interface view controller that was passed when the application was started.

Now there is the question of how the outbound plugs of StartView can be triggered from outside. As view controllers in the Web Dynpro programming model cannot be used by other controllers and therefore do not have a IPublic API, *server-side eventing* is the only possibility for non-view controllers to interact with view controllers.

View controller without IPublic API–server-side eventing as a solution

Figure 3.63 illustrates the concept of event-based view navigation:

1. In the interface view controller, the URL parameter mode is read and passed to the component controller via the method call show-InitialView(String mode) (Figure 3.63, ❶ and Listing 3.14).

2. In the called showInitialView(String mode) method, the component controller triggers the ShowInitialView event (❷). The URL parameter mode received by the interface view controller is forwarded as the event parameter to the event recipient (Figure 3.63, ❸ and Listing 3.15).

3. The StartView view controller subscribed to the event finally fires the outbound plug belonging to a URL parameter value (Figure 3.63, ❹ and Listing 3.16) to navigate to the view to be displayed.

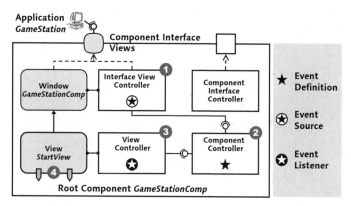

Figure 3.63 Triggering the Initial View Navigation via Server-Side Eventing When the Application Is Started

Note that the URL parameter mode received in the startup-plug event handler is transferred to the view controller via appropriate method and event parameters. There, the corresponding if query will be implemented for firing the appropriate outbound plug. If this logic were implemented in the component controller already it would have to interact with the view controller via two separate events.

According to the description above, to navigate from the StartView to the initial view assembly via URL parameter at application startup you need to implement the controller code shown in Listing 3.14, Listing 3.15, and Listing 3.16.

```
//@@begin javadoc:onPlugDefault(ServerEvent)
/** Declared validating event handler. */
//@@end
public void onPlugDefault(
  com.sap.tc.webdynpro.progmodel.api.IWDCustomEvent
    wdEvent,
  java.lang.String mode) {
  //@@begin onPlugDefault(ServerEvent)
  wdThis.wdGetGameStationCompController()
    .showInitialView(mode);
  //@@end
}
```

Listing 3.14 GameStationCompInterfaceView.java–Startup Plug Event Handler

```
//@@begin javadoc:showInitialView()
/** Declared method. */
//@@end
public void showInitialView( java.lang.String mode )
{
  //@@begin showInitialView()
  wdThis.wdFireEventShowInitialView(mode);
  //@@end
}
```

Listing 3.15 GameStationComp.java–Public Method for Firing the Event ShowInitialView

```
//@@begin javadoc:onShowInitialView(ServerEvent)
/** Declared validating event handler. */
//@@end
public void onShowInitialView(
  com.sap.tc.webdynpro.progmodel.api.IWDCustomEvent
    wdEvent,
  java.lang.String mode )
{
  //@@begin onShowInitialView(ServerEvent)
  if ("simple".equals(mode)) {
```

```
    wdThis.wdFirePlugShowSimpleLayoutOut();
    } else if ("standard".equals(mode)) {
    wdThis.wdFirePlugShowStandardLayoutOut();
    }
    //@@end
}
```

Listing 3.16 StartView.java–Triggering Outbound Plugs

3.9.4 Alternative Solutions to the Default View Problem

Maybe you have already wondered if we could solve more easily the problem of displaying different UI variants or default views when the GameStation application is started. In fact, two more alternatives are possible, which will be described here briefly.

Setting the Default View Using the IWDWindowInfo API at Runtime

In contrast to Web Dynpro UI elements, the properties of windows and the views embedded therein, as well as component interface views, cannot be bound to the context. Therefore it is not possible to bind their **default** property to a context attribute of the **Boolean** type and to set it at runtime via context programming.

No data binding for view properties in windows

However, there is a trick that enables you to dynamically set the **default** property of embedded views using application code; we use the special IWDWindowInfo API using which it is possible to access the metadata of window objects. In contrast to numerous other IWD*Info APIs, the IWDWindowInfo API even lets you change individual metadata, such as the **default** property of embedded views, using a setter call.

IWDWindow Info API trick

The solution method starts with using the Web Dynpro tools to assign a unique ID to the two views that are embedded in the Game-StationComp window, IGame.PlaygroundInterfaceView and Stan-dardLayoutView (see Figure 3.64):

Defining the id property of embedded views

1. In Web Dynpro Explorer, open the node **Main_WD-BOOK-D~tc~games~sap.com · Web Dynpro · Web Dynpro Components · GameStationComp · Windows · GameStationComp · Game.PlaygroundInterfaceView**.

2. Change to the **Properties** perspective view and assign a value of **IGameCompInterfaceView** to the **id** property.

3. In Web Dynpro Explorer, open the second view `StandardLayout-View` embedded in the `GameStationComp` window.

4. Assign a value of **StandardLayoutView** to its **id** property.

Note that the **default** property of both embedded views is set to **false** at design time.

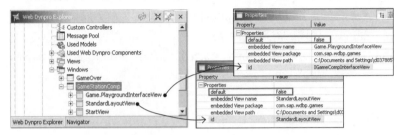

Figure 3.64 Definition of ViewUsageIDs in the Web Dynpro Tools At Design Time

By declaring the **id** property for both views used in the `GameStation-Comp` window we can access the associated `IWDViewUsageInfo` APIs in the application code at runtime. The implementation to dynamically set the default view of the `GameStationComp` window changes according to this approach as shown in Listing 3.17.

```
//@@begin javadoc:showInitialView()
/** Declared method. */
//@@end
public void showInitialView( java.lang.String mode )
{
  //@@begin showInitialView()
  IWDWindowInfo windowInfo=
    wdComponentAPI.getComponentInfo().findInWindows(
      "GameStationComp");
  IWDViewUsageInfo viewUsageInfo= null;
  if ("simple".equals(mode)) {
    viewUsageInfo=
    windowInfo.getViewUsageByID("StandardLayoutView");
  } else if ("standard".equals(mode)) {
    viewUsageInfo=
      windowInfo.getViewUsageByID(
        "IGameCompInterfaceView");
  }
  windowInfo.setDefaultRootViewUsage(viewUsageInfo);
```

```
//@@end
}
```

Listing 3.17 Listing 3.17 GameStationComp.java–Dynamically Setting the Default View in the GameStationComp Window Using IWDWindowInfo API

Dynamically setting the default view of a window is very easy. We first reference the window's runtime instance named GameStation-Comp. Then we assign the appropriate IWDViewUsageInfo instance to the viewUsageInfo variable of the type IWDViewUsageInfo depending on the passed URL parameter. Finally, we specify the default view to be initially displayed in the GameStationComp window using the IWDWindowInfo.setDefaultRootViewUsage(IWDViewUsageInfo View UsageInfo) method.

Declaration of Several Web Dynpro Applications

The easiest solution to the default view problem is to define not one but two separate Web Dynpro applications. For this approach, we do not need a URL parameter named mode for separate navigation but instead specify a separate URL for every application variant. Instead of the two applications URLs, ...sap.com/tc~games/GameStation-App?mode=simple or ...sap.com/ tc~games/GameStationApp?mode= standard with the URL parameter mode, the two application URLs ...sap.com/ tc~games/GameStationSimpleApp or ...sap.com/tc~games/ GameStationStandardApp could be used without any URL parameter for starting the GameStation application in two different UI variants.

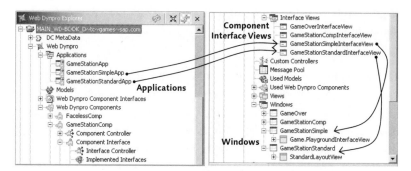

Figure 3.65 Definition of Two Web Dynpro Applications Pointing to Different Component Interface Views

Figure 3.65 represents the two declared Web Dynpro applications GameStationSimpleApp and GameStationStandardApp in the Web Dynpro Explorer.

A disadvantage of this multiple declaration of Web Dynpro applications is that it causes a high declaration effort due to the 1:1 relation between application and component interface view or window when there are several startup variants. On the other hand, the approach based on URL parameters allows us to define different initial view assemblies for a single Web Dynpro application (and thus a single component interface view) and to address them at runtime.

3.9.5 Inter-Component Navigation Between Component Interface Views

Last, we'll discuss the general topic of inter-component navigation between component interface views, the *cross-component navigation*. Although there are no such navigation transitions in the GameStation application, we can still immediately transfer the knowledge gained from the solution of the default view problem to the general inter-component navigation.

Inbound Plug Dispatching in Interface Views

Like normal views, component interface views in Web Dynpro can have inbound and outbound plugs. Navigation transitions are declared via navigation links form inbound to outbound plugs and triggered at runtime by firing outbound plugs via IPublic<Component Interface View Name>.wdFirePlug<Plug Name>() in the application code.

Inbound plugs of component interface views navigate to the default view assembly

The problem of inter-component navigation in more complex application scenarios is that the inbound plug of a component interface view addresses only the initial view assembly declared in the window (*default view assembly*). This means that all of those views are displayed that were declared as the default views in ViewContainer UI elements or in view areas at design time (see Figure 3.66). If the inbound plug of a component interface view is newly addressed after the component has been created, and if the displayed view assembly has changed due to navigation transitions inside the component, this view assembly remains unchanged.

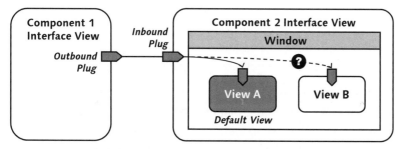

Figure 3.66 Navigation Between Two Component Interface Views

Therefore, as with in the default view problem discussed in Section 3.9.3, we again face the question of how to navigate to a *non*-default view assembly that is defined in the window when reaching the inbound plug of the component interface view. In the example shown in Figure 3.66, View B would be such a default view assembly (consisting of only one view). In this problem case, we therefore again need a mechanism that enables us to forward or to dispatch into the component the navigation events handled in the inbound plug-event handler of the component interface view.

To solve this problem, please remember the default view problem: To display different default views depending on the URL parameter value at application startup we added a third view named `StartView` as the actual default view (see Figure 3.62). The two outbound plugs of `StartView` could then be used to trigger navigation to the view assembly to be initially displayed via server-side eventing. Because component-internal navigation events in SAP NetWeaver 2004 can exclusively be triggered by view instances we need an additional auxiliary view again that is referred to as `NavDispatcherView` (*navigation dispatcher view*) in this case.[12]

Idea of the navigation dispatcher view

To be instantiated, the `NavDispatcherView` must always be visible within the component interface view (or within the window). If it were removed from the current view assembly within the component it could be destroyed at some stage, even if its **Lifespan** prop-

---

12 Future releases of SAP NetWeaver will allow the definition of outbound plugs at the window level. This enhancement of the Web Dynpro navigation model will significantly facilitate the cross-component navigation. The `NavDispatcherView`-based solution for SAP NetWeaver 2004 described here will then be possible directly at the window level.

erty were assigned a value of **createOnDemand**. If it were destroyed, it could certainly no longer trigger its own navigation events or dispatch any incoming navigation events. To make the NavDispatcher-View always visible we will use a simple trick (see Figure 3.67):

NavDispatcher-View as a window substitute

In the view layout of the NavDispatcherView we only declare a single ViewContainer UI element that exists in the user interface but is not visible and in which we then model the actual view composition. In the window, the NavTesterView is the default view at top level that embeds all other views. The view composition in the ViewContainer UI element of NavTesterView can be modeled like in a window; that is, it is possible to also use view sets and view areas and to embed views and component interface views. The NavDispatcherView thus acts as a window itself except that it additionally has its own outbound plugs for navigation control.

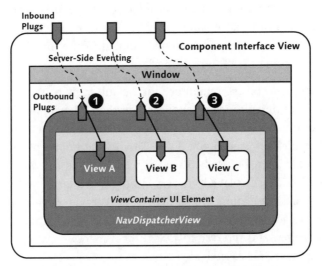

Figure 3.67 NavDispatcherView for Navigating Within a Component Interface View

Event-based inbound plug dispatching

How can we now trigger the navigation to View B in NavDispatcher-View starting from an inbound plug event handler in the component interface view controller? The solution to this problem is illustrated in Figure 3.67: Let us first assume that the component interface view exposes three inbound plugs to its embedding component for declaring navigation links. Depending on which of these inbound plugs is addressed, View A, B, or C should be the navigation target within the component.

This is enabled by declaring three separate outbound plugs in the NavDispatcherView that are connected via navigation links to the inbound plugs of the Views A, B, and C in the NavDispatcherView. If a server-side event (declared in the component controller) is now triggered in one of the inbound plug-event handlers of the component interface view controller, the NavDispatcherView can trigger its appropriate own outbound plug in a subscribed event handler that eventually navigates to one of the views A, B, or C. The information about which target view is to be displayed can be transferred to the NavDispatcherView by the inbound plug-event handler via an event parameter of the **integer** type.

Implementation of the Inbound Plug Dispatching

After this conceptual design of the *inbound plug dispatching* via NavDispatcherView we will close this topic by explaining the required controller coding. Please note that the server-side eventing concept implemented in this case is identical to the one for solving the default view problem in Section 3.9.3; the StartView corresponds to the NavDispatcherView (see Figure 3.63). After various declaration steps within the component have been performed, the implementation takes place in three controller classes:

▶ **Component controller**
In the component controller, the DispatchInboundPlug event is declared using the id parameter of the **int** type. To trigger this event in the component interface view controller, the fireEvent-DispatchInboundPlug(int id) method must be declared.

▶ **Component interface view controller**
This controller uses the component controller and can therefore trigger the DispatchInboundPlug event in every inbound plug event handler, passing the respective id parameter value.

▶ **NavDispatcherView controller**
This controller also uses the component controller and subscribes the event handler onDispatchInboundPlug(int id) to the event DispatchInboundPlug. Depending on the passed id parameter value, the corresponding outbound plug to the internal view navigation is triggered in the event handler.

This description results in the application code shown in Listings 3.18, 3.19, and 3.20, where only an exemplary navigation case (View Assembly A, **id = 1**).

```
//@@begin javadoc:onPlugDisplayViewAssemblyAIn(
    ServerEvent)
/** Declared validating event handler. */
//@@end
public void onPlugDisplayViewAssemblyAIn(
  com.sap.tc.webdynpro.progmodel.api.IWDCustomEvent
    wdEvent )
{
  //@@begin onPlugDisplayViewAssemblyAIn(ServerEvent)
  wdThis.wdGetGameStationCompController()
    .fireEventDispatchInboundPlug(1);
  //@@end
}
```

Listing 3.18 ComponentInterfaceViewController.java

```
//@@begin javadoc:fireEventDispatchInboundPlug()
/** Declared public method to trigger event
 *  from other (component interface view) controller */
//@@end
public void fireEventDispatchInboundPlug( int id )
{
  //@@begin fireEventDispatchInboundPlug()
  wdThis.wdFireEventDispatchInboundPlug(id);
  //@@end
}
```

Listing 3.19 ComponentController.java

```
//@@begin javadoc:onDispatchInboundPlug(ServerEvent)
/** Declared validating event handler. */
//@@end
public void onDispatchInboundPlug(
  com.sap.tc.webdynpro.progmodel.api.IWDCustomEvent
    wdEvent, int id )
{
  //@@begin onDispatchInboundPlug(ServerEvent)
  switch (id) {
    case 1:
      wdThis.wdFirePlugDispatchToAOut();
      break;
    case 2:
      wdThis.wdFirePlugDispatchToBOut();
      break;
```

```
    default:
      break;
  }
//@@end
}
```

Listing 3.20 NavDispatcherView.java

The essential difference between the solution of the default view problem and this one is that, in contrast to the `StartView`, the `NavDispatcherView` remains part of the displayed view assembly although outbound plugs are triggered. Irrespective of the view assembly currently shown in its child component, the embedded component can therefore navigate to another view assembly because the `NavDispatcherView` embeds all view assemblies that can be reached by navigation (and therefore the view composition). However, the event-based technique of inbound plug dispatching is applied the same way in both cases.

3.10 Summary

We will conclude this chapter about the Web Dynpro component concept using the example of the GameStation application with a short review of the essential contents.

A central target of this chapter was to introduce you to a *component-oriented* Web Dynpro developer's way of thinking and developing. Using a simple but versatile example, you gained a detailed insight into the practical and conceptual aspects of the Web Dynpro component model.

Component-oriented Web Dynpro development

You learned how more complex applications can be built in a modular way by dividing them into several components and by using visual and programmatic component interfaces. An essential prerequisite for this is the component model of the SAP NetWeaver Development Infrastructure. By using specific Web Dynpro development components, it is possible to distribute the development process to several developers working in different places in order to enable a quick and efficient development process. You learned how an inter-DC composition of Web Dynpro entities up to a complete application can be implemented by defining and using public parts.

Componentization based on the NWDI

Loose coupling using component interfaces — The architecture of the GameStation application is essentially influenced by the usage of the abstract game-component interface. Numerous advantages result from being able to implement loose coupling between the using game component (GameStationComp component) and the game implementation (SameGame component, for example). These include the modification-free exchangeability of game components at runtime and the extensibility of the application by adding game components at a later stage. After the conceptual basics of component interfaces we dealt with real-life questions regarding their usage (component usage dependencies) and implementation at design time as well as their instantiation at runtime.

Inter-component context mapping and eventing — We also dealt with the topics of data transfer (interface context mapping), interaction (eventing), and communication (methods) across several components. You have learned to distinguish internal and external interface context mapping depending on the place of the data context, to use server-side eventing between child and parent component, and to transfer component usages from the root component to several UI components via method calls. Doing so, you got to know the advanced technique of using component usages in the so-called referencing mode. This enables the usage of a central model component in several UI components.

Using component interface views and navigation — The concluding part of this chapter dealt with the UI-specific aspects of handling components and their component interface views as the visual component interfaces. You have learned to embed UI components in layout views via ViewContainer UI elements so as to be able to model component-based view compositions. Then you were introduced to alternative solutions to the default view problem of determining the initially displayed view assembly after the application is started by using URL parameters. The gained knowledge could then be transferred to the problem of navigating among Web Dynpro components to be able to navigate to different view assemblies within a Web Dynpro component based on a specific navigation-dispatcher view.

By using the web service model, you can access any web service with your Web Dynpro application. In this chapter, we want to take advantage of this functionality and create a convenient Google search application. In doing this, we'll introduce you to the various aspects of dynamic user interface creation.

4 Web Dynpro Google Search

In addition to the Adaptive Remote Function Call (RFC) model that enables you to access data in an SAP backend system, other models are available that provide access to different types of data access. As you saw in Chapter 2, regarding the model abstraction for the common model interface (CMI), the actual functionalities of the selected model are essentially transparent for the Web Dynpro application that you use.

One of the most important models here is definitely the *web service model*; just think of SAP's Enterprise Services Architecture (ESA). In the following sections, we'll use the Google web service to demonstrate how quickly and easily you can use even complex web services in a Web Dynpro application.

We'll focus our attention on various aspects of dynamic programming, that is, the dynamic creation of individual components of the Web Dynpro user interface. Lastly, we'll discuss the different options available to you for manipulating the initial screen of your Web Dynpro application.

4.1 Google Web Service

The Google web service is a part of the *Google Web APIs developer's kit* that you can download free of charge from *http://www.google. com/apis*. To use this service, you need a user ID that you can apply for at the same URL. This user ID enables you to create up to 1,000 search requests per day, which means that you cannot use the service to develop professional search services.

Google Web APIs developer's kit

The Google Web APIs developer's kit contains various examples of using the Google web service, different Java wrappers, and the *Web Service Definition Language* (WSDL) file on which we will generate the Web Dynpro web service model. Theoretically, you could also use the Java wrappers to develop a Web Dynpro-based search template. Using such a template would, for instance, be advantageous in a model component that calls the Java wrappers directly instead of using the generic Web Dynpro web service model.

You can find the Web Dynpro Google search example in the tc/search development component. The Web Dynpro component that implements the Google search is GoogleSearchComp. The required Web Dynpro project is called MAIN_WD-BOOK_D~tc~search~sap.com.

Since we don't want to focus on the componentization of a Web Dynpro application in this chapter, and we'd like to keep the example as simple as possible, we did not disassemble the Web Dynpro application into several Web Dynpro components, even though this would make a lot of sense, as you'll see in Section 4.6.

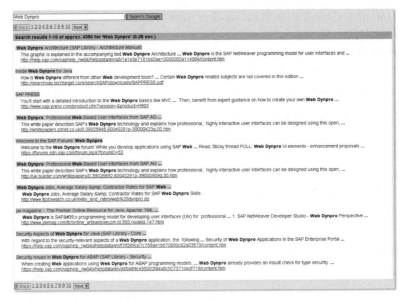

Figure 4.1 Web Dynpro Google Search

Figure 4.1 shows the final Web Dynpro Google search. When you enter a search term in the search field at the top of the screen, the search results determined via the Google web service are displayed in accordance with how you requested that they be displayed.

4.2 Generating the Google Web Service Model

The first step towards a successful Google search request consists of the creation of the corresponding web service model.

1. For this purpose, you must go to the Web Dynpro Explorer, open the context menu of the **Models** node in Web Dynpro project MAIN_WD-BOOK_D~tc~search~sap.com, and select **Create Model** (see Figure 4.2).

Figure 4.2 Creating a New Web Dynpro Model

2. Select the required model type in the first dialog step of the **New Model** window. Because we want to restrict ourselves to using the web service model here, you must select **Import Web Service Model** (see Figure 4.3).

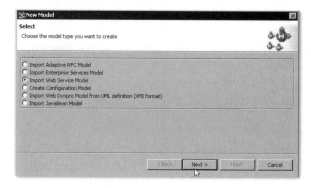

Figure 4.3 Selecting the Web Service Model Type

3. In the next step, you must define the name and the package of the model. Make sure that the specified package is empty; otherwise, you would encounter problems when generating the required model files later on. Figure 4.4 displays the definitions of **Model Name** and **Model Package**.

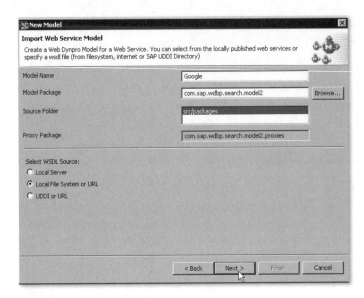

Figure 4.4 Defining the Model Name

4. Furthermore, you must define the location of the required WSDL file. For our example, you should use the option **Local File System or URL** since the WSDL file is contained in the Google Web APIs developer's kit you downloaded earlier.

Selecting the WSDL file

5. The next step defines the WSDL file you want to use (see Figure 4.5). Of course, the path you specify here depends on where you have stored the WSDL file on your hard drive.

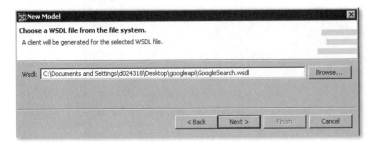

Figure 4.5 Defining the WSDL file

6. In the final step, you must define any mappings that you may require. For our example, however, you don't need to enter any further changes (see Figure 4.6).

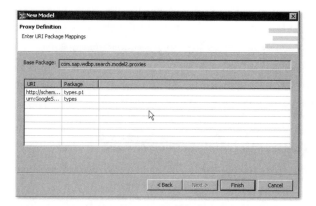

Figure 4.6 Defining the Package Mappings

Thus, all data that is required has been defined so that you can generate the web service model simply by clicking on the **Finish** button. Figure 4.7 displays the newly created model classes.

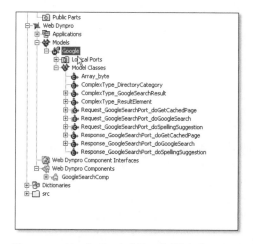

Figure 4.7 Newly Created Google Web Service Model

In addition to various classes that provide the structures required in the web service, such as `ComplexType_DirectoryCategory`, several `Request_*` and `Response_*` classes are created for each function provided by the Google web service. Those classes will enable you to call the corresponding functions. The `Request_*` classes are used to

Web service model classes

define the required input parameters, while the Response_* classes contain the determined return values.

In the following sections, we'll focus on the normal Google search that can be implemented using the Request_GoogleSearchPort_doGoogleSearch model class. The other two model classes—Request_GoogleSearchPort_doGetCachedPage and Request_GoogleSearch-Port_doSpellingSuggestion—are not addressed any further in this book, but you should feel free to play around with them. Why not develop a translation tool based on Web Dynpro?

4.2.1 Restrictions of the Web Service Model

Before we describe how to use the web service model that we just created, we should mention at this point that the Web Dynpro web service model in its current version contains some restrictions that you should take into account in your projects.[1]

Authenticating the web service calls The most important restriction is that only in a very limited way can you define whether the individual web service calls are authenticated for a specific Web Dynpro web service model; for example, you cannot use non-SAP logon tickets. Moreover, once you have generated the web service model, you cannot configure on which machine the web service is to be called. Lastly, you might also encounter problems with the model types you use, depending on the web service.

4.2.2 Regenerating the Web Service Model

When working with web service models, you may have to regenerate the web service model, for example, because the web service being used has changed. Unfortunately, the current version of SAP NetWeaver Developer Studio (NWDS) does not provide any option that allows you to regenerate the web service model quickly and conveniently. Therefore, it can prove to be a rather tedious and time-consuming task to delete an existing model and generate a new one, because you have to declare all usages of the model once again in your Web Dynpro application.

---

1 SAP NetWeaver 2004 SP16 will contain a substantially extended variant of the Web Dynpro web service model, which will eliminate the restrictions described here.

However, when using Web Dynpro development components, you can avoid this additional laborious work by performing a few simple steps. We therefore recommend that you use the following procedure:

1. Make sure that all activities of your Web Dynpro project have been checked into your Design Time Repository (DTR). If that is the case, it means that all involved files are read-only and cannot be modified inadvertently.

2. Go to the Web Dynpro Explorer, open the context menu of the model created earlier, and delete it by clicking on the **Delete** item. Note that you must memorize the exact names of the model and model package, because you will have to reuse those names for the new model that you want to generate.

3. Make sure that all files that belong to the model are deleted. To do so, go to the navigator and check the respective directories. Files that still exist must be deleted manually in the DTR view of SAP NetWeaver Developer Studio.

4. Regenerate the model. Use the exact model name and model package of the model that you just deleted.

5. Use the context menu item **Reload** of the respective Web Dynpro project to import the newly created model files and refresh the entire project.

4.3   Using the Google Model

Once the Google model has been generated successfully, you must link the model to a Web Dynpro component.

4.3.1   Using a Model Component

As we said in Chapter 3, we recommend that you use a model component here, which abstracts the generated model. In this way, the Web Dynpro component using the model component has no direct access to the generated model. This greatly facilitates a possible regeneration of the model, because the newly generated model is visible only inside the model component itself so that all the necessary changes take place within the model component. This does not affect the users of the model component because this regeneration is transparent to them.

Extending the generic Web Dynpro model API

Another advantage of using a model component is that it allows you to extend the generated model by methods and options that are currently not supported by the generic Web Dynpro model API—the common model interface described in Chapter 2. For example, it can be useful to provide filtering and sorting functions in the model component, although the (Web Dynpro) model you use does not support those functions.

To keep our example simple, however, we won't do that here. Instead, we'll link the Google model directly with the Web Dynpro component GoogleSearchComp. And, because we want to use the example primarily to describe the usage of the model, we'll accept the reduction in flexibility caused by linking the Google model directly with the Web Dynpro component.

4.3.2   Linking the Model with a Web Dynpro Component

Data Modeler

To link the generated model with Web Dynpro component Google-SearchComp, we launch the Web Dynpro Data Modeler by double-clicking on the Web Dynpro component in the Web Dynpro Explorer.

Figure 4.8 shows the basic structure of the sample application. In addition to the Web Dynpro component, the Data Modeler displays the Google model that is being used, as well as the Web Dynpro views that will enable us to implement the different display types for the search results at a later stage.

1. First you must add the Google model to the Web Dynpro component by clicking on the **Create a Model** icon on the left-hand side of the Data Modeler, and then define the required model binding.

Defining the model binding

2. To do that, you must create a *data link* between the model and the component controller (see Figure 4.9). Note that the direction of the data link defines the direction of the binding.

3. The system now displays a dialog in which you can define the *model binding*, that is, the link between the model and the component controller context. To do that, you must drag the model class Request_GoogleSearchPort_doGoogleSearch from the right and

drop it under the context node of the component controller context. This will map the data structure defined by the model in the component controller context. By default, the node and attribute names defined by the model are used, but you can also rename them per your requirements.

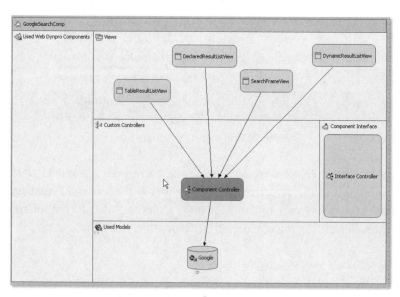

Figure 4.8 Web Dynpro Data Modeler

Figure 4.9 Creating a Data Link

Figure 4.10 shows the result of the model binding: the component controller context now contains the complete data structure required for the Google search. To obtain readable context node names, we renamed `Request_GoogleSearchPort_doGoogleSearch` into `GoogleRequest`.

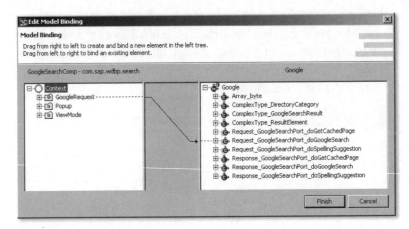

Figure 4.10 Defining the Model Binding

In the final step, you must generate the corresponding model class and bind it to the associated `GoogleRequest` context node. Typically, this happens as part of the `wdDoInit()` method of the component controller during the component instantiation (see Listing 4.1).

```
// Create model class instance
Request_GoogleSearchPort_doGoogleSearch searchRequest =
  new Request_GoogleSearchPort_doGoogleSearch();

// Set default values
searchRequest.setKey(key);
searchRequest.setMaxResults(10);
searchRequest.setStart(0);
searchRequest.setRestrict("");
searchRequest.setIe("");
searchRequest.setLr("");
searchRequest.setOe("");

// Define model binding
wdContext.nodeGoogleRequest().bind(searchRequest);
```

Listing 4.1 Creating the Model Binding

Creating the model class instance

Now that the instance of model class `Request_GoogleSearchPort_doGoogleSearch` has been created, you can define the required parameters that should *not* be modifiable through the Web Dynpro user interface. In our example, this is, for instance, the required user ID that is defined via the `setKey()` method. Furthermore, you can define default values for any other parameters that can be modified later by the user. In our example, those values are the maximum number of search results and the start index for the search results.

Note that for all parameters to which we don't assign any values, we'll transfer blank strings instead of `null` values; otherwise, the Google web service wouldn't function correctly.

Once the model class instance has been created and provided with (default) parameters, you must define the model binding between the model class instance and the component controller context. The binding between the model (class) and the component controller context enables us to transport the required input parameters of the Web Dynpro UI into the model and also to transport the search results from the model into the Web Dynpro UI. As you will see in the following sections, those tasks are carried out automatically for the biggest part.

Data transport from the model to the UI and back

Importing the User ID

We don't want to define the required user ID directly in Java code; instead, we want to make it configurable. For this purpose, we'll use the Web Dynpro configuration service that can be called via the `WDConfiguration` class. Listing 4.2 describes the access to the user ID via this class.

WDConfiguration class

```
String key = null;

try {
  IWDConfiguration keyConfig =
    WDConfiguration.getConfigurationByName(
      "sap.com/tc~search", "key");
  key = keyConfig.getStringEntry("userKey");
} catch (Exception e) {
  wdComponentAPI.getMessageManager().reportException(
    "Failed to load user key configuration.",
    true);
}
```

Listing 4.2 Importing the User ID

We import the required `userKey` configuration parameter from the configuration file *key.properties*, which we'll store in the development component `sap.com/tc~search` (see Figure 4.11).

Figure 4.11 Configuration File key.properties

Once you have deployed the development component, you can customize the *key.properties* configuration file using the Visual Administrator. Chapter 10 describes this process in great detail.

4.4 Developing the Search Interface and Defining the Scope of Usage

As we already mentioned at the beginning of this chapter, apart from describing the usage of the Web Dynpro web service model, we also want to discuss the different options available to you to create the corresponding user interface.

Declarative versus dynamic

Basically, Web Dynpro allows the use of both *declarative* and *dynamic UIs*. Before we describe the actual development based on an example, we want to briefly touch upon the basic pros and cons of using declarative or dynamic UIs.

4.4.1 Declarative Creation of the User Interface

As a rule, you should declare as many components of your user interface as possible using SAP NetWeaver Developer Studio. This enables you to ensure that the user interfaces thus created don't contain any redundancies. Moreover, all declaratively created UIs are automatically optimized for each existing Web Dynpro client.

Web Dynpro View Designer

The Web Dynpro View Designer enables you to evaluate and assess the declared user interface already during the design process without having to start the Web Dynpro application. Even though the view designer does not provide real WYSIWYG (What You See Is What You Get) in all scenarios, it does facilitate your work and enables you to accelerate the UI design process.

4.4.2 Dynamic Creation of the User Interface

Whenever you're not exactly sure during the design phase about the future look and feel of parts of your application UI, you can generate those parts dynamically using *dynamic programming*. If you do that, you can use all options of declarative programming as well; however, you should always ensure that you adhere to the following rule of thumb: "As much declarative programming as possible and as much dynamic programming as necessary." A user interface that appears to be completely dynamic at first glance can actually be declaratively generated in many parts when you take a closer look at it.

As you will see later in this chapter, we'll display the search results list in three different ways. The framework of the application that allows the entry of search terms and provides the navigation buttons, irrespective of the chosen type of search results display, will be generated via declarative programming only.

Figure 4.12 shows the Web Dynpro view SearchFrameView that integrates any type of search results display through the IWDViewContainer UI element SearchResults, in addition to the required application framework.

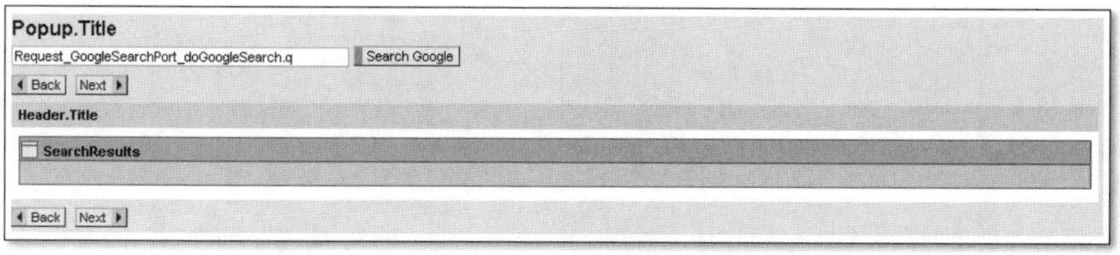

Figure 4.12 SearchFrameView

4.4.3 Developing the Search Template

In our example, the search template consists of a simple Web Dynpro UI, which, in turn, consists of an input field for the search string and a **Search Google** button that starts the search (see Figure 4.13).

Figure 4.13 Search Template

We basically need two things for the technical implementation:

▶ A corresponding Web Dynpro view that contains the displayed UI elements

▶ The definition of the context mapping between the view controller context and the component controller context to enable the transport of the search string through the component controller into the model

Defining the context mapping You can use the Data Modeler again to define the context mapping by connecting the view controller of the SearchFrameView view with the component controller of the GoogleSearchComp component via a data link.

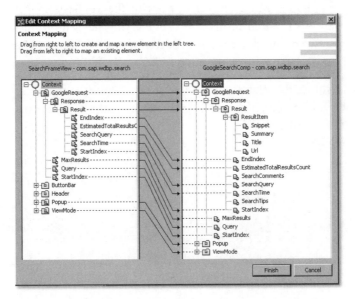

Figure 4.14 Defining the Mapping Between the View Controller Context and the Component Controller Context

Figure 4.14 shows the result. In the view controller context, the required context attributes are mapped to the corresponding attributes in the component controller context. You should generally make sure that you map only those context nodes and attributes that are actually required in the respective Web Dynpro view. Not only will you obtain a clear display by doing so, but you can also avoid unnecessary redundancies that might result in increased memory requirements for your Web Dynpro application at runtime.

For example, the `SearchFrameView` view does not require any access to the search results list. Therefore, we don't need to map the corresponding `Result` context node from the component controller context to the view controller context.

To transport the search string from the UI into the view controller, all you need to do is to bind the input field to the appropriate context attribute (see Figure 4.15).

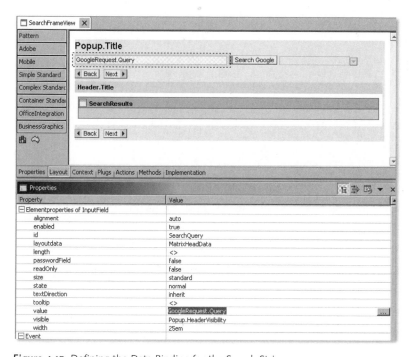

Figure 4.15 Defining the Data Binding for the Search String

4.4.4 Triggering the Google Search

To trigger the Google search, we simply need to link the **Search Google** button to the `GoogleSearch` action and implement the associated `onActionSearch` action event handler (see Listing 4.3). So we basically call the `doGoogleSearch()` method of the component controller shown in Listing 4.4.

```
updateSearchIndex(1);

wdThis.wdGetGoogleSearchCompController()
  .doGoogleSearch();

if (wdContext.nodeResultItem().size() > 0) {
  wdComponentAPI.getMessageManager().reportException(
    "No search results found for '"
      + wdContext
      .currentRequest_GoogleSearchPort
        _doGoogleSearchElement()
        .getQ() + "'",
    true);
}
```

Listing 4.3 Starting the Google Search

```
try {
  wdContext
    .currentRequest_GoogleSearchPort
    _doGoogleSearchElement()
    .modelObject()
    .execute();
  wdContext.nodeResponse().invalidate();

  wdThis.wdFireEventUpdateResultList();

} catch (Exception e) {
  wdComponentAPI.getMessageManager().reportException(
    e.getLocalizedMessage(),
    true);
}
```

Listing 4.4 The doGoogleSearch() Method

In a first step, we'll carry out the `execute()` method of the model object. Here, the context node serves as an access path to the model class instance, which is made possible due to the binding you defined between the context node and the model class. The call of the `execute()` method initiates the start of the Google web service.

The second step invalidates the `Response` context node that is supposed to contain the return values. This allows you to ensure that the determined search results are transferred from the model class to the context node. Then, the Google search has been executed successfully and the `Response` context node is filled with search results.

Importing the search results from the model

4.4.5 Creating the Navigation Bar

We now have to display this data. Figure 4.16 shows the navigation bar, which basically consists of two components. First there is the page index that allows for direct navigation to a specific page. Secondly, there are the navigation buttons that enable you to scroll forward and backward through the search results. Depending on the page index you have chosen, we want to enable and disable the navigation buttons accordingly, for example, to ensure that the user cannot navigate backwards when he or she is on the first page of the search results.

Figure 4.16 Navigation Bar

Listing 4.5 shows how you can use the `createPageIndexList()` method to generate the page index. Note the use of the *dynamic parameter mapping* for the `index` parameter that enables us to use the same `GotoPage` action for each page index entry. Figure 4.17 shows the definition of the `GotoPage` action.

Dynamic parameter mapping

```
IWDLinkToAction link = null;

for (int i = 0; i < 10; i++) {

  link =
    (IWDLinkToAction) view.createElement(
      IWDLinkToAction.class,
      null);

  link.setOnAction(wdThis.wdGetGotoPageAction());
  link.mappingOfOnAction()
```

```
    .addParameter("Index", startIndex + i);

    link.setText(String.valueOf(startIndex + i));
    link.createLayoutData(IWDMatrixData.class);

    indexList.addChild(link);
  }
```

Listing 4.5 Creating the Page Index

The `onActionGotoPage` action event handler calls the `updateSearch-Index()` method that refreshes the start index of the search. You may remember that we assigned the default value **0** to the index after we had created the model class instance.

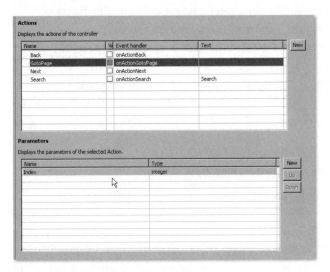

Figure 4.17 Defining the GotoPage Action

Listing 4.6 shows the `updateSearchIndex()` method.

```
private void updateSearchIndex(int pageIndex)
{
  wdContext.currentButtonBarElement()
    .setPageIndex(pageIndex);
  wdContext.currentRequest_GoogleSearchPort_
    doGoogleSearchElement()
    .setStart((pageIndex - 1) * 10);
}
```

Listing 4.6 updateSearchIndex() Method

To ensure that the navigation buttons are enabled or disabled according to the current selection, we must define the ButtonBar context node that contains a Boolean (**calculated**) context node attribute for each button that returns the required value depending on the current selection. For example, the value of the BackIsEnabled node attribute is calculated within the getButtonBarBackIsEnabled() method (see Listing 4.7).

Calculated context attributes

```
return wdContext.currentButtonBarElement().
  getPageIndex() > 0;
```

Listing 4.7 getButtonBarBackIsEnabled() Method

Tip

You should always use context attributes of the **calculated** type when the value of the attribute depends on other data (for example, on other context attributes), or on the application status in general.

Figure 4.18 shows the definition of the ButtonBar context node. You can define both the Set and Get methods for each **calculated** context attribute. Because we only need the appropriate Get method in our example, the context attributes BackIsEnabled and NextIsEnabled are declared as **readonly** attributes.

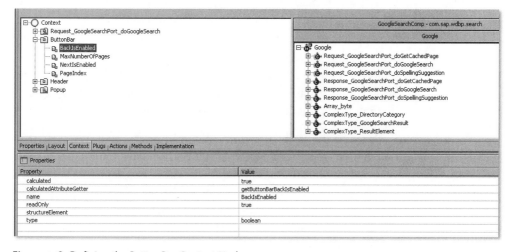

Figure 4.18 Defining the ButtonBar Context Node

133

4.5 Defining the Initial Display of a Web Dynpro Application

As we already mentioned earlier in this chapter, we'll display the search results in different ways. In this context, it makes sense to provide the user with an option to select those different types of display. In this section, we'll demonstrate the options provided by Web Dynpro for selecting the display options. We'll restrict our discussion to the definition of the initial display of the application, that is, to the display that should be used when a Web Dynpro application is started.

There are two basic options available here. On the one hand, you can define one single Web Dynpro application for all available types of display. The required initial display can then be selected using specific call parameters. On the other hand, you can define a separate Web Dynpro application for each available display type. The following sections describe both processes in greater detail.

4.5.1 Several Display Variants for one Web Dynpro Application

As we described in Chapter 2, you can use a Web Dynpro application to define an executable entity, which can be started via a specific application URL. You should always keep in mind that the Web Dynpro application does not contain any program logic by itself. Rather, the program logic is implemented completely in one or several—which is the more typical scenario—Web Dynpro components. The Web Dynpro application describes only the point of entry that is defined using the following three parameters:

▶ **Name of the Web Dynpro root component**
Whether you use one or several Web Dynpro components in your Web Dynpro application, there's always exactly one Web Dynpro component that serves as a *root component*. The root component usually embeds other Web Dynpro components. Although such a root component is a regular Web Dynpro component, it performs very specific tasks, especially in applications that consist of several Web Dynpro components.

As you can see in all the examples provided in this book, the root component often doesn't contain any or only little programming logic when the Web Dynpro application is consistently componentized. It serves instead as a framework for embedded components and is therefore often responsible for creating and deleting embedded Web Dynpro component instances.

Root component as framework for embedded components

Both the Web Dynpro GameStation (see Chapter 3) and the Web Dynpro MusicBox (see Chapter 8) are structured according to this principle—a principle that we would like to once again wholeheartedly recommend to you, because it substantially adds to a well-structured and maintainable Web Dynpro application.

▶ **Name of the component interface view**
Each Web Dynpro component can define different views based on the definition of one or several *component interface views*. A user or embedder can then choose between the different views. When defining a Web Dynpro application you must select one of the component interface views provided by the root component.

▶ **Name of the startup plug**
As we already mentioned, you can define inbound plugs and outbound plugs for each Web Dynpro view that enables you to enter and leave a Web Dynpro view. In this way, component interface views behave like typical Web Dynpro views.

When defining a Web Dynpro application, you must now use a specific inbound plug—the *startup plug*—to define the entry point into the interface view that you want to use for the Web Dynpro application.

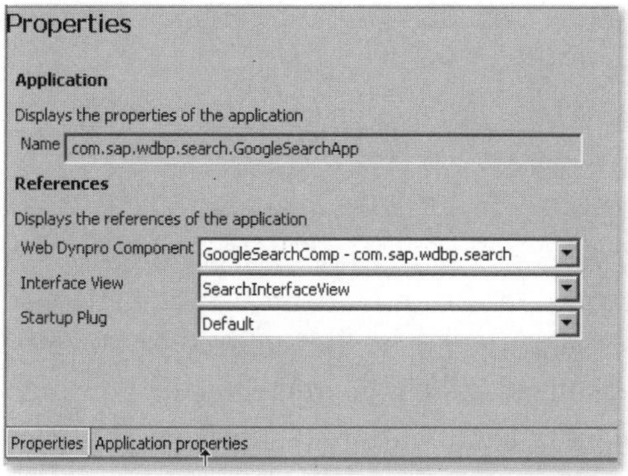

Figure 4.19 Defining the GoogleSearchApp Application

Figure 4.19 displays the Web Dynpro application `GoogleSearchApp` for which we want to define different initial display types in the following sections. Since we want to use the same Web Dynpro application for those display variants, we must control and separate the individual display variants via call parameters that we'll define as parameters of the startup plug being used.

Channeling call parameters into the Web Dynpro application

To *channel* those call parameters that are attached as URL parameters to the Web Dynpro application URL into your Web Dynpro application, you must extend the startup plug by the required parameters. The parameters must have the **String** type. Figure 4.20 shows the definition of the startup plug using the `mode` parameter.

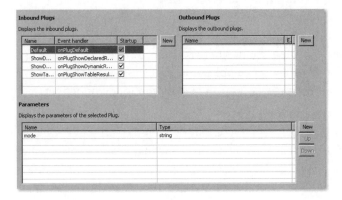

Figure 4.20 Defining the Default Startup Plug

When the Web Dynpro application is called via the appropriate call parameters, the extended startup plug is automatically provided with the transferred call parameters. You can access the transferred value directly in the `onPlugDefault()` handler of the interface view controller, as shown in Listing 4.8.

```
wdThis.wdGetGoogleSearchCompController().
    switchViewMode(mode);
```

Listing 4.8 onPlugDefault Handler

Using the WDWebContext adapter

In addition to extending the startup plug by the required parameters, you can also access the transferred call parameters directly; however, you cannot access the request parameters directly from the Web Dynpro client abstraction. To do that, you must use the `WDWebContextAdapter`. Chapter 6 describes this process in great detail.

From our point of view, the extension of the startup plug is a far more elegant method, because you don't need to contend with ensuring access to the defined call parameters. Moreover, when using the startup plug parameters, you explicitly define the required call parameters for your Web Dynpro application.

Selecting the Display Variant

Now that we have defined the necessary call parameter for our example and imported it into the Web Dynpro application via the startup plug, we must choose the desired display variant depending on the selected value. To do that, we'll perform the following steps:

1. The required call parameters are imported into the Web Dynpro application via the mode startup plug parameter.

2. Depending on the value of the call parameter or parameters, you must fire a corresponding event in the startup plug handler of the interface view controller by calling a method in the component controller of the root component. In our example, we call the switchViewMode() of the component controller in which we use wdFireEventSwitchViewMode(mode) to fire the SwitchViewMode event.

3. For the SearchFrameView view, we'll define an onViewSwitchMode event handler for the SwitchViewMode event that is called whenever the Web Dynpro application is launched.

4. In the final step, we'll make the Web Dynpro view that represents the required display variant visible within the onViewSwitchMode event handler. Figure 4.21 shows the three available display variants. The selected Web Dynpro view is displayed within the onViewSwitchMode event handler by calling the corresponding outbound plug.

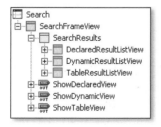

Figure 4.21 Available Display Variants

4.5.2 Several Web Dynpro Applications for Several Display Variants

Using different startup plugs

Sometimes it makes sense to implement different display variants by different Web Dynpro applications. The advantages of this approach are readily apparent. Instead of using the often rather cryptic call parameters, you can launch the required display variant via the corresponding Web Dynpro application URL. If you use meaningful names for the applications, you can make it much easier for the user to start the required display variant or application.

In our example, we'll use the same logic to obtain the initial display; however, because we now have to define a separate startup plug for each Web Dynpro application, it is no longer necessary to define specific startup plug parameters.

Defining additional startup plugs

To create an additional startup plug, you must generate a simple inbound plug for the SearchInterfaceView interface view and set the type to **Startup Plug**. Figure 4.22 shows a list of created startup plugs.

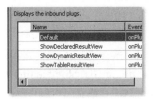

Figure 4.22 Defining Additional Startup Plugs

In the startup plug handlers, we then fire the corresponding event that is responsible for the display of the required display variant. As an example we use the startup plug handler onPlugShowTableResultView() that ensures the display of the search results in a table (see Listing 4.9).

```
wdThis.wdGetGoogleSearchCompController().switchViewMode(
    "TABLE_RESULT_VIEW");
```

Listing 4.9 Startup Plug Handler onPlugShowTableResultView

Using different interface views

In addition to defining the different Web Dynpro applications via the different startup plugs of an interface view, you can also define a separate interface view for each Web Dynpro application. We don't recommend this approach, however, because the definition of several interface views automatically generates different Web Dynpro windows. Furthermore, since the entire navigation structure of your Web Dynpro application is defined for exactly one Web Dynpro window, you might have to redefine the navigation structure completely when using several interface views. The extra work involved and the more complex maintainability of your Web Dynpro application are strong arguments for not using this variant.

4.6 Displaying the Result List

Now that we have discussed the implementation of the application framework and the manipulation of the initial arrangement of the Web Dynpro views, we want to describe three different options to display the search results, including their advantages and disadvantages.

We decided to implement the different types of search result displays by using simple Web Dynpro views. We could also use different Web Dynpro components here, but because we don't want to discuss the potential increase in flexibility here, we decided against that approach.

Using Web Dynpro views

Note that, however, it's completely up to you whether you want to extend our sample application in this way. For example, you could implement the different displays of the search results via separate Web Dynpro components that are embedded into the application framework via a Web Dynpro component interface. The use of the Web Dynpro component interface would then enable you to embed new display variants at any time. We decided to follow that approach for the Web Dynpro GameStation (see Chapter 3).

4.6.1 The TableResultListView View

The easiest way to display the search results list is most probably the use of the IWDTable UI element. Once you have positioned the IWD-Table UI element in the Web Dynpro view, you must bind the table to the data to be displayed via data binding in the view controller context.

Defining the table-
data binding

1. To do that, select the **Create Binding** entry from the context menu of the IWDTable UI element ResultList (see Figure 4.23).

Figure 4.23 Starting the Table Binding Dialog

2. Then select the required context attributes. In our example, we want to display all attributes of the ResultItem context node (see Figure 4.24).

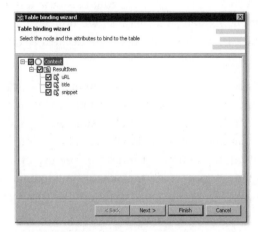

Figure 4.24 Defining the Required Context Attributes

Displaying the
attributes

3. Then you must define the sequence and type of the display of individual node attributes (see Figure 4.25). You can use the two arrows to change the sequence of the attributes. In the **Editor** column, you can define the required display and the required UI element you want to use to display the relevant attribute in the table column.

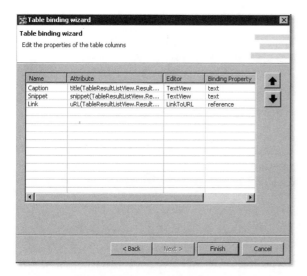

Figure 4.25 Defining the Display Type for Individual Context Attributes

Figure 4.26 shows the created table columns. The selected `Table-CellEditors` match your settings exactly. Of course, you can change those settings at a later stage if you want, either by calling the table binding dialog again or by manipulating the relevant UI elements.

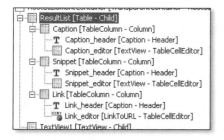

Figure 4.26 Created Table Columns

The great advantage of this display variant is the simplicity of the solution. You can define a simple and efficient display of the search results by using declarative programming only. On the other hand, your room to maneuver is certainly limited by the options provided by the `IWDTable` UI element. Therefore, you cannot produce an attractive display based on the HTML formattings, for example, as you can see in Figure 4.27.

Evaluating the display

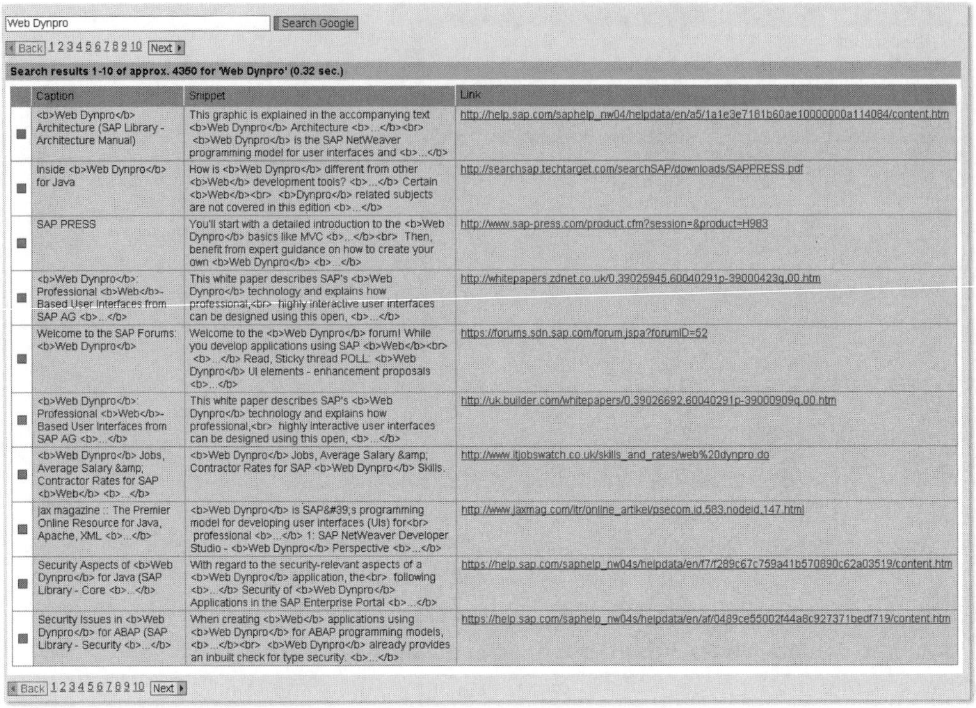

Web Dynpro | Search Google

Back 1 2 3 4 5 6 7 8 9 10 Next

Search results 1-10 of approx. 4360 for 'Web Dynpro' (0.32 sec.)

	Caption	Snippet	Link
■	<b>Web Dynpro</b> Architecture (SAP Library - Architecture Manual)	This graphic is explained in the accompanying text <b>Web Dynpro</b> Architecture <b>...</b> <b>Web Dynpro</b> is the SAP NetWeaver programming model for user interfaces and <b>...</b>	http://help.sap.com/saphelp_nw04/helpdata/en/a5/1a1e3e7181b60ae10000000a114084/content.htm
■	Inside <b>Web Dynpro</b> for Java	How is <b>Web Dynpro</b> different from other <b>Web</b> development tools? <b>...</b> Certain <b>Web</b> <b>Dynpro</b> related subjects are not covered in this edition <b>...</b>	http://searchsap.techtarget.com/searchSAP/downloads/SAPPRESS.pdf
■	SAP PRESS	You'll start with a detailed introduction to the <b>Web Dynpro</b> basics like MVC <b>...</b> Then, benefit from expert guidance on how to create your own <b>Web Dynpro</b> <b>...</b>	http://www.sap-press.com/product.cfm?session=&product=H983
■	<b>Web Dynpro</b>: Professional <b>Web</b>-Based User Interfaces from SAP AG <b>...</b>	This white paper describes SAP's <b>Web Dynpro</b> technology and explains how professional, highly interactive user interfaces can be designed using this open, <b>...</b>	http://whitepapers.zdnet.co.uk/0,39025945,60040291p-39000423q,00.htm
■	Welcome to the SAP Forums: <b>Web Dynpro</b>	Welcome to the <b>Web Dynpro</b> forum! While you develop applications using SAP <b>Web</b> <b>...</b> Read, Sticky thread POLL: <b>Web Dynpro</b> UI elements - enhancement proposals <b>...</b>	https://forums.sdn.sap.com/forum.jspa?forumID=52
■	<b>Web Dynpro</b>: Professional <b>Web</b>-Based User Interfaces from SAP AG <b>...</b>	This white paper describes SAP's <b>Web Dynpro</b> technology and explains how professional, highly interactive user interfaces can be designed using this open, <b>...</b>	http://uk.builder.com/whitepapers/0,39026692,60040291p-39000909q,00.htm
■	<b>Web Dynpro</b> Jobs, Average Salary & Contractor Rates for SAP <b>Web</b> <b>...</b>	<b>Web Dynpro</b> Jobs, Average Salary & Contractor Rates for SAP <b>Web Dynpro</b> Skills.	http://www.itjobswatch.co.uk/skills_and_rates/web%20dynpro.do
■	jax magazine :: The Premier Online Resource for Java, Apache, XML <b>...</b>	<b>Web Dynpro</b> is SAP's programming model for developing user interfaces (UIs) for professional <b>...</b> 1: SAP NetWeaver Developer Studio - <b>Web Dynpro</b> Perspective <b>...</b>	http://www.jaxmag.com/itr/online_artikel/psecom,id,583,nodeid,147.html
■	Security Aspects of <b>Web Dynpro</b> for Java (SAP Library - Core <b>...</b>	With regard to the security-relevant aspects of a <b>Web Dynpro</b> application, the following <b>...</b> Security of <b>Web Dynpro</b> Applications in the SAP Enterprise Portal <b>...</b>	https://help.sap.com/saphelp_nw04s/helpdata/en/f7/f289c67c759a41b570890c62a03519/content.htm
■	Security Issues in <b>Web Dynpro</b> for ABAP (SAP Library - Security <b>...</b>	When creating <b>Web</b> applications using <b>Web Dynpro</b> for ABAP programming models, <b>...</b> <b>Web Dynpro</b> already provides an inbuilt check for type security. <b>...</b>	https://help.sap.com/saphelp_nw04s/helpdata/en/af/0489ce55002f44a8c927371bedf719/content.htm

Back 1 2 3 4 5 6 7 8 9 10 Next

Figure 4.27 Displaying the Search Results in a Table

4.6.2 The DeclaredResultListView View

Composite display

In Section 4.6.1, we saw that using the `IWDTable` UI element enables you to quickly define a simple, but very limited display of the search results. We now want to introduce another display variant in which we'll define the required user interface declaratively. Contrary to using the `IWDTable` UI element, we will now compose the display variant from several UI elements, as shown in Figure 4.28. Each search result is then displayed by using two `IWDTextView` UI elements for the caption (e.g., **ResultItem1.Caption**) and the text excerpt (e.g., **ResultItem1.Snippet**), as well as an `IWDLinkToAction` UI element (e.g., **ResultItem1.Link**) for displaying the URL.

In contrast to the previous variant, we now get a much more attractive display, although we still cannot display the HTML formattings correctly (see Figure 4.29).

Figure 4.28 DeclaredResultListView in the View Designer

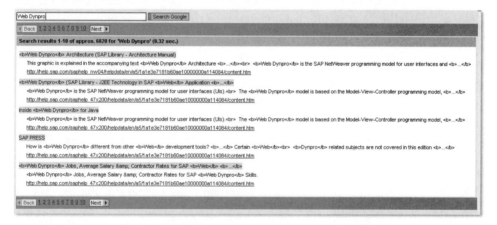

Figure 4.29 Displaying the Search Results via a Declaratively Created User Interface

We declare all required UI elements explicitly so we can display a maximum of five search results at the same time. Two basic options are now available to provide the corresponding UI elements with data. The use of dynamic programming enables you to provide the UI elements with those search results that exist in the ResultItem context node of the view controller context. Because our objective is a completely declarative display variant, however, we must define a separate context node in the view controller context of the Declared-ResultListView view in order for each search result to be displayed (see Figure 4.30).

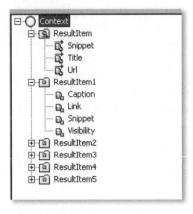

Figure 4.30 View Controller Context

ResultItem1 defines the first search result; ResultItem2 defines the second search result; and so forth. In addition to the attributes provided by the ResultItem context node, we must also define the **Visibility** attribute that enables us to control the visibility of individual search results.

Although we can create the user interface completely declaratively due to the use of additional context nodes, we have to compensate for using additional context nodes by filling the corresponding context nodes ResultItem1, ResultItem2, ... explicitly with the search results provided by the ResultItem node. To do that, we can use the updateResultItem() method that fills a specific node, ResultItem<Index>, with data (see Listing 4.10). For this purpose, we must first determine the corresponding node element of the ResultItem node. If the necessary data exists for this process, the associated ResultItem<Index> node is filled and made visible.

```
private void updateResultItem(int index) {
  IPrivateDeclaredResultListView.IResultItemElement
    resultItem =wdContext.nodeResultItem()
      .getResultItemElementAt(index - 1);
  String nodeName = "ResultItem" + index;
  IWDNodeElement nodeElement =
    wdControllerAPI
      .getContext()
      .getRootNode()
      .getChildNode(nodeName, 0)
      .getCurrentElement();
  if (resultItem != null) {
```

```
nodeElement.setAttributeValue(
   IPrivateDeclaredResultListView.
      IResultItem1Element.CAPTION,
   resultItem.getTitle());

nodeElement.setAttributeValue(
   IPrivateDeclaredResultListView.
      IResultItem1Element.SNIPPET,
   resultItem.getSnippet());

nodeElement.setAttributeValue(
   IPrivateDeclaredResultListView.
      IResultItem1Element.LINK,
   resultItem.getUrl());
nodeElement.setAttributeValue(
   IPrivateDeclaredResultListView.
      IResultItem1Element.VISIBILITY,
   WDVisibility.VISIBLE);
} else {
nodeElement.setAttributeValue(
   IPrivateDeclaredResultListView.
      IResultItem1Element.VISIBILITY,
   WDVisibility.NONE);
   }
}
```

Listing 4.10 updateResultItem() Method

Contrary to the use of the IWDTable UI element, the combination of several UI elements provided a much more elegant display variant. And yet, the HTML formattings are still not displayed correctly because none of the Web Dynpro UI elements provides such a function. The declaratively created user interface is only made possible by the introduction of new context nodes to which the original data is copied. This, of course, increases the memory utilization of the Web Dynpro Google search.

Evaluating the display

4.6.3   The DynamicResultListView View

Figure 4.31 shows the display of search results that is enabled by using the Web Dynpro view DynamicResultListView. As is readily apparent, this variant provides the most elegant and complex display of the three variants introduced here.

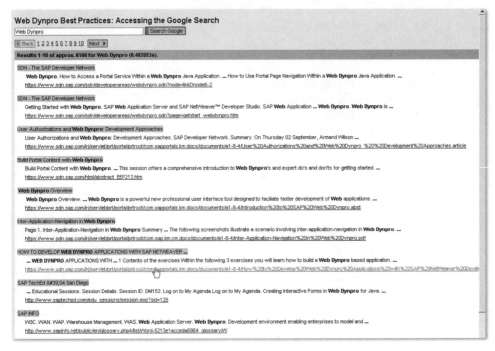

Figure 4.31 Dynamically Created Display of the Search Results

Dynamically created display

This type of display is made possible due to a completely dynamically created user interface, which we'll now describe in greater detail. Basically, we have to provide the following resources:

▶ The search results are returned in HTML format. However, Web Dynpro based on SAP NetWeaver 2004 does not provide any HTML renderer UI element, which means we have to dynamically create such an HTML renderer by ourselves.

▶ To create a completely dynamic UI, we'll also generate the entire list of search results dynamically in this display variant, as opposed to the `DeclaredResultListView` view in which we had declared the individual search results upfront.

4.6.4 Displaying HTML-Based Search Results

Let's take a closer look at the display of a search result (see Figure 4.32). First, the found string is displayed and the search string that was entered is highlighted. Then a part of the found document is added. Again, the search string is highlighted. Finally, a link to the found document is provided. If you click on that link, the corresponding URL is called in a new window of the web browser.

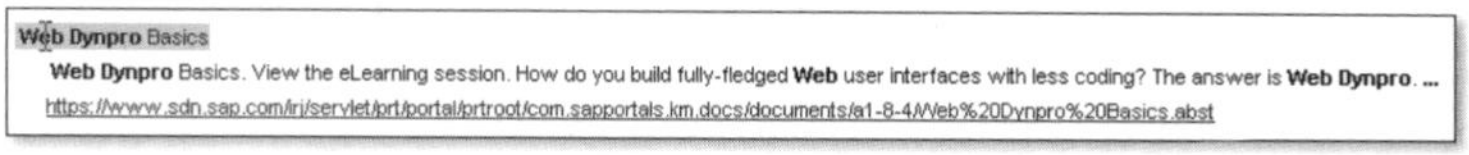

Web Dynpro Basics
Web Dynpro Basics. View the eLearning session. How do you build fully-fledged Web user interfaces with less coding? The answer is Web Dynpro. ...
https://www.sdn.sap.com/irj/servlet/prt/portal/prtroot/com.sapportals.km.docs/documents/a1-8-4/Web%20Dynpro%20Basics.abst

Figure 4.32 Displaying a Search Result

Google web service returns both the title and the excerpt of the found document in HTML format. Nevertheless, because SAP NetWeaver 2004 doesn't provide any corresponding UI element, we must resort to dynamic programming to implement the displayed UI.

Displaying texts in HTML format

The underlying idea is pretty straightforward. We'll decompose the texts that are available in HTML format into separate components and display each of those components in different `IWDTextView` UI elements. The `IWDTextView` UI elements support the relevant formattings such as bold, italics, and so on, so that we can implement the required typeface. The dynamically generated `IWDTextView` instances are eventually combined in an `IWDTransparantContainer` UI element.

All this can be created dynamically without any problem. This is a good example of how important it can be in certain scenarios to create dynamic UIs despite all the benefits of a declarative UI. The dynamic UI is created in method `createHTMLViewer()` of view controller `DynamicResultListView`, as shown in Listing 4.11. In addition to the HTML text fragment, we also need the corresponding `IWDTransparentContainer` instance that combines all text fragments at the end of the process. Moreover, we need the `IWDView` instance so that we can dynamically create the corresponding UI elements. And finally, we must define the color in which we want the text fragment to be displayed.

```
private static void createHTMLViewer(
  String htmlfragment,
  IWDTransparentContainer container,
  IWDView view,
  WDTextViewSemanticColor color) {
  container.removeAllChildren();
```

```
htmlfragment
    = StringUtil.searchAndReplace(
        htmlfragment, "<br>", "");

String[] parts =
    StringUtil.divide(htmlfragment, '<');

WDTextViewDesign design = null;
String part = null;

for (int i = 0; i < parts.length; i++) {

    if (parts[i].startsWith("b>")) {
        design = WDTextViewDesign.EMPHASIZED;
    } else {
        design = WDTextViewDesign.STANDARD;
    }

    part = StringUtil.
        searchAndReplace(parts[i], "/b>", "");
    part = StringUtil.
        searchAndReplace(part, "b>", " ");
    part = StringUtil.
        searchAndReplace(part, "&quot;", "'");

    addHTMLPart(part, container, view, design, color);
    }
}
```

Listing 4.11 createHTMLViewer() Method

First we must remove all line breaks from the HTML text fragment. Then we decompose the entire text fragment into the components that are defined by HTML tags. For this purpose we'll use the "<" character, which defines the beginning of an HTML tag. Then, we'll implement iterations via the newly created subfragments and determine the required WDTextViewDesign. In our example, we'll process only the <b> HTML tag (bold), which we'll need to highlight the search strings. The addHTMLPart() method finally enables us to generate the IWDTextView UI element (see Listing 4.12).

```
private static void addHTMLPart(
    String htmlPart,
    IWDTransparentContainer container,
    IWDView view,
    WDTextViewDesign design,
```

```
WDTextViewSemanticColor color) {

IWDTextView textView =
  (IWDTextView) view.createElement(
    IWDTextView.class,
    null);
textView.setText(htmlPart);
textView.setDesign(design);
textView.setSemanticColor(color);
container.addChild(textView);
}
```

Listing 4.12 addHTMLPart() Method

Now that we have defined the `IWDextView` instance, we can define the text, design, and color. The instance that we created is then assigned to the encompassing `IWDTransparentContainer`, which you can extend to meet your requirements.

At this point, we'll mention the two options that you can use to provide the created UI element instances with data in the context of dynamic programming. In the aforementioned example, we have consistently used the corresponding `Set` methods such as `setText()` or `setDesign()` to define the text and design of the `IWDTextView` instance. In this example, these methods are available and are used correctly, because static data, which cannot be modified by the user, is used here.

Assigning data to dynamically created UI elements

However, if the user should be able to modify the displayed data, you *must* use the corresponding `bind…()` methods to provide the dynamically created UI elements with data. The use of `bind…()` methods is also beneficial, because these methods enable you to separate the real data that is bound to the relevant UI elements from the purely visual definition of the user interface. You can use this ability to separate data to optimize the data quantities to be transferred.

4.7 Summary

In this chapter, we described the use of the Web Dynpro web service model in great detail. Despite some restrictions, this model allows for the simple integration of any type of web service.

Using the Google web service as an example, we also demonstrated how you could use a combination of declarative and dynamic programming to create modern and user-friendly application UIs.

In this context, we discussed the pros and cons of these programming techniques that can be summarized in the following adage: As much declarative programming as possible and as much dynamic programming as necessary.

Before we outline the various aspects of integrating Web Dynpro applications into SAP NetWeaver Portal via numerous examples in the following chapters, we will discuss some basic principles of SAP NetWeaver Portal and how it interacts with Web Dynpro applications.

5   Web Dynpro and SAP NetWeaver Portal

Many new possibilities become available to you when you run Web Dynpro applications within SAP NetWeaver Portal. Using SAP NetWeaver Portal is especially helpful if you want to aggregate or structure different Web Dynpro applications that can run in different SAP NetWeaver installations, or if you want to combine them with other types of applications.

Even though we cannot provide a complete and detailed overview of the capabilities of SAP NetWeaver Portal here, we will describe the basic concepts and options in this chapter. The integration of your Web Dynpro applications will be a running theme throughout this book.

You can find additional information on SAP NetWeaver Portal in the SAP Help Portal at *http://help.sap.com*, as well as in the SAP Developer Network at *http://sdn.sap.com*.

Additional information

5.1   SAP NetWeaver Portal

As part of your SAP NetWeaver installation, SAP NetWeaver Portal provides numerous options for integrating different types of applications in a structured and role-specific manner, and for providing different users with access to those applications. The major advantages that result from running your applications within SAP NetWeaver Portal can be summarized as follows:

▶ **Execution of any type of application**
Within SAP NetWeaver Portal, you can run any type of application, whether it is based on one of the SAP UI technologies such as WebGUI, BSP, HTMLB, or Web Dynpro, or on any other web technology such as Java Server Pages (JSP) or servlets.

▶ **Role-based access**
The use of portal roles enables you to customize your applications according to different user requirements and to provide users with exactly those applications that they need in order to fulfill their roles, for example, as a purchaser or a team leader. The often long and inconvenient search for the required functionality or application, therefore, becomes unnecessary and a thing of the past.

▶ **Single sign-on**
Particularly when you start applications within SAP NetWeaver Portal that run on different SAP NetWeaver installations, it is very useful to use single sign-on (SSO) because this helps you to ensure that the user only needs to log on to the SAP NetWeaver Portal. Therefore, no further logon is required if the user launches an application on another SAP NetWeaver installation.

5.1.1 Content Model

To be able to consistently structure different types of applications, the SAP NetWeaver Portal defines a number of entities that we'll describe in the following sections.

iViews

Different iView types

You must generate an iView to launch an application within SAP NetWeaver Portal. An iView is the entity within SAP NetWeaver Portal that can be started or executed. In this context, each type of application defines a separate type of iView with application-specific or type-specific properties. In the simplest scenario, an application can be a regular URL (for example, *http://www.sap.com*) that can be launched via a *URL-iView*. Web Dynpro applications are launched through *Web Dynpro iViews*.

Editing iView properties

Regardless of the type of iView, the SAP NetWeaver Portal defines specific iView properties that are always valid. For example, for each iView, you can define the size in which it is to be displayed. In addition, the SAP NetWeaver Portal provides the *iView Editor* as a consistent functionality for all types of iViews that enables you to define or change the properties of an iView. Section 5.2.3 discusses the options provided by the iView Editor, particularly regarding Web Dynpro iViews.

Portal Pages

As soon as you want to display more than one iView concurrently, you need a portal page. A portal page enables you to arrange any number of iViews on one page. The Page Editor, in turn, helps you to define and change the contents of a portal page, which is the list of displayed iViews, as well as the layout in which you want to display the different iViews.

Using the Page Editor

Furthermore, the SAP NetWeaver Portal provides countless communication options so that iViews that are called on one portal page can exchange data with one another.

Communication between iViews of a portal page

Lastly, you can also embed portal pages into other portal pages and thereby create complex page layouts. For example, the portal UI, which we'll describe in Section 5.1.2, consists of several nested portal pages. This feature enables you to customize the general layout of your SAP NetWeaver Portal installation using the Page Editor.

Worksets

You can group several iViews or portal pages using *worksets*. A workset is a logically related group of applications. Worksets are particularly useful if you use many iViews and portal pages. With regard to (portal) roles, the use of worksets allows for a better structuring of the roles. Moreover, you can use worksets to provide components that can be made into entire roles later on.

Roles

The (portal) role defines the contents that are to be made available to a specific group of users, or to a specific individual user. For example, in Section 5.2.4, we'll define the role **Web Dynpro Best Practices**, which contains all the examples described in this book. Each user who is assigned to this role in SAP NetWeaver Portal is therefore given access to the iViews and portal pages contained in that role.

Using the Role Editor A role defines both the actual contents—the available iViews, portal pages, or worksets—and their structure and arrangement. You can define and change the contents and structure using the Role Editor.

5.1.2 User Interface

Figure 5.1 shows the Web Dynpro MusicBox (see Chapter 8) within the SAP NetWeaver Portal. Here, the user interface consists of fixed components that enable the user to call specific portal functions, regardless of the displayed content. We'll describe the most important components in greater detail in the following sections.

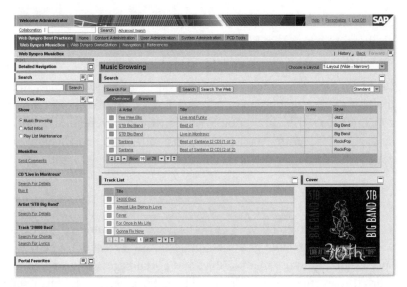

Figure 5.1 SAP NetWeaver Portal

Top-Level Navigation

The top-level navigation enables the user to navigate between the different types of content provided by the roles assigned to that user (see Figure 5.2). Top-level navigation always displays the two top levels, which is where the different iViews, portal pages, or worksets are structured within a role. Above the top-level navigation, several links are provided that enable you to run generic portal functions such as **Help**, **Personalize**, or **Log Off**.

Figure 5.2 Top-Level Navigation

You can use the **Personalize** link to change central functions and other basic settings of the SAP NetWeaver Portal. For example, Figure 5.3 shows change of the portal theme that defines the required graphical display of the used UI elements.

Defining the portal theme

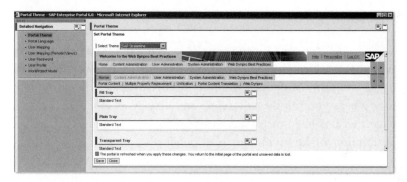

Figure 5.3 Personalizing the Portal Theme

Besides the portal theme, you can also define the language to be used. All the properties that define the portal environment chosen by the user are transferred to the Web Dynpro runtime environment when a Web Dynpro application is launched within SAP NetWeaver Portal. This ensures that your Web Dynpro application automatically uses the portal theme that you have defined or the language that you have selected, for example.

Inner Page

Below the top-level navigation, there is the inner page that consists of the page header, the navigation panel, and the working area or content area (see Figure 5.4).

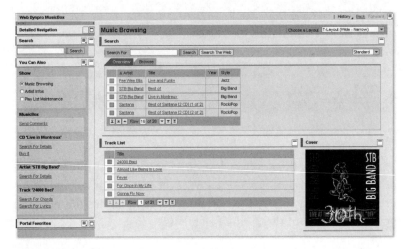

Figure 5.4 Inner Page

Elements of the page header The page header contains the generic forward and backward navigation that enables you to navigate between the iViews and portal pages you visit. Moreover, the page header provides the portal history where you can directly select and display an iView or a portal page that has been displayed earlier. Chapter 6 contains a detailed description of how you can manipulate the portal history within your Web Dynpro application and how you can navigate to any iView or portal pages within the Web Dynpro application.

Last but not least, the page header displays the title of the currently active iView or portal page. Furthermore, it provides access to specific functions of the displayed iView or portal page. Figure 5.5 shows the iView tray of the **NavigationTester** iView (see Chapter 6).

Figure 5.5 iView Tray

Nested portal page The inner page is a good example of the use of nested portal pages because it is defined as a regular portal page that embeds, among other things, the working area as a portal page.

Navigation Panel

The most important component of the navigation panel is the *detailed navigation*. Whereas the top-level navigation displays the two top levels where the different iViews, portal pages, or worksets are structured within a role, the detailed navigation displays all other structure levels. Typically, you don't want to define more than three levels so that the detailed navigation always displays the lowest level (see Figure 5.6). If your role defines only two levels, the detailed navigation contains the same entry as the second level of the top-level navigation.

Detailed navigation

Figure 5.6 Detailed Navigation

Moreover, you can define for each iView and portal page if you always want to hide the detailed navigation, or if you want to hide it periodically (if no third navigation level has been defined). This is particularly useful if the iView or portal page requires a lot of space within the working area. Section 5.2.3 describes how you can manipulate the visibility of the navigation panel for a Web Dynpro iView.

Because the navigation panel is also defined as a portal page—similar to the inner page—you can display any iView within the navigation panel. This is useful in scenarios in which you want to provide specific navigation options that depend on the displayed iView or portal page. We'll take advantage of this option in Chapter 8, for example, when we embed a special Web Dynpro (navigation) iView into the navigation panel for the Web Dynpro MusicBox.

Extending the navigation panel

Working Area

The working area or content area of the SAP NetWeaver Portal displays the selected iView or portal page, that is, it displays the area in which you will use your Web Dynpro applications.

5.2   Creating Portal Content

This section provides a detailed description of how you can run your Web Dynpro application within SAP NetWeaver Portal by generating a Web Dynpro iView and embedding it into the relevant portal pages, worksets, and roles.

5.2.1   Creating a System in the Portal Landscape

Separating the portal and the Web Dynpro application

Typically, you would run your Web Dynpro applications on a different SAP NetWeaver installation than the SAP NetWeaver Portal itself. Among other things, the advantage of separating the portal from the Web Dynpro application is that the different installations can be upgraded independently of each other. Moreover, because your Web Dynpro application does not have any influence on the SAP NetWeaver Portal, you can ensure that even if errors occur in your Web Dynpro application, SAP NetWeaver Portal will still function correctly, and vice versa.

However, as we'll see in Chapters 7 and 8, if you want to use specific SAP NetWeaver Portal features in your Web Dynpro application, you must run all your Web Dynpro applications on the same SAP NetWeaver installation as the SAP NetWeaver Portal itself.

Portal landscape

To enable the SAP NetWeaver Portal to launch your Web Dynpro application as a Web Dynpro iView, you must first tell the portal landscape on which SAP NetWeaver installation you want to run your Web Dynpro application. You can do that by defining a corresponding system in the portal landscape.

1. To start the definition process for that system, first go to **System Administration · System Configuration** and then select the item **New · System** in the context menu of the directory in which you want to store the system, that is, the system definition (see Figure 5.7). In this example, we want to store the system in the *Web Dynpro Best Practices* directory, which is where we'll create all required iViews, portal pages, and roles at a later stage.

Selecting the system type

2. In the next step you must select the required system type. Note that your SAP NetWeaver installation is not directly displayed as such. Instead you must select one of the existing **SAP system** entries (see Figure 5.8).

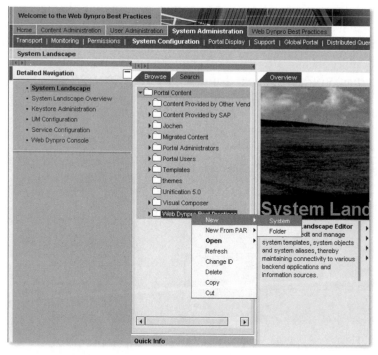

Figure 5.7 Creating a System

As long as your SAP NetWeaver installation is a pure Java installation, it doesn't matter which entry you select. However, if it is a composite Java-ABAP installation, you must select the entry that corresponds to your ABAP installation.

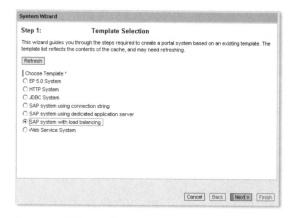

Figure 5.8 Selecting the System Type

3. Once you have selected the system type, you must define the **System Name** and **System ID**, and optionally the required namespace (**System ID Prefix**) as well as the language and description in the subsequent dialog step. In Figure 5.9, we define the **Web Dynpro Best Practices** system that describes our SAP NetWeaver installation on which we'll run all the examples used in this book.

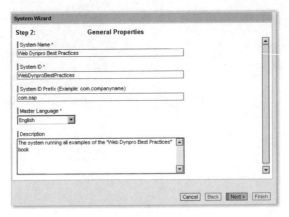

Figure 5.9 Defining General System Properties

4. The dialog step that is displayed next summarizes the settings you made. You can then generate the system by clicking on the **Finish** button.

Figure 5.10 shows the generated **Web Dynpro Best Practices** system in the *Web Dynpro Best Practices* directory that we had previously selected. As you can see, the directory already contains several subdirectories that we created, which will help us to structure the content we're going to create later on.

Figure 5.10 Created System

Changing system properties

Now that we have created the **Web Dynpro Best Practices** system, we must define several different system properties. To do that, you must open the context menu of the system and select **Open · Object** to launch the *System Editor* (see Figure 5.11). Like every other type-specific editor in SAP NetWeaver Portal, the System Editor also allows the maintenance of the respective object properties using the Property Editor. As you'll see in this chapter, you can do that consistently, irrespective of the selected object.

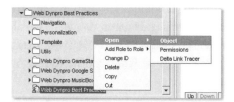

Figure 5.11 Launching the System Editor

One of the essential characteristics of the Property Editor is that it divides the available properties into different *categories*. Each category describes a set of semantically related properties of the corresponding object. Figure 5.12 displays a selection of the possible categories for the **Web Dynpro Best Practices** system.

Division into categories

Figure 5.12 Selecting the Web Application Server Category

Most categories described here do not play any role in the execution of a Web Dynpro application. For this reason, we'll describe only those categories in greater detail that are important for our purposes.[1]

---

1 Please refer to the SAP Help Portal (*http://help.sap.com*) for a complete overview of the categories.

Figure 5.13 shows the properties of the **Web Application Server
(WAS)** category. The following parameters are important for us:

▶ **WAS Host Name**

The **WAS Host Name** defines the host name of your SAP NetWeaver installation. Make sure that you enter the fully qualified host
name including the corresponding domain. Host names that are
not fully qualified may cause problems later when you want to call
one of the client-side APIs provided by the SAP NetWeaver Portal.
Note that you must specify the **WAS Host Name** in the following
structure: <Hostname>.<Domain>:<Port>.

▶ **WAS Protocol**

The **WAS Protocol** property helps you define the protocol used
for your SAP NetWeaver installation.

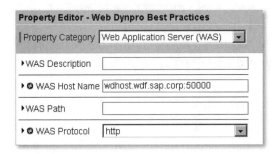

Figure 5.13 Defining the Web Application Server Properties

The **User Management** category (see Figure 5.14) enables you to
define how you want to authenticate your Web Dynpro application
within SAP NetWeaver Portal. The **Logon Method** property defines
whether you want to use the SAP Logon Ticket (**SAPLOGONTICKET**),
a specific user (**UIDPW**), or an X.509 client certificate (**X509CERT**)
for this purpose.

Figure 5.14 Defining the User Management Properties

> **Tip**
>
> We generally recommend using the SAP Logon Ticket when you run your Web Dynpro application on the same SAP NetWeaver installation as the SAP NetWeaver Portal. If your Web Dynpro application and the SAP NetWeaver Portal run on different installations, using the SAP Logon Ticket becomes much more complex because it requires you to set up a *trust relationship* between the two installations. You can find detailed information on this subject at the following URL:
>
> *http://help.sap.com/saphelp_nw04/helpdata/en/89/ 6eb8e1af2f115993 700508b6b8b11/frameset.htm* (**Single Sign-On with SAP Logon Tickets**).

The **User Mapping Type** property should always be set to **admin, user**.

Now that we have defined all the required system properties, we must create the so-called *system alias* in the last step. The system alias represents a logical name that can be used to address the defined system. By using such a system alias, you can make the portal objects that build on them independent of the actually defined systems.

Defining a system alias

As you'll see in Section 5.2.2, we will use a system alias to define a Web Dynpro iView so we can describe the system on which we want to run the Web Dynpro application that's launched by the Web Dynpro iView. This will enable you to run the now defined Web Dynpro iView on other SAP NetWeaver Portal installations without encountering any problems; you will only need to ensure that the corresponding system alias is available. You can also define the system alias for an already existing system, which could then provide several system aliases.

To define a system alias for our **Web Dynpro Best Practices** system, you must first go to the **System Aliases** view in the **System Editor** (see Figure 5.15).

Figure 5.15 Selecting the System Alias

Different views in the System Editor

The **System Editor** provides different views, most of which contain specific properties of the selected object that are displayed in different ways. The **Object** view is always the default view. It displays the available object properties in a generic name-value view.

Figure 5.16 shows the **System Alias Editor** that allows the definition of any system alias. For our example, we used the **Add** button to define the **WebDynproBestPractices** system alias, which we'll use in the next chapter to create our Web Dynpro iViews.

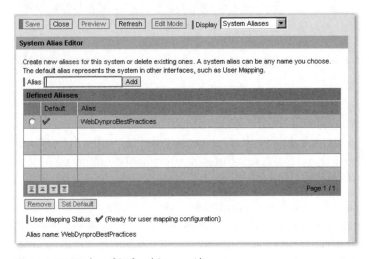

Figure 5.16 Display of Defined System Aliases

5.2.2 Creating a Web Dynpro iView

We'll now describe how you can create a Web Dynpro iView through which you can launch our Web Dynpro application within the SAP NetWeaver Portal.

Structuring the Web Dynpro content

From the start, you should determine how you want to structure the Web Dynpro-based portal content. Figure 5.17 shows the portal content structure that we selected and which helps you to display the examples used in this book in the SAP NetWeaver Portal.

Portal content catalog

You can generally create and change all kinds of portal content in the **portal content catalog** that can be opened via **Content Administration · Portal Content**. To create a Web Dynpro iView, open the context menu of the corresponding directory in the content catalog (see Figure 5.18) and select the item **New · iView** to start the **iView Wizard**.

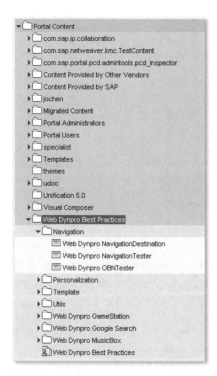

Figure 5.17 Structuring Portal Content

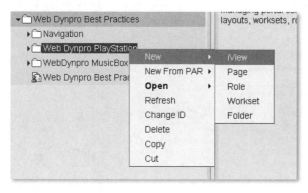

Figure 5.18 Creating an iView

Figure 5.19 shows the first dialog step of the iView Wizard, which is where you select the required iView template. Corresponding to the selected iView type, an iView template defines specific default settings and values for certain iView properties. We select the **SAP Web Dynpro iView** template.

Selecting an iView template

Figure 5.19 Selecting the Web Dynpro iView Template

Defining application-specific iView templates

In Chapter 8, we'll use the Web Dynpro MusicBox to describe scenarios in which creating application-specific Web Dynpro iView templates would be recommended.

General iView properties

Once you have selected the Web Dynpro iView template, you must define the name and ID of the iView in the next dialog step (see Figure 5.20). The iView name will be used later as a title in the portal. You can change the name at any time, for example, when you embed the iView into a portal page, or when you assign it to a role. All other parameters displayed in this dialog step are optional.

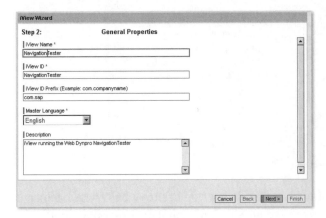

Figure 5.20 Defining General Properties

Click on the **Next** button to go to the next dialog step in which you must decide whether you want to integrate a Web Dynpro for Java

application or a Web Dynpro for ABAP application (see Figure 5.21).
We select **Web Dynpro for Java**.

Figure 5.21 Selecting Web Dynpro for Java

In the next dialog step (see Figure 5.22), you must define the follow-ing technical parameters to specify your Web Dynpro application for which you want to create the iView:

Defining the Web Dynpro application

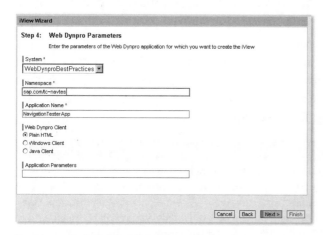

Figure 5.22 Defining the Web Dynpro Application

▶ **System**

The **System** parameter is used to define the system alias of your Web Dynpro iView. For the examples in this book, you must use the **WebDynproBestPractices** system alias. For test purposes only, you can use the **SAP_LocalSystem** system alias that always describes the local SAP NetWeaver installation. In that case, you would always run your Web Dynpro application on the same installation that also runs the SAP NetWeaver Portal.

> **Tip**
>
> We recommend that you use the **SAP_LocalSystem** system alias for test purposes only. For Web Dynpro iViews that you want to distribute to different systems later on, you should always define a separate system alias. By defining the required system alias or aliases for the corresponding systems, you will later be able to adjust the defined iViews to the specific system landscape without incurring any problem.

▶ **Namespace**

The **Namespace** parameter defines the Web Dynpro development component or the Web Dynpro Eclipse project respectively, which contains the required Web Dynpro application.

The selected value must correspond to the ⟨Vendor⟩/⟨DC-Name⟩ schema: ⟨Vendor⟩ is the vendor of the Web Dynpro development component; if a Web Dynpro Eclipse project is used, it is local. ⟨DC-Name⟩ is the name of the Web Dynpro development component or of the Web Dynpro Eclipse project respectively. We'll choose com.sap/tc~navtes for the Web Dynpro NavigationTester.

▶ **Application Name**

The **Application Name** parameter defines the application name of the required Web Dynpro application. To select the Web Dynpro NavigationTester, as shown in the example, we'll set the parameter to **NavigationTesterApp**.

> **Tip**
>
> We have often been asked whether there is an easy way to determine the parameters required for defining a Web Dynpro iView. The most elegant method is certainly using the *Web Dynpro Content Administrator* (see Chapter 10). In the next release of SAP NetWeaver, it will be much easier to create Web Dynpro iViews, and it will also be possible to do that more or less automatically.

▶ **Web Dynpro Client**

The **Web Dynpro Client** parameter defines the required Web Dynpro client that is to be used for displaying the Web Dynpro application. As we have described in Chapter 2, due to the client abstraction of Web Dynpro a Web Dynpro application can always be run on different clients without any changes.

However, since SAP NetWeaver 2004 does not contain any other Web Dynpro clients, you can use only the default browser-based client here.

▶ **Application Parameters**

You can use the **Application Parameters** parameter to define any number of transfer parameters that must be transferred when the Web Dynpro application is started. In Section 5.3.3 you'll see that you can use different parameter templates, which are provided by the SAP Application Integrator.

The transfer parameters must be specified using the following syntax: `<Name1>=<Value1>&<Name2>=<Value2>`.... Contrary to the transfer parameters that you specify for a portal navigation (see Chapter 6), you don't need to encode the parameter values here. For example, the transfer parameters could have the value `shoe-size=46&season=winter`.

By clicking on the **Next** button, you will go to the final dialog step where you can once again check all your entries. By clicking on **Finish** you can then create the Web Dynpro iView, which will be automatically displayed in the portal content catalog directory you specified earlier.

5.2.3   Editing the Properties of a Web Dynpro iView

Now that you have successfully crated the Web Dynpro iView, you can change and adjust any of its properties using the iView Editor. The iView Editor may open automatically once the Web Dynpro iView has been created; however, you can also launch it at any time by opening the context menu of the relevant iView and selecting the item **Open · Object**.

Launching the iView Editor

As we have seen in Section 5.2.1, you use the Property Editor in the SAP NetWeaver Portal to maintain the properties of any object. The properties of a Web Dynpro iView can be divided into several categories, as shown in Figure 5.23. The following sections describe the most important categories in greater detail.

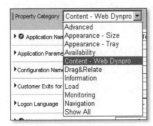

Figure 5.23 Available Property Categories of a Web Dynpro iView

Specific Properties

Figure 5.24 shows the available properties specific to Web Dynpro; you can access the properties by selecting the **Content - Web Dynpro** category.

Figure 5.24 iView Properties

Most of the properties displayed here correspond to the properties you defined during the creation of the Web Dynpro iView. Using the iView Editor, you can always change the properties. In addition to the properties that define the required Web Dynpro application, the following properties are particularly important:

Displaying debug information

▶ **Show Debug Screen**

Section 5.3.3 describes the different troubleshooting options that are available with the SAP Application Integrator. The **Show Debug Screen** property enables you to define for your Web Dynpro iView whether you want the SAP Application Integrator to display the relevant debug information at the start of the Web Dynpro application (**Yes/No**). The setting made in the iView is used only if **on demand** has been selected as a global setting.

▶ **Supply Portal Stylesheet**

When you start your Web Dynpro application within SAP NetWeaver Portal through a Web Dynpro iView, the selected portal theme is automatically transferred at the startup of the application. The Web Dynpro runtime environment uses the selected portal theme to display the Web Dynpro application with the same look and feel as the portal or the portal-specific user interfaces respectively.

Ignoring the portal theme

If you don't run your Web Dynpro application directly on the SAP NetWeaver Portal installation but on a second installation, the two installations may contain different versions of the selected portal theme. This might cause problems when displaying the Web Dynpro application using the version defined by the SAP NetWeaver Portal. In those particular cases, you can prevent the transfer of the portal theme for individual iViews via the **Supply Portal Stylesheet**.

In Chapter 10, we'll describe how you can suppress the theme transferred by the portal to be ignored for the entire Web Dynpro runtime environment and how you can configure a theme that you want to use for the display of your Web Dynpro applications.

▶ **Parameters Forwarded to Web Dynpro**

As we'll describe in greater detail in Chapter 6, when starting a Web Dynpro iView you must generally distinguish between transfer parameters that you want to be used directly by the SAP Application Integrator and those parameters that must be forwarded to the relevant Web Dynpro application. The **Parameters Forwarded to Web Dynpro** property enables you to define

Forwarding transfer parameters

explicitly which transfer parameters for a Web Dynpro iView are to be forwarded to the Web Dynpro application.

The parameters must be specified in the following form: `<Parameter1>,<Parameter2>, <Parameter3>,....` Furthermore, you can use the * character to specify that you want all transfer parameters to be forwarded to the Web Dynpro application.

Tip

If you know the required parameters explicitly—including their names—using the **Parameters Forwarded to Web Dynpro** property is recommended. In scenarios in which that is not possible, you can use the mechanisms described in Chapter 6 to forward any kind of parameters. You should use the * character only if you're absolutely sure that no parameters can be forwarded, which could negatively affect the correct functionality of your Web Dynpro application and, also, if you're certain that no sensitive security data will be transferred.

The **Configuration Name** and **Stylesheet** properties are not relevant to a Web Dynpro for Java iView since they're only required for Web Dynpro for ABAP iViews.

Defining the Size of Web Dynpro iViews

Predefined and variable height

To determine the size of a Web Dynpro iView, you must select the **Appearance – Size** property category (see Figure 5.25). Here you can use the **Height Type** property to determine whether you want to display your iView with a predefined fixed height (**FIXED**) or if you want the SAP NetWeaver Portal to adapt the displayed height automatically to the space requirement of the iView (**AUTOMATIC**). If you want to use a fixed height, you can define that via the **Fixed Height** property. The value you specify here represents the required height in pixels.

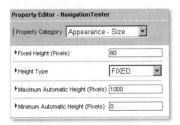

Figure 5.25 Setting the Size of the iView

If you use the automatic adaptation function for the iView height, you can specify the required minimum and maximum height in pixels via the **Minimum Automatic Height** and **Maximum Automatic Height** properties.

Finally, you can define that you want your Web Dynpro iView to fill the entire space of the working area as a so-called *full-page iView*. This only makes sense if you don't display the Web Dynpro iView together with other iViews within a portal page.

Defining a full-page iView

> **Tip**
>
> We recommend that you use the automatic height adaptation for your Web Dynpro iView. This will help you to ensure that your iView doesn't occupy more space in the working area than is actually necessary. Moreover, even if you change the height of the Web Dynpro application, your Web Dynpro iView will still be displayed correctly and completely. In contrast to other iView types, the height of the Web Dynpro iView is not only adapted initially, but also after each user interaction.

Defining the iView Tray

For each iView, the SAP NetWeaver Portal provides certain generic functions that you can select and start using the iView tray (see also Section 5.1.2). Apart from selecting those generic functions, you can also use the iView tray to expand and collapse the Web Dynpro iView to enable the user to hide an iView that is currently not needed. The **Appearance - Tray** property category (see Figure 5.26) enables you to manipulate the appearance and content of the iView tray for your Web Dynpro iView.

▸ **Add Padding Inside Tray**
You can use the **Add Padding Inside Tray** property to specify whether you want to add *padding*—a small margin between the iView content and the tray frame—to your Web Dynpro iView. Note that the space requirement of your Web Dynpro iView will increase when you use the tray padding.

▸ **Initial State - Open or Closed**
It only makes sense to use the **Initial State - Open or Closed** property if you want to display your Web Dynpro iView together with other (Web Dynpro) iViews on a portal page. This property enables you to determine whether you want to show or hide your

Web Dynpro iView in the initial display of the portal page. We recommend that you hide your Web Dynpro iView initially if the user doesn't need the displayed data of the (Web Dynpro) iView.

Tip

By hiding the iView initially, you can reduce the initial load time for the entire portal page as a collapsed Web Dynpro iView. Furthermore, the Web Dynpro application that is linked to this Web Dynpro iView is not called until the user expands the iView.

▶ **Show Tray**

If you don't want to use the iView tray for your Web Dynpro iView, you can use the **Show Tray** property to define the iView tray.

▶ **Tray Type**

You can use the **Tray Type** property to manipulate the appearance of the tray. In Section 5.3.3, we'll describe how you can transport the selected tray type to your Web Dynpro application to customize the application correspondingly.

The different **Show … Option** properties enable you to define those functions that you want the iView tray to provide.

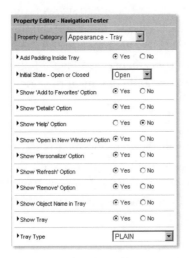

Figure 5.26 iView Tray Properties

For Web Dynpro iViews, the **Refresh** function represents a restart of the Web Dynpro application that is linked to the iView. As soon as the user has removed the iView from the portal page by using the

Remove function, the removed iView can be displayed again through the personalization dialog of the corresponding portal page. You can launch the personalization dialog of a portal page via the corresponding **Personalize** item in the tray menu of the portal page. Similar to the iView Editor, you can use the Page Editor to manipulate the appearance and the provided functions of the page tray.

The **Personalize** function launches the generic personalization dialog of an iView. Chapter 8 uses the Web Dynpro MusicBox to demonstrate how you can define application-specific properties for your Web Dynpro application that can then be customized by a user via the personalization dialog of the iView. Chapter 8 also describes how you can create and start an application-specific personalization dialog as a Web Dynpro application.

Defining an application-specific personalization

Defining the Navigation Properties of a Web Dynpro iView

The **Navigation** property category (see Figure 5.27) enables you to define the different navigation aspects of your Web Dynpro iView.

When you assign your Web Dynpro iView to a role, the role is displayed in the top-level navigation or the detailed navigation of those users who are assigned the role. In certain scenarios, it can be useful not to display an iView that has been assigned to a role, for instance, if you use *object-based navigation* (see Chapter 7).

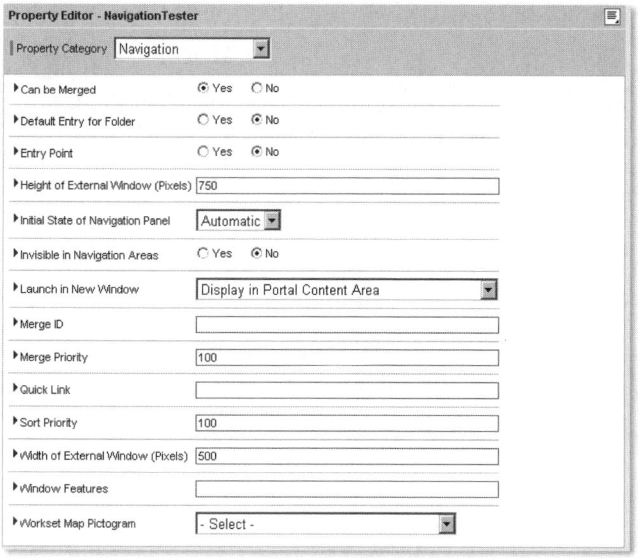

Displaying the iView in the navigation menu

Figure 5.27 Navigation Properties of the iView

You can therefore use the **Invisible in Navigation Areas** property to determine whether you want to display your Web Dynpro iView in the navigation menu. You should however note that an invisible iView is also part of the role that can be called by the user, for example, if you use the portal navigation, which is described in greater detail in Chapter 6.

Displaying the navigation panel

Depending on the defined role structure or hierarchy, it can happen that the detailed navigation in the navigation panes contains only one entry. In those instances, you can often forego displaying the navigation panel and instead provide additional space to the content of the working area in the current window.

You can achieve this by using the **Initial State of Navigation Panel** property. If you select **Automatic**, the navigation panel displays only if the detailed navigation contains more than one entry. If you select **Closed**, the navigation panel never displays. By selecting **Open**, the navigation panel is always displayed. Moreover, the user can show or hide the navigation panel at any time.

Launching the iView in a new window

Besides the option that allows you not to display an iView in the navigation menus, the **Navigation** category also enables you to determine whether you want your (Web Dynpro) iView to be displayed in a new window of your web browser as soon as the user selects the iView—either explicitly via the top-level navigation or detailed navigation respectively, or via the program by using the portal navigation or object-based navigation respectively.

You can use the **Launch in New Window** property to define the behavior according to your requirements. You can select the following values for this property (see Figure 5.28):

▶ **Display in Portal Content Area**
The iView is displayed in the portal content area (or working area) of the current web browser window.

▶ **Display in Separate Window**
The iView is displayed in a new window of the web browser without any additional portal frame for the top-level navigation and the navigation panel.

▶ **Display in Separate Portal Window**
The iView is displayed in a new window of the web browser with an additional portal frame.

▶ **Display in Separate Headerless Portal Window**
The iView is displayed in a new window of the web browser with an additional page header.

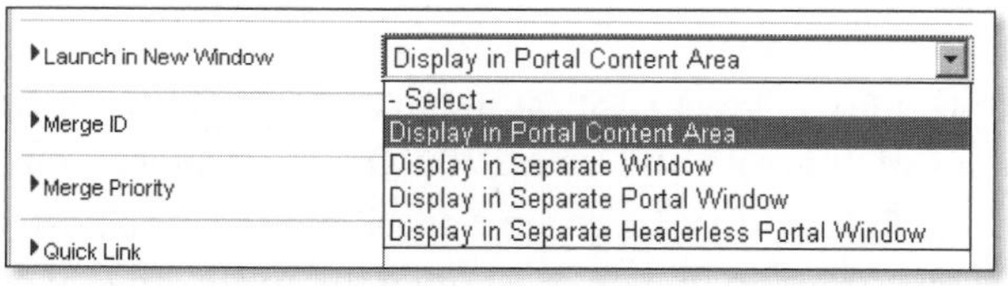

Figure 5.28 Launching the iView in a New Window

In Chapter 6, we'll describe how you can display specific iViews or portal pages using the portal navigation. In this respect, we'll discuss the details of the differences between the various display modes.

If you want to display your Web Dynpro iView in a new window of the web browser, you can define the appearance and size of that window. The **Height of External Window (Pixels)** and **Width of External Window (Pixels)** properties enable you to define the height and width of the new window. The **Window Features** property allows you to define the appearance of the window. For example, you can define whether the new window should contain a toolbar, or whether you the user should be allowed to change the size of the window.

Manipulating the additional window

Now that we have discussed all the important settings that you can make for your Web Dynpro iView, we'll embed the Web Dynpro iView into a role and make it available to the SAP NetWeaver Portal users.

5.2.4 Defining a Role

Similar to creating an iView or a portal page, you can create a role by opening the context menu of the required portal content catalog directory and selecting the item **New · Role** (see Figure 5.29). You must then define the name and the role ID in the dialog that displays next.

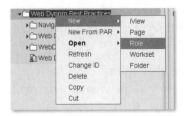

Figure 5.29 Creating a Role

Adding an iView to
a role
To assign a Web Dynpro iView to a specific role, you must first open the context menu of the role and select the **Open · Object** item, which launches the Role Editor. To assign a specific iView or a portal page to the role you just opened, you must open the context menu of the relevant iView or the relevant portal page and select the item **Add iView to Role** or **Add Page to Role** respectively. Here you can choose whether you want to insert the iView as a delta link or as a copy.

Delta link versus
copy
If you use a delta link, you only insert a reference to the original object. All changes you make to the original object—in other words, to the iView or portal page—are then automatically used as the respective role would be used as well. Delta links can be nested in any way and are especially useful if you want to customize specific settings for your (Web Dynpro) iView in different roles or uses.

If you use a copy, a separate object is generated during the insertion into a role. That object no longer has any relationship to the original object. This means that changes to the original object have no effect on the copy.

> **Tip**
>
> We generally recommend the use of delta links. The options made available by using delta links are necessary for adding your Web Dynpro iViews into other portal pages, worksets, or roles.

Figure 5.30 displays the Role Editor for the **Web Dynpro Best Practices** role. As you can see, we use several additional directories to better structure the role contents. Those directories will later be displayed as navigation levels. You can launch the Role Editor by opening the context menu of the role in question and selecting the item **Open · Role**.

Like the iView Editor, the Role Editor also provides a **Navigation** category (see Figure 5.31) that enables you to define how you want to display the structure defined in the role both in the top-level navigation and in the detailed navigation.

Including the role into the navigation structure

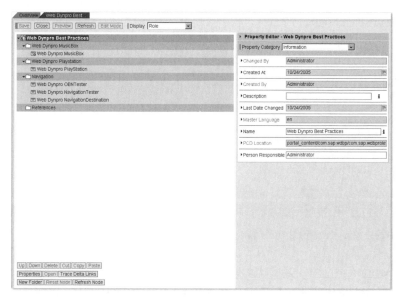

Figure 5.30 Role Editor

Figure 5.31 Navigation Properties of a Role

You can use the **Entry Point** property to define if you want to include the role in the navigation structure. The navigation structure defined in the role is then displayed without any change in the top-level and detailed navigations.

In our **Web Dynpro Best Practices** role, for example, the Web Dyn-pro OBNTester can be accessed through three hierarchy levels. The **Web Dynpro Best Practices** role represents the first level, below which we define a **Navigation** directory that determines the second level. Finally, the **Web Dynpro OBNTester** iView defines the third level (see Figure 5.32).

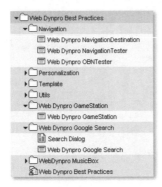

Figure 5.32 Defining a Three-Level Navigation Hierarchy

As soon as you define that you want to include the role directly into the navigation structure via the **Entry Point** property, the three lev-els are distributed to the top-level and detailed navigations. The first two navigation levels are always displayed by the top-level naviga-tion, while the detailed navigation displays every other level. Figure 5.33 shows the corresponding display.

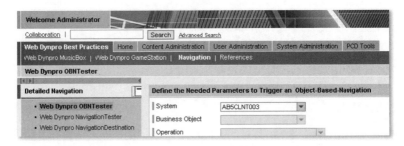

Figure 5.33 Three-Level Display of the Navigation Hierarchy

Basically, you can include any hierarchy level of a role into the naviga-tion structure. If, for example, you included only the second level of the **Web Dynpro Best Practices** role into the navigation structure, you would only define two navigation levels. The detailed navigation would not display any content in that case, as you can see in Figure 5.34.

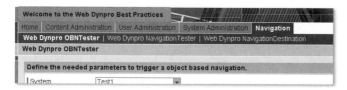

Figure 5.34 Two-Level Display of the Navigation Hierarchy

Role-Specific Adaptation of iView Properties

Once you have inserted an iView into a role, you can customize a property of that iView so that they can actually be used in the role. The consistent use of delta links ensures that all changes to the original object are automatically transferred unless you have explicitly customized the property in question for a particular usage.

Using delta links

To customize individual properties of an iView for a specific role, you must open the context menu of the iView and select the **Properties** item to launch the Property Editor (see Figure 5.35). The changed properties refer to the specific usage of the iView in that role. Theoretically, you can add each iView several times to the same role and then customize each of these usages differently.

Changing iView properties in the Role Editor

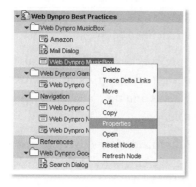

Figure 5.35 Changing iView Properties in the Role Editor

In addition to directly opening the Property Editor of an iView, you can also launch the entire iView Editor of the corresponding iView via the **Open** item in the context menu (see Figure 5.36). This allows you to carry out any number of changes to the iView, but only for the specific usage of this iView in the role.

Launching the iView Editor from the Role Editor

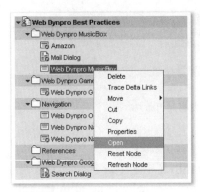

Figure 5.36 Launching the iView Editor from the Role Editor

Adding a Web Dynpro iView to a portal page

Besides adding a Web Dynpro iView to a role, you can embed every Web Dynpro iView into any portal page. To do that, you would typically use delta links to connect the original iView to the specific usage of an iView.

5.2.5 Assigning a Role to a User

Now that we have created the required Web Dynpro iViews and the corresponding role, including the required navigation structure, you must assign the role to the relevant users so that those users can call and use the role, or rather, the content defined therein.

At this point, we can't describe all the specific details of the user management role within SAP NetWeaver Portal, but, as an example, we'll create a user in the following sections and then assign that user to our **Web Dynpro Best Practices** role.

Creating a user

You can create a new user via **User Administration · Users · Create User** (see Figure 5.37). In our example, we enter "wdbook" as a user ID and "initial" as the initial password. You must change this initial password the first time you log on to SAP NetWeaver Portal. Furthermore, you must select the first and last name, email address, and preferred language of the user. The entire portal content is displayed in that language, provided the required translations are available for each piece of content.

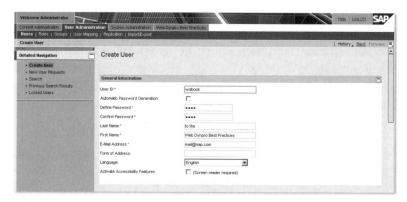

Figure 5.37 Creating the User wdbook

When you start your Web Dynpro application within SAP NetWeaver Portal, the system uses the defined portal language. If that language is not available, a specific schema determines the language to be used. Chapter 10 describes this process in great detail.

Language used in Web Dynpro

By clicking on the **Create** button, you can create the **wdbook** user. To assign the required roles to this user, in the next step you must first select the user via **User Administration · Roles**. Figure 5.38 shows the dialog that opens next and from which you can select the required roles. We'll select the roles **super_admin_role**, **eu_core_role**, and **com.sap.wdbprole** (this is our **Web Dynpro Best Practices** role).

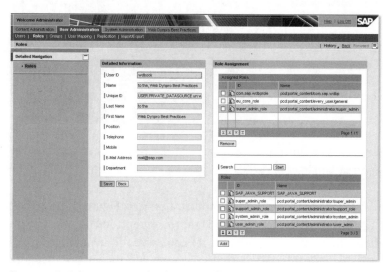

Figure 5.38 Role Assignment for the User wdbook

Click on **Save** to assign those roles to the user **wdbook**. You can now log off from SAP NetWeaver Portal by clicking on the **Log Off** link in the portal header and then select the newly created user **wdbook** when you log on again. If you assign roles to the current user, you must reload the web browser window by pressing the **F5** key or by clicking on the **Refresh** button in the toolbar so that the top-level and detailed navigations are adjusted correspondingly.

5.3   Available Web Dynpro Applications

Apart from the Web-Dynpro-based portal content that you created, several Web Dynpro applications are available, which are installed with SAP NetWeaver Portal and can be used immediately. We will briefly describe these applications here. For more information, you should refer to the SAP Help Portal (*http://help.sap.com*) and the SAP Developer Network (*http://sdn.sap.com*).

5.3.1   Administration Tools

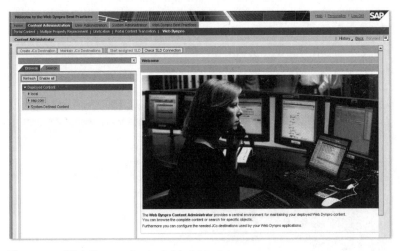

Figure 5.39 Web Dynpro Content Administrator

Web Dynpro Content Administrator

The Web Dynpro Content Administrator (see Figure 5.39) allows you to access all deployed Web Dynpro content. In addition to providing extensive search options, it enables you to maintain the Java Connector (JCo) destinations that are needed for all Web Dynpro applications, which access data in the SAP backend system via the Adaptive Remote Function Call (RFC) model.

You can call the Web Dynpro Content Administrator via **Content Administration · Web Dynpro** in the SAP NetWeaver Portal. Chapter 10 describes the Web Dynpro Content Administrator in greater detail.

The Web Dynpro Console provides many options for checking the current settings and configurations of the Web Dynpro runtime environment. Furthermore, it allows you to read comprehensive performance data that you can determine for your Web Dynpro application; Chapter 10 also contains detailed information on this topic.

Web Dynpro Console

You can launch the Web Dynpro Console within SAP NetWeaver Portal via **System Administration · System Configuration · Web Dynpro Console** (see Figure 5.40).

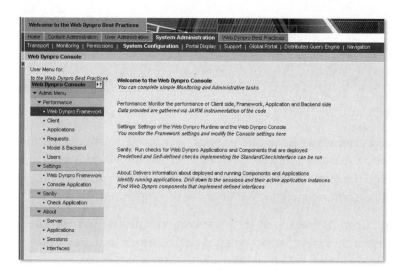

Figure 5.40 Web Dynpro Console

5.3.2 Test Applications

In addition to the administration tools, SAP NetWeaver Portal provides numerous Web Dynpro-based test applications that you can use to test the various aspects of integrating Web Dynpro applications into SAP NetWeaver Portal. If you encounter any problems while running your Web Dynpro applications within SAP

NetWeaver Portal, you can use the test applications described here to test the basic functionality of the different options.

As you can see in Figure 5.41, the Web Dynpro test applications are stored at the following location: **System Administration · Support · Web Dynpro Test Tools**.

Testing the portal eventing

The **Portal Eventing** section contains test applications that you can use to test the usage of the *portal eventing* (also referred to as *client-side eventing*) between two Web Dynpro applications or between Web Dynpro applications and non-Web Dynpro applications. Chapter 8 uses the Web Dynpro MusicBox example to describe how you can use portal eventing within your Web Dynpro application.

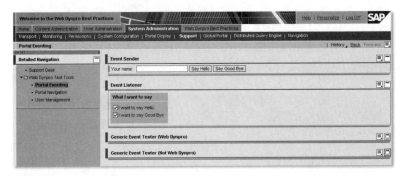

Figure 5.41 Portal Eventing

Testing the portal navigation

The **Portal Navigation** link provides various test applications that you can use to test the portal navigation and the object-based navigation. Chapters 6 and 7 contain more detailed information on using the navigation functions in a Web Dynpro application.

The **User Management** test application enables you to check whether the roles that are assigned to the current user are displayed correctly for your Web Dynpro application.

5.4   SAP Application Integrator

The previous sections have described the steps you have to carry out in order to provide your Web Dynpro application within SAP NetWeaver Portal. Now we want to discuss how you can launch your Web Dynpro application within SAP NetWeaver Portal by using a Web Dynpro iView.

5.4.1 Launching a Web Dynpro Application in SAP NetWeaver Portal

Basically, a Web Dynpro application is always represented as an *isolated iView* within SAP NetWeaver Portal. The Web Dynpro application is displayed within an iFrame, while the corresponding URL is calculated by the SAP Application Integrator.

Isolated iViews

To display your Web Dynpro application in SAP NetWeaver Portal using a Web Dynpro iView, the following steps are performed:

Start process

1. The iView properties of the iView to be displayed are read and then used for the correct display of the iView, for instance, to obtain the required iView size.

2. As the iView is a Web Dynpro iView, the SAP NetWeaver Portal calls the SAP Application Integrator.

3. Based on the iView properties, the SAP Application Integrator calculates the correct Web Dynpro application URL and extends this URL by several transfer parameters that define different aspects of the current portal environment.

4. The SAP NetWeaver Portal then launches the calculated URL within an iFrame.

The contents of the URL, which has been calculated by the SAP Application Integrator, are determined using a URL template. Because the SAP Application Integrator can launch different types of SAP applications in addition to Web Dynpro applications, a specific URL template is available for each type of application. Listing 5.1 contains the URL template for Web Dynpro iViews.

Web Dynpro URL template

```
URL = <System.Access.WAS.protocol>://
  <System.Access.WAS.hostname>\
  /webdynpro/dispatcher<Request.DistributionZone>/
    <WebDynproNamespace>/<WebDynproApplication>\
  ;jsessionid=<Request.JSessionID>?\
  sap-ext-sid=<ESID[URL_ENCODE]>&\
  sap-wd-cltwndid=<ClientWindowID>&\
  sap-locale=<Request.Locale>&\
  sap-accessibility=<User.Accessibility[SAP_BOOL]>&\
  sap-rtl=<LAF.RightToLeft[SAP_BOOL]>&\
  sap-ep-version=<Request.Version[URL_ENCODE]>&\
  sap-cssurl=<LAF.StylesheetUrl[URL_ENCODE]>&\
  sap-cssversion=<LAF.Version[URL_ENCODE]>&\
  <Authentication>&\
```

```
<DynamicParameter[PROCESS_RECURSIVE]>&\
    <ApplicationParameter[PROCESS_RECURSIVE]>
```

Listing 5.1 URL Template for Web Dynpro iViews

Once the URL template has been processed by the SAP Application Integrator, the following URL could, for example, be calculated which could be used to launch the Web Dynpro NavigationTester within SAP NetWeaver Portal:

```
http://wdhost.wdf.sap.corp:50000/webdynpro/dispatcher/
    sap.com/tc~navtes/NavigationTesterApp;
    jsesionid=(WDFD00146855A_P37_00)
    ID1615564250DB00783426715781195164End?
    sap-extsid=w5pCYOL2j191%2FB28gt1HhA%3D%3Dv
    Vf%2B0Ky5v%2BiZ268a%2BYvFjA%3D%3D&
    sap-wd-cltwndid=WID1138899091639&
    sap-locale=en_US&
    sap-accessibility=&
    sap-rtl=&
    sap-ep-version=6.4.200509182320&
    sap-cssurl=http%3A%2F%2Fwdfd00146855a%3A50000%2
    Firj%2Fportalapps%2Fcom.sap.portal.design.urdesigndata
    %2Fthemes%2Fportal%2Fsap_tradeshow%2
    Fur%2Fur_ie6.css%3F6.0.15.0.0&
    sap-cssversion=6.0.14.0.0
```

Transferred portal settings Based on the transferred parameters, different portal settings are transferred to the Web Dynpro runtime environment. In addition to the preferred portal language and the selected theme, these settings also include information on the preferred display variant (left-to-right or right-to-left) and on determining whether a barrier-free display is required.

Reading the transferred parameters In Chapter 6, we'll use a sample application to demonstrate how you can access these transferred parameters from within your Web Dynpro application. However, you should note that you usually don't need to include these parameters in your Web Dynpro application because they are automatically analyzed by the Web Dynpro runtime environment.

5.4.2 Extending the URL Template

You extend the predefined Web Dynpro URL template per your requirements in order to transfer additional information on the SAP NetWeaver Portal to your Web Dynpro application.

For this purpose, the SAP Application Integrator provides numerous variables that are grouped in what is referred to as contexts. In the following sections, we'll describe the contexts that are most relevant to a Web Dynpro iView. But please note that these contexts have nothing to do with Web Dynpro contexts.

The `<iView>` context enables you to determine additional information on the Web Dynpro iView and transfer that information to the Web Dynpro application:

`<iView>` context

▶ `<iView.ID>`

As mentioned in Section 5.2.2, all objects that you create for the SAP NetWeaver Portal are stored in the Portal Content Directory (PCD). Each object can be described by a unique path that is also used to specify navigation targets in the portal navigation.

The `<iView.ID>` variable contains exactly this path for the called Web Dynpro iView. Using this path, you can directly access the iView object in the PCD within your Web Dynpro application. We'll use this variable in Chapter 8 for personalizing the Web Dynpro MusicBox.

▶ `<iView.PCDUnit>`

The `<iView.PCDUnit>` variable provides access to the roles assigned to the iView within your Web Dynpro application. If the iView that is called has not been assigned to any role, the `<iView.PCDUnit>` variable provides the iView by itself.

You can use the `<Profile>` context to transfer the values of any iView property. The `<Profile.xyz>` variable determines the value of the iView property **xyz**.

`<Profile>` context

You can use the `<Request>` context to determine how and where the SAP NetWeaver Portal was launched. This can be particularly useful in scenarios when you don't run your Web Dynpro application on the same SAP NetWeaver installation as the SAP NetWeaver Portal.

`<Request>` context

`<Request.Protocol>` provides the protocol (HTTP or HTTPS), while `<Request.Server>` provides the fully qualified host name on which the SAP NetWeaver Portal was launched (for example, portal.domain.com). You can use the `<Request.Port>` variable to determine the port that is used. In addition to these technical parameters, you can also use the `<Request.xyz>` variable to obtain the value of any parameter that was transferred when the SAP NetWeaver Portal was launched; `<Request.xyz>` provides the value of the `xyz` transfer parameter. If no `xyz` transfer parameter has been defined, the SAP Application Integrator will ignore the variable when processing the URL template.

<System> context

As described earlier in this chapter, you use a system alias for each Web Dynpro iView in order to define the SAP NetWeaver installation on which you want to run the Web Dynpro application. The `<System.xyz>` variable of the `<System>` context enables you to determine any property of the system that is used in the iView, which has been launched. `<System.xyz>` determines the value of system property **xyz**.

<User> context

The `<User>` context helps you to transfer the various pieces of user information to the Web Dynpro application. This is especially useful on those occasions when the SAP NetWeaver installation that runs your Web Dynpro application is different from the SAP NetWeaver Portal and does not use the same User Management Engine (UME) user store. The `<User>` context defines the variables listed in Table 5.1. You can infer the meaning of these variables from their names.

Variable Name	
`<User.displayname>`	`<User.uniquename>`
`<User.firstname>`	`<User.lastname>`
`<User.salutation>`	`<User.jobtitle>`
`<User.department>`	`<User.email>`
`<User.telephone>`	`<User.mobile>`
`<User.fax>`	`<User.streetaddress>`
`<User.city>`	`<User.zip>`
`<User.country>`	`<User.state>`
`<User.timezone>`	

Table 5.1 Variables of the <User> Context

5.4.3 Defining URL Template Variables

To be able to use the variables introduced in the previous section when launching our Web Dynpro application, you must define the required variables as **Application Parameters**.

In Chapter 8, we'll use the `<iView.ID>` variable to implement an option for the Web Dynpro MusicBox that enables you to customize the behavior of the MusicBox via portal personalization. Figure 5.42 shows the definition of the corresponding **Application Parameters** value.

Usage for personalization

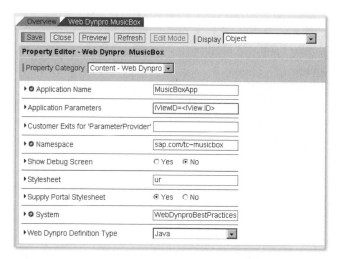

Figure 5.42 Using the <iView.ID> Variable

Section 5.2.3 described, among other things, the options that are available for customizing the iView tray of your Web Dynpro iView. However, the SAP Application Integrator does not forward all those settings automatically to your Web Dynpro application. But if you use the different URL template variables proficiently, you can make any iView property available in your Web Dynpro application.

Using enhanced tray properties

Let us demonstrate this with the **Tray Type** property for which we'll use the `<Profile.xyz>` variable described above. The **xyz** describes the name of the relevant iView property. **Tray Type**, however, is only the readable name of the property, but we need the technical name instead.

Fortunately, the Property Editor enables us to display the technical name of any (iView) property along with other meta attributes. Figure 5.43 shows the available meta attributes of iView property **Tray Type** that can be displayed by expanding the corresponding iView property.

Determining the technical name of an iView property

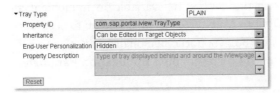

Figure 5.43 Determining the Technical Name of the Tray Type Propety

The meta attribute **Property ID** describes the technical name for our example. Because `com.sap.portal.iview.TrayType` contains special characters (.), you must specify the URL template variable using the following syntax: `<Profile."com.sap.portal.iview.TrayType">`. By doing this, you can ensure that the URL template will be processed correctly (see Figure 5.44).

Figure 5.44 Using the <Profile.xyz> Variable

You can then use transfer parameter `trayType` within your Web Dynpro application to access the required tray display and design the layout of your Web Dynpro application accordingly.

Meanings of meta attributes At this point, we want to briefly outline the meanings of the individual meta attributes. As we have already seen, the meta attribute **Property ID** defines the technical name of an iView property. The meta attribute **Inheritance** can be used to define whether the corresponding iView property can be modified in potential delta links of the iView, or whether the iView property in question can no longer be modified. You can use the meta attribute **End-User-Personalization** to define whether and how the relevant iView property can be personalized by the user. Here you have the following three options:

▶ **Hidden**
The iView property is not displayed in the personalization dialog of the user.

▶ **Read-Only**
The iView property is displayed in the personalization dialog, but cannot be changed by the user.

▶ **Read/Write**
The iView property is displayed in the personalization dialog and can be changed by the user.

5.4.4 Debugging the SAP Application Integrator

Various options are available to find the potential causes of an erroneous start of your Web Dynpro application. Usually, the problems that occur during the start-up of a Web Dynpro application within the SAP NetWeaver Portal can be divided into three categories:

Potential error sources

▶ Due to an incorrect definition of the system, the URL calculated by the SAP Application Integrator cannot be launched correctly. The typical error message displayed in such cases is "Page not Found." If that is the case, you should check the relevant system properties, as well as the availability of the corresponding SAP NetWeaver installation (Are we having a network problem? Has the installation been launched correctly?).

▶ The Web Dynpro application that has been defined within the launched Web Dynpro iView has been deployed incorrectly, or the corresponding iView properties contain errors (the specified application name can be wrong, for instance). You can check the list of deployed Web Dynpro applications using the Web Dynpro Content Administrator.

▶ The Web Dynpro application starts up correctly, but not all transfer parameters are forwarded. In that case, you can use the mechanisms described in the following sections to check which of the parameters have been transferred by the SAP Application Integrator.

To activate the debug mode of the SAP Application Integrator, you must select **System Administration · Support** from the menu to launch the SAP Application Integrator Support Desk (see Figure 5.45).

Activating the debug mode

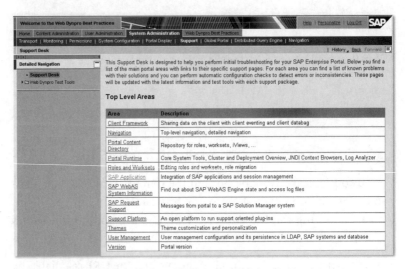

Figure 5.45 Launching the Support Desk in the SAP Application Integrator

In addition to displaying additional information and notes, the Support Desk also allows you to activate the required debug mode. Figure 5.46 shows the available settings.

Change Debug mode (current mode = off)	Description
off	Debug Mode is off (default)
on demand	Debug Mode on demand. You can set the Debug Mode per iView or just add "DebugMode=true" to the iView-URL — use with care!
always on	Debug Mode is always on, regardless the settings in the iViews — use with care!

Figure 5.46 Activating the Debug Mode of the SAP Application Integrator

Apart from switching the debug mode to **off** or **always on**, you can use the **on demand** setting to ensure that only specific iViews are started in the debug mode. This setting is especially useful if your SAP NetWeaver Portal installation is used by several users. A global activation of the debug mode would be displayed to all users. In Section 5.2.3, we described how you could activate the debug mode for individual Web Dynpro iViews by using the **Show Debug Screen** property.

Using the debug information

As soon as you launch a Web Dynpro iView in the debug mode of the SAP Application Integrator, the SAP Application Integrator displays a wealth of debug information prior to starting the corresponding Web Dynpro application. You can use the buttons shown in Figure 5.47 to navigate through the different steps the SAP Application Integrator performs in order to calculate the required URL.

Figure 5.47 Step-by-Step Process of the SAP Application Integrator

With each step, the SAP Application Integrator displays the used or calculated parameters or parameter values. In the example shown in Figure 5.48, for instance, you can see the calculated **URL** that starts the required Web Dynpro application.

TargetQuery	sap-ext-sid=JVz5d81eHINsay4n4078XQ%3D%3Dogv4ioEGG8tyrWMrj0%2BjAA%3D%3D&sap-wd-cltwndid=V
TargetScheme	http
Technique	Java
TopLayer	WebDynpro/TopLayer
URL	http://wdfd00146855a.wdf.sap.corp:50000/webdynpro/dispatcher/sap.com/tc~musicbox/MusicBoxApp?sap-ext
URL type	string
UnsupportedUserAgents	
Use_CustomerExit_ParameterProvider	false
User	
ValidityPeriod	-1

Figure 5.48 Display of Used Parameters

The step-by-step process can be very useful in identifying and localizing potential errors, especially if you use the URL template variables described earlier.

5.5 Summary

In this chapter, we described the basic components of the SAP NetWeaver Portal user interface. We also demonstrated how you could manipulate the UI within your Web Dynpro application.

Then, we outlined the options that are available to you for launching your Web Dynpro application within SAP NetWeaver Portal by using a Web Dynpro iView. Furthermore, we explained how you could structure those Web Dynpro iViews and provide users with access to them via roles.

Next, we described the significance of the SAP Application Integrator and discussed how you can use the URL template variables to customize the information transferred by the SAP NetWeaver Portal to meet your requirements.

Lastly, we discussed several error scenarios and introduced the most important troubleshooting strategies.

This chapter discusses the various options for navigating between Web Dynpro applications. Particular attention is paid to the differences between starting the Web Dynpro application inside or outside the SAP NetWeaver Portal. We will also examine how to display very large hierarchical datasets.

6 Web Dynpro NavigationTester

6.1 The Web Dynpro NavigationTester

You can use the Web Dynpro NavigationTester to try and test different options for navigating between two Web Dynpro applications. The NavigationTester also enables you to select your desired Web Dynpro application and define navigation behavior.

As with all other examples in this book, the NavigationTester can be used independently of the SAP NetWeaver Portal; however, it offers many more options for defining navigation behavior when used with the SAP NetWeaver Portal. You will find the NavigationTester in the `NavigationTesterComp` Web Dynpro component, which is stored in the `MAIN_WD-BOOK_D~tc~navtes~sap.com` Web Dynpro project. The relevant Web Dynpro development component (DC) is `tc\navtes`.

Figure 6.1 shows the Web Dynpro NavigationTester in the SAP NetWeaver Portal. The NavigationTester essentially comprises two screen areas. In the left pane, you can select a navigation target of your choice, that is, either a Web Dynpro application or an iView or portal page. In the right pane, you can define the desired navigation behavior in more detail.

Figure 6.2 shows the `NavigationTesterComp` Web Dynpro component in the Web Dynpro Data Modeler. The basic structure is clearly identifiable.

Basic structure of the Navigation-Tester

Figure 6.1 The NavigationTester in the SAP NetWeaver Portal

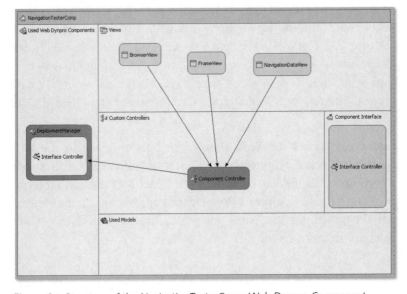

Figure 6.2 Structure of the NavigationTesterComp Web Dynpro Component

A total of three Web Dynpro views are used for display: the `Browser-View` displays the existing navigation targets; the `NavigationData-View` allows you to define the desired navigation behavior; and lastly, the `FrameView` is a combination of the two aforementioned views.

In the Data Modeler, you can see that the `DeploymentManager` component usage is also used. This allows you to detect the available Web Dynpro applications (see Section 6.5.3).

6.1.1 Defining the Runtime Environment

As mentioned above, you can run the Web Dynpro NavigationTester either inside or outside the SAP NetWeaver Portal. But, because you have to consider many details when navigating between Web Dynpro applications with different runtime environments, checks are required within the NavigationTester at multiple stages to detect the runtime environment in which it was started (i.e., either inside or outside the SAP NetWeaver Portal).

You can generally use the `WDPortalUtils` utility class to obtain this information. The `isRunningInPortal()` method allows you to determine whether your Web Dynpro application is called inside in the SAP NetWeaver Portal. The Boolean value returned is often sufficient; however, if you want to make individual areas of the application visible or invisible, depending on the runtime environment, you can use a **calculated** attribute. This returns the corresponding value for `IWDVisibility`, depending on the `isRunningInPortal()`method.

Using WDPortal-Utils

In the NavigationTester, you define a **calculated** attribute in the view controller context of the `NavigationDataView` view. The `IsRunningInPortalVisibility` context attribute of the `RuntimeEnvironment` context node maps the Boolean value to the corresponding `IWDVisibility` value, as in the implementation of the `getRuntimeEnvironmentIsRunningInPortalVisibility()` method shown in Listing 6.1.

Mapping to IWD-Visibility

```
return WDPortalUtils.isRunningInPortal()
    ? WDVisibility.VISIBLE
    : WDVisibility.NONE;
```

Listing 6.1 Determining IWDVisibility Based on the Runtime Environment

This mapping allows you to make any UI elements of your application visible or invisible, depending on the runtime environment. You do this by using purely declarative programming and binding the **visibility** property of the relevant UI element to the IsRunning-InPortalVisibility attribute.

Nevertheless, we have decided to enable or disable the relevant UI elements in the NavigationTester, rather than hiding them. This gives us a consistent UI design, which is independent of the runtime environment selected. The EnabledInPortal context attribute of the RuntimeEnvironment context node is used for this purpose. It is bound to the **enabled** property of the relevant UI element, as shown in Figure 6.3. The IWDInputField UI element ContextInputField is shown here as an example.

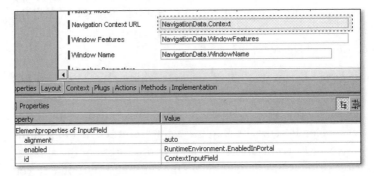

Figure 6.3 Using the EnabledInPortal Context Attribute

6.1.2 Selecting a Navigation Target

The runtime environment is also taken into account in the display of the possible navigation targets. If you start the NavigationTester outside the SAP NetWeaver Portal, only the available Web Dynpro applications are displayed (see Figure 6.4).

Figure 6.4 Displaying Navigation Targets Outside the SAP NetWeaver Portal

If, however, you start the NavigationTester inside the SAP NetWeaver Portal, the available iViews and portal pages that can be used as navigation targets are also displayed (see Figure 6.5).

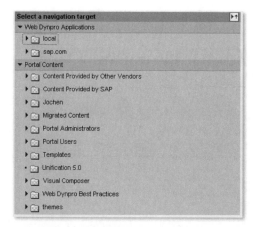

Figure 6.5 Displaying Navigation Targets Inside the SAP NetWeaver Portal

The hierarchical display of possible navigation targets is discussed in detail in Section 6.6.

6.1.3   Defining Navigation Behavior

As well as allowing you to define a navigation target, the Navigation-Tester also offers a range of options for defining the desired navigation behavior in more detail. Outside the SAP NetWeaver Portal, these options are limited to deciding between relative and absolute application URLs, defining additional transfer parameters, and determining whether the navigation target is to be started in the same window or in a new window of the web browser.

Figure 6.6 shows the settings you can make. Note that, in this case, the options available within the SAP NetWeaver Portal have been disabled using the mechanism described above.

Tip
Although we generally recommend that you use the SAP NetWeaver Portal, you should always ensure that your Web Dynpro application is structured in a way that caters to both runtime environments, for example, using the mechanism described above for disabling or hiding UI elements.

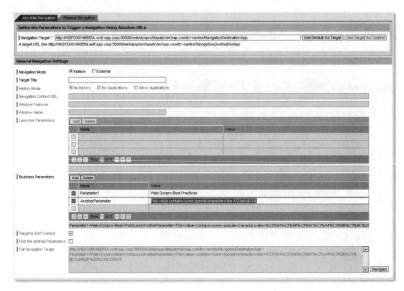

Figure 6.6 Defining Navigation Behavior Outside the SAP NetWeaver Portal

The options for navigating between two Web Dynpro applications are discussed in detail in the next section. At the end of this chapter, we will then describe the hierarchical display of the possible navigation targets (Web Dynpro applications and iViews or portal pages).

6.2 Navigation Outside the SAP NetWeaver Portal

If you start your Web Dynpro application outside the SAP NetWeaver Portal, it is very easy to navigate between two Web Dynpro applications.

6.2.1 Combining Web Dynpro Applications

You should always bear in mind, however, that you can make navigation much more efficient by combining your Web Dynpro applications in one single Web Dynpro application. To do this, combine the corresponding root components of the applications in question in another (third) Web Dynpro component. This Web Dynpro component serves only as a shared framework for the components it contains.

With this approach, the relevant Web Dynpro components are started within one Web Dynpro application instance, which results in a much tighter integration of the components involved. This is particularly useful if the Web Dynpro applications or Web Dynpro components in question will be using large volumes of the same data concurrently.

Combining Web Dynpro applications

You can also combine several Web Dynpro components in one Web Dynpro application if the different components are created in different teams. Using corresponding Web Dynpro component interfaces gives you greater flexibility and reduces direct and unwanted dependencies as far as possible.

This procedure is discussed in the chapters that pertain to the Web Dynpro GameStation (see Chapter 3) and the Web Dynpro MusicBox (see Chapter 8).

6.2.2 Defining a Web Dynpro Application URL

If you want to navigate between two Web Dynpro applications outside the SAP NetWeaver Portal, you must define the target of this navigation step in the form of a *Web Dynpro application URL*. Since this application URL must satisfy certain conditions, you should *always* use the WDURLGenerator utility class to generate this URL. Here, a basic distinction must be made between relative and absolute application URLs.

Using WDURLGenerator

Defining a Relative Application URL

You can always use relative application URLs if the target application is to be executed on the same server node of your SAP NetWeaver installation, or if the application URL is not to be used as a bookmark or is not to be otherwise persistable (for example, in order to be sent in an email at a later stage).

Listing 6.2 shows the definition of a relative application URL for the Web Dynpro NavigationTester.

```
try {

  // Option 1
  String navigationTesterUrl =
```

```
      WDURLGenerator.getApplicationURL(
        "sap.com/tc~navtes",
        "NavigationTesterApp");

    // Option 2
    WDDeployableObjectPart navigationTesterApp =
      WDDeployableObject.getDeployableObjectPart(
        "sap.com/tc~navtes",
        "NavigationTesterApp",
        WDDeployableObjectPartType.APPLICATION);

    navigationTesterUrl =
      WDURLGenerator.
        getApplicationURL(navigationTesterApp);

  } catch (WDURLException e) {
    wdComponentAPI.getMessageManager().reportException(
      "Failed to get application URL -
        please check the defined parameters",
      true)
  } catch (WDDeploymentException e) {
    wdComponentAPI.getMessageManager().reportException(
      "Failed to load deployable object
      'sap.com/tc~navtes'",
      true);
  }
```

Listing 6.2 Generating a Relative Application URL

In this example, the relative application URL can be defined in two different ways. You can enter the required name of the Web Dynpro DC and the application directly. Alternatively, you can generate an instance of the corresponding WDDeployableObjectPart for the NavigationTester first. Note that both options ultimately produce the same navigationTesterUrl:

*../../../sap.com/tc~*navtes/*NavigationTesterApp*

Components of a relative application URL A relative application URL therefore comprises the following components:

`../../../<vendor>/<DC name>/<application name>`

You define the `<vendor>`, `<DC name>`, and `<application name>` variables. If you use local Web Dynpro Eclipse projects, `<vendor>` always has the value `local`. The `<DC name>` is the name of your local Web Dynpro Eclipse project. If you use Web Dynpro development components, define the `<vendor>` as part of the definition of the development component. The `<DC name>` is the name of the development component used.

Defining an Absolute Application URL

If you require a persistable application URL, you must generate an absolute application URL as shown in Listing 6.3. When compared with the definition of a relative application URL, the essential difference here is that you use the `getWorkloadBalancedApplicationURL()` method of the `WDURLGenerator` utility class.

```
try {

  // Option 1
  String navigationTesterUrl =
    WDURLGenerator.getWorkloadBalancedApplicationURL(
      "sap.com/tc~navtes",
      "NavigationTesterApp");

  // Option 2
  WDDeployableObjectPart navigationTesterApp =
    WDDeployableObject.getDeployableObjectPart(
      "sap.com/tc~navtes",
      "NavigationTesterApp",
      WDDeployableObjectPartType.APPLICATION);

  navigationTesterUrl =
    WDURLGenerator
      .getWorkloadBalancedApplicationURL(
        navigationTesterApp);

} catch (WDURLException e) {
  wdComponentAPI.getMessageManager().reportException(
    "Failed to get application URL -
      please check the defined parameters",
    true);
} catch (WDDeploymentException e) {
  wdComponentAPI.getMessageManager().reportException(
    "Failed to load deployable object
    'sap.com/tc~navtes'",
    true);
}
```

Listing 6.3 Generating an Absolute Application URL

In this example, `navigationTesterUrl` contains the following URL after `WDURLGenerator` is called, provided that the Web Dispatcher has been configured accordingly:

*http://wdhost.wdf.sap.corpt:50000/webdynpro/dispatcher/sap.com/
tc~navtes/NavigationTesterApp*

Components of an
absolute URL An absolute Web Dynpro application URL therefore comprises the following components:

```
<protocol>://<server name>.<domain>:<port>/webdynpro/dis-
patcher/<vendor>/<DC name>/<application name>
```

The `<protocol>`, `<server name>`, `<domain>`, and `<port>` depend on your SAP NetWeaver installation. Although specification of the `<domain>` is optional, we recommend that you use the fully qualified server name by specifying the `<domain>`, especially if you start the Web Dynpro application inside the SAP NetWeaver Portal.

As with relative application URLs, you define the `<vendor>`, `<DC name>`, and `<application name>`. If you use local Web Dynpro Eclipse projects, `<vendor>` always has the value `local`. In this case, the `<DC name>` is the name of your local Web Dynpro Eclipse project. If you use Web Dynpro development components, define the `<vendor>` as part of the description of the development components. The `<DC name>` is the name of the development component used.

Tip

You should only use the `getWorkloadBalancedApplicationURL()` method to define an absolute application URL. In this way, you ensure that the URL is always valid, even if you use a Web Dispatcher for your SAP NetWeaver installation. Chapter 10 describes in detail the configurations that you require to access your Web Dynpro applications correctly with a Web Dispatcher. If you have not configured these settings, `getWorkloadBalancedApplicationURL()` returns the same (relative) application URL as `get ApplicationURL()`.

Defining URL Aliases

At this point, you should address a frequently asked question regarding Web Dynpro application URLs, namely, "How can you define shorter and more meaningful URL aliases?" This question often arises because it may not take very long for the resulting application URLs to become rather cryptic, particularly if you use Web Dynpro development components. Unfortunately, you can only define shorter and more meaningful URL aliases if you use another servlet, which you then must redirect to the relevant Web Dynpro application URL.

Note that you can save the desired (absolute) application URL in your browser as a bookmark so that you don't need to remember or type in the full application URL each time that you access your Web Dynpro application.

6.2.3 Transferring Parameters

If you want to navigate between Web Dynpro applications, you will usually need to define additional parameters to transfer certain information from one Web Dynpro application to another. You can do this very easily by simply specifying the corresponding application URL of the target application as shown in the following example:

http://wdhost.wdf.sap.corp:50000/webdynpro/dispatcher/sap.com/ tc~search/GoogleSearchApp?query=Web%20Dynpro& viewModeSwitch=true

In this example, you call the `GoogleSearchApp` Web Dynpro application with the desired search term that is specified by transferring the `query` parameter with the desired value. In addition, the `viewModeSwitch` parameter is used to specify that the selection of the desired display variant be displayed.

As you can see, you add the parameters that you want to the defined (absolute) application URL as query strings. Note here that you may have to URL-encode the desired parameter values (see Section 6.3).

6.2.4 Importing Parameters

The `tc\navtes` Web Dynpro development component contains a second Web Dynpro application in addition to the Web Dynpro NavigationTester. This is used here as an example to illustrate the options at your disposal for importing transferred parameters within the Web Dynpro target application.

Figure 6.7 shows the `NavigationDestinationApp` Web Dynpro application, which uses the `NavigationDestinationComp` Web Dynpro component as the root component.

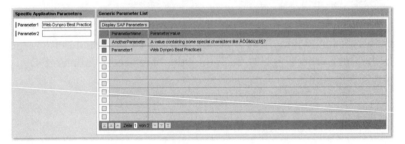

Figure 6.7 The NavigationDestinationApp Web Dynpro Application

You essentially have two options for accessing the transferred parameters within your Web Dynpro application. You can either explicitly define the desired parameters as parameters of the startup plug of the root component used, or you can access all transferred parameters generically using the `WDWebContextAdapter`.

The `NavigationDestinationApp` application is used to illustrate both options in Figure 6.8. On the left, it shows two explicitly defined parameters, **Parameter1** and **Parameter2**. On the right, all transferred parameters are displayed in a table. You can also decide whether you want the transferred system parameters to be displayed automatically.

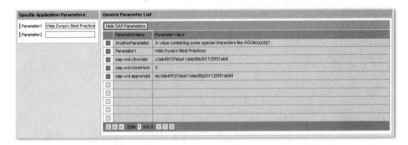

Figure 6.8 Transferred System Parameters Outside the SAP NetWeaver Portal

Transferred system parameters

Figure 6.8 shows the system parameters that are transferred when you start the application outside the SAP NetWeaver Portal. The `sap-wd-cltwndid` and `sap-wd-appwndid` parameters are required by the Web Dynpro runtime to determine the correct application instance.

The `sap-wd-norefresh` parameter indicates that the request does not start the Web Dynpro application instance.

> **Tip**
>
> As a general rule, you should *not* change or delete the transferred system parameters, that is, all parameters beginning with `sap-wd`. If you do, your Web Dynpro application may not function correctly.

If you start your Web Dynpro application inside the SAP NetWeaver Portal, several additional system parameters are transferred, as shown in Figure 6.9. These additional system parameters are ultimately used to define the current portal environment.

Transferred system parameters inside the SAP NetWeaver Portal

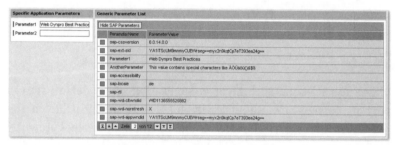

Figure 6.9 Transferred System Parameters Inside the SAP NetWeaver Portal

For example, the `sap-locale` system parameter defines the selected portal language, while the `sap-rtl` parameter determines whether the user has configured left-to-right support in the portal. The Web Dynpro runtime adopts these (portal) settings automatically and displays your Web Dynpro application with the correct language or selected left-to-right setting. Chapter 5 provides more details about the individual system parameters in the SAP NetWeaver Portal.

Defining Explicit Startup Plug Parameters

If you know exactly which parameters your Web Dynpro application needs to access (for example, to define a specific display variant, as with the Web Dynpro Google search that was described in Chapter 4), you can define these parameters explicitly as parameters of the startup plug used. In the `NavigationDestinationApp` application, the relevant parameters are `Parameter1` and `Parameter2`.

Figure 6.10 shows the definition of the default startup plug with the relevant parameters. Note that the startup plug parameter names must be identical to the names of the transfer parameters. In addition, the startup plug parameters must be **string** parameters.

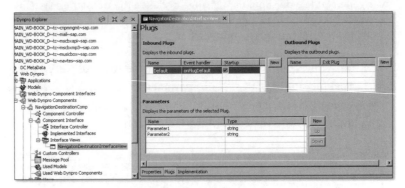

Figure 6.10 Defining the Startup Plug Parameters

When you start the Web Dynpro application, these default startup plug parameters are automatically filled and are available in the onPlugDefault() event handler. In our example, the values are written into the context provided by the interface component controller of the root component, as shown in Listing 6.4.

```
wdThis
  .wdGetNavigationDestinationCompInterfaceController()
  .wdGetContext()
  .currentParametersElement()
  .setParameter1(Parameter1);

wdThis
  .wdGetNavigationDestinationCompInterfaceController()
  .wdGetContext()
  .currentParametersElement()
  .setParameter2(Parameter2);
```

Listing 6.4 Using Explicitly Defined Startup Plug Parameters

Accessing All Parameters Generically

In addition to accessing transfer parameters explicitly, you can also access all transfer parameters generically using the WDWebContext-Adapter.

Tip

As you saw in Chapter 2, one of the strengths of Web Dynpro is that it is not dependent on a specific protocol or display client. You can display the same Web Dynpro application without any adjustments both in a conventional web browser based on HTTP and in a Smart Client, which can use any protocol (even a proprietary protocol). To avoid violating this *Web Dynpro client abstraction*, you should *always* use the WDWebContext-Adapter to access transfer parameters.

In our NavigationDestinationApp application, the WDWebContext-Adapter is used to import all transferred parameters and to copy these parameters into the relevant context node. In the last step, the parameters are then displayed using the IWDTable UI element.

The updateParameterList() method in the view controller of the DestinationView Web Dynpro view imports all transferred parameters and fills the RequestParameter context node, as shown in Listing 6.5:

```
IPrivateDestinationView.
  IGenericParametersElement parameter = null;
wdContext.nodeGenericParameters().invalidate();

// Import transfer parameters
Map parameters =
  WDWebContextAdapter.getWebContextAdapter()
    .getRequestParameterMap();

for (Iterator paras = parameters.keySet().iterator();
  paras.hasNext();) {
  String key = (String) paras.next();

  if (!key.startsWith("sap-wd") ||
    wdContext.currentContextElement()
      .getShowSAPParameters()) {

    if (key.equals("eventQueue")) {
      continue;
    }

    String value =
      WDWebContextAdapter.getWebContextAdapter()
        .getRequestParameter(key);
```

```
        wdContext.nodeGenericParameters()
          .createGenericParametersElement();
      parameter.setValue(value);
      parameter.setName(key);

      wdContext.nodeGenericParameters()
        .addElement(parameter);
    }
  }
```

Listing 6.5 Importing All Transfer Parameters

6.2.5   Using the Exit Plug

After you have defined the preferred application URL along with the required transfer parameters, you must trigger the navigation you want. To do this, use the *exit plug* to exit the application.

Exit plug   The exit plug is the counterpart of the startup plug you used to start the application instance. In addition to using an exit plug without any parameters, you can extend the exit plug and define the target URL that you want to access after you exit the Web Dynpro application. In principle, you can use any URL; however, if you want to navigate to another Web Dynpro application, you must enter a valid Web Dynpro application URL.

Like the startup plug, the exit plug is defined as part of the interface view controller of a Web Dynpro component. To do this, follow the steps below:

1. In the Web Dynpro Explorer, navigate to the relevant interface view controller and double-click to open the appropriate editor. In the editor, select the **Plugs** tab to define the desired exit plug. Here, click on the **New** button next to the list of outbound plugs.

2. Figure 6.11 shows the dialog box that appears. Here you define the NavigationToApplication exit plug required in our example. Remember to select the relevant checkbox to indicate that the outbound plug is an **exit plug**.

Figure 6.11 Defining the Exit Plug

3. Click on **Next** to define the desired exit plug parameters. Figure 6.12 shows the definition of the Url parameter. You *must* enter the Url parameter so that the URL is recognized as the target URL when the exit plug is triggered.

URL parameter in the exit plug

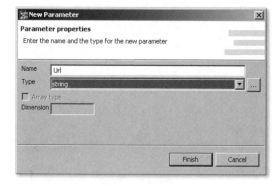

Figure 6.12 Defining the Url Parameter

4. In our NavigationTester example, the required exit plug, NavigateToApplication, is defined in the NavigationTesterInterfaceView interface view controller of the NavigationTesterComp component (see Figure 6.13).

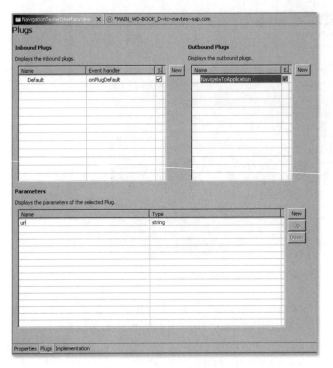

Figure 6.13 NavigationToApplication Exit Plug

5. Lastly, you trigger the exit plug. To do this, you must access the relevant `wdFirePlugNavigateToApplication()` method of the component interface view controller.

Creating the controller usage — Since you want to trigger navigation from the `NavigationDataView` Web Dynpro view in the NavigationTester example, you must first create a *controller usage* to call the `NavigationTesterInterfaceView` component interface view controller in the view controller.

1. To do this, double-click on the `NavigationDataView` Web Dynpro view in the Web Dynpro Explorer to open the view editor (see Figure 6.14). Alternatively, select the **Edit** option in the context menu of the Web Dynpro view.

Figure 6.14 NavigationDataView in the Web Dynpro Explorer

2. In the view editor, select the **Properties** tab and click on **Add**. Figure 6.15 shows the dialog box that appears. Here you select the `NavigationTesterInterfaceView` interface view controller.

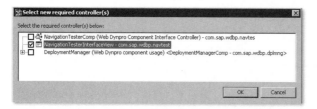

Figure 6.15 Defining the Controller Usage

3. After you have successfully created the required controller usage, it is displayed on the **Properties** tab in the view editor. Figure 6.16 shows the controller usages defined for the NavigationDataView Web Dynpro view.

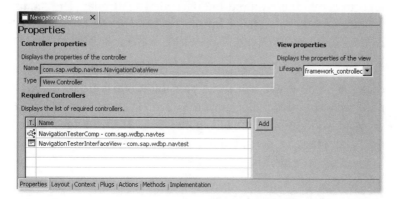

Figure 6.16 List of the Defined Controller Usages in the View Editor

4. As an alternative to using the view editor, you can also display the defined controller usages in the Web Dynpro Explorer directly by expanding the relevant views, as shown in Figure 6.17.

Figure 6.17 List of the Defined Controller Usages in the Web Dynpro Explorer

Calling the
exit plug After you have created the controller usage, you can access the interface view controller directly in the view controller and use the
`wdFirePlugNavigateToApplication()` method to trigger the exit
plug. This exit plug is part of the `onActionNavigate()` event handler,
as shown in Listing 6.6 below:

```
// Navigate to the selected Web Dynpro application
// using the Exit-Plug
  wdThis
    .wdGetNavigationTesterInterfaceViewController()
    .wdFirePlugNavigateToApplication(
      wdContext
        .currentNavigationDataElement()
          .getFullNavigationTargetString());
```

Listing 6.6 Calling the Exit Plug

First, `wdThis.wdGetNavigationTesterInterfaceViewController()` is
used to access the required interface view controller. The required
application URL is defined by the `FullNavigationTargetAsString`
context attribute of the `NavigationData` context node.

The `FullNavigationTargetAsString` context attribute is a good
example of how you can use a **calculated** attribute to define the
required value depending on other context attributes. Listing 6.7
shows the definition of the full application URL, including any transfer parameters, as part of the `getNavigationDataFullNavigation-
TargetString()` method.

```
fullNavigationTarget.append(
  wdContext.currentNavigationDataElement().
    getAbsoluteTarget());

String businessParameters =
  wdContext.currentNavigationDataElement()
    .getBusinessParameterString();

if (!StringUtil.isEmpty(businessParameters)) {
  fullNavigationTarget.append('?')
    .append(businessParameters);
}
```

Listing 6.7 Defining the Full Application URL

6.2.6 Starting the Web Dynpro Target Application in a New Window

The exit plug is used to exit the Web Dynpro application that triggered navigation as soon as the desired target application has been reached. However, if you don't want to exit the navigating Web Dynpro application but continue to use it concurrently, you must open the desired target application in a new window of the web browser. This is easily done using the IWDWindowManager, as shown in Listing 6.8:

```
IWDWindow browserWindow =
  wdComponentAPI.getWindowManager().
    createNonModalExternalWindow(
      wdContext.currentNavigationDataElement()
        .getFullNavigationTargetString(),
      wdContext.currentNavigationDataElement()
        .getTargetTitle());

browserWindow.open();
```

Listing 6.8 Starting the Target Application in a New Window

There is also another option you can use to start the target application in a new window. With the IWDLinkToURL UI element, you can use the **target** attribute to define the window in the web browser in which the specified URL is to be called. If you use the _BLANK value, which is the default value, the URL is displayed in a new window.

Using the IWDLinkToURL UI element

Figure 6.18 shows the definition of a IWDLinkToURL UI element. In this case, the URL is the application URL defined above.

Figure 6.18 Using the IWDLinkToURL UI Element

We have addressed navigation between Web Dynpro applications outside the SAP NetWeaver Portal in detail. In the next section, we'll focus on the encoding of transfer parameters, followed by a discussion of the options available to you if your Web Dynpro applications are called inside the SAP NetWeaver Portal.

6.3 Encoding Transfer Parameters

To ensure that the defined transfer parameters are transferred correctly, the relevant parameter values must be encoded.

Using the JDK 1.3- encode() method

Since the SAP NetWeaver Developer Studio (NWDS) is based on the *Java Development Kit 1.3* (JDK), only the standard URLEncoder. encode() call is available in this case, which does not allow the desired code page to be defined. However, since your SAP NetWeaver 2004 installation is based on JDK 1.4, you can use Java reflexion to call the extended encode() method, which allows you to define the desired code page.

Since this functionality is required at various points (and in various examples in this book), we have defined the com.sap.wdbp.encode. URLEncode utility class, which is available for all examples in this book from the tc~utils Web Dynpro development component. Appendix A explains in detail the points to be considered when defining this development component.

The steps involved in using the URLEncode utility class are described below. This is followed by a discussion of how you actually encode the parameter values.

6.3.1 Integrating the tc~utils Web Dynpro Development Component

To use a specific function from another (Web Dynpro) development component, you must define a relevant link between the development component that provides this function and the development component that needs to use this function.

Defining public parts and public part entities

A development component uses *public parts* to make certain functions available to other development components. A public part uses *public part entities* to define the objects and functions that should be visible from the outside to other development components.

Many different types of public part entities can be defined, based on the type of the development component. For example, a Web Dynpro development component may define public part entities for Web Dynpro components or Web Dynpro component interfaces. In addition to these Web Dynpro entities, a Web Dynpro development component can also use a public part to offer simple Java classes, which is precisely what the Utils public part of the tc~utils development component—which you now need to use in the Web Dynpro NavigationTester—does. First, you must generate a reference, the *Used DC dependency*, for the Utils public part.

1. In the Web Dynpro Explorer, navigate to the **Used DCs** directory, which is located under **DC MetaData · DC Definition** in the NavigationTester Project. Use the **Add Used DC...** option in the **Used DCs** context menu to define this dependency (see Figure 6.19).

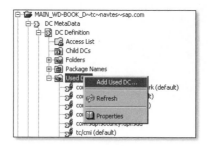

Figure 6.19 Adding a Reference to a Development Component

2. In the dialog box that appears, select the **Utils** public part of the tc~utils development component, which is displayed here as **tc/utils**. As shown in Figure 6.20, you can select a public part on the **Active** or **Inactive** tab.

As soon as you have finished developing a (Web Dynpro) development component, you can activate it and thus officially release it for use in other development components. Typically, you should access only active (i.e., released) public parts or development components. Otherwise, you may have to adjust your own (Web Dynpro) development component at a later stage if changes are made to the inactive public part that you are using. In our example, the Utils public part is selected from the list of inactive development components, because we develop all of the development components used in our examples ourselves.

Active and inactive development components

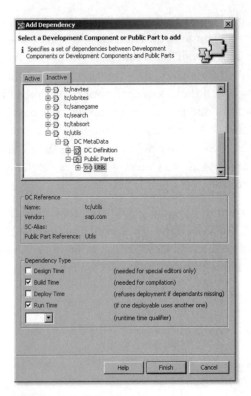

Figure 6.20 Defining the Utils Public Part

When you define a Used DC dependency, you must always pay attention to the **dependency type** selected. Because we want to use the URLEncode utility class in our example, which is part of the Utils public part, we must select **Build Time** and **Run Time**. This ensures that the URLEncode utility class is available during compilation of the NavigationTester project.

3. Click on **Finish** to generate the reference required. Figure 6.21 shows an extract from the defined reference. As you can see, a Used DC dependency always has the following form:

```
<DC name> (<public part name>)
```

In our example, the dependency is therefore tc/utils (Utils).

Figure 6.21 Defined Public Parts

To ensure that the Utils public part and the Java class it contains (for example, the URLEncode utility class) can be used by the Navigation-Tester at runtime, you must define a *sharing reference*. A sharing reference defines a runtime dependency for a specific (Web Dynpro) development component, web application, or portal service.

Using a sharing reference

From a technical point of view, a sharing reference to one of the aforementioned entities always implies a reference to the relevant Java classloader of the (Web Dynpro) development component, web application, or portal service. Without this classloader reference, the NavigationTester application cannot, for example, load or use any classes from the Utils public part.

Reference to the Java classloaders used

Without a correct definition of the required sharing reference, a ClassNotFound exception occurs at runtime when you try to use a class from the (Web Dynpro) development component, web application, or portal service that is not correctly referenced.

1. To define the sharing reference required for the NavigationTester project, select the **Properties** option in the project's context menu to open the Properties dialog (see Figure 6.22)

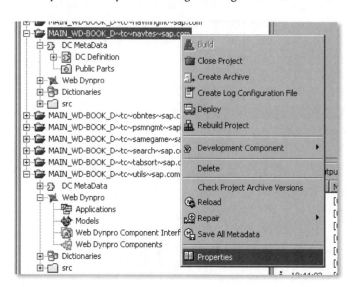

Figure 6.22 Editing the Properties of the Web Dynpro Project

2. In the dialog box that appears, select **Web Dynpro References** on the left and then select the **Sharing references** tab on the right (see Figure 6.23). Click on **Add** to create the new sharing reference.

Creating a sharing reference

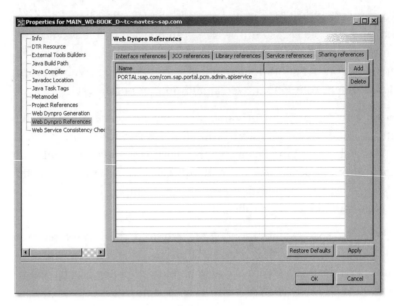

Figure 6.23 Properties Dialog of a Web Dynpro Project

3. Figure 6.24 shows the definition of the sharing reference for the Utils public part of the tc~utils development component. As you can see, you always reference the relevant development component (or web application) rather than the relevant public part. Sharing references to portal services have a special syntax of their own, which is discussed in Chapter 7.

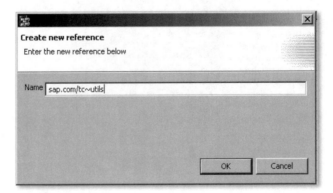

Figure 6.24 Defining a Sharing Reference

4. When you click on **OK**, the desired sharing reference is created and displayed in the Properties dialog of the project, as shown in Figure 6.25.

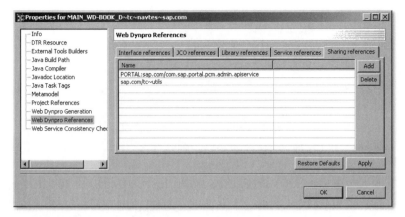

Figure 6.25 Defined Sharing References

6.3.2 Description of the portalapp.xml File

The practical steps involved in using the URLEncode utility class, which is part of the Utils public part, is discussed below, following an explanation of how and where the defined sharing references are stored in your Web Dynpro project.

1. Go to the Navigator and open the NavigationTester project. The **gen_wdp** directory contains the generated files of your Web Dynpro project. The **packages** subdirectory contains the required Java classes and the *portalapp.xml* file (see Figure 6.26).

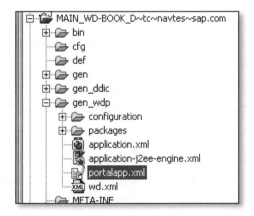

Figure 6.26 The Generated portalapp.xml File

2. To display the *portalapp.xml* file, select **Open With · Text Editor** in the context menu (see Figure 6.27).

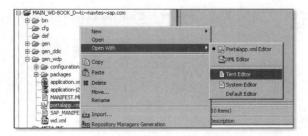

Figure 6.27 Displaying the portalapp.xml File

3. Figure 6.28 shows an extract from the *portalapp.xml* file of the NavigationTester project. As you can see, the sharing reference that you have just defined for *sap.com/tc~utils* appears in the list of defined sharing references.

```
tion-config>
    <property name="SharingReference"     value="sap.com/tc~wd~dispwda"/>
    <property name="SharingReference"     value="sap.com/tc~utils"/>
    <property name="SharingReference"     value="sap.com/tc~wd~corecomp"/>
    <property name="SharingReference"     value="sap.com/tc~dplmng"/>
    <property name="SharingReference"     value="PORTAL:sap.com/com.sap.porta
```

Figure 6.28 Defined Sharing References

Sharing references defined by default

In addition to the sharing references you define, two sharing references are automatically defined for each Web Dynpro project. Without these, no Web Dynpro application can be successfully executed. sap.com/tc~wd~dispwda indicates the required resources, such as the various files belonging to the different themes. sap.com/tc~wd~corecomp, meanwhile, contains important generic Web Dynpro components, for example, for various input helps that are available to all Web Dynpro applications.

Chapter 10 provides a detailed description of the individual components of these two (generic) Web Dynpro development components.

6.3.3 Encoding the Parameter Values

Using UTF-8 encoding

Once you have used the Utils public part of the tc~utils development component to ensure that the URLEncode utility class can be used in the NavigationTester, the relevant parameter values of the transfer parameters have to be encoded. The URLEncode utility class normally uses UTF-8 encoding.

As specified above, it is very easy to define any transfer parameters with the Web Dynpro NavigationTester. Figure 6.29 shows the definition of the application-specific `Parameter1` and `AnotherParameter` parameters. You can use the **Add** and **Delete** buttons to define or delete any parameters. The NavigationTester also shows the URL-compliant display based on the current parameter definition below the table where you define the various parameters.

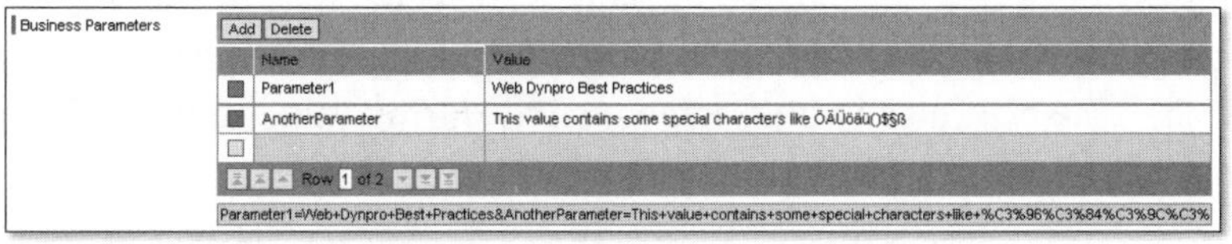

Defining transfer parameters in the NavigationTester

Figure 6.29 Defining Transfer Parameters

This URL-compliant display is defined using the `BusinessParameter-AsString` **calculated** attribute of the `NavigationData` context node. This provides a simple way for you to ensure that the relevant value is automatically adjusted each time a change is made to the individual parameters.

Listing 6.9 shows the implementation of the `getNavigation-DataBusinessParameterString()` method of the `NavigationTester-Comp` Web Dynpro component, in which the URL-compliant display is defined.

```
businessParameters.setLength(0);
for (int i = 0;
    i < wdContext.nodeBusinessParameter().size();
    i++) {

  IPublicNavigationTesterComp.IBusinessParameterElement
    parameter = wdContext.nodeBusinessParameter()
              .getBusinessParameterElementAt(i);

  if ((parameter.getName() != null)
      && (parameter.getValue() != null)) {

    businessParameters
      .append(parameter.getName())
      .append('=')
      .append(urlEncode.encode(parameter.getValue()));
```

225

```
if (i < wdContext.nodeBusinessParameter().size() - 1) {
    businessParameters.append('&');
    }
  }
}
return businessParameters.toString();
```

Listing 6.9 Encoding the Transfer Parameters

As you can see, all parameter values are generated by calling the encode() method of the URLEncode utility class. The required urlEncode instance, meanwhile, is generated during initialization of the NavigationTesterComp component.

In the example shown in Figure 6.29, the URL-compliant display corresponds to the defined transfer parameter:

```
Parameter1=Web+Dynpro+Best+Practices
  &AnotherParameter=A+value+containing+some+special
  +characters+like+%C3 %84 %C3 %96 %C3 %9C%C3 %A4 %C3 %B6 %C3 %BC
  %29 %28 %26 %C2 %A7 %3F
```

This encoding of the transfer parameters is always required, regardless of whether you start your Web Dynpro application inside or outside the SAP NetWeaver Portal.

6.4   Navigation Inside the SAP NetWeaver Portal

Chapter 5 discussed the various options available to you in the SAP NetWeaver Portal for accessing your Web Dynpro applications inside the portal in the form of a Web Dynpro iView, grouping them in worksets or roles, assigning them to specific user groups, and defining the desired navigation structure that will allow users to navigate between the different applications using top-level navigation or detail navigation.

Programmatic triggering of portal navigation

In addition to top-level navigation and detail navigation, you can trigger programmatic navigation steps from each Web Dynpro application. In this case, the navigation target can be defined as a (relative or absolute) URL to an iView or a portal page, or as an abstract operation of a *business object* (BO). This option of *object-based navigation* is discussed in Chapter 7.

In most cases, you can only navigate to an iView or a portal page within the SAP NetWeaver Portal; however, in Section 6.4.5, we address the possibility of navigating directly to a specific Web Dynpro application within the SAP NetWeaver Portal, without first creating a corresponding iView.

Direct navigation to a Web Dynpro application

6.4.1 Triggering Portal Navigation

Within your Web Dynpro application, you can use one of the methods of the WDPortalNavigation utility class to trigger portal navigation. Since Web Dynpro-based iViews in the portal are generally displayed as isolated content within an iFrame, communication between your Web Dynpro application and the SAP NetWeaver Portal can only occur via a client-side mechanism.

Due to the client abstraction of Web Dynpro, which we addressed earlier in this book, a Web Dynpro application cannot access this client-side mechanism directly, but can do so using the WDPortalNavigation utility class. The steps are essentially as follows:

Client abstraction and portal navigation

1. In any Web Dynpro action event handler, one of the methods of WDPortalNavigation could be called and the relevant data is transferred in accordance with the signature used.

2. The Web Dynpro runtime returns this data to the client with the current Web Dynpro response.

3. The Web Dynpro client recognizes this data and calls the relevant client APIs of the SAP NetWeaver Portal to trigger the desired navigation.

Although this process is totally transparent to you (as a Web Dynpro application developer), you should note that triggering a portal navigation within a Web Dynpro application always warrants an additional server roundtrip.

After this rather theoretical digression, the next section returns to the practicalities of portal navigation in the NavigationTester.

6.4.2   Absolute Portal Navigation

You can use one of the `navigateAbsolute()` methods of the `WDPortalNavigation` utility class to trigger absolute portal navigation. The navigation target is specified as an absolute URL to an iView or portal page in this case.

In addition to the navigation target, you can define many other parameters, for example, to determine whether the navigation target is to be displayed in the same window (of the web browser) or in a new window. The following sections explain how navigation behavior can be defined in more detail.

Defining an absolute target address

The `navigationTarget` parameter (of one of the `navigateAbsolute()` methods) allows you to define the absolute address of the navigation target for absolute portal navigation. The target address defines the location where the target iView or portal page is stored in the portal content directory (PCD). The prefix `ROLES://` is required to address iViews or portal pages. Accordingly, a valid (absolute) target address is as follows:

```
ROLES://portal_content/com.sap.wdbp/com.sap.navigation_
folder/com.sap.navigationdestination
```

Problems with absolute addressing

In practice, the use of absolute target address is sometimes problematic. If you use absolute target paths to iViews or portal pages in your Web Dynpro application, these paths are only valid as long as the iView or portal page addressed is stored in *exactly* this location in the PCD. Because the target address of an iView or portal page also defines the actual usage of this iView or portal page in a particular role, this may cause problems if the iView or portal page is moved to another role, or if you want or need to perform a basic restructuring of your portal content.

> **Tip**
>
> We generally recommend that you use relative portal navigation or object-based navigation.
>
> But, if you decide to use absolute portal navigation, you should plan on making the absolute target addresses configurable, for example, using the `WDConfiguration` service, which is discussed in relation to the Web Dynpro Google search in Chapter 4. This means that you can adjust these target addresses later on without having to change your Web Dynpro application.

6.4.3   Relative Portal Navigation

Using absolute target addresses may cause problems as described above if the portal content that is addressed is moved or restructured. Therefore, it frequently makes more sense to use relative addressing.

If, for example, you want to navigate between two portal pages that are both defined in the same directory in the PCD, relative addressing between the two pages continues to be valid even if the entire directory is moved within the PCD. This would not be the case if absolute addressing were used. In the worst-case scenario, you would have to change your Web Dynpro application (which may already have been delivered).

To trigger relative navigation, use one of the `navigateRelative()` methods of the `WDPortalNavigation` utility class. The relative target address is always defined by the following three parameters in this case:

Defining a relative target address

▶ `baseURL`

You use the `baseURL` parameter to define the base of the relative target address. The same rules used to define an absolute target address apply here also. The following is an example of a valid `baseURL`:

```
ROLES://portal_content/com.sap.wdbp/com.sap.navigation_
folder/com.sap.navigationdestination
```

▶ `levelsUp`

The `levelsUp` parameter defines how many levels are to be navigated upwards in the PCD structure.

▶ `path`

The `path` parameter defines the path to the desired navigation target relative to the selected `baseUrl`.

6.4.4   Defining Navigation Behavior

In addition to specifying an absolute or relative target address, you can define navigation behavior inside the SAP NetWeaver Portal in many different ways. An overview of the available options is provided below. The parameters specified always correspond to the parameters of one of the `navigateAbsolute()` or `navigateRela-tive()` methods of the `WDPortalNavigation` utility class.

Defining the Navigation Mode

The `mode` parameter allows you to define where the specified target address is to be displayed. You can use the following modes:

▶ `WDPortalNavigationMode.SHOW_INPLACE`
▶ `WDPortalNavigationMode.SHOW_EXTERNAL`
▶ `WDPortalNavigationMode.SHOW_EXTERNAL_PORTAL`
▶ `WDPortalNavigationMode.SHOW_HEADERLESS_PORTAL`

SHOW_INPLACE If you use `SHOW_INPLACE`, the navigation target is displayed in the current window of the web browser. Top-level navigation and detail navigation are adjusted accordingly where possible and the addressed iView or portal page is displayed in the working area of the SAP NetWeaver Portal.

If the navigation target specified is not contained in one of the roles assigned to the user, top-level navigation and detail navigation are *not* adjusted. In this case, you can determine top-level navigation and detail navigation only by defining the navigation context.

Handling incorrect target addresses If the specified target address does not refer to a valid iView or portal page, an error message is not issued in the current version of the SAP NetWeaver Portal. The working area simply remains blank and top-level navigation and detail navigation are not adjusted. You can also navigate using the generic **Forward/Back** navigation function in the page header (see Figure 6.30).

Figure 6.30 Generic Forward/Back Navigation

SHOW_EXTERNAL With `SHOW_EXTERNAL`, the navigation target is displayed in a new window in the web browser without the portal frame, that is, without top-level navigation or detail navigation.

Handling invisible parts of the portal frame Note that if you use `SHOW_EXTERNAL`, it is not only the visible parts of the portal frame that are not displayed. The invisible parts that are usually loaded together with the portal frame are also unavailable.

For example, use of the portal's work-protect mode is no longer supported.

> **Tip**
>
> We generally recommend that you avoid using SHOW_EXTERNAL because important (hidden) parts of the portal frame are not loaded in this case and, consequently, you have only a very limited access to portal functionality.

With SHOW_EXTERNAL_PORTAL, the navigation target is displayed in a new window of the web browser, together with the standard portal frame. Top-level navigation and detail navigation are adjusted, where possible, in accordance with the defined navigation target. Meanwhile, the iView or portal page addressed (or a blank page if the target address is invalid) appears in the working area.

SHOW_
EXTERNAL_
PORTAL

The generic Forward/Back portal navigation function cannot be used in this case to navigate back to the original iView or portal page because this is in the original window.

With SHOW_HEADERLESS_PORTAL, the navigation target is displayed in a new window with the generic portal page header only. If you use SHOW_EXTERNAL_PORTAL or SHOW_HEADERLESS_PORTAL, meanwhile, all required hidden parts of the portal frame are loaded. The work-protect mode is therefore supported with both of these modes.

SHOW_
HEADERLESS_
PORTAL

Using the Portal History

With the historyMode parameter, you can determine whether and how the triggered navigation step is to appear in the portal history. The portal history is part of the generic page header. The possible values are as follows:

▶ WDPortalNavigationHistoryMode.NO_HISTORY

▶ WDPortalNavigationHistoryMode.NO_DUPLICATIONS

▶ WDPortalNavigationHistoryMode.ALLOW_DUPLICATIONS

With NO_HISTORY, the navigation step does not appear in the portal history. However, you can still use the generic Forward/Back navigation function in the portal.

NO_HISTORY

With NO_DUPLICATIONS, the navigation step is shown in the portal history. If the same navigation target, that is, the same target address

NO_DUPLICA-
TIONS

is accessed several times, only one entry appears in the portal history. If the same target addresses are specified in different navigation steps with (potentially) different parameters, these appear as a single entry in the portal history. This entry then corresponds to the target address and the different parameters of the individual navigation steps are ignored.

ALLOW_DUPLI-CATIONS

With ALLOW_DUPLICATIONS, the navigation step appears in the portal history and multiple navigation to the same navigation step is indicated by several entries in the portal history if the parameters are different each time.

Differentiating between navigation steps

This option is particularly useful in scenarios where the same navigation target is to be accessed with different parameters and you want users to have the option of navigating (back) from the portal history to one of the navigation targets that appear there.

The display of search results for an artist in the Web Dynpro MusicBox (see Chapter 8) illustrates this option. You can use ALLOW_DUPLICATIONS to ensure that various entries will appear in the portal history and that users can go directly from the portal history to the search results for a particular artist.

Determining the entry displayed in the Portal history

The targetTitle parameter allows you to define how the navigation step will appear in the Portal history. If WDPortalNavigationHistoryMode.ALLOW_DUPLICATIONS is used, this entry should also specify which parameters were used for navigation.

To differentiate between the various search results for the various artists in the Web Dynpro MusicBox (see Chapter 8), for example, add the selected artist to the title to ensure that the entries in the portal history are easily identifiable.

Defining the Navigation Context

You use the contextURL parameter to define the *navigation context*. The navigation context determines which entries are selected in top-level navigation and detail navigation.

Automatic adjustment of the navigation context

As mentioned above, the navigation context is normally adjusted automatically to the defined navigation target. If this automatic adjustment is not desired or not possible because, for example, the navigation target is not part of the role assigned to the user, a corresponding contextURL can be used to show any navigation context. This is particularly useful in scenarios where the specified navigation target does not appear in top-level navigation or detail navigation and the navigation context is therefore not changed by the navigation step.

The same rules used to define the address of the navigation target apply to the definition of the navigation context. To define the con-textURL in the NavigationTester, select a navigation target of your choice. Next, choose **Use Target As Context** to define the selected navigation target as a contextURL (see Figure 6.31).

Figure 6.31 Use Target As Context

Manipulating the New Window

If the navigation target is displayed in a new window in the web browser, you can use the windowFeatures parameter to define the appearance of this window. You can, for example, adjust the position or size of the window to meet your specific requirements. Table 6.1 shows the main options:

Name	Value	Description
location	**no** or **yes**	Determines whether the URL/location bar is to be displayed.
menubar	**no** or **yes**	Determines whether the menu bar is to be displayed.
toolbar	**no** or **yes**	Determines whether the toolbar is to be displayed.
status	**no** or **yes**	Determines whether the status bar is to be displayed.
resizable	**no** or **yes**	Determines whether the size of the window can be adjusted.
scrollbars	**no** or **yes**	Determines whether the window scrollbars are to be displayed.
width	value in pixels	Defines the width of the window.
height	value in pixels	Defines the height of the window.

Table 6.1 Options for Defining the Web Browser Display

Name	Value	Description
posX	value in pixels	Defines the horizontal position of the top left corner of the window. The value **0** indicates the left border of the screen.
posY	value in pixels	Defines the vertical position of the top left corner of the window. The value **0** indicates the top border of the screen.

Table 6.1 Options for Defining the Web Browser Display (cont.)

Defining the name of the browser window

The `windowName` parameter defines the name of the new window in the web browser. This is the *technical name* of the window, *not* the displayed window title. Manipulation of the window title is not currently supported. It is not very useful to define the `windowName` parameter in a Web Dynpro application, because you don't have the option of using this value in a Web Dynpro application, for example, with JavaScript calls.

Reusing an open window

However, you can use the `windowName` parameter to ensure that a new window is not opened with each navigation. Instead, you can use a window that has already been opened. To force this behavior, simply specify the same value for the `windowName` parameter for all navigation steps triggered.

Defining Parameters for the SAP Application Integrator

In addition to defining the target address, you will usually need to define optional application-specific parameters, which can then be used in the navigation target, that is, in your Web Dynpro application in our example.

For portal content based on SAP UI technology (for example, SAP GUI, WebGUI, BSP, HTMLB or Web Dynpro), you must distinguish between two different types of parameters. First, some parameters must ultimately be made accessible to the calling application (regardless of the technology used). Secondly, other parameters are required by the SAP Application Integrator to start the relevant application (see Chapter 5).

You use the `launcherParameters` parameter to define the parameters that are required by the SAP Application Integrator and that are not to be passed on to the calling Web Dynpro application. The `launcherParameters` parameter may have the following value, for example:

Using launcher parameters

`NameSpace=local&ApplicationName=MyTestApp.`

Two parameters, `NameSpace` and `ApplicationName`, are defined in this case. These parameters are required by the SAP Application Integrator to start the relevant application. Note that the values of these parameters (`local` and `MyTestApp`) may have to be URL-encoded.

Section 6.4.5 describes in detail how you can use the `launcherParameters` to start each Web Dynpro application in the SAP NetWeaver Portal without first having to create a special Web Dynpro iView. If the defined navigation target consists of SAP-based portal content, you must set the `useSAPLauncher` parameter to **true**. In all other cases, set it to **false**.

Starting a Web Dynpro application directly

Defining Application Parameters

The `businessParameters` parameter defines the application-specific parameters that are to be passed on to the calling Web Dynpro application. Starting the artist search in the Web Dynpro MusicBox, where the artist to be found is defined (see Chapter 8), is an example of where this parameter is used. As with the `launcherParameters` parameter, the parameter values must be URL-encoded.

If you use many parameters (defined as `launcherParameters` or `businessParameters`), they may have to be posted because of the URL length restriction of most web browsers. This means that they are transferred within the request itself, rather than as part of the called URL. If you use the `WDPortalNavigation` utility class, this occurs automatically once a length of 1,024 characters is exceeded. If you want to force posting in other cases, use the `postParameter` parameter. It may be useful to post parameters, for example, to ensure that security-related parameter values do not appear in the URL of the navigation target.

Posting the defined parameters

6.4.5 Direct Navigation to a Web Dynpro Application

As a rule, the navigation target for (relative or absolute) portal navigation always represents an iView or a portal page. Therefore, you must also create a corresponding iView for your Web Dynpro application to navigate to this application using portal navigation.

Problems starting a Web Dynpro application URL in the SAP NetWeaver Portal

If you use a Web Dynpro application URL to navigate directly to a Web Dynpro application inside the SAP NetWeaver Portal, the relationship between the application and the surrounding portal is lost. As a result, all portal settings, such as the defined portal language or the selected portal theme, are no longer used in a Web Dynpro application that was started directly.

In certain scenarios, however, it may be useful to navigate to a specific Web Dynpro application for which no iView is defined. To learn how you can do this in the NavigationTester, read the following section.

Using the launcherParameters Parameter

A Web Dynpro application is started in the SAP NetWeaver Portal using the SAP Application Integrator, which is responsible, for example, for transferring the portal settings. The `launcherParameters` parameter described in Section 6.4.4 allows you to define parameters that are read by the SAP Application Integrator directly and are not transferred to the Web Dynpro application. You can use this mechanism to provide the SAP Application Integrator with all of the parameters required to describe the relevant Web Dynpro application.

When you select a Web Dynpro application in the NavigationTester, this is automatically added, as shown in Figure 6.32.

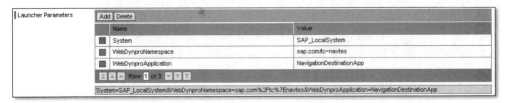

Figure 6.32 Defining Parameters for the SAP Application Integrator

The `System` parameter defines the system alias of the SAP NetWeaver installation on which the Web Dynpro application is to be executed. Since the NavigationTester only displays the Web Dynpro applications that are deployed on the local installation, `SAP_LocalSystem` can always be used here.

The value of the `WebDynproNamespace` parameter comprises the following components:

```
WebDynproNamespace = <vendor>/<DC name>
```

If you are using local Web Dynpro Eclipse projects, `<vendor>` always has the value `local`. The `<DC name>` is the name of your local Web Dynpro Eclipse project. If you use Web Dynpro development components, define the `<vendor>` as part of the description of the development component. The `<DC name>` is the name of the development component used. For the `NavigationDestinationApp` application, the relevant value is therefore the `sap.com/tc~navtes` value shown in Figure 6.32.

The `WebDynproApplication` contains the application name of the application, that is, `NavigationDestinationApp`. The Web Dynpro NavigationTester calculates the value required for the `launcherParameters` parameter from the parameters specified. For the example above, this is as follows:

```
System=SAP_LocalSystem
    &WebDynproNamespace=sap.com%2Ftc%7Enavtes
    &WebDynproApplication=NavigationDestinationApp
```

As you can see, the individual parameters were URL-encoded to ensure a correct transfer.

Using the Web Dynpro iView Template

After you have defined the parameters required for the SAP Application Integrator, you must ensure that the SAP Application Integrator is actually called during navigation.

You can, in principle, use any Web Dynpro iView. In this case, the `System`, `WebDynproNamespace` and `WebDynproApplication` parameters discussed above are already predefined according to the desired Web Dynpro application. Nevertheless, because the SAP Application Inte-

Using a Web
Dynpro iView

grator overwrites statically defined parameter values with dynami-cally transferred parameter values, the desired application is still started.

However, we want to use the generic Web Dynpro iView template, which is installed as part of the SAP NetWeaver Portal. You will find this template in the Portal Content Catalog under **Portal Content · Content Provided by SAP · Templates · iView Templates · SAP Web Dynpro iView**, as shown in Figure 6.33.

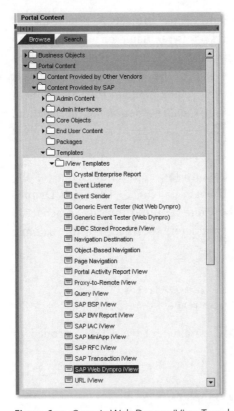

Figure 6.33 Generic Web Dynpro iView Template

As soon as you select a Web Dynpro application in the Navigation-Tester, the iView template is selected and the (absolute or relative) target address is set to `ROLES://portal_content/com.sap.pct/ templates/iviews/com.sap.portal.sap_webdynpro_iview`.

Figure 6.34 shows the NavigationTester after a Web Dynpro applica-tion has been selected.

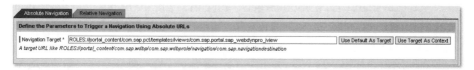

Figure 6.34 NavigationTester After the Selection of a Web Dynpro Application

6.4.6 Shared Use of Large Datasets

Before we turn to the question of how navigation targets are displayed (see Section 6.5), we will address a frequently asked question regarding navigating between different Web Dynpro applications.

As you have seen in the previous chapter, you can specify any parameters for navigating from one Web Dynpro application to another. Typically, you use these parameters to define how the target application is to be started. Again, the Web Dynpro MusicBox (see Chapter 8) serves as an example. Here, you define the name of the desired artist as an application parameter when you start the artist search. The Web Dynpro Google search (see Chapter 4) imports this value when the search is started and automatically displays the search results found for the artist defined. Therefore, provided that you want to transfer only a few parameters between two Web Dynpro applications, you should use application parameters.

Using application parameters

A different situation arises, however, if you want to use large datasets in two (or more) Web Dynpro applications simultaneously because, for example, retrieval of this data is extremely time- and resource-intensive. In this case, we can only recommend that you use Web Dynpro components and component interfaces to combine Web Dynpro applications in a single application.

> **Tip**
>
> We strongly recommend that you do not park large datasets in the HTTP session, for example. This may result in unexpected problems, in particular, if your SAP NetWeaver installation is handling a heavy load.

6.5 Display of Navigation Targets

The above sections have explored in detail the options for navigating between Web Dynpro applications inside and outside the SAP NetWeaver Portal. In this section, we'll look at the display of the available navigation targets. Since the number of possible navigation targets may be very large, they are displayed in a tree structure in the Web Dynpro NavigationTester, as shown in Figure 6.35.

At the highest level, a basic distinction is made between **Web Dynpro applications** and the available iViews and portal pages (**Portal Content**).

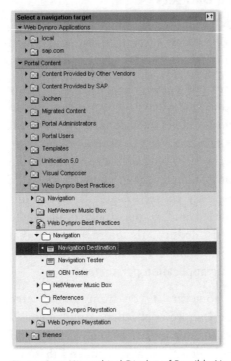

Figure 6.35 Hierarchical Display of Possible Navigation Targets

Structure of the Web Dynpro applications

The available Web Dynpro applications are displayed at three levels. The first level comprises the existing vendors. The second level represents the Web Dynpro development components and Web Dynpro Eclipse projects, and the third level is made up of the Web Dynpro applications that are defined within a Web Dynpro development component or within an Eclipse project. This basic structure is shown in Figure 6.36.

Structure of the iViews and portal pages

The available iViews and portal pages are displayed according to their structure in the Portal Content Directory (PCD). As we will see later, the structure displayed in the NavigationTester corresponds roughly to the structure displayed in the Portal Content Catalog. The process of mapping these desired structure levels in the Web Dynpro NavigationTester is discussed below.

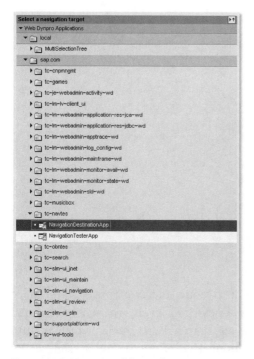

Figure 6.36 Structure of the Web Dynpro Applications

6.5.1 Mapping Hierarchical Structures in the Web Dynpro Context

All data to be displayed in a Web Dynpro application must be mapped in a Web Dynpro context. Without Web Dynpro contexts, you cannot transport data (automatically) between different Web Dynpro components or Web Dynpro views. In addition, if a relevant view controller context does not exist, data cannot be bound between the data structures and the UI elements. Without data binding, the data cannot be transported to the client and, above all, the (changed) data cannot be transported back from the client to the Web Dynpro runtime.

Meaning of the Web Dynpro context

The desired navigation targets are therefore mapped in the form of a hierarchical context in this case. Figure 6.37 shows the definition of the relevant ContentNode context node, which models the desired structure of the navigation targets. This structure of the ContentNode node very clearly matches the desired hierarchical display.

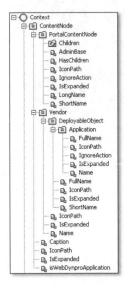

Figure 6.37 Defining the ContentNode Context Node for the Display of Available Navigation Targets

Below the `ContentNode` context node, the two `PortalContentNode` and `Vendor` nodes define the next two levels. The available portal content is then mapped using the `Children` node, which in turn recursively contains an additional `PortalContentNode`. The `Vendor` node contains the `DeployableObject` node, which defines the Web Dynpro development components or Eclipse Web Dynpro projects. Finally, the `Application` node defines the particular applications within a deployable object.

Defining hierarchical context nodes

There are essentially two different approaches to defining a hierarchical context node. The entire hierarchy can either be modeled in the form of a nested context node, or it can be based on the definition of a *recursive context node*.

A combination of these two approaches is used in the Web Dynpro NavigationTester. The available Web Dynpro applications are defined by nested nodes, while the iViews and portal pages (or the available portal content) are defined by a recursive context node.

Defining Nested Context Nodes

To define a nested node hierarchy, open the context menu of the relevant parent node and select **New · Value Node** (see Figure 6.38). In the dialog box that opens, enter the name of the desired child node, which is referred to as the *inner node.* After you have successfully created the inner node, you can define any context attributes or additional inner nodes.

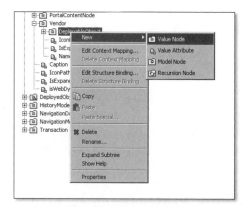

Figure 6.38 Defining an Inner Node

Defining Recursive Context Nodes

To define a recursive context node, open the context menu of the relevant parent node and select **New · Recursion Node** (see Figure 6.39). In this example, a recursive context node is created for the PortalContentNode node.

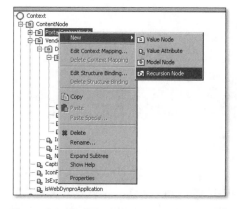

Figure 6.39 Defining a Recursive Context Node

In the dialog box that opens, define the name of the node, which is **Children** in our example (see Figure 6.40). Click on **Finish** to create the recursive node.

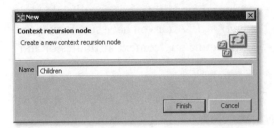

Figure 6.40 Defining the Node Name

After you have successfully created the node, you must define the desired recursion. To do this, open the Properties window of the Children context node. As shown in Figure 6.41, only two properties are defined for Children: the **name** and the **repeatedNode**, which is the node for which the recursion is to be defined.

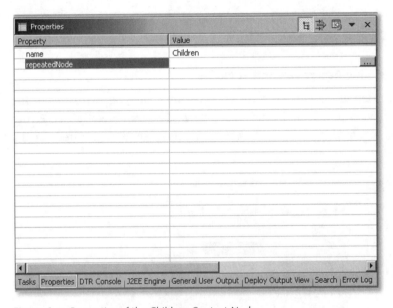

Figure 6.41 Properties of the Children Context Node

To define the relevant value for **repeatedNode**, click the **...** button at the end of this row. In the dialog box that opens, select the relevant node. In Figure 6.42, the PortalContentNode node is selected. All unavailable nodes, that is, nodes that are *not* in the direct node hierarchy of the recursive node, are automatically not available for selection. Click on **OK**. Definition of the Children node is now complete.

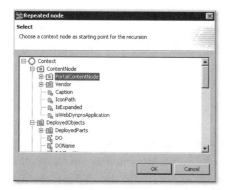

Figure 6.42 Defining the repeatedNode Value

The next section explains how to visualize the node hierarchy you have created. First, however, some special features of context nodes are discussed below, using the PortalContentNode node as an example. You must consider these features when you're defining context nodes if the context node hierarchy is to be visualized using an IWDTree UI element. Figure 6.43 shows the properties of the Portal-ContentNode context node.

Special features of hierarchical nodes

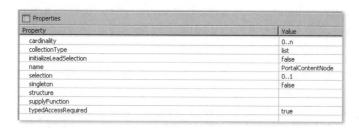

Figure 6.43 Properties of the PortalContentNode Context Node

The following properties are of particular importance if the hierarchy is to be visualized with the IWDTree UI element at a later stage:

▶ **cardinality**

You use the **cardinality** property to define the possible number of context node elements. Since you generally want to be able to display any number of elements of the PortalContentNode node at one level, you must select the value **0..n** for this property.

▶ **initializeLeadSelection**

You use the **initializeLeadSelection** property to determine whether the lead selection is to be automatically set as soon as you generate node elements for a context node. If the IWDTree UI element is used to visualize the context node hiererachy at a later stage, this results in the automatic selection of the first node element when you expand a context node. Therefore, select the value **false** for this property.

▶ **singleton**
You use the **singleton** property to define how the node elements of hierarchical context nodes are to be managed. In a typical master/detail scenario, you set the **singleton** property to **true** to ensure that only the detail node elements that correspond to the current selection of the master node are stored actively in the memory.

However, since we want to use the IWDTree UI element to visualize the context node hierarchy, the **singleton** property must be set to **false** in this case, because we want to display several subtrees simultaneously and the relevant context elements must therefore also be stored actively in the memory at the same time.

▶ **selection**
Since you want to select individual navigation targets later but also prevent automatic selection, the **selection** property is set to **0..1**. Note that the multiple selection is *not* supported in the current version of the IWDTree UI element if you use the IWDTree UI element to visualize your context node.

Required context attributes In addition to the properties described above, you should also define some special context attributes that are useful for visualization with the IWDTree UI element later. Figure 6.44 shows the PortalContentNode node as an example.

Figure 6.44 Context Attributes of the PortalContentNode Context Node

The following attributes are important for visualization at a later stage:

▶ HasChildren
The HasChildren attribute is a **Boolean** attribute that determines

whether a node has additional child nodes. As you will see in the next chapter, the HasChildren attribute is used to ensure that the icon for expanding and collapsing a node is only displayed if the node in question actually contains child nodes.

▶ IconPath

If you want to assign a special icon to each node in the tree, use the IconPath attribute, which is a **string** attribute, to define the relevant path.

▶ IgnoreAction

Because the PortalContentNode node can contain all possible types of portal content objects (that is, folders, worksets or roles, as well as iViews or portal pages), but you only want to make the iViews and portal pages selectable in the visualization of the navigation targets, the IgnoreAction attribute, another **Boolean** attribute, is used to ensure that this holds true for each individual node element. Therefore, selection is possible later for only node elements with IgnoreAction == false.

▶ IsExpanded

The IsExpanded **Boolean** attribute is used to ensure that the current tree status[1] is always retained after each server roundtrip.

▶ ShortName

The ShortName **string** attribute defines the displayed name of the tree node.

After you have defined the desired node hierarchy and assigned the required properties and attributes to the nodes, the nodes can finally be visualized, as described in the next section.

6.5.2 Displaying a Hierarchical Web Dynpro Context

The most obvious way to visualize a hierarchical context structure is to use a tree structure. The IWDTree UI element is therefore used to display the navigation targets and this visualization is defined as part of the BrowserView Web Dynpro view, which is part of the NavigationTesterComp Web Dynpro component. Figure 6.45 shows the view editor with the view designer selected.

Web Dynpro view designer

---

1 The term *tree status* as it is used here describes the status of each individual tree node with regard to the fact as to whether or not the tree node is expanded.

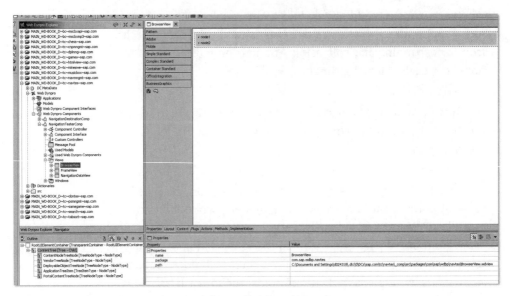

Figure 6.45 View Editor with Selected View Designer

After you have created the required IWDTree UI element, you must define the basic data binding of the UI element, that is, the link between the UI element and the context node or context node attribute that contains the relevant data. An instance of the IWDTree UI element can only visualize *one* single node hierarchy. You define the relevant root node of this hierarchy using the **dataSource** property of the IWDTree UI element (see Figure 6.46). In our example, the ContentNode context node is selected as the data source, which represents the root node of the desired context node hierarchy.

Property	Value
Properties	
Property	Value
⊟ Elementproperties of Tree	
dataSource	ContentNode
defaultItemIconAlt	
defaultItemIconSource	
defaultNodeIconAlt	
defaultNodeIconSource	
enabled	true
id	ContentTree
layoutdata	MatrixHeadData
minHeight	
rootText	
rootVisible	false
title	Select a navigation target
titleVisible	visible
tooltip	<>
visible	visible
width	100%
⊞ LayoutData[MatrixHeadData]	

Figure 6.46 Defining the DataSource of the IWDTree UI Element

After you have generated the IWDTree UI element and assigned the
relevant data source, you must define a *tree node type* for each desired
visualization level. The various visualization levels correspond to the
various inner nodes in the hierarchical context, with the Content-
Node node as the root node.

Defining the tree
node type

The tree node type can be either *tree node* or *tree item*. Tree nodes are
real nodes in the tree, that is, nodes that may in turn have child
nodes. Tree items, on the other hand, are nodes that serve only as
leaves or end nodes in the tree, that is, they have no child nodes. To
generate a tree node type, open the context menu of the ContentTree
UI element and select **Insert Node Type** (see Figure 6.47).

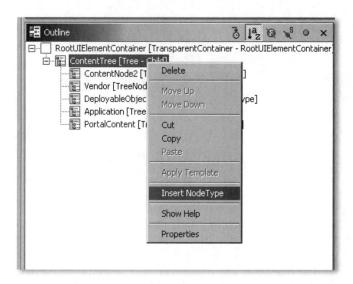

Figure 6.47 Generating a New Tree Node Type

In the dialog box that opens, select the name (**Id**) and type (**Type**) of
the tree node type. In our example, we want to create a tree node for
the ContentNode context note (see Figure 6.48).

You can, in principle, choose any name for a tree node. However, we
recommend that you use a meaningful name that clearly indicates
which context node is visualized with the tree node type.

Defining the name
of a tree node type

All other tree node types are created the same way as the Content-
Node tree node; however, you use a tree item for the Application
context node. Figure 6.49 shows the five tree node types created,
one for each level in the hierarchy of the context node.

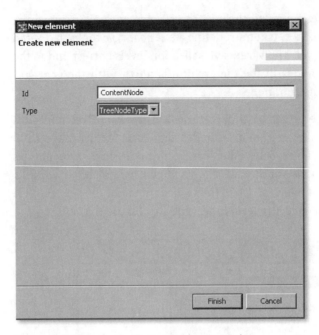

Figure 6.48 Defining the ContentNode Tree Node

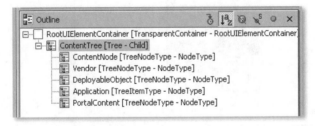

Figure 6.49 Tree Node Types Created to Visualize the Navigation Targets

Sequence of tree node types The sequence of tree node types is not crucial here. In this case, the visual display is not determined by the sequence of the individual tree node types in the outline view, but rather by the definition or structure of the context nodes used.

Section 6.5.1 used the example of the PortalContentTreeNode context node to address the question regarding which context nodes are useful and necessary for visualizing the node using the IWDTree UI element at a later stage. To use these context attributes, you must bind the relevant properties of the PortalContent tree node to the relevant context attributes, as shown in Figure 6.50.

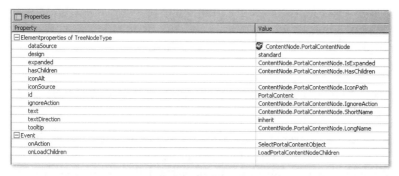

Figure 6.50 Properties of the PortalContent Tree Node

Thanks to the self-explanatory names of the individual context attributes, the process of data binding is fairly automatic. For example, the **expanded** property is bound to the `IsExpanded` attribute and the **hasChildren** property is bound to the `HasChildren` attribute.

Data binding to define the tree node types

After you have linked all required tree node types with the corresponding context attributes, you must, as a final step, fill the relevant nodes of the context hierarchy with elements. The next section therefore explores how you can obtain a list of Web Dynpro applications, before importing the available iViews and portal pages.

6.5.3 Importing the Available Web Dynpro Applications

Information about the available entities, in other words, the entities deployed in the SAP NetWeaver system, such as applications or components, is required in most of the examples used in this book.

In the Web Dynpro GameStation (see Chapter 3), for example, a list of all available Web Dynpro components that implement a special Web Dynpro component interface is required. The following sections explain how to display a list of all available Web Dynpro applications in the NavigationTester.

Using the DeploymentManagerComp Web Dynpro Component

This information is provided by the `DeploymentManagerComp` Web Dynpro component, which is discussed in detail in Appendix A. The DeploymentManager is a good example of a *faceless Web Dynpro com-*

Faceless components

ponent, that is, a Web Dynpro component that does not define any UI elements, but rather provides only data or functions, or, in other words, is similar to a service.

To use the DeploymentManager in the NavigationTester, you must first define a relevant component usage for each usage of a Web Dynpro component.

Referencing the public part

Since the DeploymentManagerComp component is contained in the tc~dplmng Web Dynpro development component rather than the NavigationTester, you must define a Used DC dependency for the corresponding DeploymentManager public part in the tc~dplmng development component, as described in Section 6.3.1 (see Figure 6.51). The DeploymentManagerComp component cannot be used until this Used DC dependency has been defined.

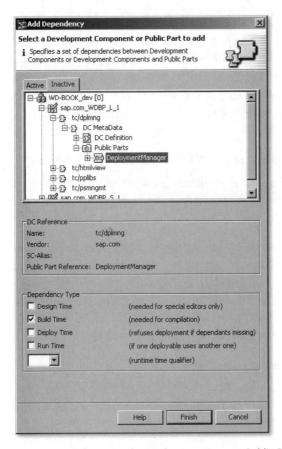

Figure 6.51 Referencing the DeploymentManager Public Part

To define the relevant component usage, select **Add Used Component** from the context menu of the **Used Web Dynpro Components** of the NavigationTester project in the Web Dynpro Explorer (see Figure 6.52).

Creating the Deployment-Manager component usage

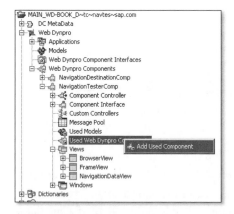

Figure 6.52 Defining a Component Usage

In the dialog box that appears, select the name of the component usage. Choose **Browse** and then select the relevant Web Dynpro component. Figure 6.53 shows the existing components. In addition to all components contained in the NavigationTester project, the DeploymentManagerComp component is also shown.

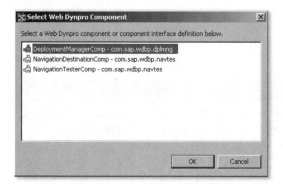

Figure 6.53 Selecting the DeploymentManagerComp Component

Select this component and click on **OK** to confirm. You have now defined all parameters required for the DeploymentManager component usage, as shown in Figure 6.54. Finally, click on **Finish** to generate the component usage.

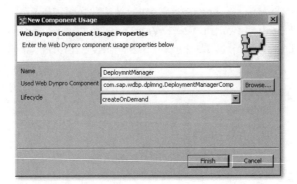

Figure 6.54 The DeploymentManager Component Usage

Accessing the DeploymentManager Data

After you have successfully defined the DeploymentManager component usage, you can access the data and functions made available by
the component. In our example, a list is required of the available
Web Dynpro applications provided by the DeploymentManagerComp
component through the DeployedObjects context node in the component interface controller context.

Using context
mapping

Although a list of the applications is ultimately required in the
BrowserView Web Dynpro view, you should not access the DeploymentManagerComp directly from this view. Instead, the component
controller context of the NavigationTesterComp component is used
as an abstraction layer. This avoids a direct dependency between the
DeploymentManager component usage and the BrowserView Web
Dynpro view.

> **Tip**
>
> Never map directly from a Web Dynpro view to an interface controller
> context of a component usage. Instead, use the corresponding compo-
> nent controller context or a specific custom controller context. This
> abstraction makes it easier to extend or change the component usage
> later.

Figure 6.55 shows context mapping between the component interface controller context of the DeploymentManagerComp component
and the component controller context of the NavigationTesterComp
component. As you can see, the complete DeployedObjects context
node is required for a list of available applications.

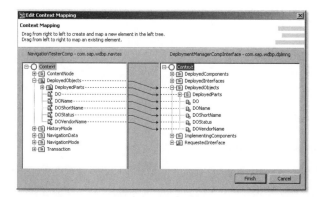

Figure 6.55 Accessing the Component Interface Controller Context of the Deployment/Manager

Finally, to transport the DeployedObjects node into the BrowserView view, you must define an additional context mapping between the view controller context and the component controller context of the NavigationTesterComp component.

Detecting the Available Applications

After you have used the relevant context mapping to transport the DeployableObject node into the BrowserView Web Dynpro view, you can obtain a list of the available Web Dynpro applications. This is done in the onActionLoadApplications() action event handler of the LoadApplications action (see Listing 6.10).

```
for (int i = 0;
    i < wdContext.nodeDeployedObjects().size();
    i++) {

  IPrivateBrowserView.IDeployedObjectsElement object =
    wdContext.nodeDeployedObjects()
      .getDeployedObjectsElementAt(i);

  if (deployableObject.getFullName()
      .equals(object.getDOName())) {

    for (int j = 0;
        j < object.nodeDeployedParts().size();
        j++) {

      IPrivateBrowserView.IDeployedPartsElement part =
```

```
      object.nodeDeployedParts()
        .getDeployedPartsElementAt(j);

    if (part.getType()
      .equals(WDDeployableObjectPartType
        .APPLICATION.toString())) {

    IPrivateBrowserView.IApplicationElement application =
      deployableObject.nodeApplication()
        .createApplicationElement();

    application.setFullName(part.getFullName());
    application.setName(part.getShortName());
    application.setIconPath(APPLICATION);

    deployableObject.nodeApplication()
      .addElement(application);
    }
  }
  deployableObject.nodeApplication().sortElements(
    new NodeElementByAttributeComparator("Name", true));
  }
}
```

Listing 6.10 Detecting the Available Web Dynpro Applications

Since the `DeployableObject` context node not only provides Web Dynpro applications, but also all other Web Dynpro entities such as Web Dynpro components and Web Dynpro component interfaces, `WDDeployableObjectPartType.APPLICATION` is used to filter the applications. Create an `Application` context node for each of the Web Dynpro applications that you want to be able to detect, and set the relevant attributes.

Sorting the application node elements

Lastly, use the **Name** attribute to sort the generated `Application` node elements. The generic `NodeElementByAttributeComparator`, to which the `URLEncode` utility has been bound using the `Utils` public part of the `tc~utils` development component, is used for this purpose.

6.5.4 Optimized Display of Hierarchy Levels

When you visualize the various navigation targets, you want to ensure that the initial display of these destinations does not take too long. Therefore, you do not want all possible navigation targets to be found and displayed when the NavigationTester is initially started. Instead, you want only those navigation targets that are explicitly requested by the user to be found and displayed. This prevents an unnecessarily high rate of memory consumption, because the relevant node elements for all possible hierarchy levels don't have to be stored in the memory at the same time. In addition, the rendering time on the client is reduced, that is, the time required by the web browser to display the transferred HTML.

> **Tip**
>
> If you want to use the IWDTree UI element to display context hierarchies with many levels, ensure that you don't generate all available levels initially. This is important because the corresponding node elements require additional memory. Furthermore, node elements may also be rendered automatically, even if the corresponding hierarchy levels will be invisible, because the tree displays only the highest levels initially.

In the NavigationTester, the required hierarchy levels should therefore only be generated when the user expands the parent node of the new hierarchy level. The onLoadChildren event of the various tree nodes is used for this purpose. This is illustrated below using the example of the DeployableObject tree node. Figure 6.56 shows the LoadApplications action of the BrowserView action assigned to the onLoadChildren event.

Using the onLoad-Children event

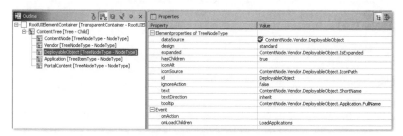

Figure 6.56 Assigning the LoadApplications Action to the onLoadChildren Event

When you have assigned a relevant Web Dynpro action to the onLoadChildren event for a tree node, this action is called as soon as the user tries to display the child node of the tree node by clicking on the icon for expanding and collapsing the tree node.

In principle, you can assign any Web Dynpro action to the onLoadChildren event. However, *parameter mapping* allows you to easily

Using parameter mapping

access the currently selected tree node (or the context node element linked to the tree node).

To use parameter mapping for the LoadApplications action in our example, you must first define a relevant action parameter, which then contains the selected context node element when the action (or the corresponding onLoadApplications event handler) is called. In our example, this is the deployableObject parameter of the type com.sap.wdbp.navtes.wdp.IPrivateBrowserView.IDeployable-ObjectElement.

The deployableObject parameter therefore describes exactly one node element of the DeployableObject node. This is precisely the element that is used for visualization by the DeployableObject tree node. Figure 6.57 shows the definition of the LoadApplications action with the required deployableObject action parameter.

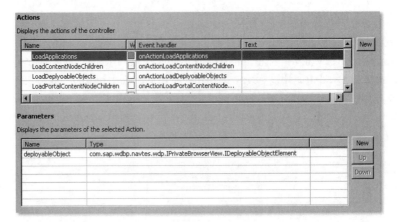

Figure 6.57 The LoadApplications Action

After you have assigned the deployableObject parameter to the LoadApplications action, you must, as a final step, ensure that this parameter is filled with the correct value as soon as the user expands the DeployableObject tree node, which causes the LoadApplications action to be called.

As mentioned above, parameter mapping is used for this purpose. It allows you to map the generic path parameter, which is transferred with each action and always contains the context node element that is currently selected, to the deployableObject parameter. This mapping is defined as standard within the wdDoModify() method.

Listing 6.11 shows the relevant parameter mapping for the `Deploy-`
`ableObject` tree node.

```
IWDTreeNodeType deployableObjectTreeNode =
  (IWDTreeNodeType) view.getElement("DeployableObject");

deployableObjectTreeNode.mappingOfOnLoadChildren()
  .addSourceMapping("path", "deployableObject");
```

Listing 6.11 Defining the Parameter Mapping for the LoadApplications Action

The parameter mapping just described is also used to define and fill
the `deployableObject` parameter shown in Listing 6.10. All other
tree nodes of the `BrowserView` use a similar parameter mapping so
that the next hierarchical level is not generated until the user explicitly requests it.

6.5.5   Selecting a Navigation Target

Ultimately, you want to provide users with an easy way of selecting
their desired navigation targets from the list displayed in the Web
Dynpro NavigationTester. In addition to navigating through the various hierarchical levels of the navigation targets, users should also be
able to select individual navigation targets. For this purpose, you use
the `onAction` event of the individual tree nodes.

Because not all of the available hierarchy levels constitute relevant
navigation targets, defining the selection behavior must be controlled separately for each of the individual tree nodes. This is easy to
do for the `PortalContent`, `Vendor` and `DeployableObject` tree nodes,
which must never be selectable. In this case, you simply don't link
the `onAction` event of this tree node with any Web Dynpro action.

Figure 6.58 Defining the onAction Event with the SelectApplication Action

For the `Application` tree item, which must always be selectable, you assign the relevant `SelectApplication` action of the `BrowserView` Web Dynpro view to the `onAction` event, as shown in Figure 6.58.

Using the ignore-Action property

A more specific distinction is required for the `PortalContent` tree node, which can potentially display all types of portal entities (such as iViews, portal pages, worksets or roles). The `ignoreAction` property, which is bound to the `IgnoreAction` attribute of the `PortalContent` context node, is used in this case (see also Figure 6.50).

Only iViews or portal pages can be selected

The `IgnoreAction` attribute is only set to **false** (see Listing 6.12 below) for context node elements that represent an iView or a portal page, in other words, selectable portal entities.

```
if (type.equals(IVIEW) || type.equals(PAGE)) {
  childElement.setIgnoreAction(false);
  childElement.setLongName(catalogNode.getId());
} else {
  childElement.setIgnoreAction(true);
}
```

Listing 6.12 Defining the ignoreAction Attribute

You generate the required `PortalContentNode` context node elements in the `createSubTreeForPortalContentNode()` method of the `BrowserView` Web Dynpro view. You generate one new hierarchy level of the hierarchical `PortalContentNode` context node in each case.

6.5.6 Executing a JNDI Lookup from a Web Dynpro Application

To import the available portal entities and generate the relevant `PortalContentNode` context node elements, you utilize the fact that the portal content directory ultimately represents a conventional *Java Naming and Directory Interface* (JNDI) provider. This means that you can use JNDI lookups to navigate through the available portal entities and import the required hierarchy levels.

Determining the JNDI root context

While a detailed discussion of these JNDI lookups lies outside the scope of this book, a brief introduction is provided below. Listing 6.13 shows the `getAdminBaseRoot()` method, in which the `adminBaseRoot` JNDI root object is determined.

```
private IAdminBase getAdminBaseRoot() {
if (adminBaseRoot == null) {
  try {
    Hashtable environment = new Hashtable();
    environment.put(
      Context.SECURITY_PRINCIPAL,
      WDClientUser.getCurrentUser().getSAPUser());
    environment.put(
      "locale",
      WDResourceHandler.getCurrentSessionLocale());
    environment.put(
      "com.sap.portal.jndi.requested_aspect",
      PcmConstants.ASPECT_ADMINISTRATION);
    environment.put(
      Constants.APPLY_ASPECT_TO_CONTEXTS,
      Constants.APPLY_ASPECT_TO_CONTEXTS);

    InitialContext ic = new InitialContext(environment);
    Object obj = ic.lookup("pcd:portal_content");

    adminBaseRoot = (IAdminBase) obj;

  } catch (Exception e) {
    IWDMessageManager msgMgr =
      wdThis.wdGetAPI().getComponent().getMessageManager();
    msgMgr.reportException(
      "Failed to load root admin base for
        'pcd:portal_content': "
      + e.getLocalizedMessage(),
      true);
  }
}
}
```

Listing 6.13 Generating the Root Object for the JNDI Lookups

While more details cannot be provided here, note the relevant definition of the *JNDI environment*. Here you define the language in which the relevant text attributes of the portal entities are defined.

Defining the JNDI environment

6.6 Summary

In this chapter, we discussed in detail all aspects that must be addressed when navigating between two Web Dynpro applications both inside and outside the SAP NetWeaver Portal.

You have seen why you must always consider the existing runtime environment in your Web Dynpro application. We have also explained the differences between defining absolute and relative target addresses, and you should now be familiar with the correct procedure for encoding the required transfer parameters. In addition, we have explored the options for defining the desired navigation behavior, which differ significantly depending on whether navigation is started inside or outside the SAP NetWeaver Portal.

Lastly, you have seen how large hierarchical data structures can be modeled within the Web Dynpro context and displayed using the `IWDTree` UI element. We have paid special attention to the dynamic reloading of hierarchy levels, which allows you to optimize the display of hierarchical data.

Apart from the options regarding the navigation between different Web Dynpro applications inside and outside the SAP NetWeaver Portal introduced in Chapter 6, you can also use object-based navigation (OBN). We will describe OBN in this chapter.

7 Web Dynpro OBNTester

As we have discussed in Chapter 6, when using absolute and relative portal navigation, you navigate to well-defined iViews or portal pages that must be known when the navigation step is triggered by a program. This way you can implement many scenarios, as you can see in the examples of the Web Dynpro NavigationTester (see Chapter 6) and the Web Dynpro MusicBox (see Chapter 8).

However, we also mentioned the problems and restrictions of the usual portal navigation in Chapter 6. Although the use of the relative addresses of the navigation targets provides a much higher degree of flexibility compared to using absolute addresses, you must always commit yourself to using concrete iViews or portal pages.

A description of the navigation target at a higher semantic level is often much more useful and even required. For example, that's the case if you want to navigate to the detail view of a displayed object instead of navigating to a specific iView or portal page. The iView or portal page that will actually implement the detail view is often not known at the time the Web Dynpro application is implemented.

Abstract description of the navigation target

Furthermore, it can be very useful to define the detail view at a later stage depending on the user and the user's (portal) roles, for instance in order to ensure that the detail view of the manager is different from that of the employee.

Reference to the role of a user

It is exactly this level of abstraction that's introduced with the *object-based navigation (OBN)*. When using object-based navigation, you do not navigate to specific iViews or portal pages because you call specific *operations* of a *business object (BO)* instead. Depending on certain

Business objects and the operations related to them

configurations, the correct iView or portal page is determined dynamically when an object-based navigation is launched. This mapping process from a rather abstract operation of a business object to the actual iView or portal page occurs completely transparently to the application developer.

7.1   The Web Dynpro OBNTester

In the following example we'll demonstrate the possibilities and usage of object-based navigation within a Web Dynpro application by using the *Web Dynpro OBNTester*. In addition to that we'll discuss the use of *portal services* within a Web Dynpro application. Those portal services enable you, for instance, to identify the list of defined business objects within the OBNTester.

Downloading the OBNTester   The Web Dynpro OBNTester is implemented in the Web Dynpro component TesterComp stored in Web Dynpro project MAIN_WD-BOOK_D~tc~obntes~sap.com. The corresponding Web Dynpro development component is tc\obntes.

You can use the Web Dynpro OBNTester to trigger any navigation step of the object-based navigation. Moreover, the OBNTester represents an elegant means of testing the correctness of existing configurations and also enables you to define any type of transfer parameter that are forwarded whenever a navigation step is triggered. This option should remind you of the Web Dynpro NavigationTester. Figure 7.1 shows the Web Dynpro OBNTester.

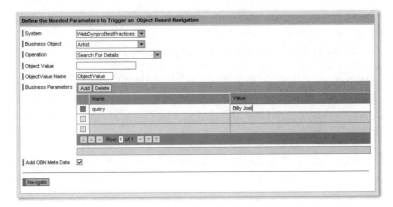

Figure 7.1 Web Dynpro OBNTester

As we'll use different portal services within the OBNTester, the Web Dynpro OBNTester can only run on an SAP NetWeaver installation that also runs the SAP NetWeaver Portal.

Figure 7.2 shows the basic structure of the Web Dynpro OBNTester. **Basic structure** It is a very simple Web Dynpro application that consists of only one Web Dynpro component and the Web Dynpro view `TesterView` that is responsible for the display.

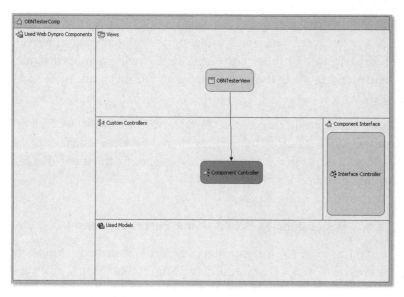

Figure 7.2 Structure of the Web Dynpro OBNTester

Before we describe the specific characteristics of object-based navigation, we'll discuss in Section 7.2 how you can access portal services in your Web Dynpro application and which interdependencies you must take into account when doing so.

7.2   Using Portal Services

In addition to the Web Dynpro runtime environment responsible for **Portal runtime** executing your Web Dynpro applications, the *portal runtime* (PRT) represents a critical runtime environment for user interfaces within an SAP NetWeaver installation.

The PRT can manage and launch *portal components*. Portal compo- **Portal components** nents enable you to implement simple user interfaces by means of a

JSP-based or servlet-based programming model. Compared to the declarative possibilities provided by the Web Dynpro programming model, the use of portal components requires more manual work from the developer. On the other hand, the open architecture of the portal components provides you an increased number of ways to implement very special requirements to your user interfaces. Naturally, you cannot use the options provided by the Web Dynpro programming model with regard to client abstraction.

Portal-specific UIs

Virtually all the portal-specific user interfaces in SAP NetWeaver 2004 have been developed using portal components. However, more and more of those portal-specific UIs will have been implemented using Web Dynpro for Java in the next release of SAP NetWeaver.

Portal services

Apart from portal components, *portal services* are available. Like the faceless Web Dynpro components, portal services usually do not define any separate UI, but they provide specific functions that can be used by other portal components.

7.2.1 Dependencies When Using Portal Services

Portal installations

As soon as your Web Dynpro application is launched within SAP NetWeaver Portal, you can call any portal service that is available. However, you should remember that when a Web Dynpro application uses a portal service, the application can only run on SAP NetWeaver installations that contain the SAP NetWeaver Portal.

> **Tip**
>
> When using portal services in your Web Dynpro application you should always check what SAP NetWeaver installations you will want for running your Web Dynpro application in the future. For example, if you want to run your Web Dynpro application on installations that do not contain the SAP NetWeaver Portal, the use of a portal service would represent a dependency that is not allowed. Note, however, that the simple integration of a Web Dynpro application into the SAP NetWeaver Portal by means of a Web Dynpro iView does *not* involve such dependencies.

As long as you don't use any portal services, you can run your Web Dynpro application without any problem on an SAP NetWeaver installation that does *not* contain an SAP NetWeaver Portal. Using the corresponding Web Dynpro iView you can run the application without a problem in the SAP NetWeaver Portal. Chapter 2 described the various options for designing the system landscape in which you want to run your Web Dynpro applications.

7.2.2 Using a Portal Service

In order to launch a portal service within your Web Dynpro application you must take two aspects into account. First, you must make sure that the required Java interfaces and classes are available at the time when your Web Dynpro application is designed in order to ensure a correct compilation of your application. Second, you must make sure that the portal service you want to use is available and running when you launch your Web Dynpro application. Let us first take a look at the aspects related to the time of design.

Design-Time Aspects

Unfortunately, SAP NetWeaver Developer Studio does currently not provide any standard way to make the required Java interfaces and classes of a portal service visible to your Web Dynpro application. If you use Web Dynpro Eclipse projects, we recommend you include the required Java Archives (JARs) that contain the Java interfaces and classes directly in the class path of your Web Dynpro project.

Extending the class path of a Web Dynpro project

Because we have developed all examples in this book on the basis of Web Dynpro development components, we decided on a different way for the Web Dynpro OBNTester as well as for all other examples used in this book that access portal services: We have to define a specific development component, tc~pplibs, that provides the Java Archives (JARs) of all required portal services centrally. To make this development component available to the Web Dynpro OBNTester, you must define a public-part relationship to the PortalLibraries public part of the development component tc~pplibs[1], as shown in Figure 7.3. This process is similar to the use of the tc~utils development component in the Web Dynpro NavigationTester (see Chapter 6).

Referencing the public part "Portal-Libraries"

---

1 Chapter 9 describes how to create the tc~pplibs development component and discusses its definition in greater detail.

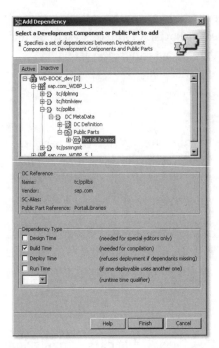

Figure 7.3 Referencing the PortalLibraries Public Part

Including the JARs into the class path

Once you have defined the reference to the `PortalLibraries` public part, the JARs contained therein are automatically included into the class path of the Web Dynpro project (see Figure 7.4).

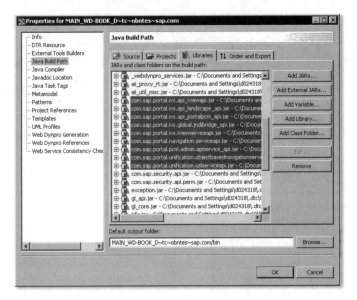

Figure 7.4 Referenced JARs

Runtime Aspects

As soon as you use a portal service within your Web Dynpro application, you must define specific references. This requirement is similar to using Web Dynpro components across different development components. Based on those references, the Web Dynpro runtime environment can then determine the required class-loader dependencies. For portal services you must define specific sharing references that describe the portal services being used.

Defining sharing references

Figure 7.5 shows the defined sharing references for the Web Dynpro OBNTester. As you can see, a sharing reference to a portal service consists of the following elements:

```
PORTAL:<Vendor>/<Fully qualified name of the portal service>
```

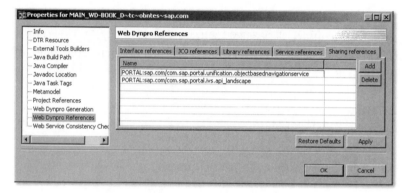

Figure 7.5 Required Sharing References to Portal Services

`<Vendor>` describes the vendor; for portal services that's usually `sap.com`. Theoretically, you can also use customer-specific portal services, but you must also select the corresponding `<Vendor>` value for those services. The fully qualified name of the portal service corresponds to the directory of the portal service located below the following directory:

```
C:\usr\sap\<SystemName>\JC<InstanceName>\j2ee\cluster\
   server<Node>\apps\sap.com\irj\servlet_jsp\irj\root\
   WEB-INF\portal\portalapps.
```

To be able to appropriately deploy a Web Dynpro application that calls one or more portal services, you must make sure that all portal services being used have also been deployed correctly and that they

Dependencies in deployment

have been started. If that is not the case, errors can occur, and your Web Dynpro application cannot be started because the referenced portal services are not available. Chapter 10 describes the available options for identifying and resolving such error situations in great detail.

7.2.3   Accessing a Portal Service

Portal services being used

We need two portal services in the Web Dynpro OBNTester: We'll use the portal service `com.sap.portal.ivs.api.landscape` to access the list of systems and system aliases defined in the portal landscape. The service `com.sap.portal.unification.objectbasednavigation-service` will be used to determine the list of valid navigation targets for any business object.

To access a portal service within your Web Dynpro application, you must use the utility class `WDPortalUtils` (see Listing 7.1). This class is called in the `wdDoInit()` method of the component controller of component `TesterComp`.

```
IUserObjectBasedNavigation obnService =
  (IUserObjectBasedNavigation)
    WDPortalUtils.getServiceReference(
      IUserObjectBasedNavigation.KEY);
wdContext.currentPortalServicesElement()
  .setOBNService(obnService);

ISystems landscapeService =
  (ISystems) WDPortalUtils.
    getServiceReference(ISystems.KEY);
wdContext.currentPortalServicesElement().
  setLandscapeService(landscapeService);
```

Listing 7.1 Accessing Portal Services

The `getServiceReference()` method provides an untyped reference to the required portal service. You can define the required key via `<Portal-Service-Interface>.KEY`.

Saving the service references

In the above example we'll save the determined references in the `PortalService` context node of the component controller which then forwards the references to the Web Dynpro view `OBNTester-View`. This way you can make sure that the required references to the portal services are only generated when the Web Dynpro component OBNTesterComp is instantiated.

Tip

If possible, you should avoid repeated getServiceReference() calls for identical portal services within a Web Dynpro application instance. Depending on the portal service you use, this can cause unnecessary memory consumption and a decrease of system performance.

7.2.4 Importing the Defined Systems

We want to finish this section with a brief description of using the portal service ISystems that enables you to access the (system) information of the portal landscape. Listing 7.2 shows the updateSystems() method of the view controller of Web Dynpro view OBNTesterView. The view controller is called to determine the list of available systems and system aliases when the Web Dynpro OBNTester is launched.

```
private void updateSystems() {
  // Access to portal service
  ISystems landscapeService =
    wdContext.currentPortalServiceElement()
      .getLandscapeService();

  // Invalidate system context node
  wdContext.nodeSystem().invalidate();

  IPrivateOBN TesterView.ISystemElement system = null;

  // Import all defined system aliases
  String[] aliases = landscapeService.getAliases();

  // Create required node elements
  for (int i = 0; i < aliases.length; i++) {
    system =
      wdContext.nodeSystem().createSystemElement();
    system.setCaption(aliases[i]);
    system.setName(aliases[i]);
    wdContext.nodeSystem().addElement(system);
  }
}
```

Listing 7.2 Importing the Defined System Aliases

7.3 Triggering Object-Based Navigation

To trigger an object-based navigation the utility class
WDPortalNavigation provides several methods. You can use one of
the navigateToObject() methods to trigger a navigation for the
default operation of a business object. Using navigateToObjectFor-
SpecificOperation(), you can explicitly determine a specific operation. The business object is always determined via the following
parameters:

▶ system

You can use the system parameter to define the system alias for
which the business object has been defined.

▶ businessObjectType

The businessObjectType parameter determines the actual business object. The combination of system and businessObjectType
must be unique as it uniquely defines the required business
object. In Section 7.4.1, we'll describe in great detail how you can
create the required business objects.

▶ objValue

Because you typically use several instances of a business object,
you must also define the actual instance when defining an object-
based navigation. You can do that by using the objValue parameter, which—in most cases—contains an instance ID of some type.

▶ operation

In addition to the definition of the business object, you must
select the required operation, which can be done using the operation parameter.

7.3.1 Defining Transfer Parameters

Moreover, similar to the absolute or relative portal navigation, the
object-based navigation also provides the option to define any type
of transfer parameter.

▶ objValueName

If you use the objValue parameter, you can define the required
instance of the selected business object. Because the object-based
navigation will be mapped to a usual portal navigation, that value
is transferred to all parameters. The objValueName parameter can

be used to define the name of the parameter. Here, the default value is `ObjectValue`.

Figure 7.6 shows the definition of the `objValueName` parameter within the Web Dynpro OBNTester. In this case, we want to call the **Search for Details** operation of business object **Artist**. Because we want to run the operation for a specific instance—i.e., for a specific artist—we must define the artist by using the `Object Value` parameter (**Billy Joel**).

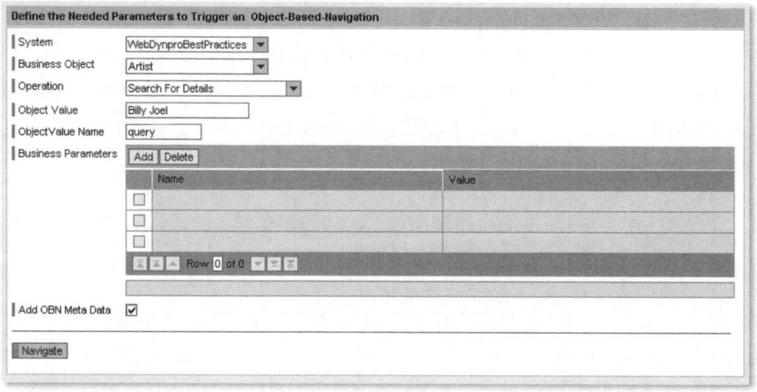

Figure 7.6 Using the objValueName Parameter

By allocating the value **query** to the `Object Value Name` parameter, the iView or portal page that executes the operation which has been called will be started, using the transfer parameter `query=Billy Joel`.

▶ `businessParameters`

As is the case with the `businessParameters` parameter in the absolute and relative portal navigations, you can also define any type or parameter in object-based navigation that are transferred to the navigation target. Concerning the URL encoding, the same rules apply as for the portal navigation.

7.3.2 Forwarding OBN Metadata

It can sometimes be useful to provide the iView that has been called (or the Web Dynpro application launched by it) with additional information on the object-based navigation that is being carried out. You can use the `forwardOBNMetaData` parameter to specify whether the metadata listed below should be defined as additional transfer parameters in the following manner.

▶ obn.system

obn.system describes the system alias that is used to define the business object.

▶ obn.bo_type

obn.bo_type defines the business object that is used in the triggered OBN.

▶ obn.operation

The operation to be executed is defined using the obn.operation parameter. If you don't define the operation so that the default operation is executed instead, the value of obn.operation will be **_default_**.

You can import all those parameters into your Web Dynpro application by using the methods described in Chapter 6.

The use of explicit plug parameters is always helpful when you want to use the transferred metadata to display different views of your Web Dynpro application. For example, if your Web Dynpro provides both a detail view and an overview view which you want to use for the corresponding operations of a business object, the use of the obn.operation parameter enables you to choose the relevant view in the start-up plug.

7.4 Defining Business Objects

Now that you have learned how to trigger an object-based navigation within your Web Dynpro application, we'll describe how to define the required business objects and operations.

7.4.1 Creating Business Objects

As is the case with iView and portal pages, you can also access your business objects within the portal content catalog. You can create new business objects by selecting the context menu item **Import Business Objects** of the **Business Objects** node (see Figure 7.7).

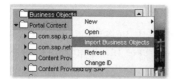

Figure 7.7 Creating a Business Object

Basically, you can import the relevant business objects from any backend system. Those backend systems can either be SAP backend systems or third-party systems.

Importing business objects

However, in the following sections we want to focus on the direct creation of the required business objects. Figure 7.8 shows the definition of business object **Artist**. Here, you must make sure that the combination of **Business Object ID** and **System Alias** defines a unique ID. The (technical) ID of business object **Artist** is `WebDynproBestPractices.Artist`. You then can use the **Business Object Name** to define the displayed name of the business object.

Creating business objects directly

As you'll see in Chapter 8, we'll use the business object **Artist** within the Web Dynpro MusicBox in order to represent the artist or the band of a specific CD or track.

Figure 7.8 Defining the Business Object "Artist"

You can define additional business objects by clicking on the **Add** button. Figure 7.9 shows the list of business objects that we'll use later on within the Web Dynpro MusicBox. Chapter 8 describes the different business objects and their meanings in greater detail.

Figure 7.9 Business Objects Used in the Web Dynpro MusicBox

7.4.2 Defining Operations

Now that we have successfully defined the business object **Artist**, we want to use the *Business Object Editor* to create the required operations. You can launch the Business Object Editor by opening the context menu of the relevant business object and selecting **Open · Object** (see Figure 7.10).

Figure 7.10 Launching the Business Object Editor

As is the case with the other editors, the Business Object Editor also provides the Property Editor that you can use to change the majority of properties. In addition, the Business Object Editor provides two additional views that display the definitions of the required operations and an overview of the linked iViews or portal pages respectively (see Figure 7.11).

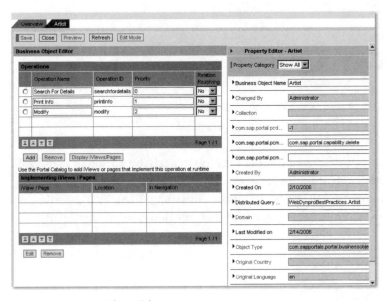

Figure 7.11 Business Object Editor

We'll define a total of three operations for the business object **Artist**. We'll use the **Search For Details** operation within the Web Dynpro

MusicBox to search for additional information on the selected artist. The **Print Info** operation prints the most important information on the artist, and the **Modify** operation enables us to change the information on the artist (see Figure 7.12).

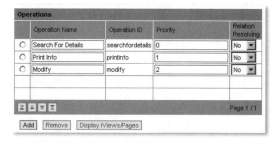

Figure 7.12 Operations of the Business Object "Artist"

The definition of those operations does not yet involve any statement on the future technical completion or implementation of the individual functions. By using the business objects and their operations, you can rather model the required objects and their existing functions without taking into account the technical implementation. It is especially this separation of the modeling and implementation tasks that guarantees the incomparably higher degree of flexibility inherent in object-based navigation, compared to the usual portal navigation.

Separating modeling and implementation

In addition to the **Operation Name** that defines the displayed name of an operation, you must define a unique ID for each operation via **Operation ID**. You can prioritize the individual operations of a business object to match your requirements by using the **Priority** property of an operation: **0** representing the highest priority, and one that should be assigned to the operation that is to be run as default operation. For the business object **Artist** we defined the **Search For Details** operation as default operation.

Prioritizing operations

Now that we have defined the business object and associated operations and thus modeled the required functionality, the next section describes how you can link the defined functionality to actual iViews or portal pages.

7.4.3   Defining the Implementation of an Operation

The use of object-based navigation generally consists of two steps. First, the required functionality is defined using corresponding business objects and their operations. You then use those business objects and operations in your Web Dynpro application in order to call the functionality they describe (see Section 7.3).

iViews or portal pages implement operations

However, in order to actually execute an object-based navigation, a second step is necessary in addition to modeling the required functionality, namely the definition of the required implementation. This can be done by assigning any number of iViews or portal pages to the relevant operation of a business object. Thus, the implementation of an operation is always represented by a specific iView or portal page.

There are two ways to define the implementation of an operation: You can either assign an iView or a portal page to an operation, or you can assign an operation to an iView or a portal page. We'll discuss the differences between these two procedures in the following sections.

Assigning an iView or a portal page to an operation

As soon as you want to assign an iView or a portal page to an operation *irrespective* of a specific role, you can directly assign the iView or portal page to the required operation. To do that, open the context menu of the business object and select the item **Open · Object** in order to launch the Business Object Editor. Then select the required operation. You can now assign the relevant iView or portal page to the selected operation by opening the context menu of the iView or portal page and selecting **Add iView to Operation** or **Add Page to Operation** respectively (see Figure 7.13).

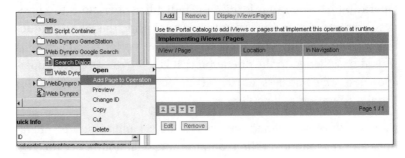

Figure 7.13 Assigning a Portal Page to an Operation

Role-independent assignment

Because you don't assign any specific usage of the iView or portal page (for example, within a specific role) in this procedure, the assignment is independent of a role.

To carry out a role-dependent assignment of an operation to the implementing iView or portal page, you must open the usage of the iView or of the portal page in the required role. Chapter 5 describes the process of embedding a (Web Dynpro) iView or a portal page into a specific role in great detail. Typically, to do that you must create a delta link; that is, a reference between the original object and the corresponding usage. In order to implement a role-dependent assignment between the operation and the iView or portal page, you must then start the iView Editor or Page Editor respectively from the corresponding role.

Assigning an operation to an iView or a portal page

Then use the dropdown menu to go to the **Object-Based Navigation** view (see Figure 7.14).

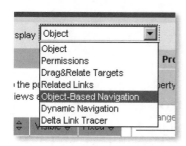

Figure 7.14 Selecting the Object-Based Navigation View

Figure 7.15 shows the **Object-Based Navigation** view for the **Search Dialog Page** from the **Web Dynpro Best Practices** role. As you can see, the **Search Dialog Page** implements a total of four operations of three business objects.

Once the **Object-Based Navigation** view is opened, you must open the context menu of the operation in question and select the item **Add iView to Page** or **Add Operation to Page** to assign an operation to the usage of an iView or to a portal page (see Figure 7.16).

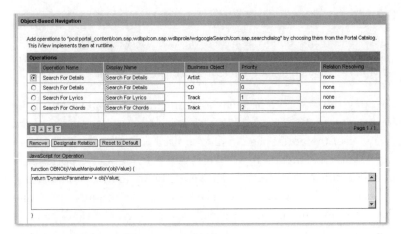

Figure 7.15 Object-Based Navigation View

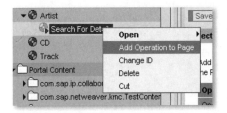

Figure 7.16 Assigning an Operation to a Portal Page

7.4.4 Mapping Transfer Parameters

There's one special characteristic in object-based navigation we'd like to draw your attention to. As you have seen in Section 7.3.1, you can define any number of transfer parameters within your Web Dynpro application that you want to transfer when triggering an object-based navigation. In contrast to the usual portal navigation, in which you have to know the called iView or portal page at the time it is called, in object-based navigation you have no information as to which iView or portal page is actually executed. This means you cannot ensure that your transfer parameters actually match the called iView or portal page.

For example, if you transfer color=green&size=medium as a transfer parameter, you cannot be sure that the iView or portal page called via object-based navigation does actually expect to receive the two parameters, color and size. Perhaps this iView or portal page needs color and sizeDefinition as parameter names instead. For this reason, it can be necessary to map the transferred parameters to the ones that are actually needed.

This mapping of parameters must also be defined in the **Object-Based Navigation** view of an iView or a portal page. In this context, you must define a JavaScript method, OBNObjValueManipulation, for each assigned operation.

Defining the parameter mapping

To generally ensure the correct transfer of parameters for Web Dynpro iViews you must define the OBNObjValueManipulation method as shown in Figure 7.17. You can find this method in the **Object-Based Navigation** view.

Specific Web Dynpro mapping

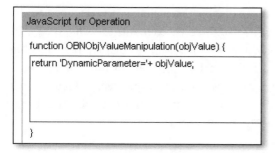

Figure 7.17 Mapping the Transfer Parameters for Web Dynpro iViews

7.5 Importing the Required Data

Now that you have learned how to trigger an object-based navigation within your Web Dynpro application and to create the business objects and operations required for that, we'll describe how the Web Dynpro OBNTester accesses and manages the required data.

As you have seen, you need at least three parameters for the object-based navigation:

Three-level data hierarchy

▶ The system for which you define the business object

▶ The business object itself

▶ The required operation

This three-level hierarchy is mapped via a corresponding three-level hierarchical context in the Web Dynpro OBNTester, as you can see in Figure 7.18.

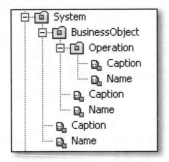

Figure 7.18 Defining the Three-Level Context Hierarchy

Note the contrast to the hierarchical data structure used in the Web Dynpro NavigationTester to display the available Web Dynpro applications or iViews using the IWDTree UI element (see Chapter 6). In the Web Dynpro OBNTester, we only want to display the available business objects for exactly one selected system or the defined operations for exactly one business object respectively. Figure 7.19 shows, for example, the valid operations of business object **CD** that we defined for the **WebDynproBestPractices** system.

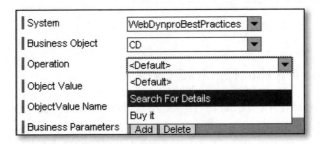

Figure 7.19 Selecting the Required Data

Using singletons — Thus, the context node hierarchy being used has to manage exactly one set of child nodes for each hierarchy level. We therefore define the BusinessObject and Operation context nodes as *singleton nodes* by setting the corresponding **singleton** property of the corresponding nodes to **true**. Figure 7.20 shows the result for the BusinessObject context node.

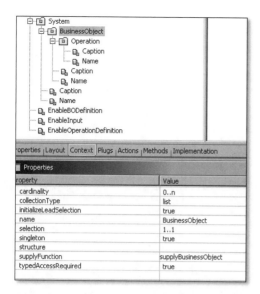

Figure 7.20 Assigning the Supply Function supplyBusinessObject

In addition to using the **singleton** property, we'd like to draw your attention to another special characteristic of the context hierarchy used here. In the OBNTester, we want to refresh the list of available business objects every time the user selects a system. Similarly, we want to adjust the list of displayed operations whenever the user selects a business object. This means that in both cases we must refresh the list of available child nodes every time the parent node is renewed.

This behavior can be implemented quickly and easily by using *supply functions*. Figure 7.20 shows the definition of the BusinessObject context node. You can use the **supplyFunction** property to define the required supplyBusinessObject() method that is called every time the superordinate system node or the currently selected node element changes. Listing 7.3 shows the supplyBusinessObject() method.

Using supply functions

```
// Import selected system
String currentSystem = parentElement.getName();

// Import current user
IUser user = null;
try {
  user = WDClientUser.getCurrentUser().getSAPUser();
```

```
    } catch (WDUMException e) {
      wdComponentAPI.getMessageManager().reportException(
        "Failed to get user",
        true);
      return;
    }

Enumeration searchResult = null;
try {
  Hashtable env = new Hashtable();
  env.put(Context.SECURITY_PRINCIPAL, user);

  DirContext ictx = new InitialDirContext(env);
  DirContext folder = (DirContext)
    ictx.lookup("pcd:Business_Objects");

  // Define search within PCD
  PcdSearchControls cons = new PcdSearchControls();
  cons.setSearchScope(
    PcdSearchControls.UNIT_ROOTS_ONLY_SCOPE);

  // Start search for defined business
  // objects
  searchResult =
    folder.search(
      "",
      "("
        + IPcdAttribute.OBJECT_CLASS
        + "="
        + "com.sapportals.portal.businessobject"
        + ")",
      cons);
} catch (NamingException e1) {
  wdComponentAPI.getMessageManager().reportException(
    "Failed to search for business objects: " +
      e1.getLocalizedMessage(),
    true);
  return;
}

while (searchResult.hasMoreElements()) {
  SearchResult result = (SearchResult)
    searchResult.nextElement();

  // For all business objects found
  // that have been defined for the required system,
  // we'll create the corresponding node elements of
  // the BusinessObject context node
```

```
if (result.getName().startsWith(currentSystem)) {
  IPrivateOBN TesterView.IBusinessObjectElement bo =

    wdContext.nodeBusinessObject().
      createBusinessObjectElement();
    bo.setCaption(result.getName()
      .substring(result.getName().indexOf('.') + 1));
    bo.setName(result.getName()
      .substring(result.getName().indexOf('.') + 1));
    wdContext.nodeBusinessObject().addElement(bo);
  }
}
```

Listing 7.3 Determining the Defined Business Objects

The element parameter that is automatically transferred at the call of the supplyBusinessObject() method provides access to the currently selected System node element.

Like the supplyBusinessObject() method, we'll use the supplyOperation() method to determine the defined operations of the business object we have just selected (see Listing 7.4).

```
// Access to OBN service
IUserObjectBasedNavigation obn =
  wdContext.currentPortalServiceElement().
    getOBNService();
IUser user = null;
try {
  user = WDClientUser.getCurrentUser().getSAPUser();
} catch (WDUMException e) {
  wdComponentAPI.getMessageManager().reportException(
    "Failed to get current user: " +
      e.getLocalizedMessage(),
    true);
}

// Import current system and the required
// business object
String system =
  wdContext.currentSystemElement().getName();
String bo = parentElement.getName();

// Import valid operations
List operations = obn.getTargets(system, bo, user);

IPrivateOBN TesterView.IOperationElement
```

```
     newOperation = null;
if (operations != null && operations.size() > 0) {

  // Create default operation
  newOperation = wdContext.nodeOperation()
    .createOperationElement();
  newOperation.setCaption("<Default>");
  newOperation.setName("<Default>");
  wdContext.nodeOperation().addElement(newOperation);

  // For each valid operation we
  // create a corresponding node element of
  // the Operation context node
  for (Iterator iter = operations.iterator();
    iter.hasNext();) {

    IOBNTarget target = (IOBNTarget) iter.next();

    newOperation = wdContext.nodeOperation()
      .createOperationElement();
    newOperation.setCaption(
      target.getOperationFriendlyName());
    newOperation.setName(
      target.getOperationName().substring(
        target.getOperationName().
          lastIndexOf('/') + 1));

    wdContext.nodeOperation().addElement(newOperation);
  }
```

Listing 7.4 Determining the Valid Operations

Valid operations   We can use the portal service IUserObjectBasedNavigation to identify the valid operations for the selected business object. By valid
operations we mean those operations to which at least one iView or
portal page is linked for the current user or the user's role respectively.

7.6   Summary

Based on a description of the OBNTester, this chapter has demonstrated how you can implement a much higher degree of flexibility
when navigating between your Web Dynpro iViews by using object-
based navigation instead of the usual portal navigation. In object-
based navigation, you define the navigation target through a specific

operation of a business object instead of using iViews or portal pages.

In addition to role-independent assignment of iViews and portal pages to operations, you can choose a role-specific assignment that lets you provide different implementations of the same functionality to users of different roles, without having to change the Web Dynpro applications that call the implementations.

Furthermore, this chapter has described how to call any type of portal service within your Web Dynpro application in order to access specific portal functions. Integrating portal services into your Web Dynpro application involves additional dependencies that have the effect of allowing you henceforth to run your Web Dynpro application only on SAP NetWeaver installations that contain the SAP NetWeaver Portal.

In the previous chapters, we discussed the componentization of Web Dynpro applications on the one hand, and the options available to you with the SAP NetWeaver Portal on the other. Now we would like to examine the countless possibilities that arise when you combine these features and functionalities within a Web Dynpro application.

8   Web Dynpro MusicBox

In Chapter 3, you saw how—by using the Web Dynpro GameStation—you could use Web Dynpro components and component interfaces to build reusable and configurable Web Dynpro applications. In the subsequent chapters, we also discussed what additional possibilities become available if you start your Web Dynpro applications within the SAP NetWeaver Portal.

We will now unite these possibilities, with the primary emphasis resting on the subsequent configurability of your Web Dynpro applications. We will also provide you with a detailed illustration indicating how you can use these options (i.e., those available with the SAP NetWeaver Portal within a Web Dynpro application), as we focus on the use of the portal personalization within your Web Dynpro application.

8.1   MusicBox Structure

As for the similarity between Web Dynpro GameStation and Web Dynpro MusicBox, we make intensive use of Web Dynpro components and component interfaces. You will find the necessary component interfaces in the Web Dynpro development component `tc~mscbxapi`. The corresponding Web Dynpro project is called `MAIN_WD-BOOK_D~tc~mscbxapi~sap.com`. You will find the Web Dynpro components that build on this in the Web Dynpro development components `tc~mscbmp3` and `tc~musicbox`.

MusicBoxComp
component
The `MusicBoxComp` Web Dynpro component within the `tc~musicbox` development component assumes a special role here, since it represents the central root component of the Web Dynpro MusicBox that administers all embedded components. We will discuss the implementation of these components in detail in Section 8.3.

Basic functionality
Figure 8.1 shows the Web Dynpro MusicBox, which you can use to find and play any music files you like. The MusicBox also allows you to define playlists and maintain other information on the musicians and bands.

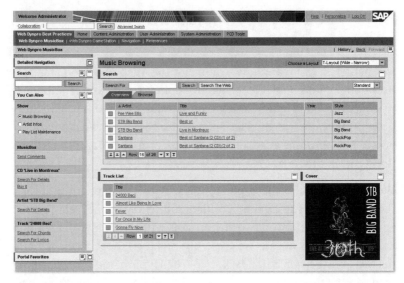

Figure 8.1 Web Dynpro MusicBox

Before we look at the specific implementation of the various aspects of the Web Dynpro MusicBox, we will discuss the component interfaces used that enable us to configure the Web Dynpro MusicBox later on.

8.2 Component Interfaces Used

The component interfaces used within the Web Dynpro MusicBox are located in the `tc~mscbxapi` development component. This development component contains only the definition of the component interfaces, that is, the *Standalone Component Interfaces*.

As we mentioned in Chapter 3 when describing the Web Dynpro GameStation, a separation of the component interfaces and the corresponding components, which are to be implemented into different development components, is always useful if you want to implement the component interfaces and the various implementations independently of each other.

Separation of interface and implementation

We essentially want to be able to configure three aspects within the Web Dynpro MusicBox:

Configuration options of the Web Dynpro MusicBox

▶ The Web Dynpro MusicBox should be independent of the specific storage or the existing format of the music files used. The Web Dynpro MusicBox uses a *Music Store* for this, which does exactly that.

▶ The display of the available music files should not be defined directly by the Web Dynpro MusicBox; instead, we use the *Detail Viewer* to display the existing data in a way that is defined within the various detail viewers. The MusicBox itself does not display any data.

▶ The detail viewers used should be summarized in so-called *perspectives*. A perspective defines both the list of detail viewers used and their composition and layout. The Web Dynpro MusicBox can manage any number of perspectives. Users can choose from among these perspectives as they like, and can adapt them to their needs via the portal personalization.

Based on these requirements, we define a total of three Web Dynpro component interfaces that enable the behavior described above.

8.2.1 MusicStoreCompI Component Interface

The MusicStoreCompI component interface defines the data used within the Web Dynpro MusicBox. In certain respects, we use this interface to define the data model of the MusicBox. As we have already explained in Chapter 3, it is generally helpful to use *model components* to abstract the specific data model used. This is particularly useful when you use Web services or Adaptive Remote Function Call (RFC) models, as this allows you to exchange these models a lot easier; for example, if the Web services or RFC modules, which are provided in the backend system that is called, have changed.

Using model components

Since we want to make the Web Dynpro MusicBox independent of a specific implementation of this model, we only describe the used data structure(s) via the `MusicStoreCompI` component interface, and not their specific storage or format. Furthermore, since we only want to provide data through this interface, we do not define any interface view. We describe the data provided using the context node hierarchy of the interface controller (see Figure 8.2).

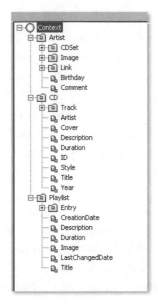

Figure 8.2 Definition of Data Provided

Here, the `Artist` node describes the information that can be defined for the individual artists. The `CD` node contains the list of available music files. The `Playlist` node describes the playlists created by the user.

Sample implementation

Within this example, we implement the `MusicStoreCompI` interface in the Web Dynpro component `FileSystemMusicStore`, which is located in the `tc~mscbxmp3` development component. As its name implies, we import all existing MP3 files that are located under a root directory of our choice. The `FileSystemMusicStore` component anticipates a directory structure as shown in Figure 8.3, which is searched for available MP3 files: Under the root directory, there is a directory for each artist that contains the available CDs.

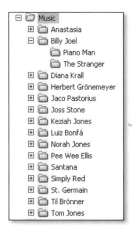

Figure 8.3 Anticipated Data Structure of the FileSystemMusicStore Component

You can import the root directory used with the WDConfiguration service and adapt it within the visual administrator (see Chapter 10).

Definition of the root directory

The model provided by the FileSystemMusicStore component does not contain any persistence. All of the changes you make when you use the MusicBox are lost when you restart the application. Although this restriction is certainly unacceptable during production, we accept it here because we don't want to place the emphasis (in this example) on possible implementations of such persistence. Rather, we want to be able to present and discuss all desired functions, regardless of this restriction.

You can easily define a separate module that provides such a persistency, however. Thanks to the flexibility of the Web Dynpro MusicBox, it is very easy for you to use your own implementation of the MusicStoreCompI component interface, as we will see in Section 8.2.3. Moreover, because of the use of the MusicStoreCompI interface and the abstraction this allows, the precise model used for the Web Dynpro MusicBox is entirely transparent.

Exchanging the music store used

8.2.2 DetailsViewerCompI Component Interface

The DetailsViewerCompI component interface describes the detail viewers mentioned above, which display the data provided by the MusicStoreCompI component interface as you wish. We define the visual part of such a detail viewer here using the DetailsInterface-View interface view.

Within the interface controller, we also define three methods that can later be used, for example, to allow the portal to be personalized for the individual detail viewers or to ensure access to the available data (see Figure 8.4).

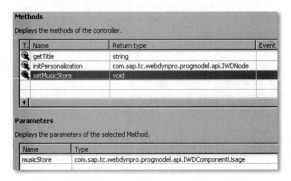

Figure 8.4 Methods of the DetailsViewerCompI Interface Controller

Sample
implementation

Within this example, we define many different detail viewers, which we all summarize in the tc~musicbox development component. In Section 8.4, we describe an example of what you should consider when you implement your own detail viewer.

Using the option to define many of the perspectives that are presented in the following section, you can also very easily add your own detail viewers to the Web Dynpro MusicBox.

8.2.3 PerspectiveConfigurationCompI Component Interface

The PerspectiveConfigurationCompI component interface allows you to define perspectives. A perspective describes a certain combination and configuration of different detail viewers. Users can switch between the defined perspectives by using the *Contextual Navigation Panel* that we discuss in Section 8.6.2.

Description of the
perspectives

The desired perspectives are defined within the interface controller using certain context nodes, through which the Web Dynpro MusicBox obtains access to the required information. Figure 8.5 shows the context node hierarchy defined within the interface controller context.

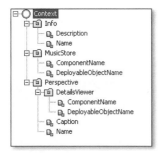

Figure 8.5 Definition of the Desired Perspectives

The `Info` node describes general information; the `MusicStore` node determines the data model used (i.e., the desired implementation of the `MusicStoreCompI` component interface); and the `Perspective` node defines the desired perspectives that are each composed of a list of detail viewers that are determined through the relevant `DetailsViewer` node elements.

Within this example we define the desired perspectives using the `BookPerspectivesComp` component, which implements the `PerspectiveConfigurationCompI` component interface. As is the case for all of the detail viewers we provide, the `BookPerspectivesComp` component is also located in the `tc~musicbox` development component.

Implementation provided

Within the `BookPerspectivesComp` component, we define a total of three perspectives (see Figure 8.6) that represent the corresponding entries within the contextual navigation panel.

Figure 8.6 Perspectives Provided

In Chapter 3, we recommended that you keep the interface controller of a Web Dynpro component as slim as possible. In particular, you should ensure that you do not create any context node elements within the interface controller. We satisfy this requirement by implementing the `BookPerspectivesComp` component. The interface controller maps to the node elements defined in the component controller, as shown in Figure 8.7.

Definition of the context node elements

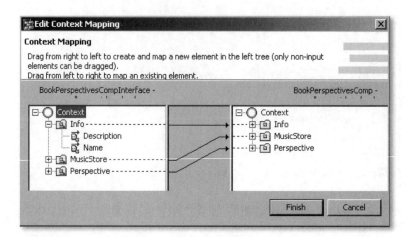

Figure 8.7 Mapping Between the Interface Controller and the Component Controller

Selecting the defined perspectives

The perspectives used within the MusicBox are determined via the corresponding implementation of the `PerspectiveConfiguration-CompI` component interface. Since the `MusicBoxComp` component represents the central component of the Web Dynpro MusicBox, which manages all embedded components, when we initialize `MusicBox-Comp`, we determine the desired perspectives within the `wdDoInit()` method of the component controller, as shown in Listing 8.1.

```
String deployableObjectName = null;
String componentName = null;

// Import perspective configuration
try {
  IWDConfiguration perspectiveConfig =
    WDConfiguration.getConfigurationByName(
      "sap.com/tc~musicbox",
      "perspectives");
  deployableObjectName =
    perspectiveConfig.getStringEntry
      ("deployableObjectName");
  componentName =
    perspectiveConfig.
      getStringEntry("componentName");
} catch (Exception e) {
  wdComponentAPI.getMessageManager().reportException(
    "Failed to load configuration
      of used perspectives: "
    + e.getLocalizedMessage(),
    true);
```

```
}

// Create component instance for definition
// of existing perspective
wdThis.wdGetPerspectivesComponentUsage()
  .createComponent(
    componentName,
    deployableObjectName);

// Create component instance for
// used Music Store
wdThis.wdGetMusicStoreComponentUsage()
  .createComponent(
    wdContext.currentMusicStoreElement().
      getComponentName(),
    wdContext.currentMusicStoreElement()
      .getDeployableObjectName());

wdContext.nodePerspective().setLeadSelection(0);
initPerspective(wdContext.currentPerspectiveElement());
```

Listing 8.1 Determining the Perspectives

We determine the implementation used of the Perspective-ConfigurationCompI component interface using the WDConfiguration service. You can include your own implementation at any time using the visual administrator. Figure 8.8 shows our default settings in which we define the use of the BookPerspectivesComp component.

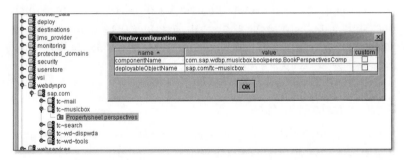

Figure 8.8 Definition of the PerspectiveConfigurationCompI Implementation Used

Having now described the component interfaces used and having shown the configurations that are available within the Web Dynpro MusicBox, we will now discuss the tasks and the implementation of the MusicBoxComp component.

8.3   MusicBoxComp Web Dynpro Component

The `MusicBoxComp` component is the core Web Dynpro component of the MusicBox. Accordingly, it also serves as the root component of the Web Dynpro application `MusicBoxApp`, through which you start the Web Dynpro MusicBox. The main tasks of the `MusicBoxComp` component are as follows:

▶ Instantiation of the desired perspectives.

▶ Creation of the configured data model.

▶ Creation and management of the individual component instances that are necessary to realize the various detail viewers. Each of these component instances must be supplied with the corresponding data model. Furthermore, the required data from the portal personalization must be adjusted.

▶ Creation of the desired layout in which the detail viewers of a perspective are to be displayed.

Note that the `MusicBoxComp` component is primarily responsible for the administration of the embedded components; the MusicBox's actual logic is implemented in these embedded components. The design of the `MusicBoxComp` component can therefore also be used in entirely different scenarios without too much difficulty.

For example, the employee self-services (ESS) within mySAP Enterprise Resource Planning (mySAP ERP) 2004 are implemented exactly in accordance with the same model. A central component, which does not contain any application logic, assumes the administration of the individual components of the application, which is entirely composed of Web Dynpro components.

8.3.1   Basic Structure

Figure 8.9 shows the basic structure of the `MusicBoxComp` component in the Web Dynpro Data Modeler.

Component usages used

You will notice the many component usages, through which the `MusicBoxComp` component can create and monitor the individual components of the MusicBox. The `MusicStore` component usage provides the data model used and the `Perspectives` component usage or the component instantiated through it returns the definition of the individual perspectives. In Section 8.2.3, we discussed how the `MusicBoxComp` component creates the component instances required for this.

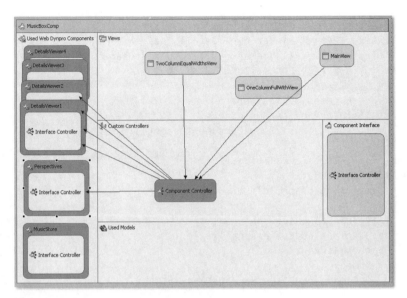

Figure 8.9 Components of the MusicBoxComp Component

Although the `MusicBoxComp` component could theoretically manage any number of detail viewers, to simplify matters, we limited the number of possible detail viewers of a perspective to four. Through the corresponding component usages `DetailsViewer1` to `Details-Viewer4`, the `MusicBoxComp` component generates the required component instances within the `initDetailViewer()` method and supplies these with the corresponding data model, as shown in Listing 8.2.

Number of possible detail viewers

```
// Determine required component usage
 Component-Usage
IWDComponentUsage componentUsage =
  getComponentUsage(index + 1);
if (componentUsage == null) {
  throw new WDRuntimeException(
    "Failed to get component usage for index: "
      + index);
}

// Create new component instance
if (componentUsage.hasActiveComponent()) {
```

```
    componentUsage.deleteComponent();
  }
  componentUsage.createComponent(
    componentName, deployableObjectName);

  // Access component interface
  IExternalDetailsViewerCompI detailsInterface =
    (IExternalDetailsViewerCompI) componentUsage.
      getInterfaceController();

  // Assign used Music Store
  detailsInterface.setMusicStore(
    wdThis.wdGetMusicStoreComponentUsage());

  // Initialize Personalization
  IWDNode persDataRoot =
    detailsInterface.initPersonalization();

  if ((persDataRoot != null)) {
    p13NHelper.updatePersonalization(
      persDataRoot,
      true,
      wdComponentAPI.getMessageManager());
  }

  IWDNode node =
    wdContext.nodeContent().getChildNode(
      "DetailsViewer" + (index + 1), 0);
  node.getCurrentElement().setAttributeValue(
    "Title",
    detailsInterface.getTitle());

  node.getCurrentElement().setAttributeValue(
    "IsActive", Boolean.TRUE);
```

Listing 8.2 initDetailViewer() Method

Here, you should note that the access to the `IexternalDetails-VievewerCompI` component interface enables you to have a typed access to the component instance created, without even knowing the specific implementation.

Dynamic generation of component usages

By restricting the number of possible detail viewers, we can declare the corresponding number of component usages required within the `MusicBoxComp` component.

> **Hint**
>
> In principle, the Web Dynpro programming model allows you to create the component usages used dynamically, similar to the dynamically created user interface. However, we do *not* recommend that you do this at this point, because an entirely dynamic approach will ultimately lead to cryptic code when the corresponding interface views are embedded in the `IWDViewUIContainer` UI elements that are required.

As the example of the Web Dynpro MusicBox shows, you can achieve very flexible and customizable applications, even with a restricted and declared number of component usages (and the related possibilities of the declarative use of these component usages within your Web Dynpro application).

8.3.2 Provision of the Data Model

As we saw in Listing 8.2, the `MusicBoxComp` component assigns the data model used to every detail viewer created via the `setMusicbox()` method of the `IExternalDetailsViewerCompI` component interface. Therefore, the `setMusicbox()` method receives a reference to the `MusicStore` component usage, which refers to the previously created component instance. Within a detail viewer, this component usage is addressed via the `enterReferencingMode()` method.

Listing 8.3 shows an example of the implementation of the `setMusicStore()` method in the component controller of the `SearchComp` component, which implements the `Search` detail viewer.

```
wdThis.wdGetMusicStoreComponentUsage()
  .enterReferencingMode(musicStore);
```

Listing 8.3 setMusicStore() Method

In Section 8.4, we will look more closely at the implementation of a detail viewer. Here, we would merely like to point out that due to the referencing of the assigned component usage, the related component instance is used in both components: `MusicBoxComp` and `SearchComp`.

Although we can fix the number of detail viewers, depending on the perspective chosen, we do not want to automatically display all four possible detail viewers. Therefore, we'll define a context node for

Defining the visibility of a detail viewer

each detail viewer in the component controller context of the MusicBoxComp component. Figure 8.10 shows the definition of the DetailsViewer1 to DetailsViewer4 context nodes, with whose **Visibility** and **Title** attributes we determine the visibility or the title displayed of the individual detail viewer.

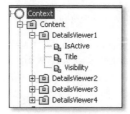

Figure 8.10 Content Context Node

As we saw in Listing 8.2, the MusicBoxComp component sets the is Active attribute to **true** for every defined detail viewer of a perspective. We calculate the value of the **Visibility** attribute based on this value in the getDetailsViewer1Visibility() method, for example (see Listing 8.4).

```
return element.getIsActive()
 && wdContext.currentShowDetailViewer1Element().getValue()
    ? WDVisibility.VISIBLE
    : WDVisibility.NONE;
```

Listing 8.4 Calculating the Visibility of a Detail Viewer

In addition to the value of the IsActive attribute, we also use the ShowDetailViewer1 node to check whether the user has shown or hidden the corresponding detail viewer via the portal personalization. In Section 8.5, we'll look in more detail at using portal personalization within the Web Dynpro MusicBox.

8.3.3 Defining the Layout

In addition to managing the component usages presented in the last two sections, the MusicBoxComp component also provides the desired layout of the existing detail viewer. The different layouts are defined via different Web Dynpro views that are all embedded in the MainView Web Dynpro view through a IWDViewUIContainer UI element.

Figure 8.11 shows the *View Composition* of the MusicBoxComp component, which illustrates the structuring of the different views and the navigation between the individual views.

View composition used

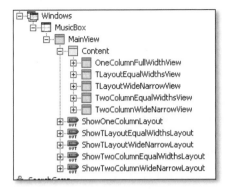

Figure 8.11 View Composition of the MusicBoxComp Component

Each layout is realized through a particular Web Dynpro view. The MainView view can switch between these layouts by calling the corresponding outbound plug. For example, the ShowTwoColumnEqualWidthsLayout outbound plug displays the TwoColumnEqualWidthsView view.

We define the list of available layouts using the simple type Layout, which we also create in the tc~musicbox development component. By using simple types, you can also define any types for Web Dynpro applications, similar to the Data Dictionary, and then also enter a valid value set, for example (see Section 8.4.2).

List of defined layouts

As we mentioned earlier, we implement each layout using a special Web Dynpro view. Figure 8.12 shows the TwoColumnEqualWidthsView view within the view designer as an example. A maximum of four detail viewers are then included using four IWDViewUIContainer UI elements.

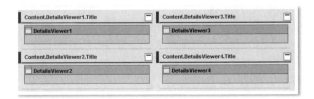

Figure 8.12 TwoColumnEqualWidthsView Web Dynpro View

Predefined list of
layouts Of course, the implementation of the various layouts using a list of firmly predefined Web Dynpro views limits the expandability of the Web Dynpro MusicBox regarding the possible layouts. Unlike the data model used or the detail viewers displayed, here we dispensed with abstracting the displayed layouts using a special component interface. This is primarily due to a restriction of the Web Dynpro programming model, although this restriction should be removed with the next release of SAP NetWeaver.

Controlling the
visibility In the last section, we described how the individual detail viewers are made visible depending on the perspective chosen. To use the value that is calculated of the corresponding **Visibility** attribute in a layout, we map the corresponding attributes from the component controller of the MusicBoxComp component to the corresponding view controller.

In the view designer, we then bind the **visible** characteristic of the relevant IWDTray UI elements against the corresponding **Visibility** attribute of the DetailsViewer<i> context node. Figure 8.13 shows an example of this for the DetailsViewer1 node.

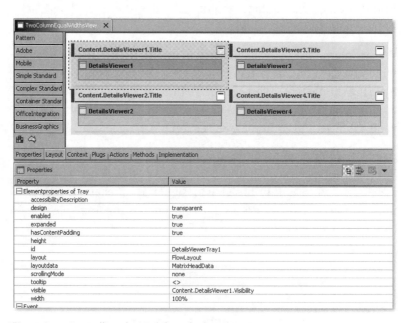

Figure 8.13 Controlling the Visibility of a Detail Viewer

304

In addition to the embedding of the desired layout, the `MainView` view also displays the header shown in Figure 8.14. Besides selecting a perspective (i.e., one is currently selected), you can also choose the layout you want.

Switching the layout

Figure 8.14 Selecting the Desired Layout

The chosen layout is selected within the `setLayout()` method of the view controller of the `MainView` view (see Listing 8.5).

```
private void setLayout() {
  String layout = wdContext.currentLayoutElement()
.getValue();

  if (layout.equals("ONE_COLUMN")) {
    wdThis.wdFirePlugShowOneColumnLayout();
  } else if (layout.equals("TWO_COLUMNS_EQUAL_WIDTHS")) {
    wdThis.wdFirePlugShowTwoColumnEqualWidthsLayout();
  } else if (layout.equals("TWO_COLUMNS_WIDE_NARROW")) {
    wdThis.wdFirePlugShowTwoColumnWideNarrowLayout();
  } else if (layout.equals("T_LAYOUT_EQUAL_WIDTHS")) {
    wdThis.wdFirePlugShowTLayoutEqualWidthsLayout();
  } else if (layout.equals("T_LAYOUT_WIDE_NARROW")) {
    wdThis.wdFirePlugShowTLayoutWideNarrowLayout();
  } else {
    wdComponentAPI.getMessageManager().
      reportException("Unknown layout '" + layout
        + "'",
      true);
  }
}
```

Listing 8.5 Choosing the Selected Layout

Depending on the layout that is currently chosen, the desired layout is displayed through the corresponding outbound plug. Since the different Web Dynpro views that we use to implement the different layouts ultimately always use the same interface views of the same component usages, the same (component) instances of the detail viewer are used even if you switch layouts.

8.4   Implementing a Detail Viewer

Throughout this section, we will use the `Cover` detail viewer to describe the most important steps required to implement a detail viewer that we can use later in the Web Dynpro MusicBox.

Functions offered   The `Cover` detail viewer displays the cover of a selected CD. If no cover is available for the selected CD, the user can load the selected cover using Web Dynpro's file upload function. Figure 8.15 shows the `Cover` detail viewer.

Figure 8.15 Cover Detail Viewer

8.4.1   CoverComp Web Dynpro Component

We implement the `Cover` detail viewer within the `CoverComp` Web Dynpro component, which we group in the `tc~musicbox` development component as we do for all of the detail viewers that we provide. Once you have successfully created the `CoverComp` component, use the context menu entry **Add** of the `Implemented Interfaces` node to define the required component interface (see Figure 8.16).

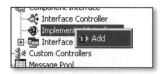

Figure 8.16 Adding a Component Interface Implementation

As we explained in Section 8.2.2, all detail viewers are described using the `DetailsViewerCompI` component interface. We select this interface in the following dialog (see Figure 8.17). Incidentally, the dialog contains the list of all local component interfaces—those interfaces that are defined in the current Web Dynpro project or in the current development component—as well as all component interfaces that are available via the referenced public parts.

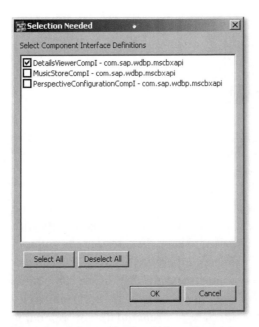

Figure 8.17 Selecting the DetailsViewerCompI Component Interface

When you click on **OK**, the default methods and events from the DetailsViewerCompI component interface and the DetailsInterfaceView interface view are generated automatically. The CoverComp window, which is created automatically when the CoverComp component is created, can now be deleted because we want to provide the UI via the Details window (see Figure 8.18). The deletion of the CoverComp window automatically also deletes the corresponding CoverCompInterfaceView interface view.

Deleting windows

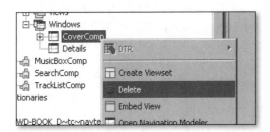

Figure 8.18 Deleting the CoverComp Window

Now that you have created the CoverComp view, you can embed it into this window via the context menu entry **Embed View** of the Details window (see Figure 8.19).

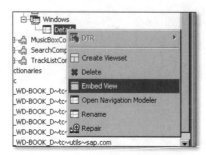

Figure 8.19 Embedding the CoverView View

Implementing the
component inter-
face methods

In the next step, you must implement the default methods and events from the `DetailsViewerCompI` component interface. As with all examples in this book, we want to keep the interface controller of a component as slim as possible and therefore define the 1:1 methods, which are defined in the interface controller, in the component controller of the `CoverComp` component (see Figure 8.20), and delegate the method calls in the interface controller to the corresponding methods in the component controller.

Figure 8.20 Default Methods

Creating the
component usage
MusicStore

The default data model that is copied to the `CoverComp` component through the `setMusicStore()` method will now be managed via a corresponding component usage. We generate the required component usage with the context menu entry **Add Used Component** of the `Used Web Dynpro Components` node in the Web Dynpro Explorer (see Figure 8.21).

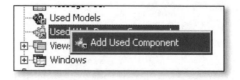

Figure 8.21 Creating a Component Usage

In the following dialog, we select the `MusicStoreCompI` component interface, because even within the `CoverComp` component, we don't want to define any direct dependency on an actual implementation of the data model (see Figure 8.22).

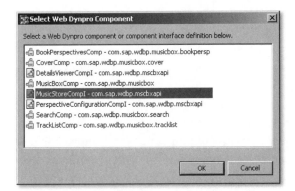

Figure 8.22 Selecting the MusicStoreCompI Component Interface

As we saw in Section 8.2.2, within the components that realize the different detail viewers, we always want to use the same instance of the data model (which is also implemented via a component). This allows us to ensure that all of the detail viewers involved work on the same data, and that selecting a particular CD, for example, within the `Search` detail viewer will automatically result in an update of all other detail viewers. In Listing 8.3, the `setMusicStore()` method within the component controller was implemented, which is the same for all components that implement a detail viewer.

Referencing mode for component usages

8.4.2 Defining the Cover Size

Within the `Cover` detail viewer, we want to show the cover displayed in a total of three different sizes. Users can later choose the size they want through the portal personalization. We define the possible sizes using a special `CoverSize` simple type, which we create using the **Create Simple Type** context menu entry (see Figure 8.23).

Figure 8.23 Creating a New Simple Type

In the following dialog, we define the three possible sizes: **SMALL**, **MEDIUM**, and **LARGE** (see Figure 8.24).

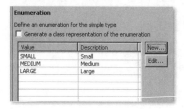

Figure 8.24 Defining the Possible Screen Sizes

Accessing the iView characteristic

In Section 8.5.3, we describe in detail how you can define application-specific iView characteristics within your Web Dynpro application. Within the CoverComp component, we only define the **Size** iView characteristic via the corresponding Size context node. Without wanting to jump ahead to the details given in Section 8.5.3, the **Value** attribute of the Size node gives you access to the specified value for the desired cover size. In order to use this value in the CoverView view, we simply need a conventional mapping between the view controller context and the component controller context (see Figure 8.25).

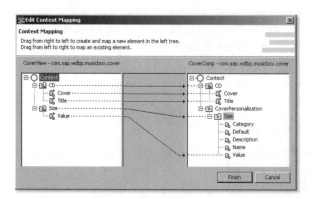

Figure 8.25 Required Context Mappings

In addition to the mapping of the **Value** attribute of the Size node, the CoverView view has access to the CD that is currently chosen through the corresponding mapping to the CD node. Here again we map only those attributes that are actually used in the view. The following Figure 8.26 shows the **Cover Size** characteristic that has just been defined within the iView Editor. As you can see, the values that are defined through the simple type `CoverSize` are transferred automatically.

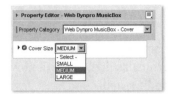

Figure 8.26 Selecting the Screen Size in the iView Editor

Having looked at the Web Dynpro-specific aspects of the Web Dynpro MusicBox, we would now like to examine the enhanced possibilities available to you when you start your Web Dynpro application within the SAP NetWeaver Portal. We'll focus on the integration of the portal personalization.

8.5 Personalizing Web Dynpro iViews

8.5.1 Role-Specific Adjustments versus User Personalization

As we discussed in Chapter 5, the Web Dynpro iViews you create can be embedded in any portal pages, worksets, or roles. By using the *Delta Links*, you can adjust each characteristic of your Web Dynpro iView to its respective use within a portal page, a workset, or a role. These changes are always visible for *all* users of the corresponding role, which is why they are also referred to collectively as *role-specific customization*. You always perform role-specific adjustments for iViews using the iView Editor.

Role-specific customization

Unlike the role-specific adjustments, each user can use the corresponding **Personalize** entries in the top-level navigation in the SAP NetWeaver Portal, or the tray menus of each iView or each portal page to make user-specific adjustments. These adjustments then always apply to only that specific user. Here we therefore talk about the so-called *end-user personalization*. The end-user personalization for an iView is always determined via the *personalization dialog*, which appears in the iView tray after the **Personalize** entry is selected.

End-user personalization

Interplay Role-specific adjustments and end-user personalization naturally complement each other here. For example, all adjustments to a Web Dynpro iView for a particular role are of course visible for all users who are assigned to this role. The changes from the end-user personalization are also managed for each user. The overall behavior of a Web Dynpro iView is therefore determined by the product of the role-specific adjustments and the user personalization. We will now describe the possibilities of role-specific adjustments and user personalization together as *portal personalization*.

Default iView attributes As long as the adjustments you want to make pertain only to the default iView attributes such as the title, or the size, or the display of the iView tray, for example, you can easily set these using the iView Editor (see Chapter 5). Furthermore, by using the URL template variables within your Web Dynpro application (also described in Chapter 5), you have access to any iView attribute that you want.

Application-specific enhancements However, we want to use the Web Dynpro MusicBox to define application-specific iView attributes, which you can then use for role-specific customization or end-user personalization. For example, we want to make the default layout, in which the various detail viewers are to be displayed, adaptable by utilizing the potential of the portal personalization. In the following sections, we'll describe the steps that we need to do in order to achieve this enhancement.

8.5.2 Including the P13NUtils Public Part

Development component tc~p13nmng All examples in this book have access to different Java classes through the Utils public part of the tc~utils development component. Among other things, these classes allow the sorting of tables or the encoding of transfer parameters. The Java classes and Web Dynpro entities required for the portal personalization can be defined similarly in the tc~p13nmng development component, which you can access using the P13NUtils public part.

In addition to various Java classes, the tc~p13nmng development component contains the P13NDialogContainerComp Web Dynpro component, through which we will later implement a Web Dynpro-specific personalization dialog (see Section 8.5.6). In Chapter 9, we'll use the tc~utils development component to describe the particular things you should note when you define Web Dynpro development components, which, like Web Dynpro entities, also contain individual Java classes. These features apply similarly for the `tc~p13nmng` development component.

To access the Java classes provided within the Web Dynpro MusicBox, define a reference to the `P13NUtils` public part (see Figure 8.27).

Accessing the P13NUtils public part

This gives you access to the `P13nHelper` Java class, in particular, which will play a central role for using the portal personalization, as we will see in Section 8.5.4.

P13nHelper Java class

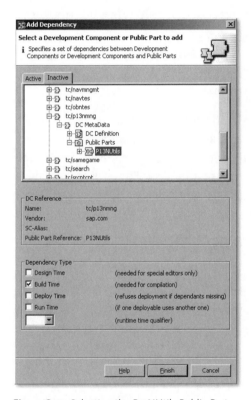

Figure 8.27 Selecting the P13NUtils Public Part

Here we would like to briefly point out possible problems that can arise when you use public parts. Figure 8.28 shows a section of the **Deploy Output View** in the SAP NetWeaver Developer Studio (NWDS). As soon as warnings appear during the deployment of your Web Dynpro application or Web Dynpro development component, this is usually because the development component deployed cannot

Warnings during deployment

be started correctly. Typically, this occurs when referenced development component also cannot be started correctly, or are not even deployed. In Chapter 10, we'll explore ways of analyzing and then solving this problem.

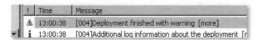

Figure 8.28 Problem During the Deployment of a Web Dynpro Development Component

8.5.3 Definition of Application-Specific iView Attributes

Before we tackle the runtime issues regarding using the portal personalization within your Web Dynpro application, we'll explain how you can define the desired iView attributes within your Web Dynpro application.

Significance of the meta attributes of an iView attribute

Here you should note the significance of the *meta attributes*, which you can define for every iView attribute; for example, you can use the meta attribute to determine the title, the type, or the description of an iView attribute. Furthermore, the iView Editor uses these meta attributes to ensure a type-specific and correct display of the different iView attributes.

Figure 8.29 shows the category **Web Dynpro MusicBox - Search**, which, in addition to several Boolean attributes, contains the **Display Size** attribute, for which a default value quantity is defined.

Figure 8.29 Search Category of the Web Dynpro MusicBox

Changeability and visibility of an iView attribute

In addition to the meta attributes mentioned above, you can determine for each iView attribute whether and how this attribute becomes changeable or visible within the iView Editor or the personalization dialog. For example, you can define for an iView attribute that it is only visible within the iView Editor in the context of role-specific adjustments, or that the attribute is visible but cannot be changed in the personalization dialog. Within the iView Editor, you can also control this behavior, as Figure 8.30 shows us with an example for the **Display Size** attribute.

Figure 8.30 Defining the Changeability of an iView Attribute

Through the **Inheritance** meta attribute, you can define whether the corresponding attribute can be changed when you define additional delta links. The meta attribute **End-User Personalization** determines whether the attribute is no longer visible in the personalization dialog (**Hidden**), or whether it is changeable (**Read Write** or **Read Only**).

Using Context Nodes

In addition to defining the required meta attributes, we want to address the specific value of an iView attribute defined by us within our Web Dynpro application or component in a simple and declarative way. Therefore, we decided to define every iView attribute via a special context node. We determined the required meta attributes by using corresponding node attributes. Figure 8.31 illustrates this hierarchical display using the iView attributes defined for the Search detail viewer.

Accessing the iView attribute

Figure 8.31 Defining the DisplaySize Attribute

Within the component controller context of the SearchComp component, which implements the Search detail viewer, we define a context node under the SearchPersonalizationData node for each iView attribute of a context node that you want, whose node attributes define the required meta attributes. The various node attributes that are listed here (see Figure 8.31 again) describe the following meta attributes:

▶ **Category**

You use the **Category** attribute to define the desired category in which the attribute is to be displayed in the iView Editor. We recommend that you use application-specific categories to ensure a better structuring of the iView attributes.

Use of the **Category** attribute is optional. If you don't define any special category for the iView attribute, it becomes visible in the **Content - Web Dynpro** category.

▶ **Default**

You use the **Default** attribute to define the default value of the iView attribute. You should essentially determine useful default values for all of the iView attributes you define. The **Default** attribute must have the same type as the **Value** attribute.

▶ **Description**

You can use the **Description** attribute to define the explanatory text of the iView attribute, which appears as a tooltip of the iView attribute, for example, in the iView Editor.

▶ **Inheritance**

The **Inheritance** attribute defines whether the iView attribute can be changed when new Delta links are created. The type of the **Inheritance** attribute is determined by the simple type Inheritance, which defines the possible values **NON_FINAL** and **FINAL**.

The **Inheritance** attribute is optional. If you don't define an **Inheritance** attribute for the iView attribute, you can change the iView attribute when new Delta links are created.

Incidentally, the simple type Inheritance is also defined in the tc~p13nmng development component and made available via the public part P13NUtils.

▶ **Mode**

You can use the **Mode** attribute to determine the visibility and changeability of the iView attribute in the personalization dialog. The possible values are determined here via the simple type

`P13NMode`, which we define for the simple type `Inheritance` within the `tc~p13nmng` development component.

The following values are possible: When you use **HIDDEN**, the iView attribute is not visible in the personalization dialog. With **READ_ONLY**, the attribute is only displayed, and with **READ_WRITE,** the corresponding attribute can also be changed by the user.

▶ **Name**

The **Name** attribute defines the visible name of the iView attribute. As for the **Description** attribute, you should also define the value of the **Name** attribute within the message pool of the component to ensure that the displayed name of the iView attribute can also be defined in different languages.

▶ **Value**

The **Value** attribute allows you to access the specific value of the iView attribute within your Web Dynpro application. The default value that is fixed via the **Default** attribute is then transferred automatically, when the corresponding iView attribute was not changed using the portal personalization. The **Value** attribute and the **Default** attribute must be of the same type.

In principle, you can choose absolutely any Java type such as **string,** **integer,** or **Boolean** for the **Value** and the **Default** attribute. Furthermore, you can also use any simple types you like if you want to use a fixed value quantity.

Possible Types

▶ **Mapping the Boolean Type**

When you use the **Boolean** type, the corresponding iView attribute is displayed with the corresponding **Yes/No** options (for example, the attribute **Show Year Column** in Figure 8.30).

▶ **Mapping the Integer Type**

The **integer** type is also displayed in typed form in the iView Editor or in the personalization dialog, in that it is only possible to enter integers.

▶ **Mapping Simple Types**

If you use simple types with a default value quantity, this value quantity is also copied for the iView attribute (for instance, the **Display Size** attribute in Figure 8.30).

▶ **Other Types**

All other types are mapped to iView attributes of the type **String**. The **long** type, for example, is displayed in the iView Editor or in the personalization dialog as an iView attribute of the type **string**. The type-specific and easy-to-use input helps you are familiar with from your Web Dynpro applications are not available here.

However, as we will see in Section 8.5.6, you can use the existing type-specific value helps when you define Web Dynpro-specific personalization dialogs.

Defining the iView Attribute

initPer-
sonalization()
method

Each Web Dynpro component that implements a detail viewer must implement the `DetailsViewerCompI` component interface (see Section 8.2.2). Here, the `initPersonalization()` method plays integral role in the integration of the portal personalization. Within this method, you define the desired iView attributes by filling the context nodes or node attributes introduced in the last section with the values you want.

Listing 8.6 shows a sample of the definition of the iView attribute **Display Size** within the component controller of the `SearchComp` component. As we already mentioned, you should define the attributes **Name**, **Description**, and **Category** using texts that you can define in the message pool of the corresponding component.

```
wdContext.currentDisplaySizeElement()
  .setName(
    wdComponentAPI.getTextAccessor()
      .getText("DISPLAY_SIZE_TITLE"));

wdContext.currentDisplaySizeElement()
  .setDefault("STANDARD");

wdContext.currentDisplaySizeElement()
  .setDescription(
    wdComponentAPI.getTextAccessor()
      .getText("DISPLAY_SIZE_DESCRIPTION"));

wdContext.currentDisplaySizeElement()
  .setCategory(
    wdComponentAPI.getTextAccessor()
      .getText("SEARCH_CATEGORY"));
```

```
wdContext.currentDisplaySizeElement()
  .setInheritance("NON_FINAL");

wdContext.currentDisplaySizeElement()
  .setMode("READ_WRITE");
```

Listing 8.6 Defining the iView Attribute Display Size

Since we want to keep the interface controller of a Web Dynpro component as slim as possible, we implement the actual method initPersonalization() in the component controller. The corresponding method in the interface controller calls only the method of the component controller.

Implementation within the component controller

You define all context nodes that describe the desired iView attributes under a parent node that you return at the end of the init-Personalization() method. As we'll discuss in the next section, the Java class P13nHelper obtains access via this node to the defined iView attributes. Listing 8.7 shows the return of the SearchPersonalizationData node.

```
return wdContext.nodeSearchPersonalizationData();
```

Listing 8.7 Return from the SearchPersonalizationData Node

The description of the desired iView attributes in this section is not part of the Web Dynpro programming model; however, it is the convention that we have used to implement the use of the portal personalization within the Web Dynpro MusicBox. The P13nHelper Java class in Section 8.5.4 also builds on this convention.

Convention

Note that the methods that we have employed here are only possible ways of implementing the use of the portal personalization within the Web Dynpro MusicBox. Therefore, you should feel free to adapt it to your own needs.

8.5.4 P13nHelper Java Class

Having described how you define the desired iView attributes within your Web Dynpro application, we will now look at the use of the Java class P13nHelper, which you can access via the public part P13NUtils of the tc~p13nmng development component.

Access via the P13NUtils public part

The main task of the P13nHelper Java class is to link the context nodes defined in the last section with the desired iView attributes that are stored in the Portal Content Directory (see Chapter 5).

As we discussed in Section 8.3, the MusicBoxComp component takes over the instantiation of the individual detail viewers. During this instantiation, the defined iView attributes of the detail viewer are also reconciled with the values stored in the PCD. Previously, the required P13nHelper is created within the wdDoInit() method of the component controller of the MusicBoxComp component, as shown in Listing 8.8.

```
iViewPath =
  WDWebContextAdapter.getWebContextAdapter()
    .getRequestParameter("iViewPath");
if (StringUtil.isEmpty(iViewPath)) {
  wdComponentAPI.getMessageManager().reportWarning(
    "Failed to get iView path.
      iView personalization is not be supported.");
} else {
  wdComponentAPI.getMessageManager().reportSuccess(
    "Used iView path is " + iViewPath);
}
p13NHelper = new P13nHelper(iViewPath);
```

Listing 8.8 Instantiation of P13nHelper

iView path An important prerequisite for using the portal personalization within your Web Dynpro application is the so-called *iView path*, through which the P13nHelper can address the Web Dynpro iView and the iView attributes defined for this, through which the Web Dynpro application was started, within your Web Dynpro application. In the following section, we define how you can ensure the transfer of this iView path for your Web Dynpro iView.

Within the initDetailsViewer() method of the component controller of the MusicBoxComp component, the connection of the portal personalization to the corresponding Web Dynpro component is initialized, as shown in Listing 8.9.

```
return wdContext.nodeSearchPersonalizationData();
IWDNode persDataRoot =
  detailsInterface.initPersonalization();
if ((persDataRoot != null)) {
```

```
p13NHelper.updatePersonalization(
  persDataRoot,
  true,
  wdComponentAPI.getMessageManager());
}
```

Listing 8.9 Initialization of the Portal Personalization for a Detail Viewer

Although we won't go into detail here regarding the implementation of the P13nHelper Java class,[1] we will outline the basic operation of the P13nHelper Java class to illustrate several important restrictions and basic conditions.

Basic operation

The updatePersonalization() method essentially assumes the following function: The system checks whether each iView attribute, which is defined via a corresponding context node, exists for the iView that is determined via the transferred iView path. If not, this iView attribute is created by taking into account the defined node attributes that describe the different meta attributes. The value of the **Default** attribute is set as the default value. The newly created iView attributes are created independently of the current user. Therefore, they are visible to all users who are assigned to the corresponding role and can also be adapted to specific roles within the iView Editor.

If the desired iView attribute already exists, the current value is determined and assigned to the **Value** attribute of the corresponding context node. The value that is determined always depends on the current user. Any changes that the user has made via the user personalization are considered.

The **Value** attribute will therefore always contain the current value you want after you call the updatePersonalization() method. Since we ensured from the beginning that it would be easy to use the current value of an iView attribute, you can now address and use the **Value** attribute like any other node attribute within your Web Dynpro application. In Section 8.4, we describe this using the example of the Cover detail viewer.

Accessing the current value of an iView attribute

The following basic conditions for using the portal personalization arise from this:

---

1 However, you can download the entire set of source files from the website for this book: *http://www.sap-press.com*.

▶ All iView attributes defined within a Web Dynpro application are created only when you initially start the Web Dynpro application using a corresponding Web Dynpro iView.

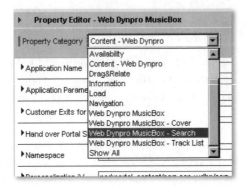

Figure 8.32 Categories Defined Within the Web Dynpro MusicBox

▶ These iView attributes become visible in the iView Editor only when the corresponding Web Dynpro iView or the Web Dynpro application has been started at least once. However, as Figure 8.32 shows, all defined iView attributes can then easily be accessed through the corresponding category. Furthermore, the defined, application-specific iView attributes are then also automatically available in all usages of the iView, for instance, in numerous roles.

We recommend that you use the following procedure:

1. Define all desired application-specific iView attributes using the corresponding context node.

2. Deploy the Web Dynpro application.

3. As described in the next section, generate the corresponding Web Dynpro iView that you can personalize.

4. Open the Web Dynpro iView in the iView Editor and click on the **Preview** button to start the Web Dynpro application linked with the Web Dynpro iView.

5. As described above, all application-specific iView attributes will then be generated automatically. As with all other iView attributes, you can then change and adjust these attributes as well.

8.5.5   Generating Personalized Web Dynpro iViews

As described in the previous section, the iView path of the called Web Dynpro iView is an essential element for using the portal personalization. Every Web Dynpro iView through which you start a Web Dynpro application, in which you want to use the portal personalization, *must* insert the iView path using the `<IView>` context (described in Chapter 5) into the URL template of the SAP Application Integrator (see Figure 8.33).

Disclosing the iView path

Step 4:	Application Parameter
	Enter the paramater(s) of the application for which you want to create the iView

System *
`WebDynproBestPractices` ▼

Namespace *
`sap.com/tc~musicbox`

Application Name *
`MusicBoxApp`

Application Parameters
`iViewPath=<iView.ID>`

Figure 8.33 Defining a Personalized Web Dynpro iView

The definition of `iViewPath=<iView.ID>` within the iView attribute **Application Parameters** allows you to ensure that—within the called Web Dynpro application—the `iViewPath` transfer parameter contains the desired value.

Because you must assign this value to every Web Dynpro iView for which you define application-specific iView attributes, you can also create a special *iView template* here in which you predefine the desired value. You can convert every iView that is created by changing the attribute **Object is a Template** into an iView template (see Figure 8.34).

Using an iView template

▶ Object is a Template   ⦿ Yes   ◯ No

Figure 8.34 Defining an iView Template

When you create a Web Dynpro iView, this iView template is then also displayed in the list of available iView templates. Figure 8.35 shows the iView template **Personalized SAP Web Dynpro iView** that we provide.

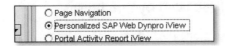

Figure 8.35 Personalized SAP Web Dynpro iView Template

8.5.6 Application-Specific Personalization Dialogs

Default
personalization
dialog

We will now look at the possibility of realizing the personalization dialog through which users can perform the user-specific adjustments as a Web Dynpro application. Figure 8.36 shows the default personalization dialog for the Web Dynpro MusicBox.

Because we define many iView attributes in this example, the generic list display quickly becomes quite complex. Moreover, the different categories, which we have defined for the detail viewers used, are not visible and this makes it harder to find a particular attribute.

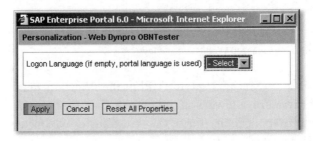

Figure 8.36 Default Personalization Dialog

In contrast, Figure 8.37 shows the Web Dynpro-specific personalization dialog provided by us through the `P13NDialogContainerComp` Web Dynpro component.

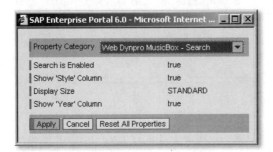

Figure 8.37 Personalization Dialog of the MusicBox

The **Personalized SAP Web Dynpro iView** iView template provided enables you—in addition to the predefined iView path—to define any iView using the **Personalization iView** attribute that you want to start as your personalization dialog (see Figure 8.38).

Assignment of the personalization dialog used

Property Editor - Web Dynpro MusicBox	
Property Category	Content - Web Dynpro
▶ Application Name	MusicBoxApp
▶ Application Parameters	iViewPath=<iView.ID>
▶ Customer Exits for 'ParameterProvider'	
▶ Hand over Portal Stylesheet	⦿ Yes ○ No
▶ Namespace	sap.com/tc~musicbox
▶ Personalization iView	pcd:portal_content/com.sap.wdbp/com.sap.personalization/com.sap.personalizationdialog
▶ Show Debug Screen	○ Yes ⦿ No
▶ System	WebDynproBestPractices

Figure 8.38 Defining the Web Dynpro MusicBox iView

P13NDialogContainerComp Web Dynpro Component

At this stage, we cannot go into detail regarding the implementation of the P13NDialogContainerComp Web Dynpro component. Nevertheless, we would like to address several key factors that will give you an idea of what you should bear in mind when you implement your own personalization dialog.

Since we want to display the user-specific adjustments within the personalization dialog, we access the corresponding values via the getEndUserPropertyContent() method of the P13nHelper Java class. If you only want to display the role-specific adjustments, you can determine these using the corresponding getRolePropertyContent() method.

Importing the iView attributes

Figure 8.39 shows the node hierarchy defined within the component controller of the P13NDialogContainerComp component.

Context node hierarchy used

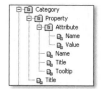

Figure 8.39 Node Hierarchy of the P13NDialogContainerComp Component

Each category is mapped via a corresponding node element of the Category node. The Property node describes the different iView attributes and the Attribute node describes the defined meta attributes. We create the required node elements here using the supply function supplyAttribute().

Dynamically-created node attributes

The P13NDialogContainerComp Web Dynpro component is a good example of displaying the dynamic creation of node attributes, which we create for each value of an iView attribute, in order to generate the typed Web Dynpro value help(s). We create the corresponding node attributes within the initProperties() method of the component controller of the P13NDialogContainerComp component.

Starting in debug mode

By adding the runsInDebugMode=true transfer parameter, you can start the personalization dialog of the Web Dynpro MusicBox in debug mode. You then have the option of checking all available iView attributes and the corresponding meta attributes, in addition to the conventional display of the personalization dialog (see Figure 8.40). Furthermore, you can choose whether you want to see only the role-specific adjustments, or the user-specific adjustments as well.

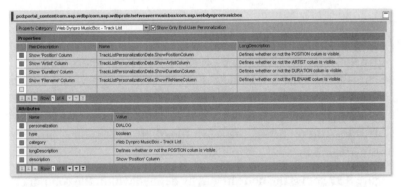

Figure 8.40 Debug View in the Personalization Dialog

Hint

When using the method that we described for defining and using application-specific iView attributes within your Web Dynpro application, the corresponding iView attributes are written directly to the PCD with the P13nHelper. This means that your Web Dynpro application will then only be able to run on the same installation as the SAP NetWeaver Portal.

Therefore, if you want to operate your Web Dynpro applications without the SAP NetWeaver Portal, you cannot use the method we describe.

8.6 Implementing a Context-Sensitive Navigation Bar

Now that you've learned how to use the portal personalization within the Web Dynpro MusicBox, we'll show you how to add a user-friendly, context-sensitive navigation bar to your Web Dynpro application as soon as you start the Web Dynpro application within the SAP NetWeaver Portal.

8.6.1 Extending the Navigation Panel

In Chapter 5, we described the Navigation Panel, which contains the default detail navigation, among other things. The SAP NetWeaver Portal also allows you to define which iView(s) or portal page(s)—for each iView or each portal page—should be displayed in the navigation panel, in addition to the detail navigation, as soon as the corresponding iView or the portal page is displayed in the working area of the SAP NetWeaver Portal.

Figure 8.41 Contextual Navigation Panel

In the Web Dynpro MusicBox, we use this option to show the **Search** and **You Can Also** iViews described further below, as soon as you start the Web Dynpro MusicBox (see Figure 8.41).

1. To display an iView or a portal page in the navigation panel, start the iView or page editor of the iView or the portal page that later appears in the working area. In Chapter 5, we described how you can do this for iViews or portal pages in a particular role. Choose the **Dynamic Navigation** view (see Figure 8.42).

Figure 8.42 Selecting the Dynamic Navigation

2. You can use the context menu entry **Add to Dynamic Navigation** of the desired iView or portal page to display the relevant iView or the portal page on the navigation panel (see Figure 8.43).

Figure 8.43 Adding an iView for Dynamic Navigation

3. Figure 8.44 shows the **Dynamic Navigation** view of the Web Dynpro MusicBox. You recognize the two iViews **Search** and **You Can Also** that we want to display in the navigation panel.

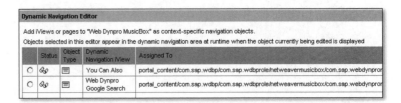

Figure 8.44 iViews for Dynamic Navigation

iView tray settings
4. As soon as you display an iView in the navigation panel, we recommend that you limit the functions offered through the iView tray to the entries **Open in New Window** and **Refresh** (see Figure 8.45).

Figure 8.45 iView Tray of an iView in the Navigation Panel

5. As soon as you want to display a Web Dynpro iView in the navigation panel, you should ensure that you use the "right" background color—the same background color as is used by default in the navigation panel—within your Web Dynpro application. Figure 8.46 shows an example of this for the Web Dynpro View `SearchTriggerCompView` of the `SearchTriggerComp` component, which we define within the `tc~cnpmngmt` development component.

Defining the background color

6. By using a `IWDTransparentContainer` UI element, we can adjust the background color to that used in the navigation panel by setting the **cellBackgroundDesign** property to **fill1**.

Figure 8.46 Defining the Background Color for the Navigation Panel

8.6.2 Contextual Navigation Panel

As we described in the last section, we show the Web Dynpro iView **You Can Also** in the navigation panel, among other things, as soon as you start the Web Dynpro MusicBox. Through this iView, you start the *Contextual navigation panel*, which we implement using the `CNPManagerComp` component, which is located in the `tc~cnpnmngmt` development component.

As you can see in Figure 8.41, the contextual navigation panel is divided into two areas: In the upper area you can select one of the

Basic operation

possible perspectives that are defined within the Web Dynpro MusicBox. In the lower part, the system displays the objects that you can select in one of the detail viewers. For each object, the system then displays additional functions that you can start by selecting the corresponding link. Normally, the functions that you choose in this way are displayed in a new window.

Depending on the relevant status of the MusicBox, the content of the contextual navigation panel therefore changes, thereby providing a *real* context-sensitive navigation bar. We will now consider two aspects we examined while implementing the contextual navigation panel.

Using Portal Eventing

Loose coupling of portal content

The Web Dynpro MusicBox and the contextual navigation panel are implemented through two independently running Web Dynpro applications. As we described in Chapter 5, Web Dynpro applications are always integrated as isolated iViews into the SAP NetWeaver Portal. Each Web Dynpro iView and the Web Dynpro application linked to it runs isolated from and independently of the remaining content that is displayed. In this context, we therefore talk about a *loose coupling* of this portal content.

But, on the other hand, we want to ensure that the contextual navigation panel adapts to the current status of the Web Dynpro MusicBox, and that it displays, for example, the functions available for the object selected in the MusicBox. We also want to use the contextual navigation panel to choose the perspective displayed in the MusicBox.

Portal eventing

Despite the aforementioned loose coupling of the two Web Dynpro iViews, we therefore need a simple communication option that allows, for instance, the MusicBox to inform the contextual navigation panel as soon as the user has chosen a CD. The SAP NetWeaver Portal offers exactly this communication option via the *portal eventing*.

The portal eventing is a client-side event mechanism that allows *portal events* to be sent and received between any iViews running within a window of the web browser. Within a Web Dynpro application you can use the WDPortalEventing help class to access the portal eventing options.

You register your Web Dynpro application as an *event listener* via the subscribe() method, which you can essentially only call within a view controller. For instance, the contextual navigation panel is registered within the wdDoInit() method of the view controller of the CNPManagerView view to the objectEvent portal event (see Listing 8.10).

Event registration

```
WDPortalEventing.subscribe(
  "urn:com.sap.wdbp.cnp",
  "objectEvent",
  wdThis.wdGetObjectEventAction());
```

Listing 8.10 Registering to the objectEvent Portal Event

In addition to specifying the **Event Name** and the **Event Namespace**, you define a Web Dynpro action of your choice that is to be called by the Web Dynpro runtime environment if the specified portal event has been sent. To access any event parameters that may have been transferred, you must define a dataObject parameter of the type **string** for the specified action (see Figure 8.47).

Using a Web Dynpro action

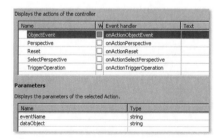

Figure 8.47 Defining the ObjectEvent Action

If you want to use the same Web Dynpro action for different portal events, you can also define an eventName parameter that then contains the name of the sent event. Furthermore, by defining an event-Namespace parameter, you can also handle events from different namespaces within a Web Dynpro action.

> **Hint**
>
> We recommend that you use an action for different portal events *only* in individual cases, as this can easily lead to very large event handlers that are difficult to read.

Event deregistration

You can use the unsubscribe() method of the WDPortalEventing help class to deregister your Web Dynpro application again from a particular portal event.

> **Hint**
>
> It is important to ensure that you always deregister for all registered portal events within your Web Dynpro application, as soon as the Web Dynpro application is shut down. You can do this in the wdDoExit() method of the corresponding view controller, for example.

Sending a portal event

You can use the fire() method of the WDPortalNavigation help class to send any portal event within your Web Dynpro application. As soon as you select an artist name in the Search detail viewer, for example, the objectEvent portal event is sent to the SearchView view within the onActionSelectArtist() event handler (see Listing 8.11).

```
Map parameters = new HashMap();
parameters.put(
  "query",
  urlEncode.encode(
    wdContext.currentCDElement().getArtist()));

WDPortalEventing.fire(
  "urn:com.sap.wdbp.cnp",
  "objectEvent",
  EventHelper.encodeObject(
    "Artist",
    wdContext.currentCDElement().getArtist(),
    "Selected",
    parameters));
```

Listing 8.11 Sending the objectEvent Portal Event

Using the Event-Helper help class

The only time that you can transfer a single string parameter is when you send a portal event, which is not always recommended for practical use. Within the Web Dynpro MusicBox we therefore use the EventHelper help class, which allows several parameter values to be bundled and read out. The `EventHelper` help class is part of the `Utils` public part of the `tc~utils` development component.

Using the Object-Based Navigation

To display the available functions of the object selected in the MusicBox within the contextual navigation panel, we use the object-based navigation described in Chapter 7, which allows operations of a business object to be activated. Figure 8.48 shows the business objects defined within the MusicBox.

Figure 8.48 Business Objects That Are Required by the MusicBox

The defined operations correspond exactly to those functions displayed in the contextual navigation panel, for instance, for the business object **Track**, as soon as a particular music title has been selected in the MusicBox (see Figure 8.49).

Figure 8.49 Available Functions for the Track Business Object

The operations of a business object available at runtime are not necessarily identical to those operations that are declared in the content catalog. Depending on the roles that are assigned to the current user, individual operations may not be available. Within the contextual navigation panels, we therefore want to display only those operations that are actually available; we use the `IUserObjectBased-Navigation` portal service to determine the operations that are valid

Displayed operations

for the current user. We will later display only these operations in the contextual navigation panel.

Listing 8.12 shows the `updateObjectOperations()` method of the view controller of the `CNPManagerView` view, in which we determine the valid operations defined for the current user for any business object and the corresponding node elements of the `Operation` context node.

```
IUserObjectBasedNavigation obn =
 wdContext.currentOBNServiceElement().getService();
IUser user = null;
try {
  user = WDClientUser.getCurrentUser().getSAPUser();
} catch (WDUMException e) {
    wdComponentAPI.getMessageManager().reportException(
      "Failed to get current user: " +
        e.getLocalizedMessage(),
      true);
    return;
}
List operations = obn.getTargets(system, objectType, user);

IPrivateCNPManagerView.IOperationNode operationNode =
  getOperationNode (system, objectType, value, parameters);

IPrivateCNPManagerView.IOperationElement
  newOperation = null;

if (operations != null && operations.size() > 0) {

  for (Iterator iter = operations.iterator();
    iter.hasNext();) {

  IOBNTarget target = (IOBNTarget) iter.next();

  newOperation =
    wdContext.nodeOperation().createOperationElement();
   newOperation.
     setCaption(target.getOperationFriendlyName());
   newOperation.
     setName(target.getOperationName()
       .substring(target.getOperationName()
         .lastIndexOf('/') + 1));
```

```
      operationNode.addElement(newOperation);
  }
}
```

Listing 8.12 Determining the Valid Operations

We use the node elements of the `Operation` node created in this way within the `wdDoModify()` method of the view controller of the `CNP-ManagerView` view, to generate the desired `IWDLinkToAction` UI elements through which you can start the desired operation or function.

In Chapter 5, we described how you could use the **Launch in New Window** attribute of a Web Dynpro iView to define whether the iView should be displayed in a window of the web browser. In this case, you can use the **Window Features** attribute to define the size, the appearance, and the behavior of this window (see Chapter 6).

Opening a new window

Unfortunately, the **Window Features** attribute cannot be used within SAP NetWeaver 2004 if the new window is opened using object-based navigation. Therefore, we use the conventional portal navigation within the contextual navigation panel to start the desired iView or the portal page that implements the selected operation. We use the portal service `IUserObjectBasedNavigation` to determine the iView or the portal page that implements the selected operation, and start it via the portal navigation, taking into account the defined **Window Features**.

Listing 8.13 shows the portal navigation being launched within the `triggerNavigation()` method of the view controller of the `CNP-ManagerView` view.

```
IOBNTarget navigationTarget =
  obn.getDefaultTargetForOperation(
    system, type, operation, user);
String iViewPath = navigationTarget.getIViewName();

P13nHelper p13nHelper = new P13nHelper(iViewPath);
IPropertyContent properties =
  p13nHelper.getEndUserPropertyContent();

String windowFeatures =
  properties.getProperty(
```

```
                    "com.sapportals.portal.navigation.WinFeatures");

WDPortalNavigation.navigateAbsolute(
  iViewPath,
  WDPortalNavigationMode.SHOW_EXTERNAL,
  windowFeatures,
  "ObjectWindow",
  WDPortalNavigationHistoryMode.NO_HISTORY,
  null,
  null,
  parameters,
  null,
  false,
  true);
```

Listing 8.13 Activating a Portal Navigation

Reusability   Although we designed and implemented the contextual navigation panel especially for combination with the Web Dynpro MusicBox, you can use it in your own Web Dynpro applications. The displayed objects and the corresponding functions are defined entirely transparently within the object-based navigation. If necessary, you may need to adjust the required portal events for communication between the contextual navigation panel and your Web Dynpro application.

8.7 Additional Remarks

As we approach the end of this chapter, we would like to provide you with two workarounds that address two questions we are often asked.

Within the Web Dynpro programming model, there is no possibility, based on SAP NetWeaver 2004, to programmatically close the window of the web browser in which the Web Dynpro application is running. However, particularly when you are using multiple windows, this often makes sense and makes the application more user-friendly. Furthermore, Web Dynpro also doesn't give you a way of accessing the default print functions of the web browser. Here's a way of solving these two problems.

8.7.1 Closing a Window

Within a JSP- or servlet-based application, it is fairly easy to implement the functions described by calling the relevant JavaScript functions. In Web Dynpro, this is *not* possible, and with good reason,
namely, because of the Web Dynpro Client abstraction that we have
already mentioned on several occasions. As soon as you start your
Web Dynpro application within the SAP NetWeaver Portal, however, we can combine these two methods.

To do this, we define a special portal component in the **Enterprise
Portal Perspective** of the SAP NetWeaver Developer Studio (see Figure 8.50), without going into detail on the possibilities available to
you when you develop a portal component.

Defining a portal
component

Figure 8.50 Selecting the Enterprise Portal Perspective

For our purposes, the critical step is defining the *eventHandler.jsp* file,
which contains the required JavaScript functions for closing the web
browser window and for calling the print functionality (see Listing
8.14).

```
<%@ page import = "com.sapportals.portal.prt.util.*" %>
<%
  String eventURN = "urn:com.sap.wdbp";
  String windowCloseEventName = "windowClose";
  String printEventName = "print";
%>
<script>
  <!--
  function windowCloseHandler(eventObj) {
    window.close();
  }
  function printHandler(eventObj) {
    print();
  }
  EPCM.subscribeEvent(
    "<%= StringUtils.escapeToJS(eventURN) %>",
    "<%= StringUtils.escapeToJS(windowCloseEventName) %>",
    windowCloseHandler);
```

```
     EPCM.subscribeEvent(
       "<%= StringUtils.escapeToJS(eventURN) %>",
       "<%= StringUtils.escapeToJS(printEventName) %>",
       printHandler);
     //-->
</script>
```

Listing 8.14 eventHandler.jsp File

Using portal event-
ing

To call these functions later from a Web Dynpro application, within
the *eventHandler.jsp* file, we register two portal events: `windowClose`
and `print`. As soon as one of these events is sent, we call the desired
JavaScript functions, which then close the current window, for
example.

To allow the window to be closed from a Web Dynpro application,
we combine the Web Dynpro application and the portal component
via the corresponding iViews on a portal page. For example, Figure
8.51 shows the **Search Dialog** portal page, which we use for the different search options within the Web Dynpro MusicBox.

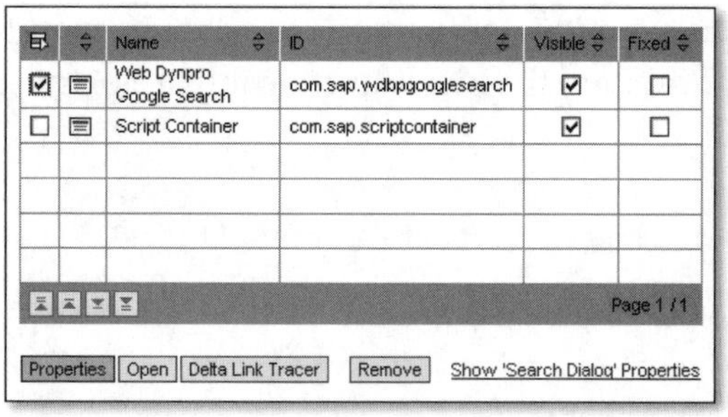

Figure 8.51 Contents of the Search Dialog Portal Page

Because we hide the iView trays of both iViews within this portal
page, and the portal component or the *eventHandler.jsp* file doesn't
contain any visible user interface, we get the desired result (see Figure 8.52): The window for the artist search only seems to contain the
corresponding Web Dynpro Google search. However, when you
click on the **Close** button, windows disappear because we send the
`windowClose` portal event in the corresponding event handler, which
is then processed within the *eventHandler.jsp* file in which the window is closed.

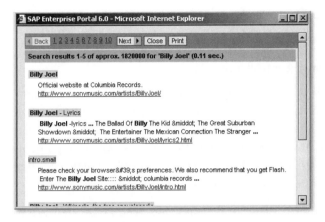

Figure 8.52 Artist Search

8.7.2   Printing the Window Content

We call the print functionality of the web browser in the same way that we do when closing the window. By sending the corresponding print portal event, the required JavaScript function is finally called within the *eventHandler.jsp* file.

Sending a portal event within a Web Dynpro application is always associated with a server roundtrip. This works in our favor, because during this server roundtrip we can also adjust the Web Dynpro application that is displayed by hiding the navigation bars and choosing to display only the actual search results (see Figure 8.53). In addition to hiding a particular area of your application UI, you can also adapt the number of table rows displayed in a special print preview to ensure that all available entries are printed.

Implementing a print preview

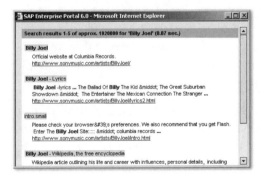

Figure 8.53 Artist Search in the Print Preview

8.8 Web Dynpro Applications in the SAP NetWeaver Portal

8.8.1 Current Restrictions

As you can see by the Web Dynpro MusicBox example, the integration of your Web Dynpro application into the SAP NetWeaver Portal—based on SAP NetWeaver 2004—allows you to implement very potent and demanding applications. Nevertheless, we must point out a number of restrictions that you should consider when designing and implementing your Web Dynpro applications.

Isolated iViews

Your Web Dynpro iViews are always displayed as isolated iViews within the SAP NetWeaver Portal, so that initially only the client-side communication options are available to you or your Web Dynpro application. Even the launch of a portal navigation or the use of the work protect mode always occurs using client-side mechanisms that are associated with at least one additional server roundtrip when they are used within a Web Dynpro application. Furthermore, problems can occur with isolated iViews if your Web Dynpro application and the SAP NetWeaver Portal are running on installations in different network domains.

Web Dynpro application versus Web Dynpro iView

Another restriction that is often the subject of discussion is that a Web Dynpro application is always assigned to exactly one Web Dynpro iView. However, as we saw with the Web Dynpro MusicBox example, a Web Dynpro application can easily, in principle, be split up into several Web Dynpro iViews. Therefore, it makes sense to map each individual detail viewer within the MusicBox to an independent iView. The Web Dynpro MusicBox would then not appear as one iView in the SAP NetWeaver Portal, but rather as a collection of several iViews that could be summarized with the conventional portal options into portal pages. The different layouts that we implemented within the Web Dynpro MusicBox could then be implemented via the default layouts of a portal page.

Of course, based on SAP NetWeaver 2004, you can also divide an application such as the Web Dynpro MusicBox into several Web Dynpro applications, and to then define a Web Dynpro iView for each of these. This gives you the flexibility outlined above, albeit you would lose the option of being able to efficiently reuse the corresponding data between the different Web Dynpro applications.

Essentially, you must therefore always decide between the narrow integration of Web Dynpro components within a Web Dynpro application, and a more flexible combination of numerous iViews.

8.8.2 Next Steps

Note that starting with the next release of SAP NetWeaver, the aforementioned restrictions will no longer apply.

Web Dynpro iViews will then no longer be displayed as isolated iViews. Instead, they will be embedded in the surrounding portal page. From the user's point of view, the portal page and all embedded Web Dynpro iViews will appear as a single unit that will only be reloaded as a whole.

Embedded Web Dynpro iViews

Closely linked to the embedding of Web Dynpro iViews are the enhanced possibilities for changing and extending certain attributes and settings of the SAP NetWeaver Portal within a Web Dynpro application. It will therefore be possible, for example, to add application-specific entries to the iView tray of a Web Dynpro iView, or to change the list of displayed iViews within a portal page.

Extended portal services

Furthermore, the options for the portal personalization will be linked more closely to the Web Dynpro programming model, so that you can use this within your Web Dynpro application with a lot less additional effort.

Improved personalization

Finally, it will be easier to generate Web Dynpro iViews, and the often painstaking search for the right parameters, which is inherent when you create an iView, will be a thing of the past.

Generating iViews

Because your Web Dynpro applications will be much more tightly integrated with the SAP NetWeaver Portal in the next release of SAP NetWeaver, there will also be new *types* of Web Dynpro iViews that exemplify this kind of integration. You can only access these new functionalities with these *new* Web Dynpro iViews; however, the Web Dynpro iViews created on the basis of SAP NetWeaver 2004 will continue to run in the future.

8.9 Summary

By using the Web Dynpro MusicBox, we explored the extensive possibilities with which you can make your Web Dynpro application flexible and adaptable through strategic componentization.

Furthermore, we looked at using the portal personalization within your Web Dynpro application and showed you how to develop Web Dynpro-based personalization dialogs.

We also discussed the possibilities offered by object-based navigation (i.e., the contextual navigation panel) and showed you how the skillful definition of business objects and operations allows you to obtain a very flexible description of the functions you provide.

Finally, we looked at the limits and restrictions that exist when you integrate Web Dynpro applications into the SAP NetWeaver Portal based on SAP NetWeaver 2004, and we also examined future integration possibilities that will unfold with the next release of SAP NetWeaver.

In this chapter we will look in more detail at the generic development components that we have used in the various examples in this book. As an example, we can use the DeploymentManager, which can be used, among other things, to determine the list of available Web Dynpro applications in the Web Dynpro NavigationTester.

9 Generic Development Components

From the beginning, we had two objectives in implementing the examples in this book. First, we wanted to illustrate the possibilities for structuring your Web Dynpro application and splitting it into reusable entities by using Web Dynpro components and component interfaces and using the SAP NetWeaver Development Infrastructure (NWDI). Second, we wanted to apply these possibilities in the individual examples themselves. To achieve this, we implemented a number of generic development components that are used in a wide range of different examples. We have described the relevant usage in the corresponding chapters. In this chapter, we now want to describe the definition of some of these generic development components.

9.1 Development Component tc~utils

Certain functions of the individual examples in our book are repeated or are not linked directly to the relevant example: The encoding of transfer parameters when you navigate to another Web Dynpro application or another Web Dynpro iView, the sorting of a table in a Web Dynpro application, or the packing of several parameters for the portal eventing are only some examples. We have implemented these functions using several generic Java classes, for which we have defined the `tc-utils` development component, to be able to use the Java classes in all examples.

9.1.1 Definition of the tc~utils Development Component

In the following sections, we will look at how to create the Web Dynpro development component `tc~utils`, and how to make the various Java classes accessible through a corresponding public part from outside; in other words, from other development components.

1. To create a development component, first go to the **Development Configurations Perspective** of the SAP NetWeaver Developer Studio (see Figure 9.1).

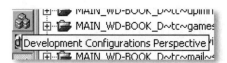

Figure 9.1 Selecting the Development Configurations Perspective

2. Since we also want to provide the source files of the `tc~utils` development component, start creating the development component using the context menu entry **Create New DC...** of the software component `sap.com_WDBP_S_1` (see Figure 9.2).

Figure 9.2 Creating a New Development Component

3. In the dialog that then appears, you define the **Vendor (sap.com)** and the required **Name** of the development component (DC); make sure you choose the correct prefix (**tc/**), as this cannot be changed later (see Figure 9.3). We define the `tc~utils` development component as a Web Dynpro development component, although (as you will see later) we will not define any additional (Web Dynpro) entities, other than the Java classes.

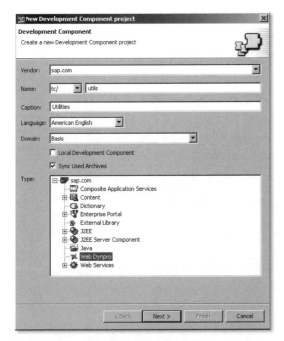

Figure 9.3 Definition of the tc~utils Web Dynpro Development Component

It is also possible to provide Java classes via J2EE or Java development components. However, we decided on a Web Dynpro variant for the `tc~utils` development component, because this is the easiest way to add the Java classes provided for your Web Dynpro project.

Development component type used

4. After you click on the **Next** button, you must assign the new development component (or the files linked to it) to an **Activity** (see Figure 9.4) by selecting the desired activity from the list of available activities or by creating a new one using the **New Activity** button.

You can use an activity to group any files you create or edit and want to check in, activate or transport as a single package. While in theory it is possible to group files from different development components in a single activity, it is often useful to separate the files according to their development component.[1]

Using activities

---

1 You can find further information on using activities at the following address, among others: *https://www.sdn.sap.com/irj/sdn/developerareas/was?rid=/webcontent/uuid/033cabec-0701-0010-5a93-b2776c29d65e.*

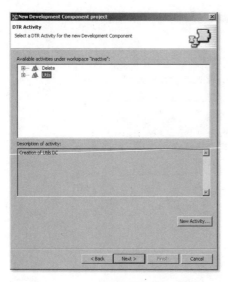

Figure 9.4 Assigning the tc~utils Development Component to an Activity

Creating the Web Dynpro project

5. After you have selected the corresponding activity, the corresponding Web Dynpro project MAIN_WD-BOOK_D~tc~utils~ sap.com is created in a final step, which will later give you access within the Web Dynpro perspective of the SAP NetWeaver Developer Studio to the content of the tc~utils development component (see Figure 9.5).

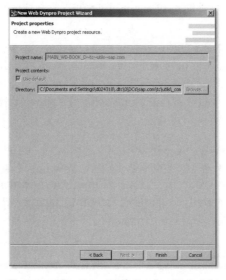

Figure 9.5 Creating a Web Dynpro Project Based on a Web Dynpro DC

6. When you click on the **Finish** button, both the development component and the corresponding Web Dynpro project are created. Figure 9.6 shows the tc~utils development component that has been created in the **Development Configurations Perspective**.

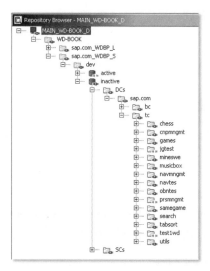

Figure 9.6 Created tc~utils Development Component

9.1.2 Definition of the Public Part Utils

A key element of the NWDI and of the use of DCs is the ability to explicitly define who has what type of access to what functions. Each development component defines public parts for this. These can be used to determine the open components of the relevant development component. In Chapter 3, we already discussed in detail the significance of a public part in conjunction with Web Dynpro development components.

Using public parts

For our Web Dynpro development component tc~utils we now want to create the public part Utils, through which we then make the required Java classes available. To do this, we must first import the corresponding Java files into the MAIN_WD-BOOK_D~tc~utils~sap.com project.

1. Go to the navigator and use the **Import...** entry in the context menu of the **src · packages** directory in the MAIN_WD-BOOK_D~tc~utils~sap.com project to start the import dialog (see Figure 9.7).

Importing the Java files

347

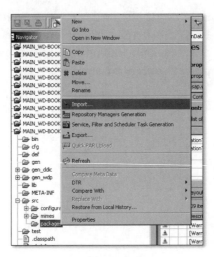

Figure 9.7 Starting the Project Import

2. Since we want to import individual Java files, choose **File system** in the dialog window that then appears (see Figure 9.8).

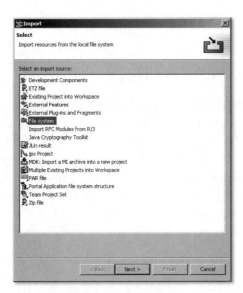

Figure 9.8 Selecting the File System Import

Choosing the Java files

3. When you click on the **Next** button, you have the option of selecting the individual Java files. In our example, they are in the *C:\Temp* directory (see Figure 9.9).

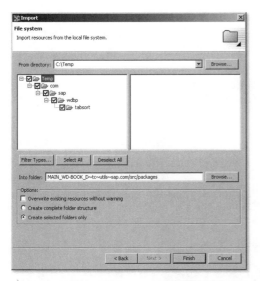

Figure 9.9 Selecting the Required Java Package

When you select Java files, make sure that the entire directory structure under the selected root directory is imported; in our example, everything under *C:\Temp*. Particularly when importing Java files, it is therefore important *not* to import the corresponding files directly from the directory where they are located, but rather from the parent directory required by the package name used.

4. When you click on **Finish**, the selected Java files are imported. The SAP NetWeaver Developer Studio then automatically recognizes that these are new files and indicates this, as you can tell in Figure 9.10. Here you are asked to assign the corresponding files to an activity, through which the files are later stored in the Design Time Repository.

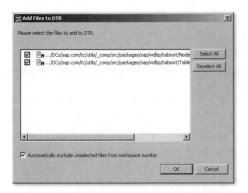

Figure 9.10 Adding new Java Files to the Utils Activity

5. Once you have confirmed with the **OK** button that you want to copy these new files, in the final step you must also select the corresponding `Utils` activity and click on **OK** (see Figure 9.11).

Figure 9.11 Selecting the Utils Activity

Figure 9.12 shows the imported Java files. You can now display and edit these by double-clicking in the Java Editor. We store the Java files in the `tc~utils` development component, but in theory you could also create and store any Web Dynpro entities you want in this DC.

Figure 9.12 Imported Java Files

Creating the public part

Once we have imported the required Java files, we must create the corresponding public part, through which the Web Dynpro components using the files can later reference the individual Java classes.

1. You essentially have two possibilities for opening the corresponding dialog. On the one hand, you can start it in the Web Dynpro Explorer with the entry **New Public Part ...** of the context menu of the **DC MetaData · Public Parts** directory (see Figure 9.13). On the other, you can also choose the dialog for creating a public part

using the entry **Development Component · Add to Public Part** of the context menu of the individual Java files.

Figure 9.13 Creating a New Public Part

2. In the next step, you define the name of the public part. If you wish, you can also specify a caption and a description of the contents of the public part (see Figure 9.14).

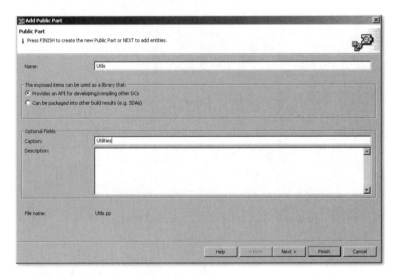

Figure 9.14 Defining the Utils Public Part

3. Clicking on the **Next** button brings you to the next dialog step, where you select the individual components that are to become part of the public part.

In our example, we select **Java Class Entity Type** and define the required Java files, as you can see in Figure 9.15.

Defining the components of the public part

Figure 9.15 Selecting the Java Files

4. After you click on **Finish,** the public part Utils is generated. To allow correct usage later, you must now rebuild the entire development component by selecting the **Development Component · Build...** entry in the context menu of the MAIN_WD-BOOK_ D~tc~utils~sap.com project (see Figure 9.16). The required files are then updated and the JAR file that is needed in our case is created.

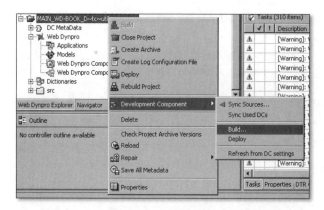

Figure 9.16 Activating the Development Component Build

The tc~utils development component is now available to any other development components. You will find the tc~utils DC being used in an example in Chapter 6.

9.2 Web Dynpro DeploymentManager

Using the Deployment- Manager in the examples Your Web Dynpro application uses the Web Dynpro Deployment-Manager to access information on the deployed Web Dynpro content. For instance, the Web Dynpro NavigationTester uses the

DeploymentManager to determine the list of available Web Dynpro applications; the Web Dynpro GameStation receives the list of available games.

The Web Dynpro DeploymentManager is implemented as a non-visual Web Dynpro component and therefore does not provide its own user interface. The corresponding Web Dynpro component is the DeploymentManagerComp component in the Web Dynpro project MAIN_WD-BOOK_D~tc~dplmng~sap.com; the DC is tc~dplmng.

9.2.1 Definition of the Information Provided

To provide all available information on the deployed Web Dynpro entities purely declaratively, the DeploymentManager uses its component interface controller to define the corresponding context nodes. However, since we do not want to create or manage any data in the component interface controller, we have defined the corresponding context nodes in the component controller itself. The component interface controller then accesses these nodes via context mapping, as shown in Figure 9.17.

Declarative access to data

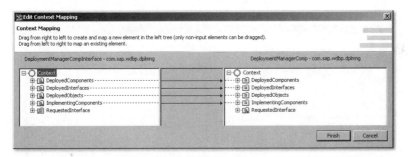

Figure 9.17 Context Mapping Between Component Interface Controller Context and Component Controller Context

The RequestedInterface context node plays a special role here, because the corresponding FullName node attribute must be determined from externally, in other words from the Web Dynpro component using it (see Chapter 3). To accomplish this, we define the RequestedInterface context node as a so-called *input element*, by setting the corresponding **isInputElement** attribute to **true** (see Figure 9.18).

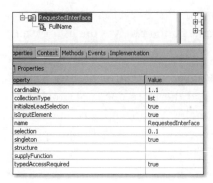

Figure 9.18 RequestedInterface Context Node

Using reverse context mappings This allows us to ensure that the `RequestedInterface` node can later be filled with a value by the user of the using Web Dynpro component via reverse context mapping.

This also explains the fact that the `RequestedInterface` node is not defined within the component controller, but rather within the component interface controller. We pass the value on via context mapping between the component controller and the component interface controller (see Figure 9.19).

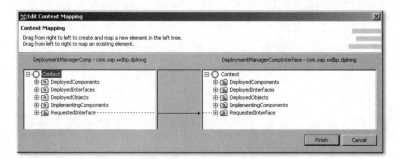

Figure 9.19 Context Mapping for the RequestedInterface Node

Bidirectional context mapping There are therefore context mappings in both directions between the component controller and the component interface controller. This is a good example of bidirectional context mapping, which then can also be seen in the Web Dynpro Data Modeler, because the data link between the component controller and interface controller is displayed accordingly (see Figure 9.20).

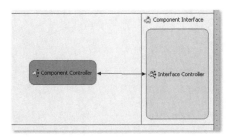

Figure 9.20 Bidirectional Context Mapping

9.2.2 Description of the Information Provided

To be able to access all deployed Web Dynpro entities generically, the Web Dynpro DeploymentManager provides the `DeployedObjects` context node. A `DeployedObjects` node element corresponds here to a Web Dynpro development component or a Web Dynpro Eclipse project.

Determining all Web Dynpro entities

For each `DeployedObjects` node element, all Web Dynpro entities contained in the relevant Web Dynpro development component or in the Web Dynpro Eclipse project are listed through the `Deployed-Parts` node. Figure 9.21 shows the definition of the `DeployedObjects` context node.

Figure 9.21 DeployedObjects Context Node

The Web Dynpro NavigationTester uses the `DeployedObjects` node, for example, to determine the list of available Web Dynpro applications (described in Chapter 6). You can get the list of available Web Dynpro components using the `DeployedComponents` context node (see Figure 9.22). Furthermore, for each Web Dynpro component the system determines, using the `ImplementedInterfaces` context node, those Web Dynpro component interfaces are implemented by the relevant Web Dynpro component.

List of available Web Dynpro components

Figure 9.22 DeployedComponent Context Node

Defined Web Dynpro component interfaces

The defined Web Dynpro component interfaces, in turn, are provided through the `DeployedInterfaces` context node (see Figure 9.23).

Figure 9.23 DeployedInterfaces Context Node

Determining all Web Dynpro components for a specific Web Dynpro component interface

In the end, you can use the `ImplementingComponents` context node to determine all Web Dynpro components that determine the component interface provided by the `RequestedInterface` context node (see Figure 9.24). The `ImplementingComponents` context node is always very useful if you want your Web Dynpro application to offer dynamic downloading of any implementations of a particular component interface. Both the Web Dynpro GameStation and the Web Dynpro MusicBox use this technology.

Figure 9.24 ImplementingComponents Context Node

9.3   Development Component tc~pplibs

As soon as you want to access a portal service within your Web Dynpro application, in addition to defining the corresponding sharing reference of your Web Dynpro application, you must make the required JAR archive accessible to ensure that the Java classes required by the portal services used are available during design time.

9.3.1 Providing the Required JAR Archives

To do this, we define the `tc~pplibs` development component, through which we make all JAR archives required available to the Web Dynpro development components in this book. This is known as an *External Library* (see Figure 9.25).

Using an External Library development component

Figure 9.25 Creating an External Library Development Component

Once you have created the `tc~pplibs` development component in the **Development Configurations Perspective** in the same way as for the development components presented in the previous sections, you must import the desired JAR archives. To do this, go to the **Resource Perspective** (see Figure 9.26).

Importing the JAR archives

Figure 9.26 Selecting the Resource Perspective

You can now import the required JAR archives into the `tc~pplibs` development component using the file import described in Section 9.1. Figure 9.27 shows all archives used.

Adding the JAR archives to the public part

```
MAIN_WD-BOOK_D~tc~pplibs~sap.com
   cfg
   def
   gen
   libraries
      com.sap.portal.ivs.api_iviewapi.jar
      com.sap.portal.ivs.api_landscape_api.jar
      com.sap.portal.ivs.api_portalpcm_api.jar
      com.sap.portal.ivs.global.jndibridge_api.jar
      com.sap.portal.ivs.iviewserviceapi.jar
      com.sap.portal.navigation.serviceapi.jar
      com.sap.portal.pcm.admin.apiservice_api.jar
      com.sap.portal.unification.objectbasednavigationserviceapi.j
      com.sap.portal.unification.uslserviceapi.jar
      gl_api.jar
      gl_core.jar
      prtapi.jar
      prtjndisupport.jar
      prtregistry.jar
   src
   test
```

Figure 9.27 JAR Archives Used

357

To now provide the required JAR archives to other development components, you must define a corresponding public part. For the development component tc~pplibs we define the public part PortalLibraries, as we did in Section 9.1.2. You can add the individual JAR archives to the public part either via the context menu entry **Development Component · Add to Public Part** of the corresponding JAR archive (see Figure 9.28) or directly when you create the public part itself (see Figure 9.29).

Figure 9.28 Adding a JAR Archive to the Public Part

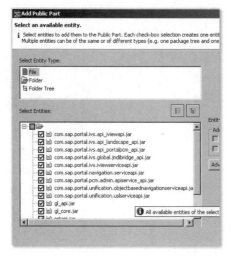

Figure 9.29 Defining the JAR Archives of the PortalLibraries Public Part

9.3.2 Localizing the Required JAR Archives

We are often asked in this context what method we recommend for finding the required JAR archives. As already mentioned, you can always call each portal service within your Web Dynpro application. Nevertheless, to our knowledge there is no general overview of the existing portal services and their functions.

General directory of existing portal services

As soon as you know the name of the desired portal service, you have two options for finding the required JAR archive:

▶ Once you have access to the file system of your SAP NetWeaver Portal installation, you can find all portal services under:

Direct access to the file system

C:\usr\sap\<SystemName>\JC<InstanceName>\j2ee\cluster\ server<Node>\apps\sap.com\irj\servlet_jsp\irj\root\WEB-INF\ portal\portalapps

For instance, the portal service used in Chapter 6 to read the valid operations of a business object can be found under:

C:\usr\sap\\<SystemName>\JC<InstanceName>\j2ee\cluster\server0\ apps\sap.com\irj\servlet_jsp\irj\root\WEB-INF\portal\portalapps\ com.sap.portal.unification.objectbasednavigationservice\lib

Here, make sure that you always read the JAR archives from the *lib* subdirectory of the portal service.

▶ When you have no direct access to the file system of your SAP NetWeaver portal installation, you can also download the required JAR archives directly via the portal UI, provided you have system administrator rights.

Downloading the JAR archives from the portal

▶ Under **System Administration · Support · Portal Runtime · Browse Deployment** you can select the existing portal service in the same way as in the file explorer, as shown in Figure 9.30.

You are here:ROOT/WEB-INF/portal/portalapps/com.sap.portal.unification.objectbasednavigationservice (download this folder)

name	action	size	last modified
lib	browse, download	0	Fri Dec 09 10:43:13 CET 2005
META-INF	browse, download	0	Fri Dec 09 10:43:13 CET 2005
portalapp.xml	view, download	1172	Fri Dec 09 10:43:13 CET 2005
private	browse, download	0	Fri Dec 09 10:43:13 CET 2005

Figure 9.30 Selecting a Portal Service via the Portal UI

> **Tip**
>
> In relation to portal services: Never import the required JAR archives directly into your Web Dynpro project or your Web Dynpro DC. These JAR archives will then be deployed together with your Web Dynpro application, which can cause problems to arise at runtime because the Java classes and interfaces of the portal services used are duplicated.

9.4   Fundamental Division of the Development Components

Use of software components

Having looked at examples of various types of development components in the last few sections, we would now finally like to look at the possibilities within the NWDI for summarizing your development components into larger units: the so-called *software components*.

Reasons for using several development components

Typically, you will not fully implement your Web Dynpro application(s) in a single development component; the examples given in this book illustrate this quite clearly. For instance, often it makes sense to separate the component interface and implement it accordingly into different development components. Furthermore, organizational or spatial aspects also play a role. Different product cycles or release strategies also can be reasons for using several development components.

Software components group development components together

You can use the software components to group your development components regardless of their type and summarize them to form delivery units. Again, a range of factors plays a role here[2]: How should the individual development components be delivered? Together with the corresponding source files? Only for use at the time of design, or also for use at runtime?

For our examples, we decided to use a total of two software components, as you can see in Figure 9.31. The software component sap.com_WDBP_L_1 contains those development components for which we do not want to provide any source files. The software

---

2 At this point we cannot describe all important factors you have to take into account when designing your development components and software components. For this reason, we would like to refer you to the very detailed documentation available at *http://help.sap.com* or *http://sdn.sap.com*.

component `sap.com_WDBP_S_1` contains our development components that we provide in this case together with the corresponding
source files.

Figure 9.31 Defined Software Components

At this point, we cannot reliably answer the question as to whether
to deliver your Web Dynpro applications with or without source
files. This will certainly also depend on your company's basic delivery strategy.

9.5 Summary

In this chapter, we have discussed how you can define and provide
different functions using development classes that can be reused in
other development components.

In addition to using Web Dynpro development components, which
we used to provide both simple Java classes and random Web Dynpro entities, you have seen how you can use an external library DC to
provide any JAR archives to your Web Dynpro projects or DCs.

We further examined how you can use software components to
group your development components and summarize them.

This chapter provides an overview of the tasks involved in installing, administrating, and maintaining the Web Dynpro runtime. The chapter contains real-life examples to illustrate the runtime configuration and provides tips and tricks for analysis and troubleshooting. Furthermore, the chapter describes different tools that are relevant for this subject.

10 Tips for the Installation, Configuration, and Administration

10.1 Overview

Based on many examples, the previous chapters have described the Web Dynpro programming techniques that are relevant in application development. In this chapter, we now want to discuss another important subject that plays a particularly significant role in the test phase and in the use of business applications in live systems: the installation, configuration, and administration of the Web Dynpro runtime and its applications. In this context, we'll focus on topics specific to Web Dynpro, but we'll also touch some other areas of the SAP Web Application Server when they directly affect the Web Dynpro runtime behavior or when they are relevant for a better understanding of the architecture and for analyzing potential problems.

10.2 Installing and Maintaining the Web Dynpro Runtime

The job of a system administrator includes the installation and maintenance of a system. A task that recurs frequently is the importing of patches and service packs for specific components. When a service pack has been installed, the administrator must be able to check whether the process was carried out successfully and completely and if the updated component is available again. To do that, the administrator must have basic knowledge of the runtime architecture, the system landscape of the application server, and of the Web Dynpro runtime. Moreover, the administrator must be able to carry out basic tests on the updated component and to analyze and troubleshoot potential problems.

This section describes the basic knowledge required to perform the tasks that are related to the Web Dynpro runtime. For this purpose, we'll first introduce the basic concepts of the SAP Web AS architecture and the Web Dynpro runtime. After that we'll describe how to import patches and check their functioning as well as how to query version information, and will then go into the details of remote debugging. We'll also provide various tips and tricks on how you can analyze potential problems.

10.2.1 The Basic Architecture of SAP Web Application Server

SAP Web Application Server[1] (Web AS) represents the technology platform on which you can deploy and run software components such as the Web Dynpro runtime and its applications. Web AS is the technological basis of all modern SAP solutions.

System Landscape of SAP Web Application Server

Web AS cluster system landscape

The sophisticated design of the Web AS allows you to merge many application-server instances into one homogeneous cluster in order to distribute the workload efficiently to the available servers, ensuring a high degree of scalability, reliability, and availability. This is an important prerequisite for ensuring a smooth flow of business-critical applications in companies where an application may be used by thousands of users and therefore has to be available around the clock. Figure 10.1 shows the main components of the Web AS in a cluster environment.

SAP Web Dispatcher

▶ The *SAP Web Dispatcher* is the central point of entry for all user requests. It distributes the load of incoming requests globally to the available dialog instances.[2]

---

1 As of Release SAP NetWeaver 2004s: SAP NetWeaver Application Server.
2 Instead of SAP Web Dispatcher, you can also use any other load balancer.

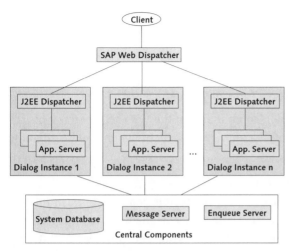

Figure 10.1 Main Components of SAP Web AS

▶ A *dialog instance* represents a logical combination of *application servers* that are linked to the outside world via a commonly used load distributor—the *J2EE Dispatcher*. The J2EE Dispatcher and the application servers of a dialog instance can be installed on the same hardware or on different hardware resources. The J2EE Dispatcher serves as a central point of entry for a dialog instance and manages the local load distribution, that is, it distributes the incoming requests from a client (for example via HTTP) as equally as possible to the connected application servers that process those requests. The supported application containers run on the application servers. In the case of Web AS, those application containers are the *web container*, the *portal runtime container*, and the *Web Dynpro container*. We'll discuss the Web Dynpro container in greater detail when we describe the runtime architecture.

Dialog instance with J2EE Dispatcher and application server

▶ *Central system database* and central services such as *message server* and *enqueue locking server*:

Central system database and services

▷ The system database is the central storage location of all deployed components, that is, of all binary data, static web resources, and configurations. Without the system database, the central administration, central deployment, central installation, or the upgrade of a cluster would not be possible.

▷ The *enqueue server* is used for a cluster-wide locking of resources that may only be used and changed by exactly one application server of a cluster at a given point in time.

> ▶ The *message server* is used for sending messages between the application servers in order to publish specific events across the entire cluster.

Central Administration Tools of Web AS

In addition to the main components of the Web AS, central tools are available for the central administration, deployment, and configuration of a cluster:

Visual Adminis-
trator and
SAP NetWeaver
Administrator

▶ **Visual Administrator**

The Visual Administrator is used for the central administration of a cluster.[3] Its graphical user interface enables you to administer all infrastructure components of a cluster and provides monitoring tools such as a central log and trace viewer and a performance monitor. Moreover, it enables remote access to non-local clusters so that it is possible to administer a system from remote. As an alternative to the Visual Administrator, SAP NetWeaver 2004 provides *SAP NetWeaver Administrator* as a web-based tool for the central administration of a cluster from Service Pack 13 onwards. SAP NetWeaver Administrator can be opened in the web browser and can be called from the Web AS home page.[4]

Software
Deployment
Manager

▶ **Software Deployment Manager**

The Software Deployment Manager (SDM) ensures the central deployment of a software component in a cluster. It consists of a client component—that is, a graphical tool that allows you to import patches and software archives[5] (SDA or SCA, see Section 10.2.2)—and a central server component for a cluster. The central server component enables the consistent deployment of a software component.[6]

Configuration tool

▶ **Configuration Tool**

The configuration tool can be used to change the configuration

---

3 You can start the Visual Administrator in Windows by using the following batch file: */usr/sap/<system name>/J<dialog instance>/j2ee/admin/go.bat*.

4 You can also start the SAP NetWeaver Administrator directly via the following URL: *http://<engine host>:<engine port>/webdynpro/dispatcher/sap.com/tc~lm~webadmin~mainframe~wd/WebAdminApp*.

5 You can launch the client in Windows using the following batch file: */usr/sap/<system name>/J<dialog instance>/SDM/program/RemoteGui.bat*

6 You can start and stop the SDM server in Windows using the SAP MMC console.

data of a cluster. For this purpose, an online tool and an offline tool are available, which means that you don't necessarily have to start a dialog instance in order to change configuration data.[7]

▶ **SAP Management Console**

The SAP MMC (SAP MMC under Windows) is a graphical user interface for the Java startup and control framework that is responsible for controlling the lifecycle of the Web AS components. You can use the SAP MMC to start and stop the entire cluster, individual dialog instances, or even individual application servers in a convenient way. In a way that's transparent to the user, the startup and control framework makes sure that all required processes are started and stopped in the correct sequence. Furthermore, you can use the SAP MMC to execute other useful functions of the start-up and control framework, such as triggering a JVM thread dump, starting the J2EE Telnet console, or switching an application server to the debug mode.

SAP Management console

▶ **J2EE Telnet Console**

The J2EE Telnet console is an expert tool that can be used to execute many administration tasks via command line commands. The tool can be launched via the SAP MMC: Select the J2EE Dispatcher node of a dialog instance, find the J2EE Telnet item in its context menu, and start the J2EE Telnet console (see Figure 10.2). You can also launch the J2EE Telnet console directly from the command prompt without using the SAP MMC by entering the following command:

J2EE Telnet console

telnet <hostname> <Port>

The host name is the name of the J2EE Dispatcher of the dialog instance, while the port can be calculated based on the HTTP port used by the instance as follows: HTTP port+8. For example, if the HTTP port is 50000, the Telnet port is 50008.

---

7 In Windows, the configuration tools can be found at the following location: */usr/sap/<System-Namen>/J<Dialoginstanz>/j2ee/configtool*. The online tool for which the dialog instance must be running can be launched through the batch file *configtool.bat*, while you can start the offline tool by using the file *offlinecfgeditor.bat*.

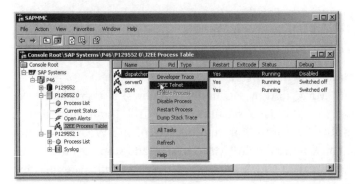

Figure 10.2 Launching the J2EE Telnet Console from the SAP MMC

Once you have launched the J2EE Telnet console, you must first log on to it using an administrator user. Then you can use the `jump <number of server node>` command to go to the server node for which you want to perform additional administration tasks (for example, the command `jump 0` takes you to server node 0). On a server node, you can use the `man` command to display an online help for the available commands. Those commands are divided into command groups, and not all of these groups are active after you logon. You can activate and use command groups using the `add <name of command group>` command. You can obtain a list of all command groups that are available via the `man -g` command. The `add deploy` command can, for instance, be used to activate the frequently used command group for deployment commands.

Runtime Architecture of the Application Servers in Web AS

To be able to run applications smoothly and to avoid common errors it is very helpful to have a basic knowledge of the application-server architecture. Potential problems, such as inability to launch a deployed application, can be analyzed and eliminated quickly with a basic understanding of the architecture. For this reason, we'll now describe in greater detail the runtime architecture of a server node in Web AS.

Software layers in Web AS

The server nodes of Web AS—whether a J2EE Dispatcher or an application server node—contain three different types of layers in which the software components are arranged: the *kernel*, *infrastructure*, and *application layers*. As shown in Figure 10.3, those layers are built on top of each other. Note, however, that the components of a lower layer do not know and cannot access components of a higher layer. In contrast, a higher-layer component can access and use the components of a lower layer.

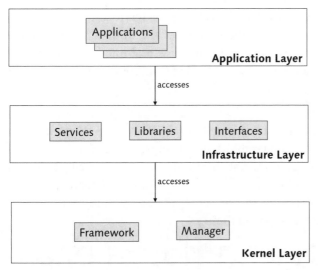

Figure 10.3 Architecture Layers of a Server Node

The layers illustrated in Figure 10.3 have the following logical functions:

▶ **Kernel layer**
The kernel layer represents the lowest level in the system and provides the basic functions of a server node such as thread management, sockets, messages, communication within a cluster, and other OS-based native functions. Those basic functions are realized by *manager components* that are activated in a fixed sequence when a server node is started. Because the kernel layer serves as the container for the superordinate infrastructure layer, it not only contains the manager components, but also an additional service framework that is used to embed and control the infrastructure components such as libraries or services. The framework controls the lifecycle of the infrastructure components and defines interfaces for the communication between those components. Furthermore, it isolates the kernel from the higher layers in that it provides an exactly defined number of APIs that enable the interaction with the kernel.

Kernel layer

Infrastructure layer
including libraries,
interfaces, and
services

▶ **Infrastructure layer**

The infrastructure layer comprises all components of the application programming model such as the supported J2EE containers or the Web Dynpro container, as well as components of other J2EE specifications, security services, or services for the administration of the system landscape or of the configuration. In total, the infrastructure layer consists of several hundreds of components that can generally be divided into three different types of components:

▶ **Libraries**

A library component usually provides commonly used utility classes and frequently used functions. Here, you should note that a library does not have a lifecycle of its own, that is, a library is either deployed so that it can be actively used or it isn't available on the server. It is not possible to activate or deactivate a deployed library.

Tip

In the J2EE Telnet console, you can display a list of all available libraries by entering the `lsl` (*list libraries*) command at the command prompt. Note that before you can do that you must activate the `DEPLOY` command group via the `add deploy` command.

▶ **Interfaces**

Interface components define contracts that describe the behavior of implementing components. An interface component consists of a unique name and a set of Java interfaces and it must be implemented by a service component. Like a library component, an interface component doesn't have its own lifecycle.

Tip

In the J2EE Telnet console, you can display the list of all active interfaces via the `lsi` (*list interfaces*) command, which is part of the `DEPLOY` command group.

▶ **Services**

Services are the most powerful components of the infrastructure layer. A service component can access other components of the infrastructure and kernel layers if it has defined *refer-*

ences to those components. Such a reference between a component A and a component B is used to define a classloader reference that enables classes of component A to access classes of component B. Some service components are referred to as *core services*. Those services always must be started in order for the server node to be started successfully. If the services are not started, the startup process of the server node will cancel with an error.

Tip

You can display the list of all deployed services in the J2EE Telnet console via the lss (*list services*) command. This command is also included in the DEPLOY command group.

Furthermore, a service component is integrated into a complex lifecycle. For example, a service can be started or stopped, but it can only be used by other components—i.e., applications or services—if it is started. Figure 10.4 illustrates in a simplified manner the lifecycle of a service.

Lifecycle of a service

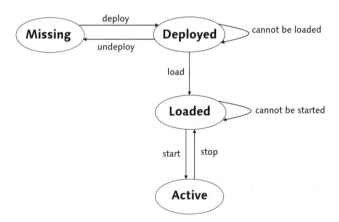

Figure 10.4 Lifecycle Stages of a Service Component

First, a service has the status **Missing** if it is not part of the system. Once it has been deployed, its status changes to **Deployed**, which means it exists on the system. If you un-deploy it here, the service returns to the **Missing** status. A service can be loaded if all of its defined references can be resolved. If that is the case, the service changes to the **Loaded** status. Technically speaking, this means that the classloader of the service is initialized. If one of the required references cannot be resolved, the classloader cannot be initialized and the service remains in the **Deployed** status. The service can be started if it is in the **Loaded** status. After a successful start the service is in the **Active** status, which means that it can be used by other services and application. If the start is not successful or if an active service is stopped, it returns to the **Loaded** status.

Application layer

▶ **Application layer**
The application layer is the layer that's relevant to the application developer, as it contains all the components of an application. An application can access other components of the infrastructure and application layers if it has defined references to those components.

The lifecycle of an application is similar to that of a service component. Figure 10.5 shows a simplified illustration of the different statuses of an application. An application can only be used—i.e., executed—if its status is **Active**. It enters this status if all the necessary defined *hard references* can be resolved. If that is not possible or if an active application is stopped, the application is in the **Inactive** status.

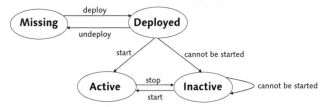

Figure 10.5 State Graph of an Application

Irresolvable references

Note

One of the main reasons why a deployed Web Dynpro application cannot be started are irresolvable references to libraries, services, or other components in the application layer. In SAP NetWeaver 2004, Web Dynpro only supports hard references: All defined references of a Web Dynpro application must actually be resolvable in order to translate the application into the **Active** status so that it can be executed. SAP Web AS can resolve a hard reference if the referenced component exists and if it is active.

If one of those two reqirements cannot be met, that is, if the referenced component hasn't been deployed or if it can't be started due to unresolvable references on its side, the Web Dynpro application will remain in the **Inactive** status. If you tried to start the application while it is in that state, the system would return an error message.

Tip

You can display a list of deployed applications, including their statuses, in the J2EE Telnet console via the `list_app` command of the `DEPLOY` command group.

We'll now conclude our overview of the basic architecture of a server node by taking a closer look at the concept of references and classloading of an application. From the point of view of the server, each component that has been deployed in a separate *enterprise application archive* (EAR) represents an application that is loaded by a separate classloader.[8] Similarly, each component of the infrastructure layer is also loaded by a separate classloader. A component can access its own classes and the classes of other components if it has defined a reference to those.

References between components and the classloader concept

Therefore, if you want to access components of the infrastructure or application layers from a Web Dynpro application, the application must have defined a corresponding *classloader reference* to the required component. The reference can be uniquely determined by the technical name of the referenced component and the component type. Table 10.1 contains a list of available Web Dynpro reference types:

Defining references in a Web Dynpro application

Referencs Type	Referenced Component
Sharing reference	Component of the application layer
Libraries reference	Library component of the infrastructure layer
Services reference	Service component of the infrastructure layer
Interfaces reference	Interface component of the infrastructure layer

Table 10.1 Web Dynpro Reference Types

---

8 Note that the term *application* does not describe a Web Dynpro application here. Web Dynpro describes a Web AS application as a deployable object. This means that is a deployable unit that can contain zero, one, or several Web Dynpro applications, components, configurations, data dictionaries, models, and static Web resources.

If you use development components (DCs) and the SAP NetWeaver Development Infrastructure, the creation of *public part dependencies* between DCs automatically causes the creation of the correct references, as we have shown in Chapter 3. In addition to this automatic maintenance of references, you can also add a classloader reference manually. To do that, go to the **Web Dynpro Explorer** view of SAP NetWeaver Developer Studio and open the context menu of a Web Dynpro project. Then select the **Properties** item. The system displays the dialog shown in Figure 10.6. If you select the **Web Dynpro References** item on the left, for example, you can add new classloader references to components of the application and infrastructure layers on the right-hand side of the dialog. The name that is used for a referenced component must match exactly the technical name on the Web AS.

> **Tip**
>
> The easiest way to identify the technical name of a component is to use the J2EE Telnet console. The commands list_app, lss, lsl, and lsi that we already have described can be used to display lists of the different component types of the application and infrastructure layers including their technical names.

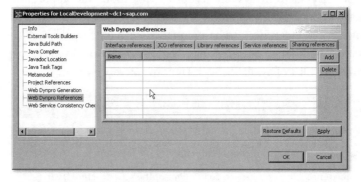

Figure 10.6 Creating Classloader References in SAP NetWeaver Developer Studio

The defined references of an application do not directly affect the lifecycle of that application. If a *hard reference* is used, the application cannot be started—i.e., activated—until the referenced component has been activated.[9] Conversely, if a hard-referenced component is

---

9 Because Web Dynpro supports only hard references in SAP NetWeaver 2004, we'll restrict our descriptions to hard references from now on.

stopped, all referencing components must be stopped first. If, on the other hand, an application has defined a *weak reference* to another component, the application can be started even if the reference cannot be resolved; that is, if the referenced component is inactive. In that case, the engine won't try to resolve the reference until the referenced component is accessed at runtime.

Thus, because of all those references a complex interdependency exists between the components of the application and infrastructure layers. Those interdependencies can be graphically illustrated using the **Classloader Viewer** service. You can use this service to analyze classloading problems that may occur when an application accesses other components.

10.2.2 Web Dynpro Runtime Components

In this section, we'll describe the various runtime components of Web Dynpro and classify them with regard to the overall architecture. To do that, we'll first describe the software components that make up the Web Dynpro runtime, including their interdependencies. This information is useful for importing service packs of the Web Dynpro runtime, and it enables you to carry out a detailed analysis of the runtime status and of the versions being used.

Web Dynpro Runtime Components

The Web Dynpro runtime in SAP NetWeaver 2004 consists of five deployable components. Some of these components are part of the infrastructure layer of the engine, while others are application components and thus belong to the application layer. Each of the five components is provided and deployed in a separate *software deployment archive (SDA)*. However, in the standard installation, they are contained in larger packages: the *software component archives (SCA)*. The following sections describe the five Web Dynpro SDAs, including their contents, interdependencies, and the associated architecture layer.

We'll start with the two SDA files that are part of the infrastructure layer of the engine and can be deployed offline. This means that once you have deployed one of these SDAs, you must restart the engine in order for the changes of the new version to take effect. In the stan-

Web Dynpro components of the infrastructure layer

dard installation, both SDAs are contained in the file *SAPJTECHF16_0.SCA* that can be deployed offline.

Web Dynpro service: webdynpro.sda

▶ **webdynpro.sda**
This SDA contains the core of the Web Dynpro runtime: the Web Dynpro service. Once deployed, the engine recognizes this service component by its technical name, webdynpro. The service contains all classes and interfaces of the Web Dynpro programming model including the publicly usable APIs.[10]

Web Dynpro container

In addition to the programming model, the archive contains the binary data of the *Web Dynpro container*. The Web Dynpro container is the application container that is responsible for controlling the lifecycle of Web Dynpro applications. Thus, it takes care of the deployment, classloading, evaluation and resolution of references, access to static web resources, and so on.

Furthermore, the SDA contains several deployment descriptors that include the *provider.xml* descriptor. This descriptor contains descriptions of all dependencies between the Web Dynpro service and other infrastructure components. If one of the hard references described therein cannot be resolved—for example because a required infrastructure component has not been deployed or isn't active—the Web Dynpro service cannot be started. At the end of this section, we'll take a closer look at how to analyze such problems when they occur.

▶ **WebDynproRrDdic.sda**
This SDA file is used to deploy database schemas in the central system database of Web AS. Web Dynpro needs these schemas for the persistent storage of runtime metadata. Apart from that, this SDA file does not contain any other infrastructure components. This means that if you deploy this archive, no other service or library will be added to the infrastructure layer of the engine.

---

10 As already mentioned several times in this book, these are all classes and interfaces whose names begin with the prefixes WD or IWD. An application should use only those public classes and interfaces, without accessing other classes of the Web Dynpro framework that are regarded as internal classes. This is because future versions of the Web Dynpro runtime will guarantee source code compatibility only for the public classes.

In addition to the infrastructure layer components, the Web Dynpro runtime consists of three components of the application layer. Those components can be deployed online, meaning that you don't need to restart the engine once they have been deployed because the changes will take effect right away. In the standard installation, these SDAs are contained in the file *SAPJTECHF16_0.SCA* that can be deployed online.

Web Dynpro components of the application layer

▶ **WebDynproDispWda.sda**

This SDA file contains the central Web Dynpro dispatcher servlet that receives client requests that have been sent via HTTP or HTTPS and delegates those requests to the Web Dynpro runtime, where they are processed. As the dispatcher servlet is the central point of entry into Web Dynpro request processing and thus represents a core component of the Web Dynpro runtime, it can be considered as a kind of "Web Dynpro system application." Once deployed, the application is recognized by the engine by its technical name, `sap.com/tc~wd~dispwda`.

Web Dynpro system application: dispatcher servlet and JavaScript resources

Furthermore, the SDA contains static web resources such as SAP icons, portal icons, and SAP standard themes. These can be used by applications for the display in user interfaces as well as by JavaScript libraries, which are required by Web Dynpro to generate the user interfaces in a web browser.

▶ **WebDynproCoreComponents.sda**

This archive consists of Web Dynpro system components that are required for generic UI services such as popups or input helps that are supported by the runtime. Once deployed, this application component is published on the application server under the technical name `sap.com/tc~wd~corecomp`.

Web Dynpro system components

▶ **WebDynproTools.sda**

This SDA file contains two applications that are required for the administration and monitoring of the Web Dynpro runtime: the Web Dynpro Content Administrator and the Web Dynpro Console. We'll describe both in greater detail in Section 10.4. The technical name of this application component on the application server is `sap.com/tc~wd~tools`.

Web Dynpro administration and monitoring tools

Interdependencies
of Web Dynpro
components
Figure 10.7 illustrates the infrastructure and application components of the Web Dynpro runtime, including their interdependencies. The `webdynpro` service component is part of the infrastructure layer and contains further dependencies to other services and libraries that are summarized as **Other Components** in Figure 10.7. The system application `sap.com/tc~wd~dispwda` references the `webdynpro` service and other components of the infrastructure layer that are automatically transferred to other Web Dynpro applications because of the transitivity of the references in the application layer. Thus, the references of `sap.com/tc~wd~dispwda` are automatically set as default references for any Web Dynpro application.

In a mapping diagram, a Web Dynpro application would thus be located at the same place as the `sap.com/tc~wd~tools` component and might have additional dependencies to application and infrastructure components.

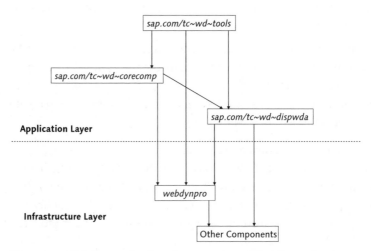

Figure 10.7 Web Dynpro Runtime Components and Their Dependencies

10.2.3 Installing the Web Dynpro Runtime and Importing Service Packs

Deploying the
Web Dynpro
runtime
After this brief introduction to the concepts of SAP Web AS and the description of the Web Dynpro runtime components, we'll now discuss the installation of Web Dynpro as well as potential problems associated to that and how you can analyze those problems. We won't describe the installation of Web AS using the SAP Installer (*sapinst*), as we assume that this has already been done so that a Web

AS system is available. We'll focus instead on installing the Web Dynpro runtime as it occurs; e.g., when you update it with a new service pack.

Querying the System and Version Information

Because the Web Dynpro runtime is part of the standard SAP Web AS installation, the system usually contains a version of the runtime after the initial installation of Web AS. The **System Information** provides you with an overview of the system landscape as well as the versions of all available components. If you want to call the system information, you must authenticate yourself as a user with administrator rights. You can launch the system-information page by calling the home page of a Web AS system. The corresponding URL is *http://<engine host>:<engine port>*. Once you have launched that page, you must click on the **System Information** link. When you have logged on successfully, the system displays an overview as it is shown in Figure 10.8.

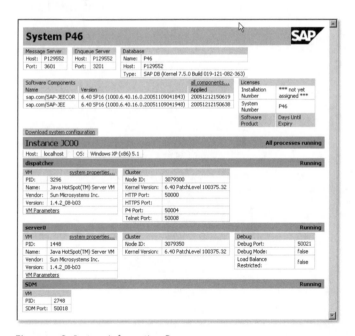

Figure 10.8 System Information Page

This page provides a brief overview of a system and its cluster landscape without your having to use any complex administration tools.

The page provides information on the central components and services of a system: the central system database, the message server and the enqueue server, the version information of the engine kernel sap.com/SAP-J2EECOR, and the dialog instances available in the cluster landscape—including their J2EE Dispatcher and application-server nodes. The information on a server node also helps you to find out whether an application server is started in the debug mode, and, if so, you can obtain the details regarding the host name of the server and its released debug port. That information is needed for remote debugging purposes, which we'll describe in greater detail in Section 10.2.4.

Querying the detailed version information for a component

If you click on the **all components** link on the system information page, you can open the subsequent page that provides a list of all components that have been deployed on the engine. These components include all available libraries, interfaces, and services of the infrastructure layer as well as all components of the application layer (see Figure 10.9). For each of those components, the system displays the relevant detailed version information and the date of installation.

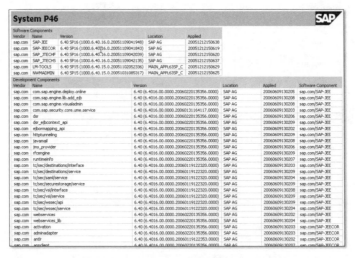

Figure 10.9 List of all Available Components and their Versions

> **Note**
>
> You should always specify the version information of a component when contacting SAP with regard to open issues or in order to analyze an existing problem. The version information is needed to determine the exact master release and the detailed patch level of a component.

Table 10.2 summarizes the items that are relevant for the Web Dynpro runtime.

Name of SDA File	Name in System Information	Contents of the Component
webdynpro.sda	`tc/wd/webdynpro`	Web Dynpro service
WebDynproRrDdic.sda	`tc/wd/rrddic`	Database schemas
WebDynproDispWda.sda	`tc/wd/dispwda`	System application
WebDynproCoreComponents.sda	`tc/wd/corecomp`	System components
WebDynproTools.sda	`tc/wd/tools`	Administration tools

Table 10.2 Web Dynpro Runtime Components and Their Names in the System Information

Deploying the Web Dynpro Runtime and Performing Basic Tests

For the SAP NetWeaver 2004 release, SAP regularly provides *service packs* (SP) that contain error corrections or partly restricted enhancements of specific components. Furthermore, SAP can also provide you with so-called *hot fixes* for individual SAP NetWeaver components outside of this regular patch cycle. Those hot fixes are made available to SAP customers through the SAP Service Marketplace (*http://service.sap.com/swdc*).

Importing service packs and hot fixes

We'll now describe how you can import a service pack or hot fix for Web Dynpro. We assume here that the service pack is already available as an SCA or SDA file and that it must now be deployed on a system.

Usually, a customer uses a two-tier, and often even a three-tier, landscape that consists of a development system, a test system, and a live system. A service pack should first be deployed on a test system where you can check whether the update of the deployed component has been completed successfully. You should not install the service pack on the live system until those tests have been run successfully.

To import a service pack, SAP Web AS provides the *Software Deployment Manager (SDM)* as a central deployment tool. You can find the SDM in your Web AS system at the following location: */usr/sap/<system ID>/<instance name>/SDM/program/RemoteGui.bat* (see Section

Deployment using the SDM

381

10.2.1). The SDM can deploy different archive formats such as EAR, SDA, or SCA. During the deployment process, the SDM creates log files that provide information on the status of the deployment and on the success or failure of its execution. You can find the log files in your system at the following location: */usr/sap/<system ID>/<instance name>/SDM/log*. You should search through those files for information on problems that may have occurred after deploying the Web Dynpro runtime as well as after the import of service packs. Figure 10.10 shows a sample entry that is written into the SDM log file after a successful deployment of the *webdynpro.sda* archive.

```
Jan 15, 2006 12:33:04... Info: Loading archive 'C:\usr\sap\P46\JC00\SDM\root\origin\sap.com\tc\wd\webdynpro\SAP
AG\6.4016.00.0000.20051108171224.0000\webdynpro.sda
Jan 15, 2006 12:33:35... Info: Actions per selected component:
Jan 15, 2006 12:33:35... Info: Update: Selected development component 'tc/wd/webdynpro'/'sap.com'/'SAP
AG'/'6.4016.00.0000.20051108171224.0000' updates currently deployed development component
'tc/wd/webdynpro'/'sap.com'/'SAP AG'/'6.4016.00.0000.20051108171224.0000'.
Jan 15, 2006 12:33:48... Info: Saved current Engine state.
Jan 15, 2006 12:33:49... Info: Starting: Update: Selected development component 'tc/wd/webdynpro'/'sap.com'/'SAP
AG'/'6.4016.00.0000.20051108171224.0000' updates currently deployed development component
'tc/wd/webdynpro'/'sap.com'/'SAP AG'/'6.4016.00.0000.20051108171224.0000'.
Jan 15, 2006 12:33:49... Info: SDA to be deployed: C:\usr\sap\P46\JC00\SDM\root\origin\sap.com\tc\wd\webdynpro\SAP
AG\6.4016.00.0000.20051108171224.0000\webdynpro.sda
Jan 15, 2006 12:33:49... Info: Software type of SDA: primary-service
Jan 15, 2006 12:33:50... Info: ***** Begin of SAP J2EE Engine Offline Deployment (Service component of SAP J2EE Engine)
*****
Jan 15, 2006 12:33:50... Info: Shutting down all the cluster processes except SDM.
Jan 15, 2006 12:33:50... Info: Shutting down the instance JC_P129552_P46_00 running on host localhost processes ...
Jan 15, 2006 12:33:50... Info: Stopping the instance JC_P129552_P46_00 processes. The instance is running on host
localhost
Jan 15, 2006 12:33:50... Info: Stopping the process dispatcher
Jan 15, 2006 12:33:50... Info: Stopping the process server0
Jan 15, 2006 12:34:21... Info: Cluster processes have been successfully shut down.
Jan 15, 2006 12:34:36... Info: ***** End of SAP J2EE Engine offline Deployment (Service component of SAP J2EE Engine)
*****
Jan 15, 2006 12:34:36... Info: Finished successfully: development component 'tc/wd/webdynpro'/'sap.com'/'SAP
AG'/'6.4016.00.0000.20051108171224.0000'
Jan 15, 2006 12:34:38... Info: Restoring the state of the instance (JC_P129552_P46_00) process dispatcher from stopped
to Running
Jan 15, 2006 12:34:38... Info: Restoring the state of the instance (JC_P129552_P46_00) process server0 from stopped to
Running
Jan 15, 2006 12:38:11... Info: J2EE Engine is in same state (online/offline) as it has been before this deployment
process.
```

Figure 10.10 Log Entry After Successful Deployment of webdynpro.sda

> **Tip**
>
> After importing a patch for the Web Dynpro runtime you should run a search through the SDM log file for information on problems that may have occurred. For example, if one of the Web Dynpro runtime components described in Section 10.2.2 cannot be successfully deployed because of a problem, you cannot use the Web Dynpro runtime to its full extent or even not at all.

Checking the status of the Web Dynpro service using Visual Administrator

After a successful deployment of the Web Dynpro runtime, the Web Dynpro service should be up and running on the engine. You can check that using the Visual Administrator in the following way: The Web Dynpro service should be displayed in the list of services of a server node by the entry **Web Dynpro Runtime.** If that is the case, the service has been started (see Figure 10.11). A service that has a symbol of a red cross next to it has been stopped. In Figure 10.11, that's the case for the **TREX Service**.

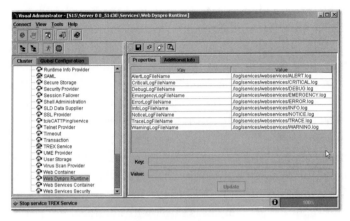

Figure 10.11 Querying the Web Dynpro Runtime Status in the Visual Administrator

The three Web Dynpro runtime components that are deployed in the application layer should be displayed in the **Deploy** service of the Visual Administrator below the **webdynpro** node (see Figure 10.12), while the system application sap.com/tc~wd~dispwda should be active. All other Web Dynpro applications are started on demand in order to reduce the server restart times. This means that they are not started after a server restart; only when they are called for the first time will they be automatically started. For this reason, the two applications sap.com/tc~wd~corecomp and sap.com/tc~wd~tools don't need to be started up front.

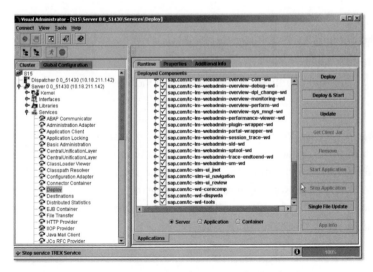

Figure 10.12 Web Dynpro System Applications in the Deploy Service

Once you have checked the SDM logs and used the Visual Administrator to make sure that all the required Web Dynpro runtime components have been deployed and can be used, you must carry out a
basic test of the operability of the Web Dynpro runtime in order to
prove that the service pack has been imported successfully. For this
purpose, we suggest you start the two administration applications—
the Web Dynpro Content Administrator and the Web Dynpro Console—that have been provided by SAP as part of the runtime. To do
that, go to the Web AS home page (*http://<engine host>:<engine port>*)
and click on the **Web Dynpro** link. The system then navigates to
another page that contains two links to the above applications. Both
applications require you to log on as a user with administrator rights.
If you can launch both applications successfully, it means that no
problems occurred during the update of the Web Dynpro runtime.
This basic test should be followed by other tests using the applications that are relevant to you.

> **Tip**
>
> If you encounter unexpected problems when importing a service pack
> that prevent the use of an updated component, you can always revert to
> the previously installed version of that component. The SDM stores all
> previously installed versions of SDAs in the following directory:
> */usr/sap/<System-ID>/<Instance-ID>/SDM/root/origin*. There you can
> find the entire history of already deployed versions of a runtime compo-
> nent.

Analyzing and Solving Potential Problems

The following sections provide guidelines that you can use for analyzing potential problems with regard to deploying and updating the
Web Dynpro runtime or Web Dynpro applications.

Problem 1: The Web Dynpro service does not start.

When importing patches for runtime components of SAP NetWeaver
or the Web Dynpro runtime, you may encounter the problem that
the Web Dynpro service won't start once the Web AS has been
updated. The SDM log files will then contain corresponding entries
that document the start failure of the service.

*Reason 1: Missing or irresolvable dependencies of the Web
Dynpro service.*
The problem often occurs because of the fact that dependent components of the infrastructure layer that are needed for Web Dynpro are
missing because of an incomplete or manually modified installation.
Another reason for this problem is that components which the Web
Dynpro service is linked to via a hard reference have not been started
themselves. See Section 10.2.1 for further information on this subject.

Non-resolvable
dependencies of
the Web Dynpro
service

Solution 1: Check the dependencies of the Web Dynpro service.
In such a problem scenario you must check the list of dependent
components of the Web Dynpro runtime by using the Visual Administrator. To do that, open the detailed view of the Web Dynpro service and go to the **Additional Info** tab, as shown in Figure 10.13. The
lower part of that window displays the **Service References**, which is
a list of dependent infrastructure components. For each of those
components you should make sure that it is available on the server
and—in the case of a hard reference—that the associated service is
started or that the library or interface has been loaded.

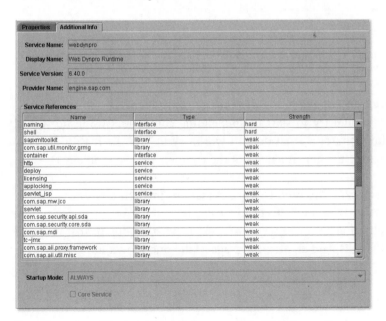

Figure 10.13 List of Hard and Weak References of the Web Dynpro Service

Problem 2: The Web Dynpro application does not start.

Web Dynpro appli-
cation does not
start

In a similar scenario you may encounter the following problem: Despite the fact that the Web Dynpro service has started, the start-up of the Web Dynpro application fails. There can be several reasons for that, as you'll see in the following sections.

Reason 2a: A component that has a weak reference to the Web Dynpro service has been stopped.

Component with
weak reference has
been stopped

An infrastructure component for which the Web Dynpro service has defined a dependency via a weak reference has not been started (in the case of a dependent service) or loaded (in the case of a dependent library or interface). If the Web Dynpro runtime then tries to access that component when executing an application, the system returns an error message similar to the one shown in Figure 10.14, where a **Web Container** service has been stopped.

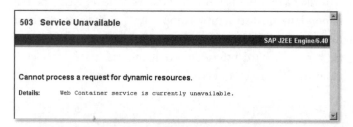

Figure 10.14 Error Message for a Web Container Service that has Been Stopped (Example)

Solution 2a: Start the depending component.

You should try to start the depending component using the Visual Administrator. If that doesn't work, try to find the reason for it by checking the dependencies of the component (see Problem 1).

Reason 2b: The Web Dynpro system application is unavailable.

Web Dynpro sys-
tem application is
unavailable

Another reason for this problem can be that the Web Dynpro system application `sap.com/tc~wd~dispwda` is not running. In that case, the system displays an error message as the one shown in Figure 10.15.

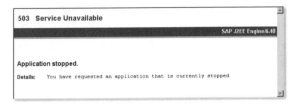

Figure 10.15 Error Message that Displays When the sap.com/tc~wd~dispwda Application is not Started

Solution 2b: Start the system application manually.

Try to start the application using the **Deploy** service of the Visual Administrator: In the detail view of the **Deploy** service, navigate to the tree node **webdynpro · sap.com/tc~wd~dispwda** and click on the **Start Application** button. The application should now be started. If not, it means that one of the hard references defined in that application cannot be resolved.

Reason 2c: Incorrect application URL or unknown development component.

If, during the start-up process of an application, an error message displays like the ones shown in Figures 10.16 and 10.17, the application was either called via an incorrect URL or hasn't been deployed on the server.

Incorrect application URL or unknown development component

Figure 10.16 Error Message Caused by an Incorrect Application URL and the Call of an Unknown Application

Figure 10.17 Error Message Due to the Request of an Unknown Development Component

Solution 2c: Run a plausibility check of the application.

First check the part of the URL that follows after "/webdynpro/dis-patcher/" for possible spelling mistakes. If the URL is correct, you then should make sure that the relevant development component has been deployed on the server.

Reason 2d: Irresolvable sharing reference.

Irresolvable sharing reference Other reasons why a deployed Web Dynpro application doesn't start are erroneous or irresolvable references between components of the application layer (sharing references). As we have shown several times in this book by using the examples of componentizing an application (see Chapter 3), Web Dynpro supports the division of an application into different development components. Each development component is then deployed as a separate runtime component on the application server. Due to their public-part dependencies, the DCs of an application define references to each other, which enables a DC to access another DC at runtime. In SAP NetWeaver 2004, Web Dynpro interprets all dependencies of a Web Dynpro DC to other components that are deployed in the application layer as hard references. Consequently, if one of the defined references cannot be resolved because the referenced component itself is not deployed or cannot be started, the referencing application cannot be started either.

Figure 10.18 shows the error message that is displayed if a sharing reference cannot be resolved. The situation that causes this problem is shown in Figure 10.19. Development component DC_1 defines a sharing reference to another development component, DC_2, which, in turn, is not deployed on the system.

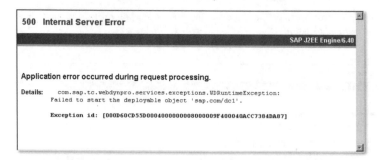

Figure 10.18 Error Message for Irresolvable Sharing Reference

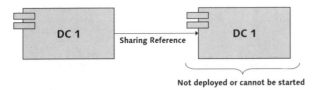

Figure 10.19 References Between Components of the Application Layer

Solution 2d: Deploy all referenced DCs.

To solve this problem, check the dependencies of the application, and match them with the application components on the server. If you find out that a referenced DC is missing, you must deploy that missing DC now.

Reason 2e: Errors in the use of component interfaces.

If a Web Dynpro application uses different components through component interfaces, each of which is deployed in a different Web Dynpro DC, the following problems can occur in case of an erroneous deployment or usage: A Web Dynpro component, UsingComponent, can use another component, UsedComponent, through a component interface, UsedComponentInterface. Each of those three entities can be deployed in a separate Web Dynpro DC. Figure 10.20 illustrates this situation: So that UsingComponent can access the UsedComponentInterface, a sharing reference must be defined between DC_1 and DC_2. A sharing reference must also exist between DC_3 and DC_2 so that UsedComponent can implement the UsedComponentInterface.

Errors in the use of component interfaces

UsingComponent can now dynamically create an instance of an implementing component of UsedComponentInterface at runtime by specifying the DC and component names of UsedComponent. Chapter 3 contains an example of the corresponding Java code. Please note that no sharing reference must exist between DC_1 and DC_3, and usually there is no sharing reference between those two. The reason is that by using component interfaces the using component can flexibly embed implementations of the interface and to exchange those, if necessary.

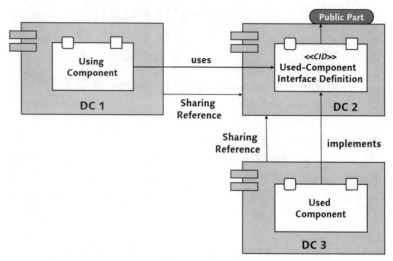

Figure 10.20 References Between Web Dynpro DCs when Using Component Interfaces

Solution 2e: Run a plausibility check of the implementing component.

If in this scenario DC_3 is not deployed on the server, you won't notice this until the used component is instantiated at runtime. In that case the system returns a runtime error message, as shown in Figure 10.21. You should then make sure that the missing DC is deployed on the application server.

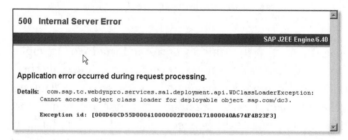

Figure 10.21 Error Message When Using Component Interfaces Caused by a Missing DC

If, on the other hand, DC_3 is deployed, but doesn't contain any component that matches the component name used in the application code, the system displays the error message shown in Figure 10.22 at runtime. In this case, you should refer to the responsible application developer groups, because either the specified DC is incomplete or the component name used for the component instantiation is incorrect.

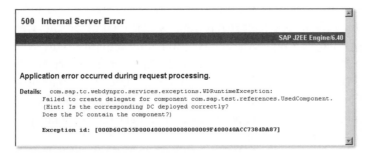

Figure 10.22 Error Message when Using Component Interfaces Caused by an Unknown Implementing Component

Analyzing the Threads and Requesting a Server Node

After this extensive troubleshooting of problems that may occur during the deployment and startup of the Web Dynpro runtime or its applications, we now want to discuss two more items that can be relevant when analyzing runtime problems:

For analysis, you sometimes may need to create a thread dump of all currently active threads of a server node. This can be useful, for instance, when a server node stops responding due to an unknown error or when queries to specific applications suddenly take longer than usual. A thread dump is a snapshot of all threads of a server node and therefore helps to analyze such problems.

Creating a thread dump

You can use the SAP MMC to create a thread dump in the following way. In the SAP MMC, select the server node for which you want to create a thread dump. Then open the context menu of that node and select the **Dump Stack Trace** item. The thread dump is then written to the file *std_server<index>.out* that is located in the directory */usr/sap/<system ID>/<instance name>/work*.

All requests processed by the web container on a server node—that is, all requests that come in via HTTP or HTTPS—are logged in the trace file */usr/sap/<system ID>/<instance name>/j2ee/cluster/server <index>/log/system/httpaccess/responses.<index>.trc*. This trace file thus also contains the requests directed to Web Dynpro applications. The logged details also provide information about which Web Dynpro

Checking the incoming requests on a server node

applications have been started on a server node and terminated via termination requests.

If Web Dynpro applications run in the SAP NetWeaver Portal and a user logs off—i.e., a page navigation is carried out or the web browser is closed—the portal sends termination requests to the Web Dynpro runtime to stop application sessions that are currently started. Thus, the information contained in the trace file can be used very effectively to analyze the requests that are being sent between the portal and the Web Dynpro runtime and that control the lifecycle of Web Dynpro application.

Because Web Dynpro applications are stateful applications, the requests of an application session that are sent one after the other must be directed to the same server node. As described in Section 10.2.1, the system landscape of a cluster can contain both a global load distributor such as the Web Dispatcher and a local load distributor for a dialog instance, such as the J2EE Dispatcher. You can use the trace file *responses.<index>.trc* to verify that consecutive requests of a Web Dynpro application session are actually directed to the same server node.

Hopefully, you are not too scared after reading these guidelines regarding potential problems. The good news is that such problems usually don't occur. If they do, they are caused in most cases by an incomplete or manually changed installation.

10.2.4 Remote Debugging

We'd like to conclude the section on the installation and maintenance of the Web Dynpro runtime with a description of *remote debugging,* a process particularly important for troubleshooting purposes in live applications. As we will see, remote debugging ensures a high degree of supportability for live applications. We'll first discuss the general concept of remote debugging and then describe how you can activate remote debugging for a server node in your Web AS cluster. Finally we'll demonstrate how you can launch a debug session from SAP NetWeaver Developer Studio.

To perform remote debugging, you can mark individual server nodes of a Web AS cluster as debugging nodes and thus isolate them from the cluster. The use of the cluster is not affected by this in any way: Debugging nodes are ignored by the message server and in the load distribution of the J2EE Dispatcher. This prevents requests for live applications being sent to a debugging node. Moreover, events that are generated on a debugging node are not distributed to other live server nodes of the cluster.

Isolating debugging nodes from the cluster

Another important aspect of remote debugging is that a debugging node remains integrated in the live cluster as long as a debugging session is started for this specific debugging node. Thus, SAP Web AS distinguishes between two statuses of a server node that are relevant for debugging: when a server node is marked as a debugging node, and when a debugging session is active on a server node thus marked. Remote debugging can only be activated, and the node can only be isolated from the cluster, if the latter status exists.

Activating remote debugging

To mark individual server nodes as debugging nodes in a Web AS cluster, the following precondition must be met for the respective server node:

Prerequisite for remote debugging

In order to use a server node for remote debugging the node must be marked as *debuggable* in the cluster configuration. You can make this setting using the configuration tool. As shown in Figure 10.23, after starting the configuration tool you must first select the server node you want to use for remote debugging in the left-hand pane, and then select the **Debug** tab in the detail view. There, you can mark the server node as a debugging node by checking the **Debuggable** check box.

Marking the server node as debuggable

To isolate a debugging node from the cluster when starting a debugging session, you must also check the **Restricted load balance** check box, which is also contained in the **Debug** tab. Furthermore, you can check the **Enabled debug mode** check box to activate remote debugging by default for the respective server node. Note that when you activate both **Restricted load balance** and **Enabled debug mode**, the debugging node is always isolated from the cluster; i.e., it cannot be used in live operations.

Restricted load balance

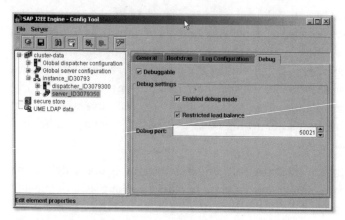

Figure 10.23 Remote Debugging Settings in the Configuration Tool

Once you have prepared a server node for remote debugging, you can launch a debugging session using SAP NetWeaver Developer Studio in the following way:

Starting a debugging session from SAP NetWeaver Developer Studio

1. In SAP NetWeaver Developer Studio, open the **J2EE Engine** view. Then open the context menu of the server node you want to use for remote debugging, and select the **Enable debugging of process** item in order to activate the debugging session.

2. This causes a restart of the server node, which is then isolated from the cluster provided the **Restricted load balancing** option has been configured for the node, as described earlier (see Figure 10.24).

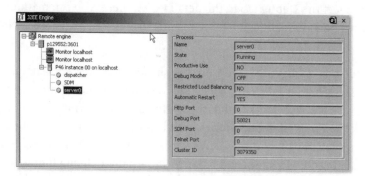

Figure 10.24 J2EE Engine in SAP NetWeaver Developer Studio

3. Then you can use the **Run · Debug...** menu item in SAP NetWeaver Developer Studio to create a debug configuration for

Web Dynpro. To do that, select the **Remote Java Application** item, as shown in Figure 10.25, open the context menu, and select **New** to create a new configuration.

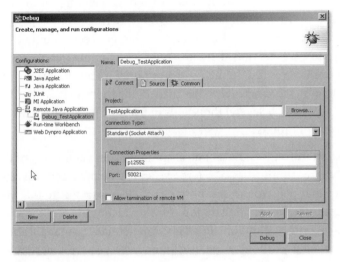

Figure 10.25 Creating a Debug Configuration for a Web Dynpro Application in Developer Studio

4. Enter the name of the debugging node and its debugging port in the **Host** and **Port** fields of the **Connection Properties** section. In the **Project** field, you must select the application whose source code you want to access in the debugging session. Finally, you can start the debugging session by clicking on **Debug**.

> **Tip**
>
> You can use the **System Information** page (see Section 10.2.3) to query whether a server node is marked as debuggable and, if so, which one. You also can query which port is to be used for remote debugging purposes.

10.3   Technical Configuration of the Web Dynpro Runtime

In addition to installing and maintaining the Web AS and the Web Dynpro runtime, another important task of an administrator is the setup of a system for test and live operation. This involves setting technical configuration parameters of SAP Web AS for actual use and

System for test and live operation

business scenarios in order to ensure a smooth operation of the application server. Those parameters include the maximum memory capacity available for the server nodes and the clearing behavior of application sessions that are no longer used. Depending on the live scenario to be used, it can be necessary and useful to set the parameters in different ways. If, for example, a server is set up only for a small group of users and if it runs only less complex applications with small resource requirements, the required memory capacity can certainly be set to a smaller value than in a system that is simultaneously accessed by several thousands of users or that runs memory-intensive applications.

This section introduces the technical configuration parameters of the Web Dynpro runtime as a reference and also provides tips and examples that help you to set those parameters. Make sure that you don't confuse the administration of the technical configuration parameters with the options to adapt or personalize an application; e.g., in order to customize the user interface for specific user roles. This kind of configuration goes beyond the pure administration of a system and requires detailed expert knowledge of business processes and usage scenarios for an application, so this process is usually carried out by business experts. We'll focus instead on those configuration tasks that are part of an administrator's job in this section: On the one hand this involves setting technical parameters that are required for specific behaviors of the Web Dynpro runtime such as the clearing behavior of running application sessions after a certain period of idle time. On the other hand, the work involves the configuration of parameters that are required for using external components in a Web Dynpro application. One example of that is the specification of the *Internet Graphics Server* (IGS) in the configuration which can then be used by Web Dynpro applications in order to create diagrams and charts.

The following three sections describe this area of the configuration work. Section 10.3.1 describes the configuration parameters specific to Web Dynpro and provides tips for setting these parameters. The application-specific configuration is described in Section 10.3.2. Section 10.3.2 concludes this part of the chapter by providing additional Web AS settings that directly or indirectly affect the Web Dynpro runtime behavior.

10.3.1 Basic Configuration of the Web Dynpro Runtime

Managing the Configuration Using the Configuration Adapter Service

The technical configuration of the Web Dynpro runtime is stored in the **Configuration Adapter** service of the engine and can be displayed and modified using the Visual Administrator. The existing configurations are arranged in a tree structure in the **Configuration Adapter**. In this tree you can find the Web Dynpro configuration at the following path: **webdynpro · sap.com · tc~wd~dispwda · Propertysheet default**. Figure 10.26 shows the detail view of the service.

Configuration adapter service

Figure 10.26 Web Dynpro Runtime Configuration in the Configuration Adapter Service

When you double-click on the **Propertysheet default** item, the Web Dynpro configuration opens in read-only mode. As shown in Figure 10.27, the individual configuration parameters are listed in a table. To change the parameters, you must first switch to the editing mode, which you can do by clicking on the **Edit** button in the toolbar (pencil icon). Then select the parameter you want to change and enter the required new value in the window shown in Figure 10.28.

Configuring the Web Dynpro runtime: Propertysheet default

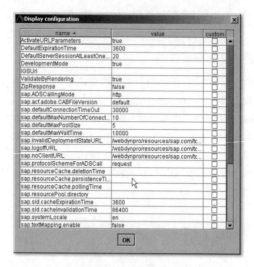

Figure 10.27 Propertysheet default: Configuration Parameters

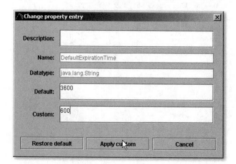

Figure 10.28 Customizing a Configuration Parameter

Confirm your entry by clicking the **OK** button in the **Display config-uration** window (see Figure 10.27) so that your changes can take effect. Then click on the **Edit** button again to return to the view mode.[11]

Note

In the rest of this chapter, we'll refer to the parameters of the **Property-sheet default** when we mean the configuration parameters of the Web Dynpro runtime.

---

11 Please note that prior to Service Pack SP15, SAP NetWeaver 2004 required a restart of the engine so that changes to the Web Dynpro configuration could take effect for the runtime. Since SP15, this is no longer necessary.

Web Dynpro Configuration and Tips for Settings

The parameters contained in the **Propertysheet default** can be divided into three different groups: The first group of parameters is required for the use of specific external components or of specific functions. The second group of parameters affects the scalability, performance, and memory utilization of a system. The third group of parameters is needed for reasons of supportability and compatibility. Following this division into three groups, we'll describe the meanings of the individual parameters in the following sections and provide tips and examples in order to explain useful settings whenever this is possible.

Web Dynpro runtime configuration parameters

▶ `IGSUrl`

This parameter enables you to make the Internet Graphics Server known to the Web Dynpro runtime. This setting is required if your applications use the `BusinessGraphics` UI element for displaying graphics and charts. As a valid parameter, you must specify a URL that points to the IGS.

Configuring an Internet Graphics Server

> **Tip**
>
> You can check the validity of the parameter by directly calling the specified URL in a web browser. The URL addresses the IGS correctly if the web browser displays the IGS home page (see Figure 10.29).

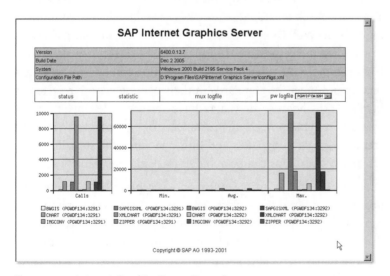

Figure 10.29 Internet Graphics Server Home Page

▶ `sap.webdispatcher.protocol`
`sap.webdispatcher.host`
`sap.webdispatcher.port`

Generating URLs from the used Web Dispatcher

These parameters are needed to generate absolute application URLs using the Web Dynpro URL Generator. Those application URLs address a Web Dispatcher that exists in the system. This is useful for applications that want to generate stable URLs that address system application and can be called by external users and stored as bookmarks. The Web Dynpro URL Generator provides the overloaded methods `getWorkloadBalancedApplicationURL()` for this purpose in the `com.sap.tc.webdynpro.services.sal.url.WDURLGenerator` class. You can use the three parameters, `sap.webdispatcher.protocol`, `sap.webdispatcher.host`, and `sap.webdispatcher.port`, to make the Web Dispatcher that's used in a Web AS system known to the Web Dynpro runtime. The generated application URLs then use the specified protocol and address the configured host and port of the Web Dispatcher; that is, URLs are generated according to the following pattern:

<sap.webdispatcher.protocol>://<sap.webdispatcher.host>: <sap.webdispatcher.port>/webdynpro/dispatcher/ <vendor name>/<DC name>/<application name>

▶ `sap.url.protocols`

Security check for used URLs

This parameter is needed by the Web Dynpro runtime to perform a security check of URLs: For all URLs generated by the runtime or called by it, Web Dynpro uses a security service to runs a check as to whether the respective URL meets the SAP security standards. For example, URLs that contain JavaScript commands or values that do not meet the standards in their parameters are rejected as invalid URLs because they may have security-relevant effects. A *cross-site scripting attack*, for instance, tries to trigger JavaScript commands by calling URLs and thus overcome the security barriers of a system. This can be avoided by using the security service.

Furthermore, the security service only accepts URLs that refer to a protocol known to the service. The `sap.url.protocols` parameter is used to specify a list of URL protocols that are to be accepted by the security service. By default, the parameter is set to the comma-separated list `http,https,ftp,mailto,file`. You can add more protocols to this list or remove protocols from it; the required valid values are the protocol names used in the URL.

▶ DevelopmentMode

This parameter specifies whether your system is currently in development mode. If the parameter is set to **true** and an error occurs, the system displays an error page that contains detailed information on the version of the runtime and code generators being used as well as information on the stack trace of the error. You should set the parameter to **false** for a live system. The default value after the initial installation is **true**, which corresponds to the setting that's recommended for the development and test phase.

Configuring the development mode

▶ sap.logoffURL

In this parameter, you can specify a URL that is called by the Web Dynpro runtime when an application logs off without explicitly specifying a *redirect URL*. An application can use the method WDClientUser.forceLogoffClientUser(String redirectUrl) to carry out a program-driven logoff. If no redirectUrl is specified for this method call, the Web Dynpro runtime automatically performs a redirect action to the URL that has been configured in this parameter. By default, the sap.logoffURL parameter is set so that it points to a default logoff page provided with the Web Dynpro runtime. Alternatively, you can specify any other static URL in this parameter. Please note that you must specify an absolute URL including host name and port if the URL references web sites or static resources outside the SAP Web AS.

Defining a logoff URL

As you will see in Section 10.3.2, you can also define a separate logoff URL for each application. For this purpose, the application-specific configuration also contains a sap.logoffURL parameter that overwrites the parameter of the same name, which is contained in the **Propertysheet default**.

> **Tip**
>
> If an application runs in SAP NetWeaver Portal, the application itself should not provide any Logoff button or carry any program-driven logoff process by using the method WDClientUser.forceLogoffClientUser(String redirectUrl). Being an integration platform for many different application, the portal carries out the tasks of starting a user session and terminating it through a logoff. For this reason, we recommend that applications only perform a program-driven logoff in well-conceived exceptional situations.

▶ sap.noClientURL

As described in Chapter 2 when discussing the basic architecture of the Web Dynpro runtime, Web Dynpro contains a client-abstraction layer that enables you to operate Web Dynpro using different clients. The *HTML client* is the standard client, while other clients are based on the business client protocol (BCP) and are supported by a *Java* or *Windows client*, for example.[12] Based on the header data of an incoming request, Web Dynpro determines which client is to be used for the runtime of an application. The sap.noClientURL parameter can be used to specify the URL of an error page that is displayed if the Web Dynpro runtime cannot determine an appropriate client when an application is launched. By default, the sap.noClientURL parameter is set so that it addresses a Web-Dynpro-specific error page.

▶ sap.systemLocale

For each HTTP session in which a Web Dynpro application is started, the Web Dynpro runtime calculates an instance of the java.util.Locale. That instance is used as a language identifier in Java and can be used to identify texts in a specific language and to determine the format of numeric values or the date format. Web Dynpro determines the locale to be used for a session on the basis of the specific processing logic. The sap.systemLocale parameter enables you to specify the locale that is to be used if the Web Dynpro runtime cannot derive any language setting from the logon or session data (see Section 10.4.1). The valid values for this parameter are defined by the ISO-639 standard (*http://www.ics.uci.edu/pub/ietf/http/related/iso639.txt*); that is, they adhere to the conventions of java.util.Locale. For example, values that make sense are **en** or **de** in order to set English or German as the system locale.

> **Tip**
>
> In this parameter, you should set the locale that is to be used as default locale if the system cannot derive any session-specific locale from the logon and session data.

---

12 At the time of writing the manuscript for this book, the Java and Windows clients were only available as prototypes.

▶ `sap.theme.default`

This parameter allows you to specify the theme to be used by Web Dynpro as default display of the user interface, provided no other theme is specified using the URL parameter `sap-cssurl` upon the startup of an application. If you don't set the `sap.theme.default` parameter, Web Dynpro automatically uses the standard SAP theme, `sap_standard`.

Setting a default theme

If you run Web Dynpro applications in SAP NetWeaver Portal, they inherit the portal theme that's currently set. Thus, the parameter is predominantly used by those applications that don't run in the portal and for which you don't want to use the standard SAP theme.

You can find a list of themes provided by SAP in your SAP NetWeaver installation by using the following path: */usr/sap/<system ID>/<instance name>/j2ee/cluster/server<i>/temp/webdynpro/web/sap.com/tc~wd~dispwda/global/SSR/themes*. Valid values for this parameter are for instance *http://<engine host>:<engine port>/irj/portalapps/com.sap.portal.themes.lafservice/themes/portal/sap_chrome* or *http://<engine host>:<engine port>/irj/portalapps/com.sap.portal.themes.lafservice/themes/portal/sap_tradeshow*.

▶ `sap.protocolSchemeForADSCall`
`sap.acf.adobe.CABFileVersion`
`sap.ADSCallingMode`

These parameters are required for integrating the *Adobe Document Service* (ADS) with the Web Dynpro runtime and for using the `InteractiveForm` UI element in Web Dynpro applications.

Integrating Adobe Document Service

The `sap.protocolSchemeForADSCall` parameter determines the protocol to be used for sending requests to the ADS. Valid values are **request**, **http**, and **https**, **request** being the default setting. For this setting, Web Dynpro uses the same protocol for requests to the ADS as the one used for the current client request. HTTP (HTTPS) is always used for the value **http (https)**.

The `sap.acf.adobe.CABFileVersion` parameter enables you to specify the ActiveX version that's needed for the `InteractiveForm` UI element. That's necessary if the versions of ADS and Web Dynpro are different, which should generally not be the case. By default, the parameter is set to the **default** value. This setting assumes that the ADS and Web Dynpro versions being used are compatible. If that's not the case, the version of the ADS being used must be specified in this parameter in order to avoid compatibility problems. In general, the parameter is used only for supportability purposes and should not be modified.

The `sap.ADSCallingMode` parameter is no longer used and can thus be ignored in the configuration process.

Using Text Mappings

The following configuration parameters are required for the use of text mappings:

▶ `sap.textMapping.enable`
`sap.textMapping.objectName`
`sap.textMapping.separators`
`sap.textMapping.systemName`
`sap.textMapping.systemNumber`

Customizing terminology

In SAP NetWeaver 2004, Web Dynpro does not yet support any general concept for a modification-free customization of an application such as the modification of terminology, the hiding of specific UI elements of a user interface, and so on. The next major release that is to follow SAP NetWeaver 2004 will provide such a concept. Yet, even in SAP NetWeaver 2004, Web Dynpro provides a rudimentary method for a modification-free customization of terminology: the *text mappings*. Using text mappings, you can customize words or texts of a deployed application without having to modify the texts that have been declared in the application and having to deploy the application once again.

If text mappings are defined, the Web Dynpro runtime only takes them into account if the `sap.textMapping.enable` parameter is set to **true**. By default, this parameter is set to **false**.

In SAP NetWeaver 2004 you must define all defined text mappings in a development component even if the text mappings are used for different Web Dynpro applications. The `sap.textMapping.objectName` parameter is used to specify the name of the DC that contains the text mapping.

Text mapping distinguishes between the following two types of text in an application:

▶ For reasons of performance, the *texts of UI elements* are always regarded and replaced in their entirety. For example, if the text of a `Button` UI element is "Search customer" and you want to replace it by "Search business partner," it is not enough to define a text mapping for "customer." You must rather define a mapping for the entire text, "Search customer."

▶ The second type of texts is *messages*. In messages you can replace individual words via text mappings. For example, you can replace the word "customer" in the message "Search for a customer successfully done" by the term "business partner." To make sure that finding individual words functions properly, you must inform Web Dynpro about the separation characters it has to take into account. You can do that by using the `sap.textMapping.separators` parameter which is set as follows by default: **!;,:-_+=)([]?**. Most often, this setting is sufficient for identifying individual words in messages and replacing them by the mapped text.

The parameters `sap.textMapping.systemName` and `sap.textMapping.systemNumber` specify the system name and the dialog instance number of an SAP Web AS for which you want to use text mapping. For example, "J2E" could be the system name and "00" the ID of the dialog instance.

Now let's take a look at how you can use SAP NetWeaver Developer Studio to create text mappings and at the restrictions you have to take into account here. As mentioned earlier, all text mappings are expected in the DC that is defined by `sap.textMapping.objectName`. For example, let's suppose this is the DC called `sap.com/TextMappings`. If it doesn't exist yet, create a new Web Dynpro DC with this name in SAP NetWeaver Developer Studio. Then switch to the **Navigator** view in the Web Dynpro perspective, and navigate to the *src/configuration* folder in the `sap.com/TextMappings` you just created. This is the location where the Web Dynpro runtime expects possible text mappings as property files that have the following fixed name structure: *TextMappings_<language>.properties*.

Creating text mappings using SAP NetWeaver Developer Studio

You can now either import existing property files or create new ones in the *src/configuration* folder. To do that, open the context menu of the *src/configuration* folder and select **New · Other... · Simple · File**. The system displays the dialog shown in Figure 10.30, which enables you to create a file.

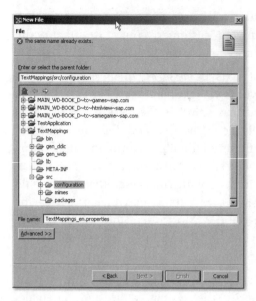

Figure 10.30 Creating a Text-Mapping File

After creating the file, you can define text-mapping entries whose format is expected to have the following structure:

<name of scope>.<original text>=<mapped text>

▸ **Name of scope**
The name of the scope specifies the Web Dynpro views to which a text-mapping entry is supposed to apply. A scope defines the name of a Java package and is used as follows:

A text-mapping entry is used only for those views whose Java package names begin with the specified scope. For example, a text mapping with the scope sap.com.ess is used for all views whose package name begins with sap.com.ess.

If you don't specify any scope, the text mapping is used globally; i.e., for all deployed Web Dynpro applications.

▸ **Original text**
This specifies the text value that is to be replaced using the map-

ping. Note the two different types of texts that must be distinguished here: the UI element texts that are either replaced completely or not at all, and the message texts in which you can replace single words.

▶ **Mapped text**
This part defines the text that is to replace the original text.

Restrictions in SAP NetWeaver 2004

> **Note**
>
> The text-mapping support provided by SAP NetWeaver 2004 has some limitations you should take into account when working with text mappings:
>
> ▶ Text mappings must be entered separately for all supported languages, because no link exists to an automatic translation process, as is the case for other text resources of an application.
>
> ▶ If you enter a mapping for an original text that contains a blank space character, the blank space must be replaced by a backslash (\). For example, to replace the value "Search customer" by "Search business partner" you must enter "Search\customer" as the original text.
>
> Despite those restrictions, the use of text mapping provides a flexible option to customize applications for different terminologies without having to modify them.

Configuration Affecting Scalability and Performance

We now want to describe the configuration parameters that affect the scalability, performance, and memory usage of a system.

▶ `DefaultExpirationTime`

This parameter is used for setting the default idle time of a Web Dynpro application until it is automatically terminated and removed from the list of currently active applications by the Web Dynpro session management. The specified expiration time is not an absolute value, as it always relates to the last interaction between a user and an application session. The value configured in this parameter defines a time interval in terms of seconds. If this interval passes by for an application and the user hasn't used the application any further, the application session is terminated by the Web Dynpro runtime and the resources that had been utilized by the application are released. When the application is terminated, its exit plug is called in which the application developer

Setting the default expiration time of an application session

should allow for releasing all used resources such as backend connections, and so on.

By default, the parameter is set to 3,600 seconds, which equals 60 minutes. This means that an application is terminated automatically after an idle time of 60 minutes has passed. If a user wants to continue using the application session that has already been removed, the system displays the SessionExpiredException error message shown in Figure 10.31: The error message says that the associated session has expired and that you can restart the application by clicking on the provided link.

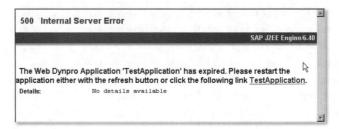

Figure 10.31 Error when Accessing a Terminated Application

Because each active application session utilizes memory on the application server, the DefaultExpirationTime parameter affects the overall required memory size. When choosing a value for this parameter, you should therefore also consider server settings such as the maximum *heap size* of the server VMs (see Section 10.3.3): As the value can be overwritten by an application, the actual application scenarios are less important here (see Section 10.3.2) than a useful default setting based on the available memory and the system load to be expected.

Tips for setting
DefaultExpiration-
Time

Tip

In scenarios where you use the server for smaller user groups or for predominantly smaller applications with a low memory utilization, it can be useful to increase the default setting of 60 minutes. However, higher values can have the effect that the configured maximum heap size of a server no longer suffices so that the system generates an OutOfMemoryError. If such an error occurs, the relevant server node is restarted. The sessions that run on this node are lost, and you cannot use the server node on productive operation while it is being restarted.

For this reason, we suggest you use a smaller value for this parameter, for example 30 minutes. This is particularly helpful if you expect a large parallel load by many users on your server. However, if you set up a system for demo or training purposes, you should use unrealistically high values in order to avoid a `SessionExpiredException` after a long break.

▶ `DefaultServerSessionAtLeastOneAppScopeExpirationTime`

The Web Dynpro runtime uses internal caches to optimize the runtime. It buffers session-independent data in those caches that then can be used by different application sessions. In Web Dynpro jargon, those caches are also referred to as *scopes*. The validity of such a scope depends on the lifecycle of a Web Dynpro session entity.

Runtime behavior of cross-application caches

The Web Dynpro session management consists of different session entities: For example, the logon session of a user is mapped as a *server session* in Web Dynpro. All applications that a user launches for instance within a login in SAP NetWeaver Portal run in the same server session. Another Web Dynpro session entity is the *application session* that describes the lifecycle of a Web Dynpro application from its start through to its termination.

Web Dynpro session management

Especially in the portal scenario you can start and end many application scenarios within one login session. A typical scenario is that a user logs on to the portal and then navigates between several portal pages using different Web Dynpro applications or iViews. As already mentioned, the Web Dynpro runtime stores specific data in the scope of the login session in order to optimize the system performance. On the one hand, this data is supposed to be deleted as soon as it is no longer needed so that the storage space can be released again; on the other hand, data should be loaded only once, if possible, and then be used by many applications. For this purpose, Web Dynpro uses the *server-session-at-least-one-application-scope* internally, that is, the scope cannot be used by an application as a publicly usable function. The data of this scope is valid as long as the login session lasts and as long as there is at least one active Web Dynpro application. The data of this scope is not deleted until the login session or the last running Web Dynpro application in the login session is terminated and a short time interval has passed. You can use the parameter

Server-Session-At-Least-One-Application-Scope

`DefaultServerSessionAtLeastOneAppScopeExpirationTime` to set the time interval in terms of seconds.[13]

By default, the value is set to 20 seconds. This interval should be sufficient so that the data of the cache that is written to can survive one navigation step in the portal. If a user navigates from one portal page to another and both pages run Web Dynpro applications, the applications of the first page are terminated first before the applications of the second page are started. This means that for a short period no Web Dynpro applications are active. To avoid deleting the data of the described scope during such a navigation step so that the data can also be used by the applications on the second page, the data is not deleted until after a certain delay.

Web Dynpro uses the described scope mainly for using imported JCo back-end metadata across different applications.

> **Tip**
>
> You should only set this value in terms of seconds and not in terms of minutes or even hours. The parameter is primarily used for the runtime optimization of Web Dynpro applications in the portal that use the *adaptive RFC model* and carry out complex read operations in the background. Since that also involves caching the JCo connections in order to collect metadata, a high value for this parameter would prevent the JCo connections from being released so that the JCo pool being used could overflow. We therefore recommend a value of between 5 and 30 seconds.

▶ `ZipResponse`

Compressing the response data

This parameter specifies whether the response sent to a client after a server roundtrip should be zipped. Possible values are **true** and **false**. Because the Web Dynpro runtime always runs on an SAP Web Application Server within an SAP NetWeaver 2004 installation and uses the HTML client by default, we don't need this parameter at the moment: The Web container of the J2EE engine already takes care of zipping the response (see Section 10.3.3). Thus, the parameter is only important for other platforms and clients, so you can ignore it for the time being in SAP NetWeaver 2004.

---

13 We must admit that the name of this parameter is somewhat intimidating.

▶ sap.resourcePool.directory
  sap.resourceCache.persistenceTime
  sap.resourceCache.deletionTime
  sap.resourceCache.pollingTime

The Web Dynpro runtime uses a cache for MIME objects that are dynamically created by applications. The cache is based on a file system. Examples of such MIME objects include diagrams that are dynamically created by the Internet Graphics Server or documents created by the InteractiveForm UI element.

MIME cache settings

For a program-based access to this cache, Web Dynpro provides the classes WDWebResource and IWDCachedWebResource, WDWebResource being used as a factory for IWDCachedWebResource objects. The cacheable entities are objects that implement the IWDCachedWebResource interface.

You can use the four configuration parameters to set different properties of the cache. sap.resourcePool.directory is used to specify the directory in the file system to which the cache is supposed to persist its data. Note that the path is platform-independent which means you must use slashes (/) instead of backslashes (\) as separating characters within a path. If you don't specify any value for this parameter, the directory */usr/sap/<system ID>/ <instance name>/j2ee/cluster/server<i>/temp/webdynpro/pool* is used by default as the file system cache.

The sap.resourceCache.persistenceTime parameter specifies the time period in seconds after which an object is to be removed from the main memory and persist in the file system cache after it has been used the last time. If you don't specify any value for this parameter, 80 seconds is used as the default value.

The sap.resourceCache.deletionTime parameter specifies the time in seconds after which an object is to be removed from the file system cache after it has been used the last time. If you don't specify any value for this parameter, 30 seconds is used as the default value.

Finally, the sap.resourceCache.pollingTime parameter defines the time intervals in terms of seconds at which the cache is to be browsed for objects that are to be persisted or deleted. If you don't specify any value for this parameter, 60 seconds is used as the default value.

▶ `sap.defaultMaxNumberOfConnections`
`sap.defaultMaxPoolSize`
`sap.defaultMaxWaitTime`
`sap.defaultConnectionTimeOut`

Default settings for JCo connections

These parameters are used by the Web Dynpro runtime to handle the connections of a JCo pool if you don't specify any specific values for the individual configurable properties of a pool during the program-based creation of a JCo connection.

Managing JCo pools

Web Dynpro acquires JCo connections from JCo pools. It administers the created pools internally using a key that contains the name of the JCo destination, the name of the current user, the current session locale, and the login mechanism used for the JCo connection. Thus, a pool can be shared by different application sessions, provided the calculated key matches the JCo pool.

API for creating JCo connections

Web Dynpro provides a service for creating and using JCo connections. This service is located in Java package `com.sap.tc.web-dynpro.services.sal.sl.api`. Among others, the service contains the `WDSystemLandscapeFactory` class that an application can use to create an `IWDJCoClientConnection` type JCo connection. In doing so, the Web Dynpro runtime reverts to the values of the four configuration parameters in the **Propertysheet default** if the values are not explicitly specified during the creation of a JCo connection.

The `sap.defaultMaxPoolSize` parameter defines the default value for the maximum number of open connections for a JCo pool. Thus, the value limits the number of potentially open JCo connections of a pool that can be used simultaneously. By default, this parameter is set to **5**.

> **Tip**
>
> To determine the default setting for this parameter, you should find out how many JCo connections your applications require on average (for example, two connections per application), and how many applications a used on average by a user within one login session (for example, four applications per user). If you multiply those two average values with each other, you obtain an estimated value that represents a reasonable value for the **sap.defaultMaxPoolSize** parameter. For our examples, the following value is used:
>
> 2 connections per application × 4 applications per session = 8.

The `sap.defaultMaxNumberOfConnections` parameter specifies the maximum number of currently used or non-used JCo connections that a pool is able to manage. Of course, the value of `sap.default-MaxPoolSize` can never be higher than that of `sap.defaultMax-NumberOfConnections`.

> **Tip**
>
> An unused connection that is buffered in the pool can be allocated faster than a connection that must be created from scratch. Therefore, it makes sense from a performance point of view to set the parameter `sap.defaultMaxNumberOfConnections` to a value that's one-and-a-half times or twice the value of the `sap.defaultMaxPoolSize` parameter. When choosing the values for those two parameters, you also should take the configuration of your ABAP backend into account.

The `sap.defaultMaxWaitTime` parameter specifies the default setting for the maximum amount of time that an application has to wait when trying to obtain a connection from the JCo pool, in terms of milliseconds. If the specified amount of time passes without the application obtaining a connection from the pool, the system displays a corresponding error message. By default, the value is set to 10 seconds.

> **Tip**
>
> If an application has to wait for a free connection, the application is blocked during this time, which mans that a user has to wait for his request to be processed. For this reason, we do not recommend choosing a value significantly higher than 10 seconds.

The `sap.defaultConnectionTimeOut` parameter specifies the default setting for the amount of time in terms of milliseconds, after which an open but unused connection closes automatically and is returned to the pool. The default setting for this parameter is 30 seconds.

> **Tip**
>
> This mechanism is supposed to prevent the pool from overflowing and thereby avoid error messages caused by programming errors such as those that occur when an application does not explicitly close unused JCo connections. We therefore recommend using a value that ranges between 10 and 120 seconds for this parameter.

▶ `sap.sld.cacheExpirationTime`
`sap.sld.cacheInvalidationTime`

SLD cache settings

The `sap.sld.cacheExpirationTime` parameter specifies the time interval in terms of seconds after which the Web Dynpro runtime invalidates data that has been read from the system landscape directory and after which the runtime re-imports this data for the next use.

The SLD contains data on the connected system landscape, including the names of the available JCo destinations of an SAP NetWeaver system. Since a read-only access to the SLD is relatively expensive and its data is rather static in live operation, it makes sense from a performance viewpoint to cache this data. For this reason, Web Dynpro keeps data that was imported from the SLD in the memory for the period of time specified in the `sap.sld.cacheExpirationTime` parameter. Once this interval has expired, the imported data is deleted and again retrieved from the SLD whenever it is needed. By default, the parameter is set to 3,600 seconds.

> **Tip**
>
> It makes sense to choose a relatively high value for this parameter in a live system. For example, you can set it to one hour because it is unlikely that the system landscape will be subject to constant changes. But you should use a smaller value for a development or test system, for instance 300 seconds.

▶ `sap.valuesetlimit.maximmediate`

This parameter is no longer used by the Web Dynpro runtime, so that you don't need to configure it.

▶ `sap.valuesetlimit.maxondemand`

Input help settings

This parameter is needed for values of a `DropDownByKey` UI element as well as for the input help (F4 help, extended value selection). It specifies the maximum size of the value sets that should be sent in a single request from the server to the client. For example, if the value set comprises several hundreds or even thousands of entries, you can use this parameter to subdivide the value set into smaller subsets that are sent to the client on demand. This way you can improve the response time and hence the system performance. By default, this parameter is set to 50.

> **Tip**
>
> We recommend you choose a value between 30 and 100 for this parameter because the system cannot display more than 100 entries per screen.

Configuration Parameters for Supportability or Compatibility Purposes

Finally, we want to introduce the third group of configuration parameters here. Those parameters are needed for reasons of supportability and compatibility.

▶ `ValidateByRendering`

This parameter was added for the purpose of rendering optimization after Web Dynpro had become generally available. The parameter specifies whether the Web Dynpro runtime retrieves and validates only the controller context data that is required for the display on screen. It can have the values **true** or **false**. By default, this parameter is set to **true** so that the runtime optimization during the rendering process is activated.

Runtime behavior during rendering

However, from time to time applications may rely on the previous behavior in such a way that the new behavior causes errors. Such errors typically have the effect that display data is inconsistent or updated with a delay. Those effects can occur for instance when—in contrast to the instructions in the Web Dynpro programming model—an application retrieves or modifies data for a **calculated** attribute in a `Get` method, which can affect other parts of the screen. In those cases, you can reactivate parts of the previous behavior for troubleshooting purposes by setting the parameter to **false**.

> **Tip**
>
> For the performance reasons described here, this parameter should always be set to **true** and should only be set to **false** for testing purposes if the display problems described above occur in the user interface.

▶ `sap.useWebDynproStyleSheet`

If Web Dynpro applications run in SAP NetWeaver Portal, you can use this parameter to specify whether you want the Web Dynpro applications to use the stylesheets provided with the portal or those provided with Web Dynpro. By default, this

Using stylesheets

parameter is set to **false**; that is, the portal stylesheets are the ones to be used. But since version problems can occur if you use different versions or service packs of Web Dynpro and the SAP NetWeaver Portal, this parameter enables you to witch to the Web-Dynpro-specific stylesheets.

> **Tip**
>
> We recommend you set the parameter always to **false** and only use the **true** value for testing purposes, if you encounter problems in the display of UI elements in your Web Dynpro applications. You can then set the parameter to **true** in order to check if a version problem exists with regard to the stylesheets. If that is the case, we recommend that you upgrade one of the two components to bring it back to a compatible service-pack level.

10.3.2 Application-Specific Definition of Configuration Parameters

Application-spe-
cific overwriting of
default settings

Some of the configuration parameters described in the previous section define default settings that are used by the Web Dynpro runtime only if the parameters have not been overwritten by a specific application. For example, the three parameters, DefaultExpirationTime, sap.systemLocale, and sap.logoffURL can be specifically set for each application. To do that, you must open the application-specific configuration of an application by selecting an application in the Web Dynpro view of SAP NetWeaver Developer Studio and activating the **Application properties** tab in the detail view (see Figure 10.32).

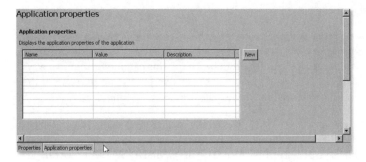

Figure 10.32 Detail View of Application-Specific Configuration Parameters

Click on the **New** button to open the dialog used for creating new configuration parameters shown in Figure 10.33. Select **Pre defined** and then click on **Browse...** to open the list of predefined application-specific configuration parameters that's shown in Figure 10.34.

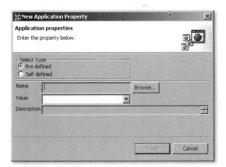

Figure 10.33 Defining an Application-Specific Configuration

The `ExpirationTime` parameter enables you to overwrite the setting of the `DefaultExpirationTime` parameter that's contained in the **Propertysheet default**. The same is true for the parameters `Logof-fURL` and `sap.logoffURL` as well as for `DefaultLocale` and `sap.sys-temLocale`.

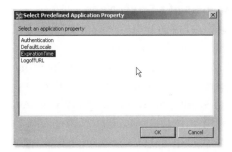

Figure 10.34 Predefined Configuration Parameters of an Application

The `Authentication` parameter can be used to define whether an application requires a user authentication when it is started. Possible values are **true** and **false**. If the parameter is set to **true** for an application, a logon screen automatically displays when the application is started. Users must first authenticate themselves successfully here before they can access the actual application.

User authentication

Self-defined
application
parameters
An application can add other self-defined application parameters to its configuration and access those parameters during the execution of the program. To do that, select the **Self defined** option shown in Figure 10.33. You then can define the name and value of a self-defined parameter by entering the corresponding data in the **Name** and **Value** fields.

10.3.3 Web-Dynpro-Relevant Configuration of SAP Web Application Server

Now that we have described the Web Dynpro-specific configuration parameters in great detail, we want to introduce some other important configuration parameters of SAP Web AS that more or less affect the runtime behavior of Web Dynpro. These include additional configurations regarding the scalability, performance, and memory usage of a system, such as the memory settings of the *Java Virtual Machine* (VM) of a server node or the *timeouts* settings of the session entities that exist on SAP Web AS. And we'll discuss configuration parameters that are required for a specific runtime behavior such as the use of HTTPS.

Configuring the Java VM Parameters of a Server Node

Changing the Java
VM parameters
using the
configuration tool
The settings of the Java VM parameters of a server node enable you to control key figures such as the maximum *heap size* and the *garbage collection* behavior of a server VM. These settings have a strong influence on the performance of a server node. For example, if the maximum heap size is too small, this can lead to undesirably frequent garbage collection runs. Because a garbage-collection run blocks other threads of the VM, the performance of a server node decreases significantly.

You can use the configuration tool of the engine to set the parameters of a server VM. Section 10.2.1 already introduced this tool briefly. As shown in Figure 10.35, you can change the parameters of a server VM in the **Java parameters** field.

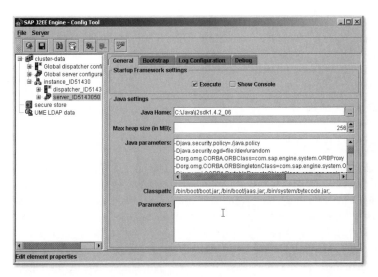

Figure 10.35 Changing VM Parameters of a Server Node Using the Configuration Tool

For your server VMs, you should check the following parameters and adjust them to the requirements of your system:

▶ **Heap Size and Its Effect on Garbage Collection**

Heap size is used to set the available disk space of a VM. Both a minimum and maximum limit can be specified for this. If the memory for a VM now becomes full over time, the VM attempts, via garbage collection, to clean up any memory that is already allocated but no longer used, in order to free up some memory space again. When you set the heap size, you should ensure that garbage collection runs do not occur too frequently. This would be evident from a significant deterioration in performance.

To be able to check how often a garbage-collection run actually occurs, the -verbose:gc parameter should always be set. The VM then logs the runs of the garbage collection in the trace file *std_ server<index>.out*, which you will find under the engine directory */usr/sap/<system ID>/<instance name>/work*.

Tip	Setting the minimum and maximum heap size
The actual value for an appropriate maximum heap size depends to a large degree on how a Web AS system is used, and can generally only be determined empirically by performing load tests.	

419

Nevertheless, based on practical experience, we recommend the following settings for SAP NetWeaver 2004: The minimum and maximum heap size should both be set to the same value. The value should not fall below the 1 gigabyte limit. In other words, a setting that might be useful as a first approximation would be

```
-Xms1024m -Xmx1024m
```

or

```
-Xms2048m -Xmx2048m.
```

To achieve the required scalability for the relevant application scenario, we recommend that you use additional server nodes rather than using server VMs with huge heap sizes of several gigabytes, because heaps that are too large would also impair the performance of the garbage collection.

If you have installed several server nodes on a server, note also that the total of the maximum heap sizes of these server nodes should not exceed the actual physical server memory space that is available. Otherwise, there may be a *paging* of memory blocks at operating-system level, which in turn would have a severe adverse impact on the performance of the affected server nodes.

▶ **Settings of the SUN HotSpot VM**

The following settings have proven useful for the server nodes of an SAP Web AS cluster for SUN's HotSpot VM:

▷ Java VM type

The SUN Hotspot VM supports both the *Server VM* and *Client VM* runtime types. These differ in their handling of the memory and garbage collection strategies.

We advise that you use the server VM type rather than the client VM type, which also corresponds to the standard setting of a server node after its installation. If you want to change the parameter, you may not use the -server or -client Java VM parameter to do so, as these are ignored by the startup framework of the SAP Web AS. Instead, the VM type in the profile of a dialog instance must be specified by the entry jstartup/vm/type=server or jstartup/vm/type=client. You will find the instance profile under the directory */usr/sap/<system ID>/<instance name>/SYS/profile/<system ID>_<instance name>_ <host name>*.

Tip

The configuration we recommend is jstartup/vm/type=server.

▶ Allocation of additional disk space

The NewSize and MaxNewSize parameters determine by how much memory space the heap grows if its current capacity is no longer enough and the configured maximum heap size is not yet used up. The parameters are thus only significant if the minimum and maximum heap sizes are not set to the same value. The SurvivorRatio and TargetSurvivorRatio parameters are also used to set the proportion of the *eden space* and *survivor space*.

Tip

We recommend that you set the NewSize and MaxNewSize parameters to around 1/6 of the available maximum heap size:

```
-XX:NewSize=160m
-XX:MaxNewSize=160m
-XX:SurvivorRatio=2
-XX:TargetSurvivorRatio=90
```

▶ Memory space for the loaded classes

The SUN HotSpot VM manages loaded classes in a special memory area, the so-called *permanent space*. This memory area must be set large enough so that the classes of all used applications and components of SAP NetWeaver can be loaded. If the setting is too low, this will cause an OutOfMemoryError during the runtime of a server node and will thus cause the VM to crash.

Tip

The configuration we recommend is -XX:MaxPermSize=208m -XX:PermSize=208m

---

▶ Settings for analyzing the garbage collection

When performance problems occur it is advisable to analyze the garbage-collection runs more closely, to be able to establish whether the performance problems observed are attributable to excessively frequent garbage-collection runs. To do this, you can specify additional parameters on a test basis that will provide a more detailed tracing of the garbage collection. The traces are then written to the file */usr/sap/<system ID>/<instance name>/work/std_server<index>.out*. However, you should not use the parameters during production operation of a server node,

Analyzing garbage collection runs

because the logging of the garbage-collection runs into the traces themselves will again adversely affect the performance of the node.

Tip

We recommend the following configuration for testing and analysis of the garbage collection:

```
-XX:+PrintGCTimeStamps
-XX:+PrintGCDetails
-XX:+PrintTenuringDistribution
-XX:+UseTLAB
```

Configuring Additional Session Timeouts

Below we describe the timeout parameters that are relevant for the session entities for Web applications on the application server. The session management of Web applications is managed on the SAP Web AS by the **Web Container** service and consists of the entities *Security Session* and *HTTP Session*. Here, a *security session* represents a user's logon session, and the *HTTP session* represents an active web application. For both session entities, there are timeout settings that specify a time period beyond which a session instance is automatically terminated.

Web Dynpro dispatcher servlet

Web Dynpro has a central servlet, the *Web Dynpro dispatcher servlet,* that receives all HTTP queries sent to Web Dynpro applications and transfers them to the Web Dynpro runtime. From the view of the **Web Container** service, Web Dynpro thereby represents a Web application. In other words, the life cycle of running Web Dynpro applications is also influenced by the session management of the Web Container.

Configuring the HTTP session timeout

▶ **HTTP Session Timeout**

In the Visual Administrator you can use the **Web Container** service to set the timeout of the corresponding HTTP session for each Web application. The configured timeout value must be understood relative to the last user interaction. In other words, it describes the time span from a user's last query beyond which, without any further user interaction, an HTTP session will be automatically terminated by the session management of the Web Container.

Figure 10.36 shows the **Web Container** service in the Visual Administrator: In the detailed view, choose the entry **sap.com/ tc~wd~dispwda** and underneath, the node **webdynpro/dispatcher**. This node represents the Web Dynpro dispatcher servlet.

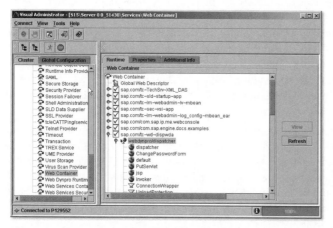

Figure 10.36 Web Dynpro Dispatcher Servlet in the Web Container Service

If you then click on the **View** button, the window shown in Figure 10.37 appears for setting the attributes of a Web application. On the **Main** tab, in the **Session Timeout** input field, you can set the HTTP session timeout for the Web Dynpro dispatcher servlet. The value is set to 30 minutes by default.

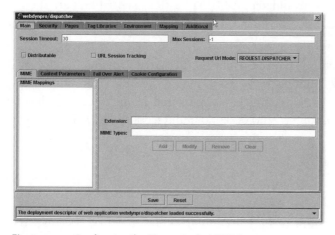

Figure 10.37 Configuring the Timeout of a HTTP Session

> **Note**
>
> Web Dynpro supports a separate timeout configuration for each Web Dynpro application, as we have already seen in the two previous sections when we explained the `DefaultExpirationTime` parameter and the application-specific ExpirationTime parameter. If this timeout value for a Web Dynpro application is higher than the timeout value of the HTTP session of the dispatcher servlet in which the Web Dynpro application is started, the Web Dynpro runtime overwrites the timeout of this HTTP session with the special value of the started Web Dynpro application. If the application is later terminated, the Web Dynpro runtime sets the timeout value of the HTTP session back to the value configured in the Web Container.
>
> Since Web Dynpro buffers data internally to the HTTP session, the setting of the HTTP session timeout nevertheless plays an important role because these data caches are not emptied until the HTTP session is "cleared." When you set the parameters, you should consider what a suitable idle time would be in view of the expected load on the system, before these are terminated automatically by the engine and their buffered data is released again.

Configuring the security session timeout

▶ **Security Session Timeout**

The setting of the security-session timeout defines the time interval in which a logon session remains valid after a user logon. Everyone must understand that the timeout value that is set takes effect from the logon time; i.e., it is not affected by subsequent user interactions. Once the set time interval has expired, the logon session is invalidated. All HTTP sessions started in it are then terminated, and the login ticket loses its validity. The user must then log on again.

The setting is made using the **Security Provider** service in the Visual Administrator (see Figure 10.38). The `SessionExpirationPeriod` parameter is measured in milliseconds. The standard setting is 100,000,000 milliseconds, i.e. a little over 27 hours.

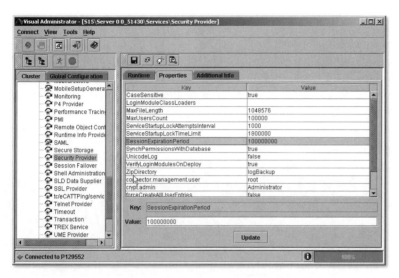

Figure 10.38 Setting the Security Session Timeout

> **Tip**
>
> For most scenarios, it does not make sense to have the value of the security session timeout set too low. For example, if the typical scenario is such that the applications of your system run in the SAP NetWeaver Portal, and this in turn runs on your company's intranet, and a user regularly works with these applications during his or her working day, a logon session that has been started should generally not end after only a few minutes or hours. This would require the user to constantly log on again and restart the required applications. In such a scenario, it is advisable to have the security session time out after around eight to 15 hours.
>
> On the other hand, in the case of security-critical applications such as applications for banks that can be reached via the Internet by any number of users, a value of minutes might make sense for the security session timeout parameter. For example, if in an online banking application a logon session is to terminate after a maximum allowed time period of 30 minutes, the timeout of the security session can be set accordingly. Note here that the security session timeout setting is a global parameter that affects all of the system's Web applications.

▸ **Validity of an SSO Login Ticket**

Another parameter that affects the behavior of applications that are running during a logon session is the validity period of a login ticket when you use *Single Sign-On* (SSO). The duration that is set specifies how long a login ticket that is issued will be accepted as valid by the security service. If you continue to use a ticket after its

425

validity period has expired, the security service generates a corresponding error message, and you must log on to the system again.

The validity period of a login ticket can be configured as follows in the Visual Administrator using the **Configuration Adapter** service: In the Configuration tree of the detail view of the service shown in Figure 10.39, choose the entry **Configuration · cluster_ data · server · cfg · services · Propertysheet com.sap.security. core.ume.service**.

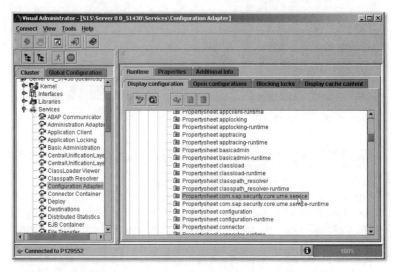

Figure 10.39 Setting the Validity of a Login Ticket in the Service Configuration Adapter

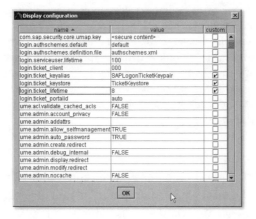

Figure 10.40 Changing the Validity Period of a Login Ticket

If you open the selected property sheet, you will find the login.ticket_lifetime parameter, which describes the validity period of a login ticket in hours (see Figure 10.40). The standard setting of this parameter is eight hours.

> **Tip**
>
> When you use single sign-on, we recommend that you set the parameter in the region of eight to 12 hours. Because SSO is usually used within companies (on the intranet) and therefore needs to avoid forcing users to constantly log on to different systems, the proposed configuration corresponds approximately to the time period of a working day.

Additional Parameters that Affect System Performance

Let's look at additional configurations of a server node that affect the performance of a system. You should check the settings of these parameters in order to obtain optimal performance during productive use of a system or when load tests are being performed.

▶ **Settings for the HTTP Provider Service**
The **HTTP Provider** service of the SAP Web AS is capable of sending compressed data to the client and of thereby reducing the time taken to transmit data over the network. The compression is already enabled by default for HTML data. The setting can be changed in the Visual Administrator using the **HTTP Provider** service using the AlwaysCompressed parameter (see Figure 10.41).

Compressing the data transferred via HTTP

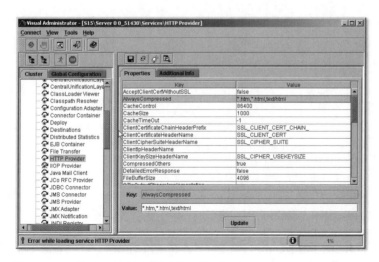

Figure 10.41 Configuring the HTTP Provider Service

427

Logs and traces ▶ **Configuration of logs and traces**

For a production system, or before running load tests in a test system, you should also ensure that the *severity level* for trace and log information is set to **Error** or, at most, to, **Warning**. If the setting is finer, the volume of logged trace and log data increases dramatically and has a noticeable adverse effect on overall system performance.

You can make the settings for logs and traces using the **Log Configurator** service via the Visual Administrator (see Section 10.4.3).

Additional Configurations that Affect Web Dynpro

System type ▶ **Configuration of the system type**

The system type of a server node specifies the application mode the node is in. The possible system types are production, test, training, or development type. The setting you choose affects the display of error pages in a system, for example: A standard error message therefore appears for the productive type if an error occurs. The message does not contain any details on the error that has occurred, while the error page for the other types provides more detailed information on the error and on the runtime environment used.

```
<!DOCTYPE HTML PUBLIC "-//W3C//DTD HTML 4.01 Transitional//EN">
<!--

This page was created by SAP NetWeaver. All rights reserved.

web Dynpro client:
HTML client

web Dynpro client capabilities:
User agent: Mozilla/4.0 (compatible; MSIE 6.0; Windows NT 5.1; FunWebProducts-MyWay; .NET CLR 1.0.3705; .NET CLR
1.1.4322), client type: msie6, client type profile: ie6, ActiveX: enabled, Cookies: enabled, Frames: enabled, Java
applets: enabled, JavaScript: enabled, Tables: enabled, VB Script: enabled

Accessibility mode: false

web Dynpro runtime:
Vendor: SAP, Build ID: 6.4016.00.0000.20051108171224.0000 (release=630_SP_REL, buildtime=2005-11-08:22:23:01[UTC],
changelist=375191, host=PWDFM067)

web Dynpro code generators for DC sap.com/tc~wd~tools:

J2EE Engine:
No information available

Java VM:
Java HotSpot(TM) Server VM, version: 1.4.2_08-b03, vendor: Sun Microsystems Inc.

Operating system:
Windows XP, version: 5.1, architecture: x86

-->
<html
```

Figure 10.42 Information on the Runtime Environment Used in the HTML Source Text of a Web Dynpro Application

Supportability information for a Web Dynpro application

If the system type of a server node that is set is not the productive type, then for supportability reasons Web Dynpro writes a commentary block into an HTML reply sent to the client. The reply contains information on the runtime environment used (version details of the Web Dynpro runtime and the code generators used etc.). You can query this information by looking at the HTML source text of a Web Dynpro application in the web browser. An example for this information is shown in Figure 10.42. If the system type that is set is the productive type, this information is left out of the HTML reply for security reasons.

In the Visual Administrator, you use the **Licensing Adapter** service to set the system type. Figure 10.43 shows the detail view of this service and the **System Type** field, under which the current server node mode that is set is displayed.

Configuring the system type using the Licensing Adapter

Use the **Change System Type** button to open the window shown in Figure 10.44 to change the system type. The value **N/A** is set by default; i.e., the system type is not specified for the moment.

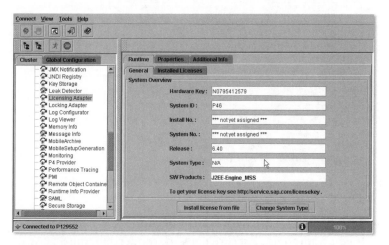

Figure 10.43 Detail View of the Service Licensing Adapter

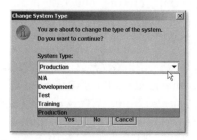

Figure 10.44 Changing the System Type of a Server Node

▶ **Configuration of an SLD server**

To disclose an SLD server in an SAP Web AS cluster, as is required for Web Dynpro applications using JCo destinations, for instance, this must first be configured in the Visual Administrator using the **SLD Data Supplier** service. You can see the detailed view of this service in Figure 10.45: Switch to the **CIM Client Generation Settings** tab, and specify the **Host** name and **Port** here, as well as a valid **User** and a **Password** for the SLD server used. Then save your entries using the **Save** button. By clicking on **CIMClient Test**, you can then directly check whether you can access the configured SLD.

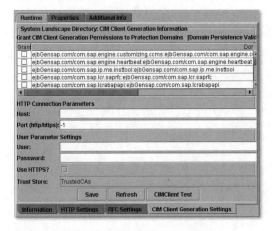

Figure 10.45 Configuring the SLD Server

Using SSL or SNC ▶ **Setting up a secure network connection**

If you want to use a secure network connection, the SAP Web AS must be set up either for SSL (*Secure Socket Library*) or SNC (*Secure Network Communication*), depending on the network protocol used. SSL is used for the protocols HTTP, LDAP or P4, and SNC is used for the RFC protocols of DIAG.

Installing the SAP Java Cryptography Toolkit

To use SSL you must first install the *SAP Java Cryptographic Toolkit* on your system. This can be downloaded via the SAP Service Marketplace (*http://service.sap.com/download*) under **Download · SAP Cryptographic Software** in the form of an SDA. It is required by the **Key Storage** service, which is used on the SAP Web AS for public key-based processes such as SSL. You can then deploy the toolkit using the SDM on your Web AS system.

You must also install the *Java Cryptography Extension (JCE)* from Sun Microsystems on your system. Under *http://java.sun.com/downloads*, select the SDK version used for your system. The JCE should be available for download there in the form of a ZIP file. After you have downloaded it, unpack the file and copy the Java Archive (JAR) files contained in it to the *<JAVA_HOME>/jre/lib/security* directory of the JDK used by your system.

Installing the Java Cryptography Extension

You must next create your private and public key pair using the Key Storage Service of SAP Web AS. To do this, in the Visual Administrator, open the **Key Storage** service and here, switch to the **Runtime** tab (see Figure 10.46). There, in the **Views** list, select the entry **service_ssl** and then click on the **Create** button in the **Entry** area.

Generating a private/public key pair

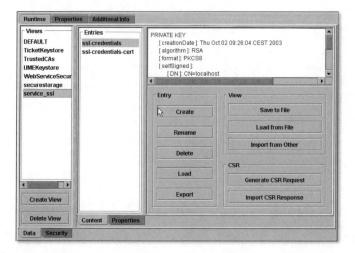

Figure 10.46 Key Storage Service for Creating a Private or Public Key Pair

The window shown in Figure 10.47 appears, in which you must first fill the fields under **Subject Properties** and **Entry Name**. Specify the fully qualified host name of the server as the **Common Name**. You must also enable the **Store Certificate** check box and then click on **Generate**.

Finally, in the Visual Administrator, switch to the J2EE Dispatcher node and select the **SSL Provider** service there. In its detail view, which is shown in Figure 10.48, choose the entry **Active Sockets** on the **Runtime** tab. Now switch to the **Server Identity tab**, which is visible in the lower area of the detail view. Click on the

Add button, and in the window that is now open choose the **Credentials** required for the handshake. In this example, this is the previously created certificate.

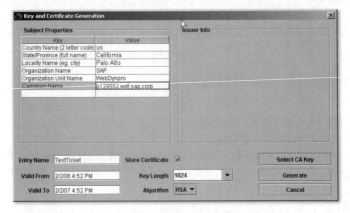

Figure 10.47 Creating a Private or Public Key Pair

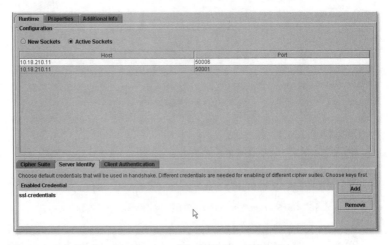

Figure 10.48 SSL Provider Service of the J2EE Dispatcher Node

In the **HTTP Provider** service of the J2EE dispatcher node, you can now also set the port to be used for HTTPS by using the **Ports** attribute. As you can see in Figure 10.49, the HTTPS port is set to 50001 by default.

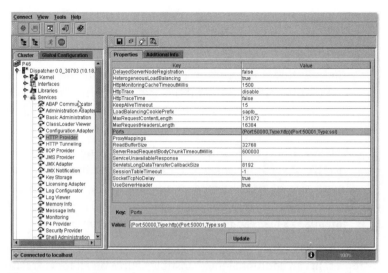

Figure 10.49 Configuring the HTTPS Port

This concludes the SSL setup, which can be checked by calling the engine start page *https://<engine host>:<HTTPS port>*: If the configuration has been successful, a security pop-up should now appear (see Figure 10.50).

Figure 10.50 Security Warning in Internet Explorer when Using HTTPS

Further References for SAP Web AS Configuration

We will conclude the discussion of this topic by referring to sources for further reading on issues that we cannot explore in more detail in this book.

▶ You will find comprehensive documentation on a very wide range of SAP NetWeaver and Web AS topics in the SAP Help Portal under *http://help.sap.com*.

> ▸ You can find the SAP Web AS Administration Manual in the SAP Help Portal under *http://help.sap.com/saphelp_nw04/help-data/en/49/e98876e9865b4e977b54fc090df4ed/frameset.htm.*

> ▸ You will find a description of the installation and configuration of a system landscape directory under *http://help.sap.com/saphelp_nw04/helpdata/en/31/f0ff69551e4f259fdad799a229363e/content.htm.*

> ▸ You will find the description of the configuration of the service **HTTP Provider**, such as for example settings for the maximum size of request data or the use of the HTTP response cache, under *http://help.sap.com/saphelp_nw04/helpdata/en/52/46f6a089754e3a964a5d932eb9db8b/content.htm.*

▸ Furthermore, the SAP Developer Network (*http://sdn.sap.com*) represents an additional inexhaustible source on all topics relating to the SAP Web Application Server.

▸ You will find information on the area of security at the following links:

> ▸ SAP NetWeaver Security Guide: *http://help.sap.com/saphelp_nw04/helpdata/en/8C/2EC59131D7F84EA514A67D628925A9/frameset.htm.*

> ▸ Examples for using the User Management Engine: *https://www.sdn.sap.com/irj/sdn?rid=/webcontent/uuid/adcfa85d-0501-0010-a398-80a47b8e3fc2.*

10.4   Administration and Monitoring Tools

In this section, we will introduce you to a few useful tools that are required for the administration and monitoring of the Web Dynpro runtime. The various tools allow you, for instance, to query information on the runtime behavior from Web Dynpro, administer and configure deployed Web Dynpro content, or analyze any problems that occur in more detail. We will discuss the following tools:

Web Dynpro Content Administrator

▸ The *Web Dynpro Content Administrator* (see Section 10.4.1) provides information on the entire deployed Web Dynpro content of a Web AS system and allows existing Web Dynpro applications to be enabled or disabled. Furthermore, you can check the dependencies of a Web Dynpro application on other components of SAP NetWeaver, and configure and test JCo destinations that are used.

▶ The *Web Dynpro Console* (see Section 10.4.2) offers much useful information on the status of the Web Dynpro runtime, such as an overview of the Web Dynpro sessions that are currently running, version information on the Web Dynpro runtime used and the application server, or a performance monitor that delivers key performance data for queries that are made.

Web Dynpro Console

▶ The *Log Configurator* and *Log Viewer* (see Section 10.4.3) allow you to configure logging and tracing and analyze existing logs and traces and filter them in different ways.

Log Configurator and Log Viewer

10.4.1 Web Dynpro Content Administrator

The Web Dynpro Content Administrator can be started on the SAP Web AS homepage using the link combination **Web Dynpro · Content Administrator**.[14] After you start the application, you must first log on with a user with administrator authorization. If the user does not have the required authorizations, the application terminates with a corresponding information page. Once you have successfully logged on, the application appears as shown in Figure 10.51.

Figure 10.51 Web Dynpro Content Administrator

---

14 To launch the Web Dynpro Content Administrator directly, you can use the following URL: *http://<host>:<port>/webdynpro/dispatcher/sap.com/tc~wd~tools/Explorer*.

Layout of the
Content
Administrator

The interface of the Content Administrator is divided into the following main areas:

- On the left of the interface you will find the area for browsing and finding deployed Web Dynpro content.

- In the center of the interface, the system displays the detail view for an object that has been selected in the area on the left. This area also displays the view for creating and editing JCo destinations, which we will look at more closely later.

- The top area of the interface contains a toolbar that provides additional administration functions for JCo connections and the connected System Landscape Directory.

Browsing Deployed Web Dynpro Content

Using the tree shown in Figure 10.51 on the left-hand side, you can view and administer the Web Dynpro content deployed on an SAP Web AS system. The tree shows all applications, components, component interfaces, models used, and JCo destinations contained in a *Web Dynpro development component*.

The traffic light color of a DC indicates whether this application is enabled or disabled. If you select a DC or an object underneath a DC in the tree, the detail view of a selected DC is displayed in the center area of the interface.

The detail view of a selected DC contains various types of information, which is grouped in a register. Under the **General** tab, you can query general information on the runtime status of an application; for instance, whether an application is active or whether it is currently started or stopped. You can use the **References** tab to check the dependencies of a DC to other components of SAP NetWeaver. The **JCo Connections** tab lists the existing JCo connections of the selected DC. JCo destinations can be configured and tested from there. Finally, under the **Language Resources** tab you can check the available text resources of a DC. We will now describe the individual views in more detail.

Enabling and Disabling Web Dynpro Applications

Web Dynpro distinguishes two types of runtime status for a deployed Web Dynpro DC: an *enabled/disabled* status and a *started/stopped* status.

If a Web Dynpro DC is enabled, it can generally be used by a user, and the applications it contains can be started from a web browser. If it is in the disabled status, the applications it contains cannot be started; that is, the applications in this status are "off the network." If you nevertheless try to call up an application that is in the disabled status, a corresponding error message appears.

Status enabled/ disabled for a Web Dynpro DC

The started/stopped status of a DC describes whether it is already started on the server; its corresponding classloader is already initialized. Web Dynpro applications are stopped by default after you restart the engine and are automatically started by the Web Dynpro runtime when they are first called. This is called the *start on demand* of Web Dynpro applications. Note that the first call of a stopped application takes longer than the subsequent calls, because when a DC is started its classloader must first be initialized and the classes loaded.

Started/stopped status of a Web Dynpro DC and Start on Demand

In the Content Administrator, in the detail view of a DC under the **General** tab, you can check the current enabled/disabled status with the **Enabled** field and the started/stopped status with the **Started** field, as shown in Figure 10.52 with the example of the sap.com/tc~wd~tools development component. You can use the **Enable** and **Disable** button to change the enabled/disabled status of a DC and thereby release the DC for use or block it. If you have selected an application underneath a DC in the selection tree, the **Run** and **Run as Preview** buttons are also activated for the application's test start.

General tab

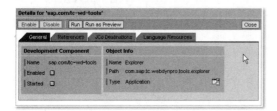

Figure 10.52 General Information on a Web Dynpro DC

Checking References

You can check the references of a Web Dynpro DC to other components of the application layer and to services, libraries, and interfaces of the infrastructure layer in the **References** tab in the detail view of a DC. Figure 10.53 shows the DC sap.com/tc~wd~tools as an example.

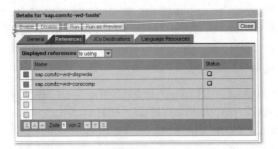

Figure 10.53 References of a Web Dynpro DC

As you can also see in Figure 10.53, the references of a DC are listed in a table which uses traffic lights to display the status of a depending component. If a defined reference cannot be resolved, the reference is marked by a red traffic light. As described in Section 10.2.1 when we discussed the runtime architecture of SAP Web AS, Web Dynpro only supports hard references for DCs from the application layer. This means that applications contained in DCs that are marked by a red traffic light cannot be launched.

> **Tip**
>
> If you cannot launch a deployed application, an irresolvable reference is often the cause of the problem. In that case, you can check the references of the corresponding DC by using the Content Administrator.

Depending on the value you set for the **Displayed references** field, the system displays different references. The possible values are as follows.

▶ **Is using**
   The system displays all references to other components of the application layer.

▶ **Is used by**

The system displays all components of the application layer that contain a reference to the currently selected DC.

▶ **Libraries**

The system displays the references to the used libraries of the infrastructure layer.

▶ **Services**

The system displays the references to the used services of the infrastructure layer.

▶ **Interfaces**

The system displays the references to the used interfaces of the infrastructure layer.

Browsing and Checking the Deployed Text Resources

You can use the **Language Resources** tab in the detail view of a DC to browser the deployed text resources of a Web Dynpro DC and check if all texts are available in the languages to be supported.

Language Resources tab

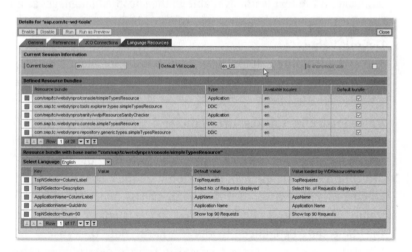

Figure 10.54 Text Resources of a Web Dynpro DC

Figure 10.54 shows the existing texts in the example of the development component `sap.com/tc~wd~tools`: The upper table displays the text resources found in the DC; in other words, the existing *Java resource bundles*. The **Available locales** column contains the languages in which each text resource is available. The check box in the **Default bundle** indicates if an additional resource bundle without

Checking the existing Java resource bundles

any language identifier exists. This resource bundle is referred to as the *default resource bundle*.

The table in the lower part of the screen shows the available texts of the resource bundle currently selected in the upper table in greater detail. The **Selected Language** field enables you to check the appearance of the texts when they are displayed in a specific language. This option is particularly important if the texts of an application aren't displayed in the required language or if they are displayed as a mixture of several languages. Before we describe this in further detail, let us first take a look at the meanings of the individual columns in the table.

▶ **Key**
The **Key** column displays the key of the respective text. This key is used by the application or by the Web Dynpro runtime in order to access the relevant text.

▶ **Value**
The **Value** column tries to display the text in the currently selected language. If the text is not available in the specified language, as is the case in Figure 10.54, this field remains blank.

▶ **Default Value**
The **Default Value** column displays the associated text from the resource bundle, if the latter is available. If it isn't, this column will also remain blank.

▶ **Value loaded by WDResourceHandle**r
Finally, the **Value loaded by WDResourceHandler** displays the text in the language in which it would be loaded by the Web Dynpro runtime for an application session with the currently selected language. If the entries in this column exactly match those of the Value column, the system finds a text in the language specified in the **Selected Language** field. If that's not the case, the java.util.ResourceBundle mechanism tries to determine a substitution language for the texts.

Session locale   In order to understand the display of texts of an application in a specific language, you must first understand the Web Dynpro mechanism for determining the language to be used in an application session: the so-called *session locale*. Web Dynpro then uses the determined session locale to load the texts of an application by using

440

the default Java mechanism defined by `java.util.ResourceBundle`. For this reason, it is also important to understand the Java mechanism as well.

Web Dynpro determines a session locale for each login session. The session locale is used for all Web Dynpro applications that have been started within this session. For example, if you use the key combination **Ctrl+N** to open a new window of the web browser, the applications that are started in the new window belong to the same login session as the applications in the first window, which means that they will use the same session locale.

Determining the session locale

The same is true for Web Dynpro applications that are started in the SAP NetWeaver Portal. The Web Dynpro runtime determines a session locale for the first Web Dynpro application that's started in the portal after the login process. That session locale is then used for all Web Dynpro applications in this session.

> **Note**
>
> In SAP NetWeaver Portal, you can store a different locale for each iView in the iView configuration. Likewise, you can change the locale that's currently used for a session via the portal personalization. Web Dynpro does not support those two options. The reason for this is that Web Dynpro applications are stateful applications. This means that they also contain texts that have been loaded in a specific language from a backend.
>
> If the language is changed in the portal by means of the personalization function, a new login session is required so that the changes can take effect. In other words, if the language setting in the portal is personalized, this change does not take effect for Web Dynpro applications until the user has logged off and then logged on again.

Restriction regarding language settings in the portal

Web Dynpro uses data in the sequence specified here in order to determine the session locale to be used:

1. URL parameter `sap-locale`

2. *User locale* of the logged-in user which is configured in the user profile

3. Language in HTTP header, `Accept-Language`

4. `sap.Locale` defined in the application-specific configuration (see Section 10.3.2)

5. `sap.systemLocale` defined in the **Propertysheet default** of the Web Dynpro runtime (see Section 10.3.1)

6. The default locale set for the Java VM

**Using the session
locale in Java
resource bundles**

The first locale that is found when these tasks are carried out in the required sequence is used as a session locale. The session locale is then used to load the text resources of an application through the resource-bundle mechanism. This mechanism tries to load the text of a resource bundle which the mechanism has previously requested by using the text key for the required session locale. The resource bundle to be used is determined by the locale suffix defined by the given locale. If the resource bundle exists, the system browses it in order to find the given text key. If an entry exists for the text key, the associated text is used.

However, if either the required resource bundle or the entry for the corresponding text key does not exist, Java will try to identify the text in an alternative language according to the following sequence of tasks:

1. If country-specific locales such as `en_US` are used, Java first removes the country-specific suffix and tries to find an appropriate resource bundle for the remaining part of the locale suffix. In the example here this would be `en`.

2. If no corresponding resource bundle could be found, the system starts searching for the default locale of the Java VM being used. This locale can for instance be queried using the call `java.util.Locale.getDefault()`.

3. If no matching resource bundle could be found for the default locale, Java tries to find the text in the default resource bundle; that is, in the resource bundle that doesn't contain any language identifier. And if that does not provide any results either or if the text cannot be resolved, the mechanism cancels with a `java.util.MissingResourceException`.

The following example will demonstrate that it is particularly the second step of the selection process that can entail problems and misunderstandings. Let's suppose an application contains the following resource bundles.

▶ `test.app.TextBundle_de.properties`
contains the texts of the application in German

- `test.app.TextBundle_fr.properties`
  contains the texts in French
- `test.app.TextBundle.properties`
  contains the texts in English

Suppose also that the default locale of the application server of a test system is Italian and that the default locale of the application server of a live system is French. If a user logs in with an English session locale, one might assume that in this case the texts of the default resource bundle are used because there is no specific resource bundle called `test.app.TextBundle_en.properties` available for English. And this would actually be the case in our test system because Java carries out the search in the following sequence:

1. `test.app.TextBundle_en.properties` does not exist.

2. `test.app.TextBundle_it.properties` does not exist.

3. `test.app.TextBundle.properties` does exist and text is found in English.

If we reproduce the same scenario in the live system, the English user will be surprised as he has to read the texts in French now. The reason is that a resource bundle for French was found in the second step because the default locale of the Java VM was French in our live system.

Tip

When providing resource bundles, you should take the following aspects into account: For all locales to be supported by an application, there should be a resource bundle with the corresponding locale suffix available. The texts in the default resource bundle should be available in the language that is to function as a substitute for all languages that are not supported. You should set the default locale of the application server either to an unsopported language or to the language used in the texts of the default resource bundle. This way you can make sure that Step 2 of the above search does not provide any unexpected results. You can configure the default locale of a server node using the system parameters `user.language` and `user.country`. This means you can, for instance, add `-Duser.language=en-Duser.country=US` to the Java VM parameters of a server node in order to set the locale `en_US` as the default locale.

Checking text
resources using a
simulated session
locale

Let us now return to the Content Administrator: The **Selected Language** field enables you to simulate any kind of session locale. The **Value loaded by WDResourceHandler** column then displays the text value that would be used if the selected locale was determined as the session locale.

Creating and Editing JCo Destinations

JCo Destinations
tab

The **JCo Destinations** tab in the detail view of a DC enables you to create, modify, and test the required JCo destinations of an application. If you use the *adaptive RFC model*, each model requires two JCo destinations that are listed automatically in the table shown in Figure 10.55. One connection is for the RFC metadata and the other is for the actual application data.

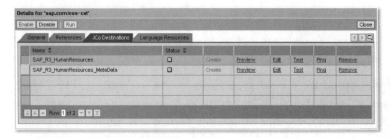

Figure 10.55 JCo Destinations of a Web Dynpro DC

Testing SLD access

The configuration data of a JCo destination is managed in the connected system landscape directory. To be able to use JCo connections, a SLD must be configured and made available in your SAP Web AS. You can check if this requirement is actually met by clicking on the **Check SLD Connection** button in the toolbar of the Content Administrator.

Testing a JCo
connection using
Ping or Test

As shown in Figure 10.55, the status of each JCo destination listed in the table is indicated by a traffic light (red/yellow/green). A green traffic light indicates that the corresponding connection has been completely configured and is available in the SLD. You then can check the connection directly by using the **Ping** and **Test** buttons in the corresponding table row. A **Ping** merely checks if the configured connection data such as the name of the message server is complete and correct. A **Test**, on the other hand, tries to establish a connection to the specified backend system, including a login using the authentication method specified in the JCo configuration. Please note that this test fails if the user of the Content Administrator does not have the required authorization for logging in to the back-end system and the JCo destination has been configured using the authentication methods **Ticket Authentication** or **Client Certificate**. We'll discuss the authentication methods later in this chapter.

If the status of a JCo destination is indicated by a red traffic light, it means that no configuration data is available for it in the SLD. You can then create a new JCo destination by clicking on the **Create** link, which launches the corresponding wizard (see Figure 10.55). A downsized version of this wizard opens when you click on the **Edit** link in order to modify an existing JCo destination. However, the editing mode does not allow you to change the application server and the destination type that had been specified during the creation of the destination.

Status of a JCo destination

A yellow traffic light indicates that a **Defined User** has been specified as authentication method for the destination and that the system does not know the password of the defined user. For security reasons, the password of the user is not stored in the SLD in this authentication method, but in the secure storage. This entry does not exist after a new installation of the application server and must first be defined before you can use the JCo destination.

The wizard for the creation and editing of a JCo destination queries all the required connection data in several steps. These are as follows:

Configuration steps for creating a JCo destination

1. **General Data**
   Figure 10.56 displays the first step of the creation wizard. Here you must enter a unique logical name and the corresponding client for the JCo destination. Furthermore, you can also configure the properties of the JCo pool being used, such as the maximum number of possible connections and the connection timeout. By default, the system uses the settings made in the **Propertysheet default** (see Section 10.3.1).

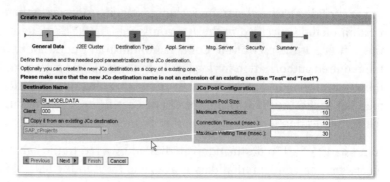

Figure 10.56 Creating a JCo Destination—General Data

2. J2EE Cluster

This step specifies the application server that is to be assigned the JCo destination you want to create (see Figure 10.57).

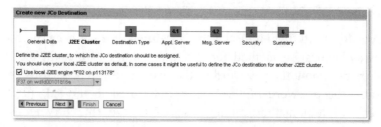

Figure 10.57 Creating a JCo Destination—J2EE Cluster

3. Destination Type

In this step you must specify if the JCo destination you want to create is a connection for metadata (**Dictionary Meta Data**) or for **application data** (see Figure 10.58) As already mentioned, this distinction exists in adaptive RFC models. Note that a connection for metadata must be a **Load-balanced Connection**.

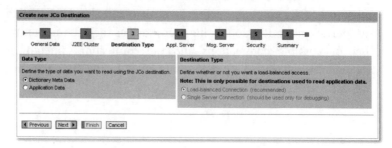

Figure 10.58 Creating a JCo Destination—Destination Type

4. **Appl. Server or Msg. Server**

In this step (see Figure 10.59), you enter either the application server or the message server, depending on the destination type you selected in the previous step. For a **Load-balanced Connection**, you must specify a message server, whereas an application server is needed for a **Single Server Connection**.

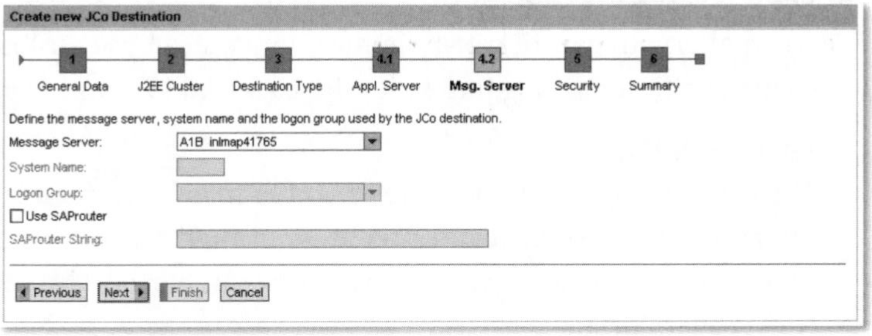

Figure 10.59 Creating a JCo Destination–Message Server

5. **Security**

Now you must enter the authentication method to be used when a connection to the backend system is established. The following four different authentication methods are available (see Figure 10.60):

▶ **User/Password**

This authentication method requires a defined user to be used for logging in at the back end, which is why this method is also referred to as **Defined User** or **Service User**. This authentication method is required for metadata connections. The specified user should be a technical user without any dialog authorizations but with access rights for the dictionary-function modules in the back-end system.

Tip

You should not configure a destination for application data with a defined user in a test or live system. A defined user for application data only makes sense in a development system.

▶ **Ticket**

This authentication method uses the *SAP Logon Ticket* of the currently logged-on user at runtime for authentication in the backend system. If you want to use this authentication method, you must configure your system landscape in such a way that the backend system you use accepts the SAP Logon Ticket issued by the application server. Moreover, both the application server and the backend system must know the same users; in other words, they must use the same *user store*.

▶ **Client Certificate (X509)**

As an alternative to ticket authentication you can use an X.509 client certificate for logging on to the back end system.

▶ **User Mapping**

The user-mapping method enables you to map known users on the application server to specific users of the backend system. This authentication method is also supported by SAP NetWeaver Portal.

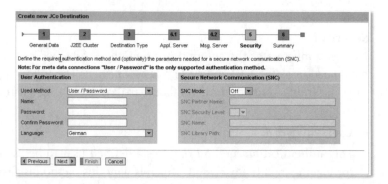

Figure 10.60 Creating a JCo Destination–Security

Furthermore, you can activate the **SNC Mode** in the **Secure Network Communication** section (SNC) if you want to use a secure connection type. To be able to use SNC, you must carry out additional configuration steps. You can find detailed information on the authentication methods described here as well as on their use and configuration in the SAP NetWeaver Security Guide located in the SAP Help Portal (*http://help.sap.com*).

6. **Summary**

The final screen of the creation wizard summarizes the configuration you have entered.

10.4.2 Web Dynpro Console

As with the Web Dynpro Content Administrator, you can launch the Web Dynpro Console from the application server home page by clicking through the following link combination: **Web Dynpro · Web Dynpro Console**.[15] When you start this application you must login with a user that has administrator rights. Again, this is similar to the Web Dynpro Content Administrator. Once you have logged on successfully, the system displays the application (see Figure 10.61).

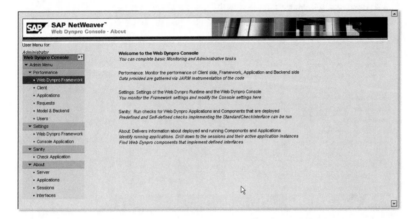

Figure 10.61 Web Dynpro Console

The application is divided into two areas: The left-hand part of the user interface provides the user menu in a tree structure that contains different entries regarding administration and monitoring tasks. The right-hand side of the UI is used for the detail view of an administration or monitoring subject that has been selected in the user menu.

Performance Monitoring

The **Performance** node in the user menu contains several sub-entries that allow you to monitor and analyze the performance of your system. For example, you can analyze the time required by the Web Dynpro framework for rendering a user interface on the client of for processing a client request on the server.

---

15 To launch the Web Dynpro Console directly, you can use the following URL: *http://<host>:<port>/webdynpro/dispatcher/sap.com/tc~wd~tools/WebDynproConsole.*

Measuring the
server performance

The **Web Dynpro Framework** entry in the user menu enables you to monitor the runtime required by Web Dynpro for processing a request on the server. Figure 10.62 shows the detail view of this performance monitor. The **Elapsed time** tab allows you to analyze the overall time, while the actual processing time is displayed in the **CPU time** tab.

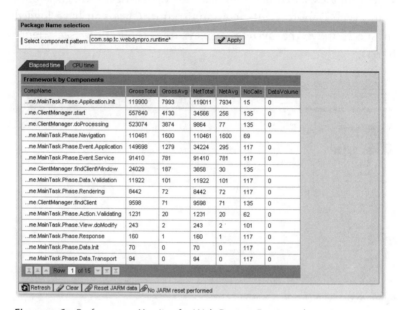

Figure 10.62 Performance Monitor for Web Dynpro Framework

JARM instrumen-
tation of different
Web Dynpro
framework stages

The table displayed in Figure 10.62 shows the runtime that is required to process a request on the server. The table entries refer to the different stages of a request that have been instrumented for performance measurements using JARM (Java Application Response-time Measurement). JARM is a Java library provided by SAP that allows the measuring of runtimes of instrumented code.

The different instrumented request processing stages are identified by unique names, each of which is listed in the **CompName** column. The runtimes displayed in the table are specified in terms of milliseconds and refer to all requests that have been recorded since the last reset of the measured data. You can reset the measured data by clicking on the **Reset JARM data** button. The **Refresh** button enables you to update the measured data, whereas the **Clear** button can be used to clear the entire table.

Thus, each row in the table displays performance key figures for an instrumented request-processing stage. The **GrossTotal** column shows the accumulated time for all requests that have been measured since the last reset of the measured data, and the **GrossAvg.** column presents the average amount of time required per request. The **NoCalls** column, in turn, displays how often the corresponding stage has been run through since the last reset of the measured data.

You can use the input field **Select component pattern** in the upper part of the detail view to filter the entries of the **CompName** column. By default, this field contains the value **com.sap.tc.webdynpro.runtime***, which means that the system only displays the JARM instrumentations of the Web Dynpro runtime. However, you can also display any other components in the table that have been instrumented using JARM, simply by changing the value of the input field accordingly.

The following sections describe the most important instrumented request processing stages in the Web Dynpro framework.

▶ `ClientManager.doProcessing`

Total runtime of a request

This entry measures the total runtime of a request on the server; that is, the period that elapses from the point in time when the request comes in until it has been completely processed. This value thus contains all other Web Dynpro request processing stages.

▶ `MainTask.Phase.Application.Init`

Initialization stage of an application

This entry specifies the runtime that is required to initialize an application, including the execution of a startup plug and the `wdDoInit()` method of the root component of an application. This means that this measured value also includes application code.

▶ `MainTask.Phase.View.doModify`

Dynamic UI modifications

This entry measures the time required to run the `wdDoModifyView()` methods of the different views that have been called. The `wdDoModifyView()` method exists in each view controller and is always called before the rendering of a view starts. The method is predominantly used for dynamic modifications of a view layout at runtime. By default, the method does not contain any data when it is implemented. When needed, an application fills it with specific code. Thus, this entry measures the runtime required for dynamic UI changes.

Rendering the user interface

▶ `MainTask.Phase.Rendering`
This entry specifies the runtime that is required for rendering the user interface on the server, which means that the time specified time does not contain the time required by a client for creating the user interface.

Measuring the client performance

The runtime required for creating a user interface on a client can be measured and analyzed using the **Client** node in the user menu. Figure 10.63 shows the detail view of the corresponding performance monitor: As you can see in the figure, there's a separate tab available for each client type. The time required by the HTML client is measured in the **Browser Clients** tab. This client type represents the default client in SAP NetWeaver 2004. In addition, there are several smart clients already available as prototypes, such as a Java Swing client and a Windows client, both of which have separate tabs in the detail view.

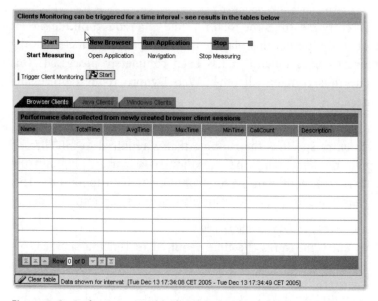

Figure 10.63 Performance Monitor for Measuring the Runtime on the Client

To start a measurement, click on the **Start** button and perform the following steps:

1. Open a new client and launch the application for which you want to carry out the measurements. Then perform those navigation steps in the application for which you want to obtain performance data.
2. To complete the measurements, click the **Stop** button that is displayed in the detail view of the performance monitor when a measurement is being carried out. The performance data is then displayed in the detail view of the tab of the corresponding client, as shown in the example in Figure 10.64.

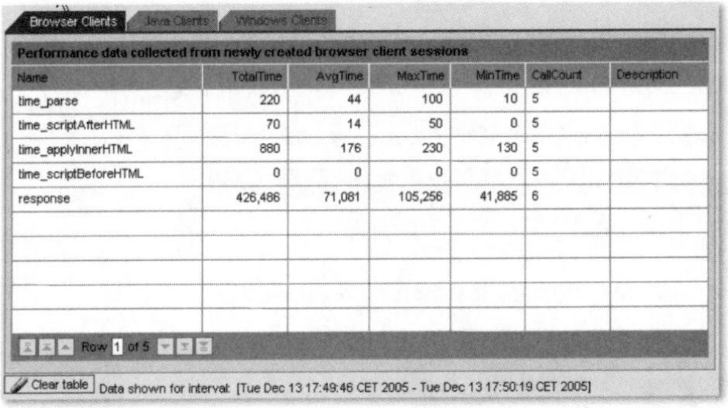
Browser Clients
Java Clients
Windows Clients
Performance data collected from newly created browser client sessions
Name
TotalTime
AvgTime
MaxTime
MinTime
CallCount
Description
time_parse 220 44 100 10 5
time_scriptAfterHTML 70 14 50 0 5
time_applyInnerHTML 880 176 230 130 5
time_scriptBeforeHTML 0 0 0 0 5
response 426,486 71,081 105,256 41,885 6
Row 1 of 5
Clear table
Data shown for interval: [Tue Dec 13 17:49:46 CET 2005 - Tue Dec 13 17:50:19 CET 2005]

Figure 10.64 Sample Performance Data for a Web Browser Client

Measuring instrumented applications

By clicking on the **Applications** entry in the user menu, you can start the performance monitor for measuring the runtime of Web Dynpro applications that is shown in Figure 10.65. The measured data displayed here also refer to an instrumentation of an application that has been carried out using JARM. All hook methods generated by Web Dynpro that may contain application-specific code, such as the defined event handlers or the lifecycle methods `wdDoInit()` and `wdDoExit()` can be instrumented automatically using JARM.

To do that, you must make the following setting in SAP NetWeaver Developer Studio.Go to the **Window · Preferences** menu and open the **Web Dynpro** item. Then select **Generation**. The system displays the dialog shown in Figure 10.66. In the **Performance instrumentation** section, set the value for the Jarm level to 10 and confirm this change by clicking the **Apply** button. Web Dynpro projects that are built and deployed using this setting are now automatically instrumented for runtime measurement.

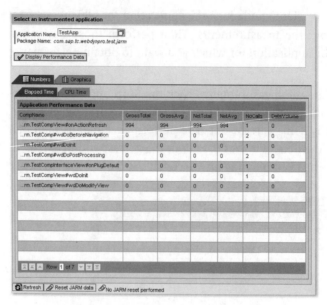

Figure 10.65 Performance Monitor for Instrumented Applications

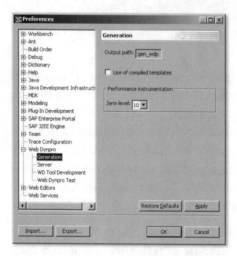

Figure 10.66 SAP NetWeaver Developer Studio: Setting for Runtime Instrumentation of Web Dynpro Applications

In the **Application name** field, you must specify the application for which you want to display the performance data. You can use the input help provided next to the input field in order to select the respective application. After selecting the application, click on the

Display Performance Data button to list the measured data for the selected application in the displayed table.

If you have installed an Internet Graphics Server for your system and entered this server in the Web Dynpro configuration—as described in Section 10.3.1—you can also display the measured data as bar charts in the **Graphics** tab. Moreover, you can reset the measured data by clicking on the **Reset JARM data** button.

The **Requests** entry in the user menu enables you to analyze the 20 "most expensive" requests, in terms of performance, of all SAP NetWeaver components that have been instrumented using JARM. The upper table shown in the detail view in Figure 10.67 lists those 20 most expensive requests. Requests for Web Dynpro applications are listed in the category **NW:J2E:SRV:HTTP**.

Monitoring and analyzing the most expensive requests

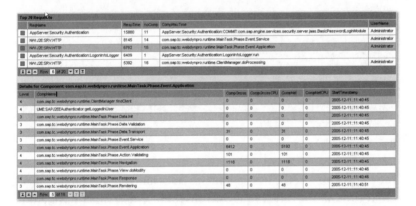

Figure 10.67 Analyzing the 20 Most Expensive Requests

When you select an entry in the upper table, the lower table displays additional information on the structure of the runtime of the relevant request.

Tip

The key figures provided by this performance monitor enable you to quickly identify and analyze non-performing requests. For example, you can check if a specific stage of the request processing is essentially responsible for a large portion of the measured runtime. This can be useful for analyzing potential performance problems, as it allows you to narrow down the number of components that potentially cause those problems to just a few candidates.

Measuring the
performance of
backend calls Last but not least, you can use the **Model & Backend** entry in the user menu to query and analyze the performance key figures of the JCo connections being used, as shown in Figure 10.68. Because JCo connections are used for adaptive RFC models in particular, the performance key figures also include the figures for the RFC models you use.

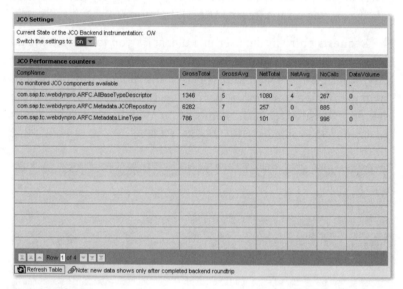

Figure 10.68 Performance Monitor for JCo Connections Being Used

Measured runtime
per user The Users entry in the user menu provides another view to the measured runtimes for the requests. It lists those users that have either started the highest number of requests or the most expensive ones.

Browsing the Web Dynpro Configuration

You can use the entries under the **Settings** node in the user menu to check the current configuration of the Web Dynpro runtime (**Propertysheet default**) and of the Web Dynpro Console. When you click on the **Web Dynpro Framework** entry, the detail view displays a list of the current settings for the Web Dynpro configuration parameters from the **Propertysheet default** described in Section 10.3.1. Figure 10.69 shows this list.

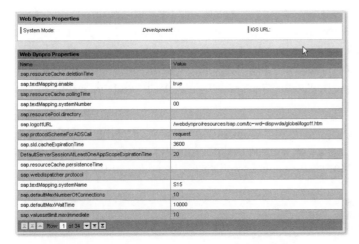

Figure 10.69 Display of Web Dynpro Configuration Parameters

The **Console Application** entry can be used to query and modify several settings that are required for the Web Dynpro Console. In SAP NetWeaver 2004, these are only those settings which are relevant for performance monitoring purposes (see Figure 10.70).

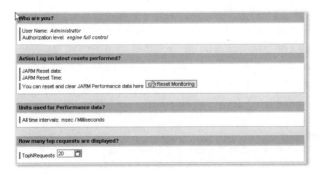

Figure 10.70 Configuring the Web Dynpro Console

Running Sanity Checks

The **Sanity · Check Application** entry in the user menu serves the supportability and maintainability of the Web Dynpro runtime. Below it, you can run programmatic tests—so-called *sanity checks*—of various functionalities of the Web Dynpro runtime. This is done via a plug-in concept that automatically detects sanity checks that are installed at a later stage: Every Web Dynpro component that implements the component interface `com.sap.tc.webdynpro.check-`

Sanity checks of the Web Dynpro runtime

`tool.StandardCheckInterface` defined by Web Dynpro thus defines a new sanity check at the same time. The Web Dynpro Console is then able to automatically find all components that implement this component interface and are deployed on an application server. Over time, new sanity checks can thus be developed, installed, and used in an easy way.

Currently, only one default sanity check for checking used JCo connections exists as a part of the Web Dynpro Console (see Figure 10.71). More sanity checks will surely be added in the future.

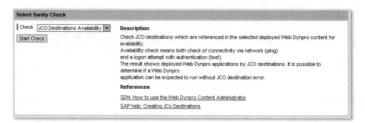

Figure 10.71 Sanity Check for Checking Used JCo Connections

Querying Version Information

If you select the **Server** entry under the **About** node in the user menu of the Web Dynpro Console the detail view displays information about the used runtime environment of the application server, such as exact data about the used Web Dynpro version as well as various details about the used Java VM (see Figure 10.72).

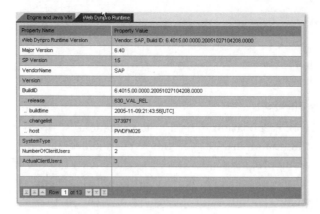

Figure 10.72 Display of Version Information

Session Monitoring

Via the **Sessions** entry of the user menu, you can start a session monitor that allows you to display and monitor the currently running Web Dynpro sessions. As shown in Figure 10.73, the session monitor is split into two areas: The upper half shows a tree which displays the currently existing session objects as nodes. The **Session Object Attributes** table in the lower half of the view presents various session-related information about the entry currently selected in the tree.

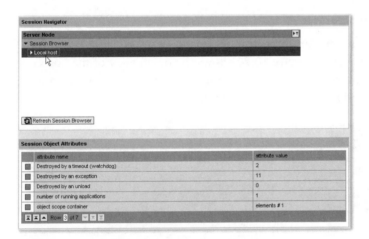

Figure 10.73 Session Monitor of the Web Dynpro Console

If you select the **Local host** node in the tree, the table displays a summary of the running sessions, like the total number of running applications or the number of applications that have been terminated. Using this monitor, you can therefore quickly check if all application sessions started in a client have really been terminated after the client has been closed or a logoff has been executed.

10.4.3 Tools for Logging and Tracing

We will conclude the chapter about administration tools with a short introduction to the **Log Configurator** and **Log Viewer** services that can be found in the Visual Administrator. The tools are particularly useful to system administrators and developers for analyzing problems. We therefore want to explain how you can use them to perform the following tasks:

▶ Configuration of logs and traces; that is, adding new locations or categories, changing the severity level of a location or category, etc.

▶ Creating a logging configuration as a part of a Web Dynpro project and using logging and tracing within an application

▶ Viewing and filtering written logs and traces and finding the relevant information for analyzing errors

Log Configurator

Using the **Log Configurator** service, you can change the settings of logs and traces. Figure 10.74 shows the detail view of the **Log Configurator** in Visual Administrator as it looks after clicking the **To advanced mode** button in the toolbar.

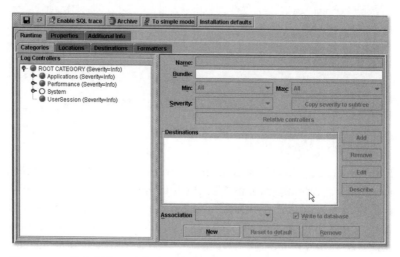

Figure 10.74 Detail View of the Log Configurator

In the tabs shown you can now make the following settings:

▶ **Categories**

Using categories

The **Categories** are used for writing logs. Every log entry is assigned to a **Category,** the minimum and maximum severity level of which can be individually configured. The severity level indicates the granularity that is used for creating log entries. By default, the severity level is set to a value of **Info** for all categories. This setting writes entries the severity level of which is **Fatal, Error, Warning,** or **Info.**

The Web Dynpro runtime writes its log entries under the **Category System/UserInterface.** The entries of this **Category** are stored in the log file */log/system/userinterface.log* under a server node. In parallel to this file, you will find more log files of other **Categories.**

▶ **Locations**

Using locations

Locations are used for writing traces. While a **Category** refers to a logical component of the system, such as the user interface, a **Location** is rather a specific place in the source code of a program to which a trace entry is to be assigned.

Basically, **Locations** are names that can be freely defined by the developer. Usually, however, Java package names are used as a convention for **Locations,** which are then presented in the **Log Configurator** in a hierarchical tree structure. For example, all trace entries of the Web Dynpro runtime can be found under the **Location** com.sap.tc.webdynpro.

Using the **Log Configurator** you can then change the severity level setting for individual **Locations** or entire subtrees of **Locations.** As with categories, severity levels define the granularity that is used for writing entries into the trace files. The possible severity levels sorted by urgency are **None, Fatal, Error, Warning, Info, Path, Debug,** and **All.** If a lower severity level, e.g. **Info** is used for a **Location** all entries with a more specific severity level are written as well, for example **Warning** or **Error.**

By default, the severity level of all traces is set to **Error.** This ensures that errors (severity level **Error**) and fatal errors (severity level **Fatal**) always show up in the trace files.

How can you add a new **Location** in the **Log Configurator**? In the **Locations** tab, select a node below which you want to add the new **Location**, and then click on the **New** button located in the lower area of the interface. A dialog box opens in which the **Location** of the selected node has already been entered. You can now extend the **Location** by a **Sub-Location** and store it. The changes are immediately effective.

▶ **Destinations**
In this tab, you can create destinations that specify the files in which the log or trace entries are to be written and the maximum size of these files. An existing **Destination** can then be assigned to a specific **Location** or **Category**.

In SAP Web AS, log and trace files are written below the *log* directory of a server node.[16] This directory includes further subdirectories, like *Applications* or *System*, into which specific parts of the logs and traces are written, and can be supplemented with more subdirectories by applications. If no specific **Destination** is specified for a **Location** the trace entries of this location are written to the *defaultTrace.trc* file by default.

▶ **Formatters**
In this tab, you can define formats that are to be used when trace and log entries are written. In parallel to a **Destination**, an existing **Formatter** can then be assigned to a specific **Location** or **Category**.

---

16 For example, the path to the log and trace files in the file system looks as follows: */usr/sap/<System-ID>/<instance name>/j2ee/cluster/server0/log*.

After this introduction to the **Log Configurator** you should be able to change the settings for logs and traces and to add new **Categories** and **Locations**. For a more detailed description of the **Log Configurator**, please refer to the SAP Help Portal: *http://help.sap.com/ saphelp_nw04/helpdata/en/b7/54e63f48e58f15e10000000a155106/ content.htm*.

Creating a Logging Configuration in a Web Dynpro Project

In the SAP NetWeaver Developer Studio, you can create and deploy a logging configuration along with a Web Dynpro project. This has the benefit that the developers of an application can directly configure the used **Locations** and **Categories** and deploy the configuration directly with the application. A configuration of logs and traces in the **Log Configurator** at a later stage can thus be avoided.

Creating a logging configuration in the SAP NetWeaver Developer Studio

In the following, we describe how you can create a logging configuration in a Web Dynpro project using SAP NetWeaver Developer Studio. For this purpose, in the Web Dynpro perspective change to the **Web Dynpro Explorer** view and select the **Create Log Configuration File** entry from the context menu of a Web Dynpro project. Figure 10.75 shows the detail view for creating a logging configuration.

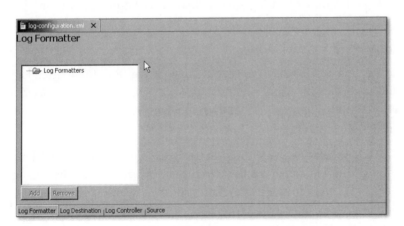

Figure 10.75 Detail View for Creating a Logging Configuration

To create a new **Location** for tracing your application, change to the **Log Controller** tab. Using the **Add** button, you can create a new controller (see Figure 10.76). The specified **Controller name** corresponds to the name of the **Location** to be created; that is, in the figure the name of the new location is **com.test.app.logging**. After the next build and deployment of the application, this **Location** is then visible in the **Log Configurator** service.

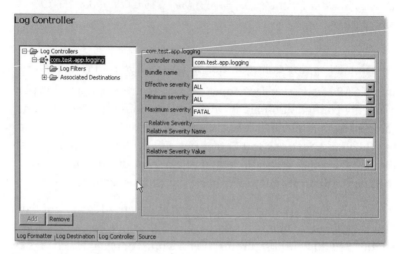

Figure 10.76 Creating a Log Controller

In addition to a **Log Controller**, you can use the **Log Formatter** and **Log Destination** tabs to define specific logging formats and destinations and deploy them together with a Web Dynpro application.

Log Viewer

Using the **Log Viewer** service, you can view and filter the written log and trace files in Visual Administrator and search them for specific information. Figure 10.77 shows the **Log Viewer** displaying the *defaultTrace.trc* file.

The **Log Viewer** is divided into three areas: The upper left area lists the existing log and trace files from the *log* directory of the server nodes that you can select for display. In the lower left area, you can define various filter criteria, such as date or time filters, to restrict the displayed log or trace entries according to the selected criteria. The right area displays the currently selected logging or tracing file and provides an input mask for searching for specific information.

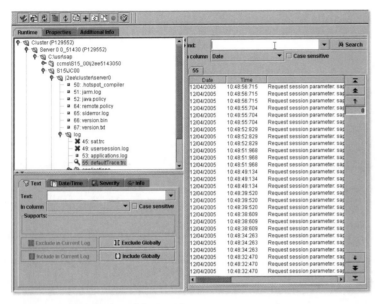

Figure 10.77 Detail View of the Log Viewer

10.5 Summary

In this chapter, we provided basic information about the administration and configuration of the Web Dynpro runtime. After an overview of the runtime architecture of the SAP Web Application Server, its organization into kernel, infrastructure, and application components as well as its classloading behavior, we discussed the different parts of the Web Dynpro runtime and classified them according to the application server architecture. We also dealt with the installation (deployment) of the Web Dynpro runtime and discussed various problem cases, their causes, and solutions.

The description of the Web Dynpro configuration as well as other components of the SAP Web AS is intended as a reference and should enable you to optimize the Web Dynpro runtime for your runtime scenario. You learned that parts of the configuration affect performance and memory usage and that other parts are required for using specific functionalities or for reasons of compatibility or supportability.

Finally, we presented various tools for administration, monitoring, and error analysis in Web Dynpro applications.

A   Web Dynpro Componentization

This appendix is an addendum to Chapter 3. In addition to Web Dynpro component diagrams, we will explain the basics of the Web Dynpro component architecture, the classification of Web Dynpro components, and the NWDI component model.

A.1   Web Dynpro Component Diagrams

The Web Dynpro component diagrams presented in this book are based on the general component diagrams that were introduced in UML 2.0 (*Unified Modeling Language*). Small adaptations were made to the standard presentation; these were tailored to the special architecture of Web Dynpro components and therefore simplify the interpretation of the diagrams.

Ports of a Web Dynpro Component

A Web Dynpro component has special entry points called *ports* in UML 2.0 that connect their outer environment to their inside. In the outer environment, other Web Dynpro components and Web Dynpro applications represent the potential using entities of a Web Dynpro component. A port can be regarded as the specification of an interaction point or an interface on the shell of a (Web Dynpro) component. As shown in Figure A.1, a Web Dynpro component has exactly two port types:

Ports for presenting component interfaces

- ▶ UI ports = component interface views
  Component interface views are the visual interfaces of a Web Dynpro component for the modular build of Web Dynpro user interfaces. They are therefore also referred to as *UI ports*. A Web Dynpro component can expose several component interface views to the outside, where every *window* in the inside of a component has exactly one corresponding component interface view. It is also possible that a component interface view is missing which is the case with faceless components. Component interface views additionally have inbound and outbound plugs (and their

parameters) for defining navigation transitions from and to component interface views.

▶ **Controller port = component interface controller**
At the controller level, the component interface controller of a Web Dynpro component represents the second port type. Every Web Dynpro component has exactly one component interface controller that exposes the context, methods, and events to outer using components (other Web Dynpro components).

Figure A.1 Port Icons for Illustrating Component Interface Controllers and Views

To distinguish between UI ports and controller ports, UI ports (component interface views) are identified with rounded corners. Controller ports (component interface controller) are still represented by squares as defined in UML 2.0.

Connectors and Usage Dependencies Between Components

Connectors for representing component dependencies

A *connector* represents the connection of a Web Dynpro component to the port of another component. The *connector* is represented by linking a *socket icon* to a *ball icon*. The socket icon starts at the component that is using the other component while the ball icon starts at the used component.

Figure A.2 illustrates the usage dependency of a parent component with its child component. The parent component embeds the component interface view of the child component in is own user interface, which is represented by a connector between the parent component and the UI port of the child component (see ❶). The parent component uses or requires the component interface controller of the child component, which is represented by a second connector between the parent component and the controller port of the child component (see ❷).

Because a connector between two Web Dynpro components implies the usage dependency the additional arrow from the parent to the child component can be omitted.

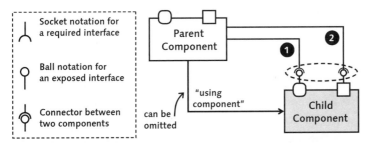

Figure A.2 Connector for Representing Usage Dependencies Between Web Dynpro Components

Component Interfaces and Their Implementation

The presentation of component interfaces for the abstract typing of Web Dynpro components takes place by inserting the stereotype *<<CID>>* as an abbreviation of *<<component interface definition>>* (see Figure A.3, ❶).

Stereotype <<CID>>

The Web Dynpro component implementing a component interface is connected to this stereotype via a dashed arrow (Figure A.3, ❷).

Because the component instance implementing a component interface is created and destroyed at the component-usage level and not at the component-interface-controller level, lifecycle control can optionally be presented by an additional arrow between the component using the component and the component interface (Figure A.3, ❸).

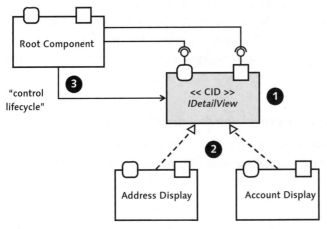

Figure A.3 Presentation of Usage and Implementation of a Component Interface

A.2   Web Dynpro Component Model

Web Dynpro components are the basic modules for developing Web Dynpro applications. In a component-based architecture, it is possible to split complex applications into single, functionally separated parts that are then developed in a distributed way using a clear task separation. This is enabled by some essential features of the Web Dynpro component model, such as its interface concept, the possibility to abstractly define component interfaces, the modularization of large applications, and the reusability of Web Dynpro components.

A.2.1   Component Architecture

The architecture of a Web Dynpro component is based on the Model-View-Controller (MVC) model, which establishes a clear separation between business data model, user interface, and controller implementation or application logic. Every Web Dynpro component has different visual and controller-specific parts. The visual facet includes the view layouts for arranging UI elements within a component. At the next level, windows provide the possibility to merge several views to an entire user interface. By connecting inbound and outbound plugs at the view level, the navigation schema in window is defined.

The controller-specific facet includes various controller types. These include the always existing *component controller*, the optional *custom controller*, as well as the *view controller* that belongs to a view layout. To easily integrate a Web Dynpro component in the backend layer, the usage of a model can be defined; e.g., an *adaptive RFC model* or a *web service model*.

A.2.2   Interfaces of a Web Dynpro Component

A Web Dynpro component provides two different types of interfaces to an external using component.[1] The using entities of a Web Dynpro component can be either other Web Dynpro components or the

---

[1] A Web Dynpro application defines which Web Dynpro component, or rather which start-up plug of an associated component interface view, is addressed during the start-up phase of the application.

entity of *Web Dynpro applications*. At a visual level, every component can offer several optional *component interface views* as interfaces. A component interface view exposes a window from within the component to the outside. Another component can then embed this visual interface like a normal view into its own window.

The *component interface controller* represents the programmatic and thus the non-visual interface of a Web Dynpro component. It enables an external component to interact with the embedded component via method calls, the reaction to events, or the exchange of context data using *internal* or *external* interface context mapping. Internal details of a component (such as the controller implementation or the internal structure of the user interface) are not visible to the outside (*black box principle*). Except via the component interface controller, it is not possible to access the inner parts of a Web Dynpro component (component controller, custom controller, or view controller).

A.2.3 Definition of Component Interfaces

In the Java programming language, an interface is a type, just like a class. Java interfaces define methods without implementing them themselves. An interface is therefore an abstraction of a class that is separated from the implementation. The major advantage of the interface approach is that an interface can be used separately from its implementation. Therefore, the implementation can be changed independently of its using component.

With the concept of the Web Dynpro component interface (*component interface definition*), this approach of loose coupling between interface-using component and interface implementation was transferred to the Web Dynpro component model. A component interface describes the functionality of a Web Dynpro component only at an abstract level. On the one hand, this includes the methods and events as well as the context structure of the component interface controller. On the other hand, these are the component interface views and its different types of plugs: *Startup plugs* for starting Web Dynpro applications, *exit plugs* for their termination, and *inbound* and *outbound plugs* for defining navigation links. Using component interfaces, usage dependencies can be defined at the component level at design time without knowing the implementing Web Dynpro components. By separating definition and implementation in the Web Dynpro component model, it is thus possible to achieve a far more flexible application architecture.

A.2.4 Reusability

The functionality implemented in a Web Dynpro component can easily be reused by other components. In the Web Dynpro programming model, reusability is only possible at the component level. It increases the efficiency of the development process and makes Web Dynpro applications less error prone by avoiding redundancies at both the definition and the implementation level.

A.2.5 Modularization

The Web Dynpro component model meets all requirements for being able to develop complex Web Dynpro applications in a modular way by separating them into different modules. By avoiding redundancies, the separation of definition and implementation as well as the separation of different functions enable Web Dynpro components to efficiently develop and maintain complex Web Dynpro applications.

A.3 Classification of Web Dynpro Components

By default, the Web Dynpro component model does not distinguish between specific types of components, which is why the construct of the Web Dynpro component is the only predefined unit. However, the component architecture provides the developer with numerous possibilities to develop different components with special characteristics. For example, it is possible to focus the function of a component on special tasks. This results in a clear logical separation of the entire application at the component level.

To distinguish specific component types, we will classify the Web Dynpro components in our own way. This is a specific concept for designing component-based Web Dynpro applications. The Web Dynpro tools do not provide any wizards for directly creating such components.

A.3.1 User Interface Components

User interface components (UI components) provide functions that are directly related to building the user interface. Such components contain at least one view themselves and in most cases provide other components—their using components—with one or several component interface views as visual interfaces. In the class of user interface components, we distinguish the following types:

Visual Components

Visual components immediately provide possibilities for interacting in the user interface. These include, for example, filling out a form or browsing a table. Visual components thus contain view layouts that are made usable to the outside via the component interface views, which are the visual component interfaces. In most cases, external using components of visual components are the main components (root components) of the application. For building more complex user interfaces, visual components can also be nested.

Root Components as Layout Components

The *root component* of any Web Dynpro application acts as the central main component within every component-based Web Dynpro application. It controls the lifecycles of the components it embeds, and it merges visual components to the entire user interface by embedding their component interface views in its own `ViewContainer` UI elements.

A Web Dynpro component is a root component if it is referenced by at least one Web Dynpro application. A Web Dynpro application specifies which startup plug of a specific component interface view of the root component is called when the application is started. At runtime, the corresponding startup plug event handler is called in the component interface view controller at startup.

UI Service Components

This component type provides UI services that can be reused by other components. In the Web Dynpro GameStation, the *HTML viewer component* is such a UI service component. It presents an

473

HTML text in a view as a dynamic series of individual TextView UI elements. The text is provided via external interface context mapping.

A.3.2 Faceless Components

Faceless components provide functionality at a non-visual level and therefore contain neither component interface views nor view layouts.

Model Components

Model components constitute a special class of faceless components. They implement the access to the back end and thus to the business logic, which is exposed to external using components via the component interface controller. Back-end data is made accessible in the context of the component interface controller so that appropriate context mapping dependencies can be defined in other components. Additionally, public methods and events provide the possibility to interact with the model component.

Library Components

Library component encapsulate the implementation of reusable, non-visual services at Web Dynpro component level. In the GameStation application, the DeploymentManagerComp component represents such a library component.

UI components and faceless components should not depend on each other, so that they can easily be exchanged if needed.

A.4   SAP NetWeaver Development Infrastructure

The development of Web Dynpro business applications for SAP NetWeaver takes place within the *SAP NetWeaver Development Infrastructure (NWDI)*.

The NWDI combines the properties and benefits of a local development environment with a server-based development landscape. It provides a central and consistent development environment to developer teams and supports the entire development process of a software product. The NWDI is composed of the following parts.

NWDI Component Model

The NWDI component model is the basis of an efficient development of component-based Web Dynpro applications. The NWDI component model provides special development units that are referred to as *software components* (SC) and *development components* (DC). While development components contain the actual development objects (like Web Dynpro components, models, component interfaces, applications, or dictionaries), software components assemble several development components into a deliverable software unit.

By using several DCs, large Web Dynpro applications can be split into clearly structured and, if necessary, reusable parts, and therefore be developed by a team. Between development components, you can define different usage dependencies that are based on a special visibility concept. *Public parts* represent the development component interfaces that are visible to the outside. Via additional *Access Control Lists* you can define which DCs or SCs are allowed to use a public part. Without the definition of an Access Control List, it is visible to all external using components.

Design Time Repository

In an NWDI-based development scenario, the development objects are stored in the *Design Time Repository* (DTR), which is the central version management system of the NWDI. In Web Dynpro, these are the various metadata files for describing a Web Dynpro project or a Web Dynpro DC. Via DTR, component-based Web Dynpro applications can be developed by several developers in a distributed way. *Development configurations* define different developer-specific views of the development infrastructure. These include the code lines relevant to a developer or a project, the versions of other used components, the versions of external third-party components, and the addresses of different systems in the NWDI development landscape.

Component Build Service

The central build process is no longer based on command-line tools and makefiles but uses the *Component Build Service* (CBS) of the NWDI. The CBS automatically builds components, i.e., development components, and the components depending on them on demand. It also creates libraries and deployable units for developers and runtime systems.

Change Management Service

The *Change Management Service* (CMS) performs the transport of software components, including the source code and the libraries, within an NWDI development landscape. Additionally, it supports the automatic deployment of executable software units in central test and production systems.

System Landscape Directory

The *System Landscape Directory* (SLD) provides services for the administration of system landscapes. These usually include several hardware and software components that depend on each other with regard to installation, software updates, and interfaces.

SAP NetWeaver Developer Studio

The *SAP NetWeaver Developer Studio* supports the development and the build process of development components and that of Web Dynpro DCs in particular. The locally built components can thus be deployed in a local runtime system for testing.

A.4.1 Component Model of the NWDI

The NWDI is based on a specific component model that enables you to structure applications as reusable development components. The NWDI component model does not change known development objects such as Java, J2EE, or Web Dynpro entities but supplements them with special metadata that defines the encapsulation of these objects and interfaces. In the NWDI, the following component types are distinguished.

Software Components

SCs are development units that group several development components to form larger, deliverable, and deployable components.

Development Components

DCs are development and build units (see Component Build Service). They combine functionally related development objects (*development objects*) to reusable and non-overlapping units. Between the individual DCs, you can define usage dependencies where no cycles may occur. The visibility concept applied for DCs is based on a black- box approach where only the DC parts exposed via public parts can be used by other DCs. The range of using components (SCs or DCs) of a public part can be limited through the use of additional access lists. Every DC has a unique type that determines on which technology the DC is based, which development tools are to be used, and how the DC is to be compiled and archived.

A DC can only use the DC of another software component if its own software component has defined its usage. Lastly, DCs can specify or restrict their visibility for specific software components by defining Access Control Lists.

Web Dynpro Development Components

For the development of Web Dynpro applications, there is the special DC type of the *Web Dynpro DC* for grouping specific Web Dynpro entities such as components, component interfaces, local dictionaries, or models. Large Web Dynpro applications with a component-based architecture are composed of several Web Dynpro DCs.

Development Objects

Development objects are created within an embedding development component and are centrally stored as versioned files in the Design Time Repository. Within Web Dynpro DCs, the following development objects can be distinguished: *Web Dynpro applications*, *Web Dynpro components*, *models*, *component interface* as well as *local* and *logical dictionaries*.

Web Dynpro DC ≠
Web Dynpro
component
Because the term "component" is used both in the NWDI and in the Web Dynpro programming model, we would like to clearly point out the difference once again. It is essential to differ between *Web Dynpro development components* and *Web Dynpro components*. Although these two terms are fairly similar they refer to two entities that are technically completely different.

▶ **Web Dynpro development component**
The Web Dynpro development component is a special DC type in the NWDI component model for storing Web Dynpro entities or, generally, for structuring Web Dynpro applications in a modular way. Outside of the NWDI, the Web Dynpro DC corresponds to a *Web Dynpro project* with the essential difference that in contrast to Web Dynpro DCs, no usage dependencies can be defined between Web Dynpro projects. This is why Web Dynpro projects quickly reach their limits in the distributed development of larger Web Dynpro applications outside of the NWDI.

▶ **Web Dynpro component**
In the Web Dynpro programming model, the entity of the Web Dynpro component is the central module for building modular Web Dynpro applications. Web Dynpro components and Web Dynpro DCs are two technically totally different units. They are only related to each other in that Web Dynpro DCs are those development components of the NWDI that are provided for storing Web Dynpro components and other Web Dynpro entities.

Figure A.4 illustrates the relational connection between the three component types of SCs, Web Dynpro development component (Web Dynpro DC), and Web Dynpro component. A software component can contain several Web Dynpro DCs that in turn can store several Web Dynpro components. It is also possible that a Web Dynpro DC does not contain any Web Dynpro components but only other Web Dynpro entities or only Java classes.

Figure A.4 Associations Between Different Components in the NWDI Component Model

Figure A.5 shows how the storage of Web Dynpro components in the NWDI is based on a three-layer component architecture. A Web Dynpro application is distributed at the top level as a software component. At the development component level underneath, this component consists of several Web Dynpro DCs. Web Dynpro DCs in turn contain individual or several Web Dynpro components as well as all other parts such as component interfaces or models.

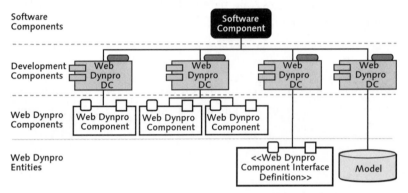

Figure A.5 Three-Layer Component Architecture of NWDI-Based Web Dynpro Applications

A.4.2 Naming Web Dynpro DCs

When naming DCs—and thus Web Dynpro DCs—you should follow some rules that are shortly introduced here.

▶ Every development component has a globally unique name. The DC names represent a hierarchically structured namespace.

▶ The DC name must be defined when a DC is created and can no longer be changed at a later stage.

▶ DC names must consist of a *vendor name* and at least one more *name segment*.

▶ Name segments are delimited with slashes (/) and may not contain more than 40 characters altogether, including the slashes.

▶ A name segment must consist of at least two characters.

▶ A name segment may consist of alphanumeric characters (a to z, 0 to 9) and the characters "-", "_", ".", "!", and "$".

▶ DC names may only contain lower-case letters.

▶ Because DC names may not be changed during their lifecycle, they should not contain any of the following information: SC name, dependencies with other DCs, version or release information, developer, team, or company name, workspace information like "dev" or "cons".

▶ When naming child DCs you should make sure that the logical relation of the child DC to its initial parent DC is not reflected in the DC name because the parent-child dependency of both DCs might change at a later stage.

▶ DC names should express the purpose and the functionality of DCs.

When naming DC name segments it is recommended to establish an individual naming convention that is followed in a Web Dynpro application project.

B Web Dynpro in the SDN

The *SAP Developer Network (SDN)* provides many Web Dynpro materials that ideally complement the subjects described in this book. To train yourself in the use of Web Dynpro for Java, you can use the specific *Feature2Sample matrix* (see Section B.2) and compile your own combination of tutorials and sample applications. This appendix is intended to give you all the information you need in order to use the SDN optimally as a knowledge platform for Web Dynpro.

B.1 Information Portal

The SDN (*http://sdn.sap.com*) represents a comprehensive information portal for numerous SAP technology areas. You can access the Web Dynpro home page via the following node: **Developer Areas · SAP NetWeaver · Application Server · Web Dynpro**.

The Web Dynpro home page (see Figure B.1) contains much material related to Web Dynpro for Java and Web Dynpro for ABAP.[1] From there, you can navigate to the following sources of information:

Web Dynpro home page

- ▶ **What's New**
  The upper part of the Web Dynpro home page is updated weekly with new materials such as articles, tutorials, or Weblogs by the Web Dynpro content strategist of the SDN team.

- ▶ **Featured Blog**
  The Web Dynpro content strategist selects a *featured Weblog* from the most recent Web Dynpro Weblogs and presents it on the Web Dynpro home page.

- ▶ **Web Dynpro Knowledge Center**
  The Web Dynpro Knowledge Center is a categorized collection of entry points to the Web Dynpro subject matter and its related technologies. The Web Dynpro Knowledge Center lets you access the majority of Web Dynpro information sources available in the SDN. You can also use the SDN search function to find them, but

Web Dynpro Knowledge Center

---

1 Web Dynpro for ABAP is provided for the first time as part of SAP NetWeaver 2004s.

the knowledge center has the advantage that its contents are maintained by SDN content strategists:

▶ **Key Topics**
The pages on *Getting Started* and on Web Dynpro specific *Key Topics* like *General Concepts, Administration, Programming Model,* or *User Interface* propagate the best sources of information to the user. They can be seen as result lists for the favorite Web Dynpro search queries.

▶ **Related JavaDoc**
You can access the **JavaDoc** for the Web Dynpro Java Runtime API through the following link in the SDN: *http://www.sdn.sap.com/irj/sdn/javadocs.* In addition to the Web Dynpro Java Runtime Environment, the APIs of the *Common Model Interface (CMI),* of the *Dictionary Runtime,* and of the *User Management Engine (UME)* are also relevant to development of Web Dynpro applications.

▶ **SAP Documentation in Help Portal**
This category lists entry points to the Web Dynpro documentation in the SAP online help.

▶ **Related Areas and IT Scenarios**
This category contains cross-references to other technology areas on SDN which are relevant within the Web Dynpro technology context.

Figure B.1 Web Dynpro Home Page in the SDN

▶ **Collection of Links**

The area on the right-hand side of the Web Dynpro home page contains a structured collection of additional sources of information on Web Dynpro:

▹ **Downloads**
This area contains links to the *Sneak-Preview Version* of SAP NetWeaver, to the *Web Dynpro Clients for Java* and *Windows*, and to the *Eclipse Theme Editor*.

▹ **How-to Guides**
The Web Dynpro **Sample Applications and Tutorials** link refers to the *Feature2Sample matrix*, which contains a breakdown of all Web Dynpro examples and tutorials according to their technical features.

▹ **Web Dynpro Discussion Forum**
The **Web Dynpro Discussion Forum** enables you to place questions and quickly receive answers from other Web Dynpro developers. As a member of the forum, you are always welcome to exchange your own experiences with other developers. You can use the automatic email-notification function to notify you about new messages in relevant threads of the forum.

▹ **Web Dynpro Blogs**
The link *https://www.sdn.sap.com/irj/sdn/weblogs?blog=/weblogs/topic/43* sums up all Weblogs related to Web Dynpro on one page. In addition to that, The Web Dynpro forum contains a specific **sticky thread** called *New Web Dynpro Weblogs* where the authors of Weblogs can enter their new Weblogs. You can use the forum function **Watch this topic** to receive automatic notifications when new Weblogs or posts are entered in this sticky thread.

▹ **Miscellaneous**
The SDN contains various other topics important for developing Web Dynpro applications. These topics include the Java Development Infrastructure forum, materials related to the Composite Application Framework, the SAP NetWeaver Portal, security topics, and SAP Web Application Server (SAP Web AS).

B.2   Web Dynpro Feature2Sample Matrix

The *Web Dynpro Feature2Sample matrix* assigns technical features of Web Dynpro to many appropriate examples and tutorials. Figure B.2 depicts the structural concept of the Feature2Sample matrix.

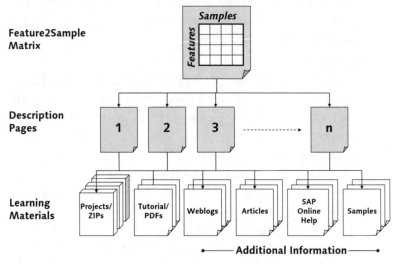

Figure B.2 Web Dynpro Feature2Sample Matrix in the SDN

Each sample application (**sample**) is identified by a number, which in turn is displayed as a link to the associated **sample description page** in the matrix. When you select a specific feature such as **Backend Access · Adaptive RFC Model**, you can use the links located next to the features to navigate to the description pages of samples Numbers 4, 5, and 9 and to obtain detailed information on the technical content of the individual samples.

A description page contains details of the content of the sample application or tutorial, download links to the associated Web Dynpro projects and Web Dynpro Development Components (DCs) and to the tutorial PDF file, and other links to related sources of information such as Weblogs, articles, and other sample applications (**Additional Information**). Many tutorials use a template concept, where the sample application and a prepared template project limit the necessary development steps to reach the actual learning content of the tutorial.

If you want to develop or test the sample applications, you must have SAP Web Application Server 6.40 installed. Alternatively, you can also use the installation of the sneak-preview edition of SAP Web AS in the SDN. All other requirements are described at the relevant locations within the articles or tutorial documents.

B.3   Web Dynpro Learning Process

The Feature2Sample matrix enables you to compose your own *Web Dynpro learning map*. Depending on the focus of your interest, your level of knowledge, or the type of technical requirements, the Feature2Sample matrix can provide you with a subset of appropriate samples. Ideally, you should work through these in a specific sequence.

Web Dynpro learning map

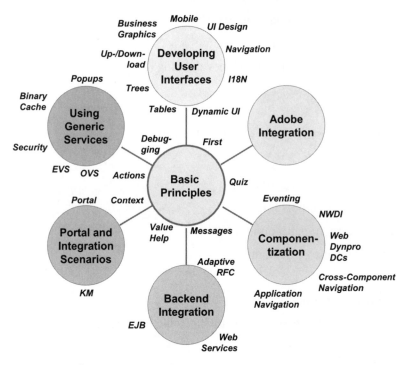

Figure B.3 Web Dynpro Learning Map

To facilitate the use of the Feature2Sample matrix for you, this section suggests ways you can subdivide the provided sample and tutorial applications into different topics. The *Web Dynpro learning map*

Subdividing the Feature2Sample matrix into different topics

485

shown in Figure B.3 groups the existing samples and tutorials around seven different topics, one of which is the basic principles of Web Dynpro. In the following sections, we'll provide a more accurate assignment of the existing sample applications to those different topics. Every sample application is listed by its number in the Feature2Sample matrix followed by its title. It is useful to work through the samples provided for a specific topic in the sequence shown, as the sample application numbers are not related with the proposed order.

B.3.1 Learning the Basics

1   – Creating your First Web Dynpro Application

2   – Creating an Extended Web Dynpro Application

18 – Context Programming and Data Binding

3   – Enabling Message and Error Service Support

8   – Enabling Value Help

33 – Using Validating and Non-Validating Actions

24 – Debugging

B.3.2 User Interface and UI Elements

Basic Principles

23 – Designing User Interfaces

13 – View Compositions

16 – Internationalization (I18N)

17 – Dynamic Programming

Specific UI Elements

11 – Creating Tables and Enhancing Table Performance

12 – Creating Trees

27 – Creating a Tree Structure in a Table

39 – Uploading and Downloading Files

21 – Using Business Graphics

22 – Using Geo Services

Mobile Clients

37 – Mobile Web Dynpro

B.3.3 Backend Access

Web Services

6   – Accessing an Email Web Service

7   – Accessing the Car Rental Web Service

Adaptive RFC Models

4   – Accessing R/3 Backend

5   – Handling Transactions with BAPIs

25 – Debugging ABAP Code from within Web Dynpro

Java Beans

20 – Using EJBs

B.3.4 Componentization

14 – Server-Side Eventing

15 – Inter-Application Navigation

38 – Designing Component-based Web Dynpro Applications

40 – Cross-Component Navigation

B.3.5 Generic Services

10 – Creating Dialog Boxes (Pop-Ups)

9   – Advanced Value Help Tutorial: OVS

36 – Yet Another EVS Value help: Showing Texts for Keys

34 – Web Dynpro Binary Cache and Excel Export

35 – Using Roles and Permissions in Applications

B.3.6 Adobe Integration

B.3.7 Portal and Integration Scenarios

C   The Authors

After his studies in mathematics, physics, and computer science at the University of Freiburg, Germany, **Bertram Ganz** finished his teacher training at a grammar school stressing technical sciences. He started his professional career as a software trainer before he joined SAP AG in 2002. Since then, he has been working as a Web Dynpro Java runtime developer. Bertram's work focuses primarily on knowledge transfer, rollout, and documentation. He regularly publishes articles on Web Dynpro in the context of SAP NetWeaver Application Server.

After graduating in computer science at the University of Karlsruhe, Germany, **Jochen Gürtler** wrote his thesis on computer center management systems (CCMS) at SAP AG. He joined SAP's technology development team in 1998. In the first two years he worked at SAP-Markets – a SAP subsidiary – where he took part in the development of a component-based user-interface framework. In the summer of 2001, Jochen joined the Web Dynpro team. Here, he was one of the driving forces for integration with other SAP NetWeaver components, in particular the SAP NetWeaver Portal integration. Jochen is currently working as a development architect and is responsible for the advanced integration of Web Dynpro and SAP NetWeaver Portal. He regularly publishes articles on the use of Web Dynpro within SAP NetWeaver.

Timo Lakner studied computer science at the University of Freiburg, Germany. He spent the first years of his professional career in the data-mining area at IBM and joined SAP AG in 2002. At SAP he has been working ever since as a software developer for the Web Dynpro runtime. His work primarily focuses on the integration with SAP Web Application Server, session management, runtime repository, and portal integration.

Index

**Improve your Design Process
with "Contextual Design"**

192 pp., 2006, US$ 49,95
ISBN 1-59229-065-5

Designing
Composite Applications
www.sap-press.com

Jörg Beringer, Karen Holtzblatt

Designing Composite Applications

Driving user productivity and business innovation for
next generation business applications

This book helps any serious developer hit the ground
running by providing a highly detailed and comprehensive introduction to modern application design,
using the SAP Enterprise Services Architecture (ESA)
toolset and the methodology of "Contextual Design".
Readers will benefit immediately from exclusive
insights on design processes based on SAPs Business
Process Platform and learn valuable tricks and techniques that can drastically improve user productivity.
Anybody involved in the process of enterprise application design and usability/quality management
stands to benefit from this book.

Provides basics as well as practical guidance for analysis and tuning of SAP BW 3.5

Contains in-depth description of BW data model, sizing, system load analysis, and DB indices

452 pp., 2006, 69,95 Euro / US$
ISBN 1-59229-080-9

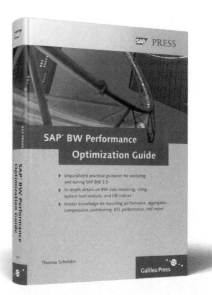

SAP BW Performance Optimization Guide

www.sap-press.com

T. Schröder

SAP BW Performance Optimization Guide

Finally, a detailed reference that gives administrators expert instruction to analyze and optimize performance in SAP BW. All the BW basics are covered such as architecture and data modelling, plus the ins and outs of systematic performance analysis, as well as volumes of valuable data design tips. Readers get an in-depth introduction to SAP BW indices, statistics, and database optimizers and learn about the key aspects of reporting performance.

Modeling and designing intuitive business applications with SAP NetWeaver Visual Composer

Practical expert advice on the various aspects of the Development Lifecycle

approx. 450 pp., US$ 69,95
ISBN 1-59229-099-X, Sept 2006

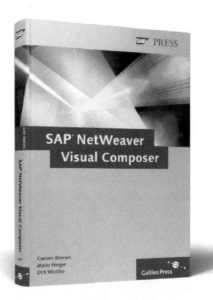

SAP NetWeaver Visual Composer

www.sap-press.com

C. Bönnen, M. Herger, D. Wodtke

SAP NetWeaver Visual Composer

Instead of conventional programming and implementation, SAP NetWeaver Visual Composer (VC) enables you to model your processes graphically via drag & drop—potentially without ever having to write a single line of code. This book not only shows you how, but also serves as a comprehensive reference, providing you with complete details on all aspects of VC. You learn the ins and outs of the VC architecture—including details on all components and concepts, as well as essential information on model-based development and on the preparation of different types of applications. Readers quickly broaden their knowledge by tapping into practical expert advice on the various aspects of the Development Lifecycle as well as on selected applications, which have been modeled with the VC and are currently delivered by SAP as standard applications.